Don Rickles

Don Rickles

The Merchant of Venom

A BIOGRAPHY

Michael Seth Starr

CITADEL PRESS
Kensington Publishing Corp.
www.kensingtonbooks.com

CITADEL PRESS BOOKS are published by

Kensington Publishing Corp.
119 West 40th Street
New York, NY 10018

All Kensington titles, imprints, and distributed lines are available at special quantity discounts for bulk purchases for sales promotions, premiums, fund-raising, educational, or institutional use. Special book excerpts or customized printings can also be created to fit specific needs. For details, write or phone the office of the Kensington sales manager: Kensington Publishing Corp., 119 West 40th Street, New York, NY 10018, attn: Sales Department; phone 1-800-221-2647.

CITADEL PRESS and the Citadel logo are Reg. U.S. Pat. & TM Off.

ISBN: 978-0-8065-4172-3

First Citadel hardcover printing: November 2022

10 9 8 7 6 5 4 3 2 1

Printed in the United States of America

Library of Congress Control Number: 2022939711

ISBN: 978-0-8065-4174-7 (e-book)

Contents

Prologue

I t is one of those old showbiz stories passed down from generation to generation, from comic to comic, recalling the glory days of nightclubs thick with cigarette smoke and celebrities, a world that does not exist anymore, where men and women, dressed to the nines, would flock to see Rowan and Martin or Louis Prima and Keely Smith. The story has been embellished over the years, as are most of these oft-told tales. But it did happen.

When and where it took place is debatable. One of its two featured players, when recounting it time and again in the ensuing forty-plus years, often painted the picture slightly differently each time, yet never failed to get a laugh from Johnny Carson, Merv Griffin, Joey Bishop, or any of the countless television interviewers or writers hearing the story. In time, it took on a life of its own and the details were expendable. Sometimes it was at Murray Franklin's nightclub in Miami Beach or at Zardi's Jazzland, the Copa, or the Slate Brothers Club. The story is timeless.

Here it is: He was in his early thirties and just starting to make a name for himself as a nightclub comic after years of bouncing around the circuit playing every dump and dive from Passaic to Pasadena and all points in-between. Word was getting around about the guy, who looked much older thanks to a hastily retreating hairline. He was only five-foot-six, but he looked taller onstage as he sweated profusely through his suit, his forehead drenched with perspiration while he prowled the stage with his microphone, looking like a caged tiger ready to uncoil. His eyes would lock on someone in the audience before verbally assaulting his prey, firing his insults in tommy-gun fashion, *rat-tat-tat*, crossing ethnic, gender, and religious lines.

"*Is that your wife, sir? What was it, a train?*"

"*You're Italian, right? I knew it. None of your clothes match. Nah, but really, we like Italians. We gotta kiss their asses so the Jews can have ice.*"

"*Got to laugh about people, Habib. I've met you before, haven't I? That's right, you hung my uncle.*"

No one was safe. And everyone loved it.

Then came *the night*. Don Rickles was onstage, doing his thing, when Frank Sinatra walked in, flanked by the guys in dark suits who no one messed with. Sinatra, as everyone knew, was moody and unpredictable, with that famously bad temper. The air was thick with tension as a hush fell over the crowed and he sat down with the boys at a table directly in Don's line of vision. Few dared to needle Sinatra to his face, and even fewer got away with it. Joey Bishop, *maybe*, in the few years that he was in Sinatra's orbit. You just never knew with Frank which way the wind was blowing.

So there was Don up on the small stage, mopping the sweat from his brow. Frank ordered a drink and turned his gaze toward the stage, waiting for (daring?) Don to level one of his trademark insults. Rickles took up the challenge.

"*Make yourself comfortable, Frank, slug somebody.*"

"*Frank, believe me, I'm telling you this as a friend: your voice is gone.*"

"*I just saw your movie* The Pride and the Passion, *and I want to tell you, the cannon was great.*"

Sinatra laughed. The tension disappeared. Everyone relaxed.

"The guys with him went, 'Frank, we find that funny,'" Don recalled years later. "Had they not, I would have been on the Jerry Lewis telethon."

Don Rickles was on his way.

CHAPTER 1

D onald Jay Rickles was born into the world, kicking and
screaming, on May 8, 1926, in the New York City borough of
Queens, the only child of Max and Etta Rickles.

Just twenty years before, at the turn of the century, Queens had
been a nearly undeveloped marshland with a few farms scattered here
and there; now, around the time that Don entered its universe, the
borough was closing in on a population of 1 million, a far cry from
the 153,000 residents cited in New York's 1900 census. Much of that
growth was spurred by the opening of the Queensboro Bridge in
1909. It was the first roadway to connect Manhattan with, as New
York Mayor William J. Gaynor called the borough then, "the corn-
fields of Queens." Six years later, in 1915, New York's IRT subway
line expanded its service to Queens, spurring yet another influx of
businesses and residents into the borough's diverse neighborhoods.

Still, Queens retained a suburban feel. Its tree-lined streets
were dotted with houses both posh and modest—one-, two-,
and three-family homes—and apartment buildings that ran the
gamut from the exclusive to the unprepossessing address in Jackson Heights into which Max and Etta Rickles eventually settled. It
was not idyllic; there were restrictive covenants in some neighborhoods that barred people by race or religion and were not struck
down until the 1940s, when more Jewish people moved into the
neighborhood, including the family of future KISS member Gene
Simmons (born Chaim Witz). The Black community would have
difficulties renting or buying a place in Jackson Heights until the
Fair Housing Act was passed in 1968.[1]

Max Rickles was born Max Ryklansky in Kovno, Russia, in 1897 to Joseph and Frances (nee Iones) Ryklansky, both natives of Lithuania. In 1903, shortly before war broke out between Czarist Russia and Japan, amid the ever-present undercurrent of Russia's anti-Semitism, Joseph and Frances decided to emigrate to America, taking with them six-year-old Max, his four brothers (Sam, Harry, Solomon, and Henry), and his sister, Katherine. They trekked to Belgium and, from Antwerp, set sail on the *Kroonland*, arriving in New York Harbor on October 4, 1903, in the midst of the city's rainiest season on record. Customs officials quickly and unceremoniously changed the family's surname from Ryklansky to the more anglicized Rickles.

As a youth, Max Rickles worked a series of jobs, eventually landing a steady gig as an insurance salesman. In the early 1920s he met and fell in love with Yettie Feldman, who was four years younger. Everyone called her Etta (or, as Don labeled his irrepressible mother, "the Jewish Patton"). She was born in New York City in 1901 to Harry Feldman, who emigrated from Austria, and Clara Feldman, née Landsberg. She had a sister, Frieda. (Don's cousin on his grandmother's side of the family, David Landsberg, later costarred with him on his NBC sitcom *CPO Sharkey*.)

Etta developed into a brash, outgoing, opinionated young woman, traits that would embarrass her son, even at an early age, making him an extremely self-conscious child. "I loved her dearly," Don recalled, "but the woman was definitely more commanding in her attitude than most."[2] She and the more soft-spoken Max were married on June 24, 1924, when he was twenty-seven and she was twenty-three.

They moved into a two-bedroom apartment in a nondescript four-story redbrick building at 89-09 32nd Avenue in Jackson Heights, a mixed community of forty-five thousand predominantly Jewish, Irish, and Italian residents located in the northwest corner of Queens. At one time, silent-screen stars Charlie Chaplin and Douglas Fairbanks Sr. lived in the neighborhood; Les Paul and Mary Ford recorded their hit instrumental "How High the Moon," in their

Jackson Heights studio. Don arrived a month short of Max and Etta's two-year anniversary, "a Mother's Day present to me," Etta said.

Their apartment was comfortable, but nothing fancy and no different from the thousands of other apartments in the city. It had a dumbwaiter in its kitchen, which thrilled Don, and their building was directly across the street from P.S. 148, which was not always appreciated by the young boy ("Whenever the school bell woke me up, I knew that I was late"). Etta Rickles, in later interviews, would say that Jackson Heights was part of Long Island, which was her attempt to make it sound posher than it was. (Queens, technically, is located at the western end of Long Island.)

Don had his own room in the apartment, which he decorated with baseball memorabilia. He was a big fan of the New York Giants, who played in the Polo Grounds in Manhattan in those halcyon days of three New York baseball teams, with the Dodgers over in Brooklyn and the Yankees in the Bronx. In 1936, when Don was ten years old and in the flush of fandom, the Giants, led by future Hall of Famers Carl Hubbell, Mel Ott, and player-manager Bill Terry, won the National League Pennant by five games over the Chicago Cubs—but lost the World Series to their cross-town rivals the Yankees in six games.

(Don's passion for baseball lasted his entire life, but he switched allegiances after the Giants and the Dodgers left New York City in 1957. When he moved to Los Angeles in the 1960s, he rooted for the Dodgers and later became good friends with the team's manager, Tommy Lasorda. Don was a regular at Dodger Stadium and even donned the team's uniform on special occasions. This usually was at Lasorda's urging when his team was slumping and needed a pick-me-up, which meant a fun tongue-lashing from Don—all in good humor, of course.)

Young Don was a quiet, shy boy, more like his father than his mother. Etta, he recalled, was "the most confident woman in Jackson Heights." Years later, well after he became a star, Etta spoke plainly when she was asked about raising a son like Don Rickles.

"Anybody you will meet who knows my son since he was a little boy, when he was 2 . . . he's never been a problem child because he was a very shy and timid youngster," she recalled. "But he did say, when you'd ask him, 'What are you going to do when you grow up?' and he would answer, 'I'm gonna be a big actor someday.' That was always what he wanted."[3]

Maybe, but Don's inherent shyness and his aloof personality kept him from making much of an impression in those early days, either on his parents or on his schoolmates. But he had a flair for performing—Etta was not wrong there—and as he grew a bit older and moved into his teen years, he began to exhibit a talent for mimicry, which he showed off when he and his parents took a drive "to the country," probably the "Borscht Belt" or, to call it by its more unsubtle name, the "Jewish Alps," an area in the Catskill Mountains whose bungalow colonies and hotels were frequented in the summer months by a largely Jewish clientele.

"No one in our family was talented along that line and we didn't pay much heed to him," Etta recalled. "But we used to go up [to] the country and he'd be in the dining room and he would mimic all the people who were sitting there and having their meals. That's how he started as a youngster, and when he was fifteen, whenever there was an amateur show, he would always win the first prize [of] a twenty-five-dollar bond in those days."[4]

The magical mimicry seemed to vanish when the family returned to the apartment in Jackson Heights, as Don fell back into his routine, with "the Jewish Patton" trying her forceful best to draw him out of his shell. "He was so shy and timid you never knew there was a child around the house," she recalled. "We had to force him to go out and meet people, to talk."[5]

"I was a very shy, very inhibited, self-conscious kid," he described himself in those days. "I had no confidence. I never believed I could be successful in school or in life. I only knew I could be successful when it happened."[6]

Don would later say that Jackson Heights was "no special place," but he had fond memories of home life with Etta and Max, who were always supportive and encouraging (especially Etta, whose faith in her son never wavered, even if he did need that extra push every now and then). This was a time when doors were not locked and everyone knew everyone else's business, when your apartment building and your street were your entire universe. The neighborhood provided fertile ground for Don to whet his appetite for performing and to closely observe people, filing away their accents, idiosyncrasies, and cultural identities for use somewhere down the road.

Max Rickles was not the most talkative individual, but he fostered a close relationship with his son. "He was quite a guy. Especially with my mother. He knew the right words with her," Don recalled."[7] Max's sense of humor was quiet and understated, his personality light-hearted. He liked to gamble on the horses and he enjoyed spending time with his family. He took great pride in his work and was beloved by his insurance clients, whose premiums he would often pay out of his own pocket if they were short that month. "He'd write their names in his debit book and carried them on his back," Don recalled. "When Dad died . . . those same customers came to his funeral and put a box next to his grave where they paid off those debits. That's how much they respected my dad."[8]

Max, to use the Yiddish expression, was a *macher* (very influential) at the family's Orthodox synagogue, which was a short walk from the apartment. At one time, he served as the congregation president, and even after his term expired, he continued to keep an eye on the synagogue's internal bookkeeping. At times, his involvement in synagogue business was of a less spiritual nature, such as the year that he sold tickets to the High Holiday services "like a scalper at a ballgame," Don remembered, and then donated the proceeds "directly to God."

Max's weakness was the horses, and with Belmont Raceway just twenty-five miles away it was easy for him to feed his habit, betting on the ponies and losing just enough to keep him returning frequently.

Don hinted that Max's gambling habit might have been more serious. "He had a little bit of a problem with it, actually," he said. When Max died, he was buried at Beth David Cemetery in nearby Elmont. It is likely not too many mourners took note of the irony that his gravesite faced the finish line at Belmont.

Etta Rickles and her dominant personality enveloped Don from the day he was born. She loved her son fiercely, and would tell anyone and everyone what a good boy he was and how he was going to be a success once he figured out a game plan. She could also be his biggest critic. (Etta asked Don, after he became famous, "Can't you be more like Alan King? He's so nice.") One time, when Don was seven or eight, she took him to Radio City Music Hall, a train ride away in Manhattan, to see a Fred Astaire–Ginger Rogers movie (and the Rockettes, of course). When they boarded the subway, she announced loudly, to no one and everyone, "We're getting off at Fiftieth Street," and then scolded Don for being too self-conscious when he shushed her.

When they arrived at Radio City, Etta noticed that the line to enter the building snaked around the corner. She was having none of it, of course, and marched up to the ticket window. "I'm Mrs. Rickles. And I must see the manager!" she announced. When the manager arrived, she turned to him and, in her best "Jewish Patton" voice, announced, "I'm Mrs. Rickles, and one day my son, Don here, will be a fine entertainer." It worked, and the cowed manager found them front-row seats for the show. When they returned home, Etta called her sister, Frieda, to tell her the story of her triumph. "Mom and Aunt Frieda loved each other, but they never stopped arguing," Don recalled. "After their conversations, Mom would cry and say, 'Why do I argue with my sister when I love her so much?' And the next night the arguing went to level two."[9]

She was also, he recalled, "the most entertaining person in my family . . . But I wouldn't say she was funny. She was the vocal star of our neighborhood and would sing, 'Some of These Days' at family parties. I still get choked up when I hear that song. She could take over a room in a matter of seconds."[10]

Don's school years flew by unremarkably. He was an athletic kid, thin and lean, and was a decent student (math was always a problem). He did not show any particular interest in anything but sports and girls until he entered Newtown High School in 1940. The school, located a few miles away in Elmhurst, was built in the Flemish Renaissance Revival style and was topped by a gothic-looking tower/spire. When it was completed in 1921, Newtown High stretched the entire length of a city block. Future *All in the Family* star Carroll O'Connor, who grew up in Forest Hills and Elmhurst, graduated two years ahead of Don; other notable alumni who would eventually walk the halls of Newtown include the aforementioned Gene Simmons, rock guitarist Johnny Thunders (John Genzale) of the New York Dolls, actress Zoe Saldana and Peter Lassally, the longtime executive producer of *The Tonight Show Starring Johnny Carson*, who graduated around six years after Don. Their paths would cross years later.

It was at Newtown High that Don's nascent acting ambitions became a reality, despite his ongoing issues with math which, as he recalled, "put me in sugar shock"—so much so that he was caught cheating on a test and given a failing grade. (Room monitor to Don: "You, what are you doing?" Don: "What am I doing? I'm cheating.")[11]

He played basketball on the school's junior varsity team and got his first mention in print in October 1943, when Brooklyn's daily newspaper, the *Brooklyn Eagle*, included Don's name among the JV basketball players hoping to make the varsity team. Most of his weekends were spent at the Forest Hills Social Hall, where Don, his cousin Jerry, and friends Sy and Spider (real name unknown) would go to listen to the swing bands and eye the girls—"some were built pretty good"—which translated to standing around awkwardly with anyone rarely making a first move. Don went on a few dates but did not have a steady girlfriend, even during this time in his life before the endless nightclub gigs in town after town, night after night, took over. He could be verbally aggressive, though, in his teenage years. "God forbid, if they let me get to second base, they worried I'd announce it to Congress," he said.[12] That did not help his romantic life.

But there was no hiding his enthusiasm for acting and his conviction that he would—*had to*—make it as an entertainer. What else could he do? In later years, he downplayed his commitment to acting ("I went to Newtown and I studied failure. I got a lucky break. World War II came. That got me out of high school."[13]), but he caught the acting bug, performed in several student productions, and was elected president of the school's Dramatic Society.

He graduated from Newtown in June 1944, but his entertaining ambitions, as strong as they were, took a backseat to his desire to fight for his country. General Dwight D. Eisenhower had just launched the massive Allied D-Day attack against the German forces on the beaches of Normandy in France, and patriotism was in the air. Eighteen-year-old Don informed Max and Etta that he was enlisting in the service as America advanced toward certain victory against the Axis powers; the Japanese were proving to be a tougher foe, but confidence was high that they, too, would be vanquished before too much longer.

His parents were not caught completely off-guard by Don's decision—not many subjects were off-limits in their two-bedroom apartment, and Etta was attuned to her son's ambitions and desires. At the very least, Uncle Sam would provide a steady paycheck.

Max Rickles advised his only child to enlist in the Navy for the simple reason that, as Don recalled him telling him, "it's cleaner than the Army. In the Army, you'll be rolling around in the mud."[14] A clever line to be sure, and probably apocryphal, but in any event, in the early summer of 1944, Don took the subway to Grand Central Station in Manhattan, entered the Navy recruiting center there to formally enlist, and . . . was forced to spend the night on a stiff cot after a routine medical checkup showed he was suffering from hypertension (high blood pressure). The Navy was not too picky, though; he was declared fit for service the very next morning and went back to Queens to proudly show off his Navy uniform, the moment captured in family photos taken outside the apartment building. In Etta's retelling of Don's decision to enlist, she and Max indulged their son, hoping that his military service would set him on a more solid course to a respectable job once the war ended. "We even let him go into the Navy," she recalled. "We thought we would let him enlist if that's what he wanted, because we thought when he came back he wouldn't want to go into show business at all. But he wanted to be an actor."[15]

Max and Etta did not have much time to spend with Don before he was ordered to report to the Naval Training Center in Sampson, New York, for basic training. It was not what the quiet kid from Jackson Heights had expected: "Who wants to run around a snowy track in your underwear at five in the morning? Husky dogs couldn't take it."[16]

Don completed his naval training over the summer, and in the fall, he reported to Norfolk, Virginia, for his assignment aboard the USS *Cyrene*, a motor torpedo boat tender that was acquired by the U.S. Navy in late April 1944. (Don: "It used to be a dock until they put a bottom under it.") The *Cyrene* counted a crew of three hundred men. It would be Seaman First Class Rickles's floating home for the next two-and-a-half years.

Don grew accustomed to life aboard the *Cyrene* as it traveled through the Panama Canal and on to Papua, New Guinea, and the Philippines—"It was so hot the crew rotted!"—and finally to San Francisco after the end of the war.

He still thought of himself as a fledgling entertainer, even as a seaman first class, and he tried his hardest to convince the higher-ups to transfer him to Special Services, the entertainment branch of the US Navy, where he was certain his talents would be needed. His many requests were ignored.

The *Cyrene* departed from Norfolk on November 10, 1944. Its first assignment was to escort two squadrons of motor torpedo boats to Hollandia, New Guinea, which went off without a hitch, before it sailed on convoy duty to Leyte, an island in the Philippines, arriving there on January 1, 1945.

I was in the Philippines. Which is a great climate. You hang around Manila and Nguyen Gulf and Cebu and you get malaria and you die, usually. It's about one hundred and five and you walk around with a little loincloth, you know, and you keep firing at anything that moves. We had a wonderful commander who said "battle stations" and when we were in action, he was below decks, under the covers, saying, "Keep firing! Keep firing!" My service days taught me a great deal.

Bonds formed quickly between the nervous young crew members on board the *Cyrene*. Don struck up a strong friendship with a first-class petty officer named Mike Flora, who was a few years older. Mike used his pull on the ship to get Don taken off scut duty scrubbing the ship's decks and assigned to the bridge as the captain's security. But that's about as far as Mike Flora's influence extended; Don's hoped-for assignment in the Special Services never came through, but he kept his shipmates in stitches with his celebrity impressions. Mike doubled as Don's protector when the kid from Queens shot his mouth off or pissed someone off with his wisecracks and mimicry.

"He was a little older. In those days, when you're twenty-two and I'm eighteen, twenty-two, twenty-three was like an old man," Don said. "And he was my bodyguard. He took care of me because I was always making jokes . . . never was a fighter . . . I always said, 'You take care of it.' And so . . . he made it so I became so popular I could say anything."[1] Don and Mike stayed friendly long after their wartime service together.

"I got to know a lot of really good people on that boat, a lot of good memories," Don recalled. "But that is not what I signed up for. One day we were out shooting the guns, and all you hear is this loud 'Boom! Boom! Boom!' and I told the guy in charge, 'Hey I can entertain, you need to send me over to Special Services.' You know what he said to me? 'Keep firing!'"[2]

In mid-January 1945, not long after docking in Leyte, the *Cyrene* was promoted to become the flagship for the commander, Motor Torpedo Boat Squadrons, carrying the flag for the 7th Fleet.

"There were two Jewish kids on the boat," Don recalled. "Every time we got a taste of action, the rest of the guys would look at us and cry, 'Do us a miracle. Part the seas and get us the hell out of here.'"[3]

The war in Europe ended on May 8, 1945—Don's nineteenth birthday—and Japan surrendered to the Allies three months later, on August 14, eight days after the US dropped its first atomic bomb on the Japanese city of Hiroshima, which was followed by a second atomic bomb on August 9 that obliterated Nagasaki nearly two hundred miles away. Near the end of the year, the *Cyrene* set sail for San Francisco, arriving there for repair work on January 7, 1946. The ship was decommissioned in July, ending the military career of Seaman First Class Don Rickles.

Even though the *Cyrene* never did see any direct combat during the war, the threat was always there, with the booming sound of shells exploding in the distance, and sometimes not so far away. It was a constant reminder to the men on the ship, which engendered a camaraderie among its crew of young men, who were, as Don recalled, "holding hands practically to stay with it and not get homesick and not worry about getting hurt or, God forbid, the other word—killed."

Don was given an honorable discharge in July and returned home to Jackson Heights. The twenty-year-old was in good physical shape—during his time on board the *Cyrene* his lean frame had filled out a bit—but his hairline was now noticeably receding.

Max and Etta were thrilled to have their son back at the apartment on 32nd Avenue, but Don needed a job while he figured out his next move: breaking into show business. Max wanted his son to join him in the insurance field; that was a questionable pursuit given Don's innate shyness in a job that would, at the very least, mean a lot of small talk, pushing himself on total strangers to cajole them into signing on the dotted line—for something they probably did not want.

But with no other immediate prospects at hand, Don was surprisingly open to the idea. He studied for, and passed, his insurance test with relative ease and started a career he hoped would be just a temporary placeholder until, somehow, he could forge ahead with his acting ambitions. Veteran insurance salesman Max Rickles was more outgoing than his son; he had the salesman's instinct to do whatever it took to get a signature on a contract. Don? Not so much.

There were problems from the get-go. If, for instance, a customer told Don to call back in a month, he would say "okay" and walk out the door—no "just five more minutes of your time" or a reminder that he was just back from serving his country, before beating a hasty retreat as the door slammed behind him. It drove Max up the wall. Once it became obvious that Don was no Willy Loman, or Max Rickles, he switched products and tried selling cosmetics door-to-door. He fared little better in this pursuit, which he followed, a short time later, with a half-hearted stab at selling magazine subscriptions. Don put it more succinctly: "I couldn't sell air conditioners on a 98-degree day."[4]

Max was exasperated by Don's failures, and he finally pulled some strings with a local butcher, who hired Don to work in his shop. The job required him to ride a bicycle and drop off customers' deliveries, and to mop the floor when he wasn't out "in the field." The bicycle deliveries proved to be a challenge. In Don's version of events, he was out on a delivery one day when his pants leg became entangled in the bicycle's chain. He crashed to the ground along with various meats, which were quickly snatched up by a hungry dog who ran off with the unexpected bounty. Several families in Queens missed out on their dinner that night. Don fared little better in mopping the shop's floor, which was second nature to the former seaman first class, who had spent countless hours swabbing the decks of the *Cyrene*. But he failed in that, too, when he knocked over his bucket filled with water and flooded the store. He was a washout.

Don's mishaps, however, did not dampen his quest to become an entertainer in some way, shape, or form, and he did what he could to keep those hopes alive.

"In those days how did you become a comedian? You had to become an actor first," he said. "I would do jokes and impressions at synagogue functions, bingo parlors, church affairs. I tried to sell insurance. I sold pots, makeup, cars. And I made the rounds. It was rejection, rejection, rejection. I thought, 'What the hell am I gonna be?' They seemed to laugh with my personality but I had nothing to fall back on. It was a frightening time of my life."[5]

Throwing caution to the wind, and hoping beyond hope, he applied for a spot at the American Academy of Dramatic Arts, a prestigious institution in midtown Manhattan that offered a two-year program for aspiring actors. The private conservatory was established in 1884 by Harvard graduate Franklin Haven Sargent with the intent of training actors for the stage. It was the oldest acting school in the English-speaking world, and after several iterations in other locations, it was currently housed at the Lyceum Theatre on West 45th Street near Times Square. The Academy was a thriving operation with plenty to brag about and a who's who of notable alumni, including Hume Cronyn, Kirk Douglas, Nina Foch, Jennifer Jones, Dina Merrill, Frank Morgan, Edward G. Robinson, Lauren Bacall, Jim Backus, Claire Trevor, Spencer Tracy, Agnes Moorehead, and Marlon Brando's older sister, Jocelyn.

Don, much to his surprise, was called in for an audition at the Lyceum—a prerequisite for aspiring applicants and a terrifying, nerve-wracking experience. Surprisingly (or maybe conveniently), he could never remember what role he read or what scene he reenacted for his Academy inquisitors, but the selection committee liked what it saw and Don was overjoyed when his acceptance letter arrived several weeks later. "The Academy gave me prestige, lifted my self-esteem," he said. He immediately quit whatever job he was laboring through at the time. Etta was thrilled, of course, since Don's acceptance into a world-renowned acting school meant bragging rights for the Rickles family and was a feather in her cap as well. Max gave his son his grudging blessing after watching him stumble aimlessly through job after job. At least the kid was happy.

Don was in good company as he prepared for his entrance into the Academy's hallowed halls and classrooms. Joining him in the Class of 1948 were future stars Conrad Bain (*Maude* and *Diff'rent Strokes*); Don Murray, who eight years later would share the big screen with Marilyn Monroe in *Bus Stop*; Jason Robards Jr., winner of two Academy

Awards (*All the President's Men, Julia*); John Ericson (*Bad Day at Black Rock*); and character actor and Oscar nominee Charles Durning. Grace Kelly was in the Class of '49; the closest Don ever got to her "was picking up the scent of her perfume when she opened her locker."[6] He remembered her wearing white gloves and being dropped off and picked up every day by a limousine. Jack Palance has been incorrectly mentioned as one of Don's classmates. He never attended the Academy and was on Broadway, appearing as a Russian soldier in *The Big Two*, around the time of Don's arrival.

Don continued to share the Jackson Heights apartment with Max and Etta and commuted to the Academy each weekday via subway and bus. The school put its students through their paces by balancing classroom instruction and acting exercises with onstage experience. (Don: "One day I was a tree and had to explain how it felt for my leaves to fall.") Don appeared in several student productions, including a supporting role as Banjo, Sheridan Whiteside's pal in *The Man Who Came to Dinner*, a role played by Jimmy Durante in the 1942 movie starring Bette Davis, Monty Woolley, and Ann Sheridan.

The actor and director Philip Loeb was teaching at the Academy during Don's time there and became his chief mentor—if only for barking at him: "Rickles, stop eating up the scenery!" It was a harbinger of things to come. At the same time, though, he admired Don's energy. In 1948, the year Don graduated from the Academy, Loeb costarred on Broadway as the loving husband, Jake, of Molly Goldberg (Gertrude Berg) in *Me and Molly* and reprised the role a year later opposite Berg in the CBS television series *The Goldbergs*, adapted from Berg's eponymous CBS radio show. He committed suicide in 1955, at the age of fifty-six, after being blacklisted, and was the inspiration for the character of comedian Hecky Brown, played by Zero Mostel opposite Woody Allen in the 1976 movie *The Front*.

During his time at the Academy, Don became friends with classmate Tom Poston, who was five years older and who would later star on television in the late 1950s on *The Steve Allen Show* alongside Louis Nye ("Hi Ho, Steverino!"), Dayton Allen, and

Don Knotts—and then rekindle his fame decades later on *The Bob Newhart Show* and *Newhart*. Jason Robards, too, became a pal, and Don invited him to the apartment in Jackson Heights to schmooze with Etta (who was more talkative than Max) and to sample her famous chopped liver. He and Don would joke about forming a comic duo, arguing over whether to call themselves "Robards and Rickles" or "Rickles and Robards." Don said later that they shared an apartment for a short time.

Don Murray's parents were show business veterans. His father, Dennis, was a Broadway dance director and stage manager, and his mother, Ethel, was a former Ziegfeld performer. Murray entered the Academy at the age of sixteen, right after graduating from high school in East Rockaway, Queens. Seventy-five years later, he vividly recalled his first encounter with Don Rickles.

"The first time I met him was when he was doing an improv routine," he said. "He was supposed to be doing a 'Mutiny on the Bounty' routine and he goes and pantomimes opening the trap door to the hold, where the men were down there, and said, 'Oooh, the stench down there!' In the middle of a dramatic scene you were doing with him, he would press up right against you and would start backing up with nowhere to go—and he would pull your pants down!"

Murray recalled Don's onstage confidence and his ability to ad-lib, which was a dicey and brave approach to playing dramatic parts and acting in sketches. But it went over well at the Academy. "It was more formal than the Actors Studio, more traditional than avant-garde," Murray said. "Only one-third of the students were invited back for the senior year. The funny thing was that Don Rickles was invited back for his senior year and Jason Robards Jr. was not invited back. What was amazing was that everybody was so nervous about being invited back but Don would be just the opposite. He would totally destroy every drama scene he was in and turn it into a farcical comedy.

"I remember one time he was playing an old man opposite another actor who was also playing an old man. In the scene, the other man is talking to him and there's dancing going on in the other room. The man says to Don, 'Do you dance?' and Don's supposed to go, 'No, I leave that to the young folks'—but instead he says, 'I thought you'd never ask' and starts to dance with the other actor, who was totally startled."

"I was amazed that I was kept in the academy," Don Rickles recalled decades later. "Most of these people were dedicated actors. We had to act out the roles of butterflies or reindeer. One day we were gypsies on a hill. I used to sit there and think, 'Are they crazy? A gypsy on a hill?' Then you had to do all these improvisations. The teacher would say, 'We are two moths on a curtain.' I was always in trouble 'cuz I was always doing the jokes. I said: 'What do I have to do, eat the drapes? I don't eat drapes.' So I was always doing the flip things and all the other people were working."[7]

Somehow he made it through, and in June 1948, he graduated from the American Academy of Dramatic Arts, just another fresh-faced wannabe thespian hoping for his big break. "The Academy keeps it quiet that I'm a member," he once said. "Spencer Tracy went there, Kirk Douglas . . . I'm sort of the Pinky Lee of the American Academy of Dramatic Arts."

CHAPTER 3

Don Rickles was twenty-two, armed with a jaunty self-confidence and a scroll of paper from an esteemed acting school. Etta Rickles never had any doubts that her son would be successful. Max Rickles was generally quiet on the subject, hoping his son would come to his senses and return to the world of selling insurance (or selling *something*). Don had no professional acting experience, but who cared? The world was his oyster, and Broadway, just a stone's throw away from the Academy, was the most exciting place to be for a young actor—even for one who was balding and who was not what anyone would call movie-star handsome. He could always be a character actor with that "interesting" face of his.

How tough could it be?

It was tough. There were a lot of aspiring actors trying out for coveted roles on Broadway or even off-Broadway. It did not matter how big or small a role might be; just getting that first credit under your belt, and maybe even a mention in the pages of the Broadway bible, *Playbill* magazine, was enough. If you were really lucky, a New York newspaper legend like Walter Winchell, Ed Sullivan, or Earl Wilson might drop your name into his nationally syndicated column, which reached millions of readers coast-to-coast. Winchell, with his clipped, staccato voice and rapid-fire delivery, also had his hugely popular Sunday night radio show ("Good Evening, Mr. and Mrs. America, and all the ships at sea!")—icing on the publicity cake if he mentioned you over the airwaves.

Television was still in its infancy. Veteran vaudevillian and radio star Milton Berle launched his NBC television show, *Texaco Star*

Theater, in June 1948 in New York City, just as Don was graduating from the Academy. Berle would, in time, earn the nickname "Mr. Saturday Night" for revolutionizing and popularizing the young medium as its first breakout star—and helping to sell millions of television sets, alarming Hollywood, which viewed this new medium providing free content with a jaundiced eye. Don loved Berle and his snarky persona, even in its earliest incarnations, and never failed to mention "Uncle Miltie" as his biggest influence. "He loved television," Etta said of her son. "His idol was Milton Berle." Their paths would not cross for many years. For now, the funnyman Milton Berle was beloved by the nation. For now, the unknown actor, Don Rickles, was beloved by . . . his parents in Jackson Heights.

The 1948–49 season on Broadway presented a world of potential opportunity to a young actor looking for his big break. The most expensive ticket to a Broadway show fetched $6.60, and the Great White Way was rife with hits, including *Gentlemen Prefer Blondes* (Carol Channing), *South Pacific* (Mary Martin and Ezio Pinza), *Death of a Salesman* (Lee J. Cobb), and *Mister Roberts* (Henry Fonda and American Academy alum Jocelyn Brando)—which was set on board a naval ship, no less. The name Don Rickles, however, was nowhere to be found on any cast list of any show—Broadway or off-Broadway or in any other stage venue. The young wannabe actor had all the ambition but none of the luck when it came to landing a part.

"*Mr. Roberts* was the right play. I knew it in my gut," Don recalled. "A wacky comedy about sailors in World War II was right up my alley. I knew the territory. I got the humor. There had to be a part for me."[1]

Don auditioned for director Josh Logan and was given the cursory "We'll call you." They did not. "It was back to Jackson Heights and hot split-pea soup in the middle of July with my father," he said. He spent the summer of 1949, according to one report, working as a busboy at the Hollywood Hills Hotel, a resort in the Adirondacks near the town of Webb, New York. One day, when the entertainment for that night's show failed to arrive, Don was asked to perform. Anything to get a laugh or to just get up on a stage. It was good experience.

When he returned to the city, Don read for a small part in the World War II comedy-drama *Stalag 17*, which was being directed by José Ferrer and costarred Don's Academy classmate John Ericson, who was making his Broadway debut. "We'll call you." They did not. And on it went, an endless parade of auditions but no one the slightest bit interested in the energy and ad-libbing that had powered Don through two years at the American Academy of Dramatic Arts. "I got a cold from taking my shirt off so many times in an effort to get a part of a sailor," he recalled years later. "My family had to pay for the training. Coming from a Jewish family, everyone was saying, 'Is he a queer?' All the uncles from the garment district said: 'He's a queer, huh? Who figured, Max, that your kid would be a queer?'[2]

It was time to make a change.

CHAPTER 4

Don Rickles was a funny man. His humor worked in the schoolyards in Queens, it worked on board the Cyrene during stressful times, and it worked at the Academy when he mimicked his friends or cut up during acting class or in student productions or impersonated celebrities (Cary Grant and Jimmy Cagney were favorites). "Make-It-Up Charlie" he called himself. Maybe he could make people laugh—and even get paid for it.

It was sometime in 1951 when he took the plunge. There were no prospects on the horizon, and he was tired—tired of waiting for that elusive callback while scarfing down a quick meal at McGinnis of Sheepshead Bay, a showbiz hangout on 48th and Broadway ("The Roast Beef King"), tired of trying out the same old gags with the actor and comic wannabes at Hanson's Drugstore on 51st Street (Jack Carter: "Hanson's was for the nothing comics, the third-raters"). Buddy Hackett, then a struggling nightclub comic, was a regular at Hanson's. So, too, was an up-and-coming comic named Will Jordan. "If you had money you went to Lindy's or the Stage Deli," he recalled. "If you were broke you went to Hanson's and hung around all day and used the telephone."[1] Milton Berle had an office above the drugstore, and Don would hang out there, hoping for a glimpse of his idol.

So close, yet so far.

Figuring he had nothing to lose, Don summoned up his courage, took a deep breath, and walked through the doors of the fabled Brill Building at 1619 Broadway, home to all types of show business people, most notably song pluggers and music publishers. He landed his first agent, whose name is lost to the winds of history, but only because Don refused to identify him for reasons of his own. "Let's say, agent Mo Lippman," Don wrote in his memoir, *Rickles' Book*, "he sounds like a Hungarian waiter who just stepped off the boat."

Whatever his name, Agent X had an offer for his new client: twenty-five bucks a night at a club Don later recalled as the Top Hat, a creaky joint across the river in New Jersey. He took it, and quickly cobbled together what passed for an act, throwing in whatever corny jokes he could remember (not his forte) and featuring his small collection of celebrity impressions, including Jack Benny and Jimmy Durante. When that failed on his opening night, he began to insult the audience: "Is that your wife? She looks like a moose." It was good enough for the club's boss, an older guy who sat near the small makeshift stage. He wore a bathrobe, according to Don, and his hacking cough was not to be confused with laughter. "He looked like he was about to go any minute but, believe me, no one was volunteering to give him mouth-to-mouth," Don recalled.

It was an inauspicious beginning, but it was enough to get started, and Agent X booked Don into dingy, second- or third-rate clubs in the area. A far cry from reciting Shakespeare on stage, for sure, and near the bottom rungs of show business, but at least Don was not selling insurance or magazine subscriptions or delivering meat on a bicycle. And, hey, you had to start somewhere, right? Joey Bishop, who was eight years older than Don, was working the circuit at the same time—and once played a place in Cleveland called El Dumpo. Really. It was that kind of life in those kinds of beaten-down, sketchy clubs.

"Really high-class places," Don said. "They smelled like a pair of sneakers after a basketball double-header at the Garden. And the owners were the kind of guys who wore $5,000 pinkie rings and beer-stained undershirts."[2]

There were extracurricular benefits for the twenty-five-year-old bachelor comic, in the form of heavy petting sessions and trysts with women whose names were forgotten in the morning or were never known in the first place. In March of 1952, he saw his name in big bold letters for the first time, in an ad for a place called the

Lamplighter in Rhode Island ("No Cover Charge At Any Time") in the *Newport Daily News*:

All-Star Show

- Don Rickles, Madman of Comedy
- Patti Travers, Voice of Romance
- Jean Mason, Daring Acrobat
- Extra Added Attraction: Lonnie Young, "Venus in Furs"
- Les Carpenter At The Piano

Don was held over at the Lamplighter, and later that month, his moniker was switched from "The Madman of Comedy" to "Your Favorite Comedian" and he became the headliner, with support from "Famous Vocalist" Mingo Maynard and "Versatile Dancer" Val Perry. Patrons could catch the show and chow down on a steak dinner for only $2.75 (excluding Monday).

It is difficult to ascertain, looking back seventy years, whether it was Don's act, his new agent, Willie Weber, or the dearth of entertainers that was responsible for the slight uptick in his popularity. Weber, who was based in New York City, "talked like a corner man in the heat of a heavyweight bout," Don said. He described him as a Damon Runyan type who believed in his client and pushed the club owners, hard, to book the young comedian with the slapdash act—a mélange of stale one-liners, impressions, and a song or two. A decade before, Weber represented Jackie Gleason and was instrumental in booking the struggling comic into the Club 18 on 52nd Street—where, according to showbiz legend, Gleason handed an ice cube to Norwegian figure skater Sonja Henie and said, "Okay, now do something." Jack Warner saw Gleason during his run at the club and signed him to a movie contract. His television fame would come later.

Willie Weber's handling of Don Rickles was a departure for the veteran agent. Parody king Allan Sherman, a former Weber client, joked in his 1965 autobiography, *A Gift of Laughter*, "Willie, as far as

I could tell, had only one single show business instinct: he was one hundred percent dead certain that the only good name for a comedian is Jackie. If a Sam, Alvin, Clyde or Montmorency walked into Willie Weber's office and signed a contract, he walked out under the name of Jackie."[3]

Willie Weber pushed Don, keeping him busy with a steady string of nightclub engagements up and down the Eastern Seaboard and even across the border into Canada—where he convinced a club owner in Montreal to keep Don on for a few more weeks after he insulted a French-speaking patron wearing a plaid shirt: "Hey fella, buy yourself an ax, chop down some trees and ride downriver."

In 1953, Don was playing the Wayne Room, a strip joint in Washington, D.C., when he received an unexpected jolt. After the show, he was startled to see his cousin, Jerry Rickles, who had flown down from New York to deliver some devastating news: Max Rickles was dead, felled by a heart attack at the age of fifty-five while walking down the street. Don learned later, after the initial shock wore off, that by an almost unbelievable coincidence, his cousin Sol, who was an intern at Bellevue Hospital, had been sent to the scene—where he found his Uncle Max crumpled on the pavement. He tried to revive him, to no avail.

Don and Etta were shocked and grief-stricken by the sudden tragedy. Don admired his father, who, while skeptical of Don's career path, was always supportive, and lately had been pleased that his son was making some headway in the entertainment business. Twenty years later, Etta recalled that, in the immediate aftermath of Max's death, Don "said he would never make people laugh again. But I said, 'Your father would have never wanted that to happen to you.' So he went back to work after his father passed away . . . We sat for the ten-day mourning period [known in Judaism as Shiva] and [then] he went back to the Wayne Room, where he was working at the time, and he was there for forty-three weeks. He made history in the nightclub world."[4]

Etta, proud mother that she was, may have been gilding the

lily a bit on that one. It is hard to fathom that a virtually unknown nightclub comic would be held over at a strip joint for ten-and-a-half months—even with Willie Weber, who Don considered "a second father," pushing hard for his client. It is true that Don returned to the Wayne Room at various times over the next three years.

In any event, following Max's death, Etta joined Don in his travels as his unofficial road manager. And the Wayne Room was, Don always claimed, the place where he first started to insult his audience—more in self-defense than in any premeditated plan. "He became an insult comedian because when he got his booking down in Washington, D.C., all the soldiers and sailors were in the audience . . . and they would heckle him back," Etta recalled. "And then he said, 'I'm in command because I have the mic,' and it caught on. Many times he was cancelled in clubs because they couldn't understand the humor."

"My dad was a religious Jew. He didn't know from entertainment," Don recalled. "He was just worried I was going to turn out a queer, traveling around in show business. I got my first big break in the Wayne Room, a burlesque joint in Washington, D.C. They'd yell at me, 'When are you going to get funny?' and I'd yell back at them. That's how I developed my style. I was there for three years and never got punched."[5]

Don's initial run at the Wayne Room went unnoticed at the time. He did, however, gain a bit of notoriety there among the locals by introducing a bizarre new character into the act. He called him "The Man with the Glass Head" and used his best Peter Lorre imitation to give voice to the character. Don claimed that he improvised the bit night after night and never really knew where it was going, changing the details and the situations in which "The Man with the Glass Head" found himself.

The setup was always the same: the Lorre character, who has a glass head, believes that everyone can see into his noggin (it is glass, after all) and, therefore, can see his thoughts. The routine was more suited for a piece of dramatic performance art than a nightclub bit and was usually greeted with polite applause (but rarely raucous laughter). Years later, after Don's death, a fan wrote to say how his mother had seen the routine in Don's nightclub act. She remembered it, he said, as "deeply disturbing and unfunny." No one knew what to make of it—not even Don.

"The Man with the Glass Head" was not created by Don. In fact, he borrowed the concept from Peter Lorre himself. In the mid-to-late 1940s, during personal appearances to promote his movies, Lorre would entertain his audiences with a dramatic monologue that, he felt, suited one of his creepy on-screen characters. One of those monologues, which was about six minutes long, was called "The Man with the Head of Glass." It was written by veteran radio writer Frank Wilson and was, Lorre said once when introducing the character, "a very powerful study of a psychopathic killer, to my mind." Perhaps Don, who was a movie buff, saw Lorre perform the monologue in person after he was discharged from the Navy. Maybe he figured that if he could not find work as an actor, this was the next best thing to a dramatic performance—a way to keep his "head" in the game until he got the Big Call.

"Many of those gin mills were sailor joints in Washington, D.C., which featured bubble dancers like Monique LaVine, who was in big trouble when her bubble pipe didn't work," Don recalled. "We had specialty acts like Zokina and Her King Cobra, which turned out to be a garter snake with dewlaps. Instead of slithering over Zokina's oiled body, it ate its own basket. And one of the strippers, Flora LaVerne, had so many stretch marks on her body she looked like the Mississippi River delta from 30,000 feet up."[6]

With Don spending more and more time on the road, when she was not traveling with him Etta was getting lonely in the two-bedroom apartment in Jackson Heights. She wanted to be closer to her sister, Frieda, who lived twenty miles away in Long Beach, so she moved into a basement apartment in Frieda's building, where Don joined her when he had a break. The place, Don recalled had "a lovely view of the sidewalk." Frieda lived directly above them, and she owned their apartment, so the rent was cheap. Don's proximity to some of the nearby clubs was an added bonus—with Etta usually in the audience, shouting to everyone that, yes, that was *her* son on stage. Wasn't he great? She was his biggest cheerleader.

Willie Weber continued to push for his client. The bookings were steady and a little more sophisticated as 1953 bled into 1954: over to New Jersey to play the Stage Coach Inn in South Hackensack; then, not too far from Long Beach, it was on to Carl Hoppl's Park Inn ("Don Rickles, M.C., Dancing Nitely to Herbie Craeger Orch.") in Valley Stream, where he was held over "with thrush Dolores Leigh, dancers Nancy and Michael Mann and ballerina Marta Nita"; then on to Detroit's Club 509 in September, where he earned a write-up in the *Detroit Free Press*. "Nomination for the entertainer with the billing most likely to pique curiosity is Don Rickles, making his first Detroit appearance . . . He's known as 'the man with the glass head,' and after his comedy, songs, impressions and dance he does a dramatic sketch with that title."

Don was also available for private parties whenever someone thought it was a good idea to have a total stranger come over and insult their guests, like the time he schlepped to Staten Island to entertain at an Italian couple's fiftieth wedding anniversary: "Look at the shape this crowd is in. If I dropped my pants and fired a rocket, I wouldn't get their attention!" Big laughs. You get what you pay for.

In the fall, he made it to the Copa. Okay, so it was not *that* Copa—not yet, anyway—but Lenny Litman's Copa Club on Liberty Avenue in Pittsburgh, where "Ambassador of ill will Don Rickles" played three nightly shows (8:30, 10:30, and 12:30) in support of the Beachcombers and Bill Kenny, leader of the popular vocal jazz/doo-wop group the Ink Spots, who had disbanded several months before. In October, Don made a triumphant return to the Club 509 in Detroit, which presented "The Sensational Don Rickles." In an advertisement for the gig that ran in the *Detroit Free Press*, Don's publicity head shot was inserted into a glass ball alongside the words "GLASS HEAD." And who could forget Don's support acts: "Little Bea, Song Dynamo," "Johnny Ak, King of The Frogs," and Margie

Bassett ("Lovely Dancers")? The following week, still at Club 509, he was billed as "Don 'Glass Head' Rickles," supporting "From the Streets of Paris: Christian and the Lamonts" giving their dramatic interpretation of the "French Apache Story." Culture, too!

Don headed north of the border, where, now billed as the "fast-talking comedian," he spent the early part of March 1955 working the Down Beat Club in Montreal with two singing comedians called the Jaye Brothers. "Comic Don Rickles starts out at a break-neck pace and with some good material but right after his opening falls into a rut of standard stuff, with a touch of melodrama a la Peter Lorre as a finale," wrote an anonymous reviewer from the *Montreal Gazette*, who was clearly not impressed with "The Man with the Glass Head." "His opening is all addressed to the ringsiders and he has some smart things to say to them. If he could keep up this first pace and quality he would have a top flight act."

Don returned to New Jersey later that month to play the Rustic Cabin on Route 9W in Englewood ("2 Miles North of the George Washington Bridge"), and then it was back to Lenny Litman's Copa in Pittsburgh in April to share the bill with singer Larry Ellis: "2 Great Stars! Comedy and Songs!" He returned there two months later billed as "The Revolting Don Rickles" . . . but in a good way.

The rapid-fire insults were now a regular part of Don's arsenal, the raison d'être for his stage act. It worked and they ate it up. Most of the time. Nightclub audiences marveled at this five-foot-six manic ball of energy who picked on everyone—Jews, Blacks, Hispanics, Asians, whoever happened to be in whatever club he was playing that night. No one had ever seen anything quite like this, certainly not in the nightclub world or on television, which was now the country's dominant form of entertainment.

The giants of mid-fifties prime-time television—Lucille Ball and Desi Arnaz, Ed Sullivan, Jackie Gleason, Perry Como, Red Skelton—were drawing upward of 30 million viewers each night. NBC ruled the morning and late-night roost with the *Today* show and *The Tonight Show* with Steve Allen, who moved to prime time with *The Steve Allen Show* in 1956 and did not miss a beat.

Television turned the entertainment industry on its head. Shows such as *Gunsmoke* and *Dragnet*, both popular radio dramas, started to falter in that medium once they were adapted for television on CBS and NBC, respectively. (James Arness replaced portly William Conrad as Matt Dillon in the small-screen version of *Gunsmoke*, but *Dragnet* stars Jack Webb and Ben Alexander made the leap to television and continued to do the radio version.) The movie industry fretted over dwindling box-office receipts and reluctantly dipped their toes into the television waters; in 1955, Warner Bros. became the first major studio to establish a television studio. In a bid to stave off the (free) TV beast, Hollywood threw whatever it could at theatergoers—3-D! CinemaScope! The industry believed it was losing the battle.

Nightclubs were, for the most part, unaffected by the dominance of television during the Eisenhower years, but the new medium did have influence, and therein lay the rub for Don Rickles. The newspaper write-ups, few and far between as they were, helped keep the Rickles train on its tracks. But there was nothing that lifted a nightclub performer more than a television appearance (or two), something to put on the marquee or in newspaper ads ("As seen on *The Ed Sullivan Show*"). That was the best publicity available, even better than a mention in Winchell's column or on his radio show, both declining in popularity as television held America in its black-and-white grip. But Willie Weber was not having much luck getting his client Don Rickles on television. He was too "small potatoes" for the network bookers, working in the smaller clubs but not in the glitzy venues where you got noticed: the Copa and the Blue Angel in New York, the Black Orchid or the Chez Paree in Chicago, the Crescendo in L.A. While Don's contemporaries—Jonathan Winters, Joey Bishop, Buddy Hackett, Jack Carter, Jack E. Leonard, Mort Sahl—were getting spots on *The Ed Sullivan Show, The Perry*

Como Show, *The Tonight Show*, and *The Jackie Gleason Show*, Don was toiling, night after night, in places like Chubby's in South Jersey or the Celebrity Room in Philly. The New Metropole in Windsor, Ontario, still billed him as "Don 'Glasshead' Rickles"—a nickname that did nothing to entice the television bookers. There was a Don Rickles working in television at the time; he was not our Don Rickles, but Donald Newton Rickles, born in Portland, Oregon, in 1927. He forged a long and successful career as an NBC staff announcer. A smattering of his credits are, to this day, erroneously attributed to Donald Jay Rickles on imdb.com. If only . . .

But there were big changes ahead.

CHAPTER 5

I n 1953, a new nightclub opened on Ocean Parkway in Brook-lyn. It was called the Elegante and was owned by brothers Joe and Charles Scandore. The Elegante sat next to the Washington Cemetery, between Avenues J and K, in the middle of a heavily Jewish neighbor-hood. The Club 100, a social organization whose members were Syr-ian Jews, was located nearby, at the eastern corner of Avenue K, on a plot of land that was purchased from Agnes Scandore for $75,000.

The Elegante ("Call CL 2-9700") was spacious and seated a capac-ity of four hundred patrons. Joe and Charles Scandore advertised their club as "A new concept of gracious dining and entertainment in Brooklyn." It soon lived up to its name, attracting a steady crowd of nightclub customers and a luminous roster of entertainers, includ-ing comedians Phil Foster, Larry Storch, and, later, Joey Bishop, and singers Mel Torme and Patti Page. Charles Scandore, meanwhile, was also in business with bandleader Guy Lombardo; they owned the East Point House, a restaurant situated on the water in East Freeport, Long Island. (In 1970, after sitting vacant for two years, the place burned down—a fire of "suspicious origins," according to reports.) Charles Scandore also had a stake in Danny's Hideaway at the Sta-dium View Inn in Queens. Word soon got around about the Elegante.

The Scandore family owned the Scandore Paper Box Company in Brooklyn, located at 21-45 Steuben Street. It was one of the largest paper-box manufacturing companies in the country. In the late 1930s, its employees unionized, which did not make its owners happy. In January 1938, the National Labor Relations Board ordered the com-pany to stop interfering with the fledgling union and to reinstate two workers allegedly fired for activities related to it. In the early fifties, the Scandore Paper Box Company workers went on strike for four weeks, claiming unfair wages. The strike was settled.

There were the persistent rumors, repeated in hushed tones, that the Scandore family was "connected" and that the Elegante was the beneficiary of friends in shadowy places. If so, it was not unusual; the Mob controlled nightclubs around the country—and, all too often, a piece of the performers who worked in those venues (see Sinatra, Frank). "[Joe] Scandore was with the Mob," claimed a comedian named Frank Man, who played the Elegante. "They provided the money and they got you the right jobs. I didn't want to get involved with anything like that but they were all Mob-connected. [Joe] seemed like a nice guy."[1]

Joe Scandore was clearly the more outgoing of the two brothers. He was slight of stature, with a high-pitched voice that people were quick to imitate (never to his face, of course). Joe was a charming, intelligent man with an easygoing manner. A natty dresser, he always wore a freshly pressed and stylish suit. He also had a law degree from Syracuse University; Don later described him as "a bright guy with a show-biz brain." "He was a character," singer Lorna Luft said of Scandore. "And he was abrasive and everybody said, 'Oh, he's got some really rough edges, but a really good heart.' I said 'Yeah, if you can get through the rough edges." He was out of a Damon Runyon novel."[2]

Joe's interest in the entertainment business grew as the Elegante blossomed into a major player on the club scene; he was the face of the enterprise and could be found there almost every night schmoozing with both the customers and the acts. His aide-de-camp was a beefy guy named Rocky (Don called him "a sweetheart") who made sure the performers got to the club on time and were taken care of once they arrived. That kind of thing.

Don turned thirty in May of 1956 and, as fate would have it, landed at the Elegante through the efforts of Willie Weber, who was blissfully unaware that he'd just lost a steady client. Don, to that point, had not played the club, but his act clicked with the Elegante's patrons from the first time he strode onto its small stage. The tough New York crowd and the wiseguys loved his zingers and his take-no-prisoners attitude as he prowled around under the hot lights, armed with nothing but a microphone and his sharp tongue. "I'll be honest, this crowd looks like a real mercy mission, so just give the kid's gifts and let me go home," he roared at one delighted Bar Mitzvah crowd seated in the Elegante. He turned it on and off like a light switch; when the act ended, he mingled with the audience and transformed back into a sweetheart of a guy, a real mensch who asked you lots of questions and was interested in hearing what you had to say—an about-face from the snarling, sweating, acid-tongued bulldog of only minutes before.

"That's where my style came together," Don recalled. "And Joe was there to witness the whole thing." Don brought Etta to the club to watch him perform, and Joe laid on the charm; he "treated her like a queen," and was so nice to her Don. She did not know that Joe was helping her "Sonny Boy" in other ways, occasionally lending Don his Cadillac for some post-show heavy-petting sessions with some woman or other in the Elegante parking lot. Joe was so impressed by Don that he booked him into his club on a semi-regular basis. Before too long Don became an extended member of the Scandore/Elegante family. He routinely took two subways from the apartment in Long Beach to Ocean Parkway to ply his trade at the Elegante—sometimes performing six shows in one weekend (three shows on Saturday and three on Sunday). It was a brutal-but-necessary schedule for a young comic getting his first big break with a patron who knew people, some of whom would figure into Don's rise to the top and who would remain part of his inner circle for decades.

"My father was an accountant in New York City and they had a client, the Scandore Paper Box Company," recalled Bill Braunstein, whose father, Jerry Braunstein, was Don's longtime business manager, a role taken on by Bill after his father's death. "Joe had a small kind of dinner theater [the Elegante] and he said, 'I got this guy, I think there's something there, why don't you come down and meet him? They met, and they were both young guys and my father started working with Don, first with his taxes. Don wasn't making much money back then but he started representing him.

"I can remember the Elegante very well, even though I was very young," Bill recalled. "It wasn't a very big place and had some tables, and I remember my father took me there because he was also doing their accounting. We would go in through the back, up this very small staircase, kind of smelly and dirty . . . and we went up around to the top, where there were books and records piled everywhere. They had this old-time German bookkeeper and she was better than any CPA I ever saw in my life. I don't even know how she figured out where the books were or what was there. That's where I saw Don for the first time . . . I was like, 'What is this?' Especially in his younger days he was really running around everywhere, he had that high, high energy. Most comedians, especially in those days, they told their jokes, you laughed and they moved on. But Don was running around the stage, sweating and dancing and weaving."[3]

Joe Scandore began to take out newspaper ads to publicize Don's appearances at the club and dubbed him "Don 'The Emperor' Rickles." The ads showed a grainy publicity head shot of Don, who was adorned with a crown and holding a scepter—the work of some semi-imaginative layout artist probably taking orders from Joe Scandore. "The Emperor" nickname stuck around for a while, at least at the Elegante, and Don's visibility grew as Joe pulled the strings behind the scenes and called in favors.

In April 1957, Scandore negotiated a deal with New York's NBC television affiliate, WNBC, to bring Jack Paar and *The Tonight Show* into the club on Ocean Parkway and air part of Don's performance to a national audience—his first coast-to-coast exposure. Don shared airtime with the sheriff's office in L.A., the NBC cameras there to document "an after-dark study of police methods." The telecast is, sadly, lost to posterity. But Don remembered it well. "When Jack Paar took over he invited me on just once. It was a disaster," he recalled.

"He didn't know me and I was a scared kid who frankly puzzled him. I came off [as] sour apples. I never went back [on his show]."[4]

As a young man, future actor Gianni Russo ran errands for mob boss Frank Costello and spent many nights at the Elegante in the 1950s during the time that Don was making his name there. Russo knew anyone and everyone—and even those in between—including Joe and Charles Scandore. "Because of Charlie's connections they helped Don along," he recalled. "Charlie was mobbed-up with the Elegante. Joe was the nicest guy [but] the bad thing was he started buying race-horses and lost a lot of money." Russo, for those steeped in the canon of *The Godfather*, played Carlo Rizzi, Vito Corleone's (Marlon Brando) oily son-in-law who set Sonny up for his bullet-riddled death at the tollbooth. Carlo was later garroted by Clemenza (Richard Castellano) in the driveway of the Corleone compound on orders from Michael (Al Pacino). Hey, it happens.

One hot June night in 1957, Joe Scandore somehow persuaded Don's hero, Milton Berle, to come over to Brooklyn and see the act. Berle's visit made Earl Wilson's nationally syndicated column the next day in the *New York Post*: "Milton Berle caught comedian Don Rickles' act at the Elegante in Brooklyn and said, 'You're a funny boy, Don, and here's a glass of poison.' Rickles replied, 'Milton, you're my idol. I know you're my idol and wouldn't want to destroy me.' Turning to the piano player he said, 'Here, you taste it.'" Wilson was an early convert to the Don Rickles school of comedy and supported his career for the next thirty years.

Joe was making things happen. Don, and Etta, took notice. Willie Weber was yesterday's news. Joe Scandore was in.

Willie, however, was not going away without a fight. In his memoir, *Rickles' Book*, Don downplayed his split from Weber. "No hard feelings," he wrote. After all, Willie was happy for him and "always wanted the best" for his client. Willie expressed his joy at Don's abrupt departure by suing him for breach of contract in Queens County court. In the case, *Cangold v. Rickles*, Weber's attorney, Benjamin Gelosky, claimed that Don had signed a contract with the

Scandore Brothers on June 1, 1956, agreeing to perform for the year at the Elegante. The contract, he alleged, gave Willie the right to exercise Don's services for a four-week period in 1957 during the months of May, June, November, or December "at a compensation of $325 for two weeks, and at $350 per week for the other two weeks." He claimed that Don, in April 1957, "through his agents refused to accept the engagement or to fix the dates." The two-count lawsuit was dismissed in New York Superior Court in May 1958.

Don never asked any questions. How Joe conducted business was, well, *his* business. He was taking good care of Don and was passionately committed to his new full-time client. His game plan for "The Emperor" was to book Don into bigger and more sophisticated clubs, to get the word out about the balding comedian who crossed so many lines in his act that no one could possibly take him seriously. If they did, Don would soften them up at the end of the act, launching into a spiel about he was really a nice guy who loved everyone, that his caustic observations and put-downs of Blacks, Hispanics, Jews, Asians, fat people, homely people (the list goes on) were just part of the act and can't we just all get along and laugh at ourselves? Once in a while he even threw God into the equation. What Joe thought about this is anyone's guess, but it worked . . . so it stayed in the act. Don was not a joke-teller. His humor was observational, in an aggressive kind of way.

"Don is the type of comic who looks around at the people watching him and then proceeds to cut them down or tear them apart," wrote a *Brooklyn Eagle* reporter profiling the thirty-one-year-old comic in 1957. "He leaves no stone unturned in making his victim uncomfortable. Yet, despite this, there is a lesson in brotherhood to be learned . . . Don says there are two types of people who don't like his type of comedy. Both the bigots and the anti-Semites are hurt because, despite the heavy laughs which follow him throughout the act, the barbs strike home. 'The good people—and thank God they're in the majority—laugh because they know I'm only kidding, or maybe because they think I'm sick in the head,' Don said. 'I never intend making a speech about brotherhood or preaching about it when I start the night's work, but I can't help it. There is always someone who just refuses to believe that other people are entitled to the same respect that they get.'"[5]

Not everyone was buying it. As his star began to rise, some critics found Don disingenuous, insufferable . . . and boring. "The guy is sensational—while he's being funny," wrote a *Los Angeles Times* reviewer. "Insulting, but not offensively so."[6]

Don finished out 1956 with a run of shows in Montreal at the Fontaine Bleau room at the Chez Paree. The reviews were good, but not great. "Mr. Rickles spends nearly all his time exchanging insults with the customers and some of his remarks are extremely sharp and witty. He is a fast and hard-driving worker, though, and he certainly knows how to deliver a line."[7]

That review in the *Montreal Gazette* ran alongside an ad for *Bus Stop*, the Marilyn Monroe movie ("Broadway's biggest hit becomes Marilyn's best!") costarring Don's pal, Don Murray, from the American Academy of Dramatic Arts, who went to see Don's act if he was in town.

"One time I heard he was playing a nightclub in east Los Angeles and I went to see him," Murray recalled. "There were only about six people in the audience and he was doing this routine where he made fun of those six people, who were Hispanic. He started making fun of them and they didn't understand what he was doing and they were getting angry at his insulting them. But he never stopped; he kept going and going. Afterwards I said, 'Don, I was afraid for your life' and he said, 'Oh, yeah, sometimes I get a tough audience.' That was par for the course for Don."

On September 29, 1957, Don's favorite baseball team, the New York Giants, played their final game at the Polo Grounds, a desultory 9–1 loss to the Pittsburgh Pirates. The team was leaving New York City and moving to San Francisco; five days before, their crosstown National League rivals, the Brooklyn Dodgers, wrapped it up at Ebbets Field (beating those same Pirates 2−0). They, too, were moving to California, where their new fans were awaiting their Los Angeles Dodgers.

Don was disappointed—what New York baseball fan wasn't?—but it was a rare low point for him that year. In those twelve months, all the pieces started to come together as the nightclub bookings, the column mentions, the celebrity fans, and the notoriety propelled him toward national stardom.

He was still romantically unattached and living with Etta in the basement apartment in Long Beach when she decided they needed their own places away from Aunt Frieda—thousands of miles away, in Miami Beach. (Don: "a tropical suburb of New York City.") So, mother and son packed up and moved to Florida; Etta shared a two-room apartment on Collins Avenue with Honey Schwartz, a friend from the old neighborhood in Jackson Heights. Don rented a small apartment nearby.

CHAPTER 6

There was a reason that Etta and Don chose Miami Beach to settle down for now. The weather was nicer, of course, but it made sense professionally—he was a hit in South Florida.

The hubbub had kicked into high gear the previous summer. Don headed south after completing a few engagements up north, including a run at the Celebrity Room in Philadelphia, two shows a night, at 9:00 p.m. and midnight.

In August, he opened at Murray Franklin's, the club in Miami Beach where Don (most likely) first met Frank Sinatra—the "Make yourself at home, Frank, hit somebody" gig recounted at the beginning of this book. Murray Franklin's was a modest place and no match for the bigger, better-known venues such as the Roney Plaza, right across the street, or Café Pompei at the Eden Roc, or the La Ronde over at the Fontainebleau Hotel. But the smart set knew where it was and kept the place crowded and buzzing. The year before, Murray and his club had launched torch singer Roberta Sherwood into stardom, and in short order, she landed a recording contract with Decca Records and herself on the cover of *Life* magazine. Murray knew what he was doing. He saw himself, Don recalled, "as the Ed Sullivan of Miami Beach." Unlike Sullivan's studio audience, the clubgoers at Murray's place watched the stage show from rocking chairs.

The *Miami News*, August 14, 1956: "Latest Franklin offering is comedian Don Rickles, who is virtually a one-man Club 18. The reference is to a now-deceased New York café noted for insults by the proprietors. People used to flock to the place to hear the owners insult the customers.

"Such is the type of Rickles' humor. Visiting showpeople catch the brunt of the guy's insults—but he throws a curve or two at anybody who happens to be around ringside or at the bar."

Two weeks later, syndicated columnist Hy Gardner led the Rickles cheerleading brigade. "The hottest nightspot in the Beach area is Murray Franklin's rocking-chair lounge from which nook Roberta Sherwood rose to belated fame and fortune. The momentum is being sustained by a whacked-up, pyramid-headed young comic named Don Rickles. His routine defies description, theft, or review. His forte is the quick insult. He's more insulting than Toots Shor, Ted Williams and Jack E. Leonard combined. Aside from that he does practically nothing—nothing, that is, except to make people laugh."

One night, the comedy team of Dan Rowan and Dick Martin, who were headlining at the newly opened Americana Hotel in South Beach (which was built for a then staggering $17 million), came to see Don at Murray Franklin's and spread the word "all up and down the beach." Larry King, a twenty-three-year-old broadcaster from Brooklyn, was now hosting an overnight radio show from a houseboat in Miami Beach. He befriended Don and invited him on to the show to schmooze and to verbally attack listeners who called in (and dared to ask a question). On another occasion, Jackie Gleason, whose live television show would, eight years later, move to Miami Beach from New York City, happened to be in town. He strolled into the club and was seated at a small table, alone, adjacent to the stage where Don was performing. "Okay, pal," he barked to the sweating comedian, "make the Great One laugh." As Gleason tossed back a few, Don joked about the Irish and did a snarky riff on Gleason's June Taylor Dancers. (Gleason married June Taylor's sister, Marilyn, in the mid-seventies.) Gleason smiled, just barely, and he lifted his glass: "To you, pally."

Bob Booker, who would go on to coproduce the JFK spoof-parody album *The First Family*—one of the fastest-selling albums in history—met Don for the first time at Murray Franklin's.

"I was working in Miami at that time. Of all things I was a disc jockey on television and I used to go over to see Don," he recalled. "It was one of the joints you had to go to. It was packed every night. Don was the talk of the beach. There were some great comics down there and it was a tremendous city. Don really had no act. He never had an act. They were talking about him the same way they would talk about [comedian] B. S. Pully. Miami, back then, was really a hot town for shows. People would have their own clubs, music, and comics. Peter, Paul and Mary were working at a bar. Louis Prima and Keely Smith were doing like eight shows a night in a bar on the beach. Henny Youngman, Alan King, Jackie Miles were all there. Joe E. Lewis would play the big gambling casinos that were just on the edge of Dade County. The whole beach was alive, and Don was building a career there, no question."[1]

Word of Don's triumphs at Murray Franklin's soon traveled north, to the New York City newspapers. The *Daily News* wrote about the city's native son in glowing terms under the headline "A New Comic." "The most unusual new comic to come along in years is Don Rickles, a master of insult, who keeps a lounge named Murray Franklin's jumping all night long. Rickles' style is very specialized, but a gift for drama which reminds one of Danny Thomas during his fine nightclub days suggests that he can move into the big league with new material."

In March 1957, the conquering hero returned to Joe Scandore's Elegante on Ocean Parkway in Brooklyn to play a few shows. He was billed as being "Direct From A Record Breaking Run at Miami Beach." Joe Scandore insisted, again, on advertising Don as "The Emperor" and running the same corny newspaper ads showing the balding "king" wearing a crown and holding his scepter. Don shared the bill with the long-forgotten Fran Leslie and Estelita & Chicuelo, whose talents are lost to posterity. In late March, he returned to the Celebrity Room in Philadelphia, sharing the lineup with Jewish American singing star Bas Sheva, who was born Bernice Kanefsky in the Bronx and was currently the flavor-of-the-month star big enough for a slot on *The Ed Sullivan Show*. Television remained out of Don's reach. But not for long. Next, though, it was off to California.

Rose Marie, who was later to costar as wisecracking comedy writer Sally Rogers on *The Dick Van Dyke Show*, recalled that she and her husband, trumpeter Bobby Guy, were instrumental in getting Don out to the West Coast. "We saw him working in Florida, and I got him a job in a club in California through some friends of mine. I knew he'd either be the biggest hit or the most smashing flop," she recalled. "And I'm glad I was right. He hit it, and big."

He sure did.

The Slate Brothers Club was located at 339 North La Cienega Boulevard, on the site of the former LaVee Club, in the city's "Restaurant Row" district on the edge of Beverly Hills. The club was small, with a capacity of about 125, and it boasted crystal chandeliers, mirrored walls, and deep, plush carpeting—a bizarre touch for a nightclub that, nonetheless, set it apart from its competitors.

The club was owned by brothers Jack, Henry, and Sid Slate— entertainers whose act mixed tap dancing and comedy and stretched back several decades, yet had taken them only to the fair-to-middling rungs of show business. The brothers, who were from New Haven, Connecticut, competed in Charleston competitions in the Roaring Twenties and eventually tap-danced their way into *The Earl Carroll Vanities* on Broadway, a popular revue that ran for nearly seventeen years and spawned stars including Sophie Tucker, W. C. Fields, Jack Benny, and Don's idol, Milton Berle.

Try as they might, the Slate Brothers never did hit the big time like their sibling comedy peers the Marx Brothers and the Ritz Brothers. They did, however, get a whiff of that rarefied air every now and then. They played the Palace Theatre in New York City— considered the Olympus of vaudeville houses—and, in 1938, they appeared on the big screen in the Hollywood farce *College Swing*, a forgettable affair that counted among its embarrassed cast George Burns, Gracie Allen, Martha Raye, Bob Hope, and Edward Everett Horton. The brothers knocked around the circuit for the next two decades, appeared on three prehistoric television shows (*Cavalcade of Stars*, *The NBC Comedy Hour*, *The Milton Berle Show*), and apparently saved their money for that rainy day when they chucked it all and opened their own nightclub. "The Slates come from an era when Charley Yates was Broadway's top flesh peddler and Danny Friendly was an office boy in the Loews office," the *Los Angeles Mirror News* noted.[2]

This is where Don comes in.

The Slate Brothers Club opened its doors the night of July 17, 1957, with a packed house including gangster Mickey Cohen, George Jessel, George Raft, and the Three Stooges. Comedian Buddy Lester was the unofficial doorman and assistant host. The inaugural entertainment lineup featured Gil Bernal and his orchestra, singer Betsy Duncan, "piano comedian" Eddie Barnes . . . and headliner Lenny Bruce. "Naturally the three Slates Henry Syd [*sic*] and Jack will be on hand nightly to heckle the acts and keep the shows moving. Nice gesture," the *Mirror News* proclaimed. Across town, Nat King Cole was holding forth at the Ambassador Hotel.

Bruce, the self-destructive, thirty-one-year-old comic who delighted in the taboo, was booked for a two-week run, two shows a night. He flamed out in spectacular fashion in his first show and turned his back to the audience to talk to the band each time one of his stream-of-consciousness riffs hung there to die in embarrassing silence. The second show went completely off the rails, when Bruce told this joke he said he'd heard from his pal Buddy Hackett: "A kid looks up to his father and he says, 'What's a degenerate?' The father says, 'Shut up, kid, and keep sucking!'" Mic drop. Gasps. Maybe a spit take or two in the stunned crowd. "During the late opus, Bruce, who usually turns in a most entertaining chore, slipped from the curb and came up covered with smut," the *Mirror News* reported. "After the show he admitted that the noisy gathering got the best of him and he just lost his head. He also lost his job."[3]

The Brothers Slate were in a panic after losing their top draw after one ignoble night. It was a disaster. Don was in L.A., bouncing around from club to club, and a frantic call went out to Joe Scandore. Don was quickly booked to replace Lenny Bruce as the club's headliner.

He was an instant success, and the word got out about the quick-witted insult comic who took no prisoners, particularly when it came to the Hollywood stars who flocked to the club to be lacerated by the sweaty, balding funnyman. "Henry [Slate] went out of his way to push me on the public," Don recalled. "I didn't know that this push would be the big one—the one I'd been waiting for."

Word of mouth about this new sensation spread quickly and followed Don to Zardi's, the jazz club over on Hollywood Boulevard. It, too, attracted A-list stars hoping to be insulted by Don Rickles and maybe even mentioned by Hedda Hopper or Louella Parsons or Harrison Carroll, the big hitters in Hollywood with nationally syndicated gossip columns.

Harrison Carroll: "Joan Collins with Arthur Loew Jr. at Zardi's again to catch that hilarious Don Rickles."

Gene Sherman, the *Los Angeles Times*: "Whenever Don Rickles spots celebrities at the Slate Brothers he slugs them unmercifully."

Mike Connolly: "Rita Hayworth and Jim Hill were at the Slate Brothers Restaurant a few nights ago to see Don Rickles."

Hedda Hopper: "Dined with Henry Ginsberg at Romanoff's, then went to Slate Brothers bistro on La Cienega . . . Then on came Don Rickles, who convulsed us all, including Judy Garland . . . She laughed so I thought she'd have a stroke."

Louella Parsons: "Gary Cooper laughed so hard when comic Don Rickles of the Slate Brothers club had him up on the floor, he couldn't speak the one line given him in the sketch. Turning to the audience, Rickles said, 'This man makes a million dollars a year as an actor, and can't speak the one line I give him.'"

And on and on.

"My mom just adored him," recalled Judy Garland's daughter

Lorna Luft. "When he was at the lounge at the Sahara my mother would go and watch his show. He was ruthless to her. The more ruthless he was, the harder she would scream laughing. People could not believe that my mother would go see Don Rickles in the lounge because, I mean, you're talking about an icon. She would take everybody with her. The more he would be ruthless about her, the more she would laugh, and she had this great laugh and Don loved her. And she loved Don. Because if you could not laugh at yourself, don't go see Don Rickles."[4]

"My first meeting [with Don] was very interesting," Carl Reiner recalled. "No one knew of him then. He had just come out here. I was doing a movie with Ernie Kovacs, and Ernie said, 'There's a guy at the Slate Brothers they say is very funny. I'm going with Frank Sinatra. Do you want to join us?' The three of us sat there and watched this guy. He just ripped people apart. Everyone was laughing and screaming. I'll never forget the first big laugh he got: Franklin Roosevelt's son was in the audience. Everyone applauded him. Don said, 'James, I was in Vegas the other day. I saw your mother there. She was standing behind the pillar waving her pocketbook over her head saying, 'Want to have some fun sailor?' The audience went nuts. He dared to do that kind of a joke in front of the son of the president."[5]

Don counted gangster Mickey Cohen among his growing legion of fans. Cohen's biographer, Brad Lewis, claimed in *Hollywood's Celebrity Gangster: The Incredible Life and Times of Mickey Cohen* that Cohen "originally promoted Rickles to the Slate Brothers." Whatever the case, Don did not care who Cohen was connected to, nor did he give a rat's ass about his (alleged, of course) mob ties. Several years later, with Cohen seated in the Slate Brothers Club audience, Don turned to him. "Fine friend! I'm up in San Francisco and you don't even invite me over to visit you"—a reference to Cohen's stint in Alcatraz after he was convicted of income tax evasion.[6]

Don's act did not go over well with everyone. Actress Janis Paige was hot off *Silk Stockings*, her new movie musical comedy costarring Fred Astaire and Cyd Charisse, when she went to see Don at the

Slate Brothers Club that first summer. Sixty years later, after Don's death, she remembered the sting of how it felt to be ripped apart by the insult comic.

> The place was small and packed as we were ushered to a tiny table near the front. Don entered, and after a few jokes, he mentioned to the audience that I was in the room. There was applause—and then began a verbal tirade that shocked and embarrassed me beyond words. Don proceeded to tear apart my ripe old "over the hill" age of 34, my looks, my talent and my successes. He left nothing to the imagination, including a few hints as to whom I had slept with "on my way to the top." I took everything personally and was left in a pool of my own insecurities. Unlike Frank Sinatra, who enjoyed Don's gutsy and one-of-a-kind routines, I just felt hurt and mad as hell.[7]

Lucille Ball and Desi Arnaz were not big Don Rickles admirers, at least in those early years. One newspaper columnist reported that Desi "found the Rickles humor in poor taste, not funny," while Lucy railed against the "sick comedians" of the day. "But I get terrified watching someone like Don Rickles, the way he perspires, as if he's going to have a heart attack. One evening Desi and I were his target, but it went right over my head. It reminded me of certain members of the English press, their faces contorted while they're asking ugly questions they're forced to ask, doing something they don't particularly enjoy." (Lucy came around to Don in later years. He guest-starred on an episode of her CBS sitcom *The Lucy Show* in 1967, and in 1975 he was invited to skewer Lucy on the *Dean Martin Celebrity Roast*.)

Groucho Marx, enjoying a career resurgence on television as the wisecracking host of *You Bet Your Life*, added his name to the list of Rickles detractors after being roasted by Don at the Slate Brothers Club one night: "Let's face it, your brothers carried you for years and when you lose the duck the show goes off the air." Groucho did not appreciate the put-down, which was ironic and thin-skinned for a legendary comedian whose bread and butter was making fun of others behind his penciled-on mustache and arching eyebrows. "A comedian will never be a star unless he is loved," he said. "It may be therapeutic to let out venom and hostility, but it's not the type of material that will make his name live through the ages. That is why Don Rickles will never be a star."

"He was very big in Florida and then he came to the Slate Brothers [Club] where he was very big," comedian Shecky Greene recalled over sixty years later. "I thought we were good friends, but we really weren't. He was jealous of Buddy Hackett and myself . . . he was frightened of us. Well, everyone was frightened of Buddy.

"I really thought Don Rickles stunk," he said. "After you saw him once, I don't care what anybody says, to me that was a bunch of shit. Yelling at people—'You're a Chink, you're a Jap'—that, to me, is all shit. To me, that wasn't talent. That was just personality. People have talent. Personality is another thing. What the public finds when they like to make a star is that personality. George Burns couldn't sing, but George Burns was great. When you call someone funny, it's the Ritz Brothers, it's the [Three] Stooges, knocking around."[8]

The vociferous Rickles bashers were in the minority. As Don's run in L.A. at the Slate Brothers, Zardi's, and elsewhere picked up steam, everyone wanted in on the action and flocked to see him that magical summer. Some stars returned to the firing line five or six times, hoping for that very public badge of honor: a tongue-lashing from Rickles, the more vicious the better so their fans could read about how they laughed at the zingers thrown their way (even if they were boiling inside). Don changed the act, such as it was, night after night, perspiring heavily and mopping his sweaty brow with a soaked handkerchief as he darted left and right with his microphone searching for his next target. "I really flatter the stars and I make ordinary people important by insulting them," he explained. It was not rocket science. And it was funny.

Don to Anthony Quinn: "I thought you were a great actor when I saw you tearing a roasted chicken apart at your table in Romanoff's. You're not an actor—you're a big slob."

Don to Zsa Zsa Gabor: "There's a bus leaving in ten minutes for Budapest. Get on it."

Don to Esther Williams: "Here's a towel, Esther, wipe your ears and show us how good you can act."

Don to Sid Luft and Judy Garland: "Look at Luft there laughing out loud. He doesn't know that Judy has cut him out of the will." (Luft, for the record, was not amused.)

Don to a hefty Slate Brothers patron: "I saw your cardiogram, you've got an hour."

They all came out to see Rickles that summer and fall: Jerry Lewis, Dean Martin, Gary Cooper, Jack Benny, the aforementioned Judy Garland ("Judy, find Mickey Rooney. I'll throw straw on the floor, and you can do a show here in the barn."), Jimmy Durante, Bob Hope, Red Skelton. Sinatra dropped by, of course, once with the newly widowed Lauren Bacall (Bogie had died in January) after a dinner at Romanoff's. (Don: "Remember the good old days, Frank, when you had a voice?") Sinatra was back several nights later, this time with Bacall and their friends Elizabeth Taylor and Mike Todd. "Don Rickles at the Slate Brothers café must be Frank Sinatra's favorite comic," Louella Parsons wrote in her column. Yes, Louella, he was.

Sinatra told Don how much it meant to him that Etta Rickles and his mother, Dolly, were friends. It meant so much to Don that Sinatra let him into the inner circle, just enough to give the young insult comic carte blanche to rip Frank a new one in the act, wherever and whenever he wanted (as long as Frank was there in person). No one else could get away with it. No one dared. Sammy Davis Jr. once criticized Frank in a Chicago radio interview—"I love Frank, but there are many things he does that there is no excuse for"—and was frozen out of Sinatra's inner circle for a stretch of time. (Shecky Greene found out the hard way. He told and retold the story of Frank "saving his life" one time in Las Vegas. Frank, he said, sicced the boys on Shecky over some slight, real or imagined, and they worked him over, but good, until Frank stepped in: "Okay, he's had enough." Cue the rim shot.)

"I had already made a lot of friends in the business," Don said. "The show biz people made me the sort of 'in' guy . . . the guy who was allowed to do this. I have always said I'm just putting someone on, a good rib. I don't like to think of it as unkind . . . All I know is what I think is funny and it goes no further. It's not something you can go home and think about. I never have anything written down."[9] As Eve Starr wrote in the *Allentown Morning Call*:

> He cuts them up into small, ragged-edged bits and pieces and leaves them lying on the floor, figuratively bleeding to death, almost literally laughing themselves to death. He also goes after unknowns in the audience, sweetly asking their names and origin—then quickly dissecting them. At the end of his act, he launches into a long—too long, actually—and fervent plea for tolerance amongst men, which serves as an apology for his own carryings on and presumably makes his victims feel better about it all.[10]

No one else was doing this in 1957. No one dared. There were the trailblazers and the rumblings of what the press, in those days, called the "sick" comedians—the scattershot, self-sabotaging Lenny Bruce . . . sardonic Mort Sahl, criticizing the establishment in his smart red sweater while holding the rolled-up newspaper . . . Redd Foxx, "The King of the Party Records," whose naughty vinyl output was sold under-the-counter, Foxx held back from mainstream visibility by the color of his skin . . . Shelley Berman . . . Tom Lehrer. But the insults? Those were Don Rickles's bread and butter—he was, as columnist Hy Gardner dubbed him, "Hollywood's burnt-toast-of-the-town." Jonathan Winters, who soon gained entry into the class of "sick" comics, was a big fan, who called Don "a very funny man. Remember . . . he insults everybody. If he picked on one or two people, then I'd agree that it's bad taste, but this way it's the act and it's fun."[11] So there.

No one did it better—in fact, no one was doing it at all. Not really. Jack E. Leonard sparred with his audience, but Don took it to an otherworldly level of withering put-downs that, with the rare exception, had the target doubled over with laughter. "With Don's humor, when he would say things, he was laughing with people and not at them," Lorna Luft recalled. "Jack E. Leonard was laughing at them. And that was the difference."[12]

He made fun of everyone—*everyone*, no matter what their income, social status, religion, ethnicity, color, gender . . . it was all fair game. You knew what to expect and you got what you paid for. The put-down. Henny Youngman asked you to "Take my wife, please"—Don told you that your wife was ugly and fat and so were you. He made fun of the Jews, the Irish, the Chinese, the Japanese, Arabs, Blacks, Hispanics, Italians . . . and he never worked blue. You got arrested for that. Just ask Lenny Bruce.

"My main problem is that my humor depends on my face," Don said. "If you take a quote from me—in print, it's different. I read it, and I say, 'Ouch.' Seeing it in cold print bothers me. It's what's not in print that's important—my honesty and my love for people. I think this comes across in my personality."[13]

"There was a gentleness to his harshness, if that makes sense," recalled Jay Leno, the veteran stand-up comic and longtime host of *The Tonight Show* following Johnny Carson's retirement in 1992. Don was a frequent guest. "Because you always realized he is not going for the throat, he is going for the funny bone. And that was the key. If you wrote his act out, I don't think it would be funny. I don't mean that in an insulting way. I just mean the fact that he made it funny through inflection and body language and just the way he reacted, the eyes bugging out."[14]

Offstage, when the lights went down and the crowd left, he transformed into a mensch, the nice, shy kid from Jackson Heights who only wanted to please everyone. "People who know Don just *love* him," said Joe Scandore, his biggest fan (right behind Etta, of course). "In reality, there are two Don Rickles—the fellow that's acting, making caustic comments and insulting people—and the real Don Rickles . . . the one the public doesn't know—a loyal, affectionate, warm man, a good man, a man who's *loved*, absolutely loved by his fellow performers."[15]

Well, not always. With Don's rapid rise up the comedy food chain came the backstage gossip, the whispers of how the comedian who could not get arrested a year ago (okay, so maybe there was a parking ticket) was suddenly the talk of the town. Never mind his raw talent, his energy, his seemingly endless reservoir of put-downs that, more often than not, hit their mark. So what was it then? Jealousy? Envy? Perhaps it was a bit of both in the backstabbing world of unhappy nightclub comics, where they eat their own and accuse each other of stealing jokes that were not all that funny to begin with. Milton Berle was "The Thief of Bad Gags" and loved the nickname so much he worked it into the act. That was one way to turn it around and throw it in their faces.

But Don did not tell jokes, so that side of the argument didn't carry much water. They whispered that it was Joe Scandore, with his "connections" to the guys no one messed with in the back rooms of the clubs. Maybe, but every comic knew you either played the game and jumped on the shady, mobbed-up bandwagon or watched your career fizzle in some strip joint in Newark . . . Delaware. Don played the game. He trusted Joe Scandore.

"Damon Runyon wrote about people like Joe Scandore," recalled producer George Schlatter. "People like Jilly Rizzo, Joe Scandore, people whose names were Guido and Carmine . . . 'colorful gentlemen' who permeated the whole café society in Las Vegas, Florida and Los Angeles. They were people to be cultivated but not offended."

Jack E. Leonard was Don's main competitor among the few "insult" comics daring to go there. Leonard was affectionately (or not) known as "Fat Jack" to his friends and detractors, for his size and girth, which he cleverly emphasized for comedic effect by wearing a too-small suit, big black-framed glasses, and a wide-brimmed hat. The schnook as Everyman. Fat Jack was fifteen years older than Don and had paid his dues—Charleston contests, vaudeville, big bands, the works. Don knew about him, of course, everybody did, and Ed Sullivan and Jack Paar invited Fat Jack onto their television shows—Sullivan in prime time on CBS and Paar during the late-night hours on NBC. (Leonard on *The Ed Sullivan Show* in 1958: "Before the show tonight I just got a late flash over the air, that Jerry Lee Lewis just brought his wife one of those new dresses . . . a sack diaper.") When he died years later, his obituary in the *New York Times* claimed that Fat Jack made fifty-four television appearances in one year.

Leonard was funny and popular and took his comedic cue from Jack Waldron, an actor and comic ("Let's play horse—I'll be the front end and you just be yourself"). Fat Jack could be cutting—"You have a very fine voice—too bad it's in Bing Crosby's throat," he told Perry Como—and as word of Don's act spread, providing the columnists with his snappy one-liners, the inevitable comparisons to Leonard began to find their way into the discussion. Soon, the community of the nightclub comics, a notoriously insecure bunch, started to wag their fingers at Don. He was appropriating Fat Jack's act, they said—which spoke more to their own insecurities and jealousies. And, save for Joey Bishop, they did not have Frank Sinatra in their corner.

Fat Jack, too, complained a lot about this kid Rickles "stealing" his material. He never got over it. "I knew Jack E. Leonard quite well," recalled comic impressionist Rich Little. "He was a very nice man. I used to see him a lot and I got to know him. He was not like he was on stage. He was a put-down comic, too, but he wasn't quite as fast as Don. He was a little milder. Jack thought that Don stole his act, which was not true. But that's a little sour grapes there, I think."[16]

Don's contemporary, Shecky Greene, was on the other side of the debate. "Jack was a friend of mine from Chicago, and when Rickles started to get really popular he said to me, 'Sheck, is he doing me?'" Greene recalled. "I said, 'Jack, he is not doing you. You are you, understand?' He lived in Vegas and I would meet him every morning at seven o'clock for coffee for him to cry into."[17]

A well-known television producer and Vegas insider who knew both men delineated the differences between Don Rickles and Jack E. Leonard. "A lot of Don came from Fat Jack Leonard. Jack was fat, he wore a hat, and he danced and sang, but he never captured the imagination and that popularity within show biz, the movie/Beverly Hills circle," he said. "He was back in New York a lot. Rickles was reminiscent of Fat Jack, but Don was an original and he was very enjoyable and very funny and very popular."

"You can't steal a guy's show and the feeling was that Don . . . stole that attitude from Jack E. Leonard," noted comedian Tom Dreesen. "I had seen Jack perform at Mr. Kelly's in Chicago one time and he was really sarcastic. But you knew he meant it. Rickles would always try to camouflage it later on with 'Oh, I'm a nice guy,' 'Laughter for love,' and all that kind of stuff. He wanted to make you think, 'I'm just having fun,' but Jack E. Leonard made you think, 'No, this is exactly how I feel.' I think if Don took Jack E. Leonard's attitude or personality, he just softened it up a little bit."[18]

In the late 1960s, when Don was being roasted at the Friars Club, Fat Jack made the introduction: "Friends . . . welcome once more to the Eichmann trial. I want to tell you what a thrill it is to be here in honor of one of America's great Americans . . . who has been doing my act for about twelve years now. I am here to make a citizen's arrest. I don't mind the guy doing my act, but the son of a bitch stole my [bald] head too. I also want to thank Johnny Carson for creating a monster."

He was only half-kidding—if he was kidding at all.

"He was a star long before I was heard of," Don said, graciously regarding Leonard. "I respect his status. We have been on the same dais together and maybe swapped some gentle jibes. But never have we battled it out, insult for insult, the way one might expect.

"Actually, our styles would clash and it wouldn't work," he said. "People may think we're alike because we go after the same thing.

But we are of different schools. Jackie is a joker. He throws one-line cracks like a buzzsaw. I circle around and zero in."[19]

Don's career kicked into high gear now, and with the success came the spoils. Burt Lancaster went to see Don at the Slate Brothers Club to be insulted—and promptly offered him a small supporting role in his next movie, a submarine drama called *Run Silent, Run Deep* that costarred Clark Gable and would begin shooting later that year. "I didn't know he was an actor," Lancaster said. "I just like being insulted for a change." Don, the frustrated thespian a decade removed from the American Academy of Dramatic Arts, was finally going to be in a picture. Better yet, the role was tailor-made for former Seaman First Class Rickles. There was the small matter of a nerve-wracking audition for director Robert Wise, which he passed with flying colors. "Don Rickles landed the prize comedy role in 'Run Silent, Run Deep,' the Clark Gable-Burt Lancaster film," faithful Earl Wilson reported in the *New York Post*.

The television doors were now starting to open, too, for the hot young comic. Eddie Fisher, a Rickles victim at the Slate Brothers Club that summer, invited Don to be a guest on *The Eddie Fisher Show*, a musical/variety series he hosted several times with his wife, Debbie Reynolds. It was not *The Ed Sullivan Show* but it was national exposure and it increased Don's visibility alongside fellow guests Tommy Sands, Marie Wilson, and actress Mary McCarty. NBC canceled Fisher's series two years later, after he left Reynolds for Elizabeth Taylor. Bad publicity and all that.

Don played it straight as a cabdriver named Eddie in an episode of *The Thin Man*, another NBC series, which aired Friday nights and starred Peter Lawford and Phyllis Kirk as the small-screen version of detectives Nick and Nora Charles—and, yes, they had a dog named Asta. It was not much of a role for Don, just a few lines, and merited little, if any, attention in the press.

There were reports that the networks were sniffing around.

Don told *Inside TV* columnist Eve Starr that he had "many" television offers, but he did not specify what those were, saying only that he had been approached about starring in his own comedy series and in a "spectacular" that never materialized (if it even existed in the first place). "I'd like to guest star with Oscar Levant but I'm warning him now, I'm sicker than he is," he joked.

He appeared on local television shows to plug his nightclub appearances. He was a guest on Tom Duggan's Friday-night show on KCOP in Los Angeles. Duggan, a controversial columnist who crusaded against Chicago's underworld, had relocated to L.A. in the mid-fifties. He either fled Chicago or was forced to leave, depending on who you asked. He also hit the sauce and sometimes failed to show up for work; one night, after he could not be located, he was replaced by a young kid named Regis Philbin. "I had a fine time on his show, and I must say his wife is the most beautiful half-blooded Indian I've ever known," Don said about Duggan. "We got along so famously we're forming our own *Wagon Train*." Don's reference to the popular ABC series starring Ward Bond was a sardonic wink to the networks' prime-time schedules, which were rife with Westerns, including *Have Gun, Will Travel*, *Bat Masterson*, *Gunsmoke*, and *The Life and Legend of Wyatt Earp*.

"Just what could be done with this gifted man on TV is difficult to say," Eve Starr wrote of Don. "NBC tried for a year to find a suitable format for George Gobel before Hal Kanter finally came up with the solution that won Gobel an Emmy. It is possible that a Kanter could do the same for Rickles. He is worth both the time and investment. He has timing, personality and a devastating collection of ad-libs."[20]

While Don was appearing at the Slate Brothers Club, Etta left Florida to join him in L.A., and they moved into a small place near the club. Their living space was separated by a curtain. Don was single and dating, which led to more than a few awkward situations: "How do you say, 'Mom, I love you very much, but do you mind not coming back till four o'clock in the morning?'"[21]

Etta was soon a regular presence at the club, cheering Sonny Boy on from the audience, laughing extra loud at his zingers and beaming with pride at her child. Remember how he was once so shy, even as a teenager, back in Jackson Heights? Look at him now, lacerating Hollywood celebrities who paid for the honor of being insulted. It was fodder for the columnists, and Don was being recognized now coast-to-coast. Sonny Boy was even going to appear on the big screen with Burt Lancaster and Clark Gable. Still, Etta could not understand why the onstage act had to be so harsh. "Why can't you be more like that nice Alan King?" she often asked him.

"One of the first times I took my wife to see Don we went to the Slate Brothers Club. It was one of Don's first engagements there," recalled George Schlatter, who was working at the Frontier Hotel at the time. "I took [my wife] Jolene to see him. I'd just bought her a beautiful mink stole for our anniversary. Don took one look at her and said, 'Who is this Jew broad in the fake fox stole?' Jolene was absolutely crushed. It took me a year to convince her that Don was just kidding. Don would pick his victims; the biggest people in the room were his favorites."

One night, after the show, Don saw Etta talking to the club's Black bartender, Harry Goins. "Harry adored my mother," Don recalled years later, after Etta became ill. "She had emphysema and I paid him $50 a week to learn to be a Jew and shop all over the place."[22] Harry, who was single, struck up a friendship with Etta; they enjoyed each other's company and he treated her like a queen, shopping for her favorite Jewish delicacies at Canter's Deli on North Fairfax. He also helped Don get dressed for his shows in the club's kitchen (there was nowhere else; it was a small place); after Don came off the stage, drenched in sweat, Harry would douse him with cold water "in the alleyway while I stood stark naked."[23]

Harry remembered, that, too, but just a little differently. "I'd take his tuxedo out to be cleaned. His dressing room was so small that it didn't have a shower, so sometimes he'd ask me to get a bucket and sprinkle some water on him after a show."

Such was Harry's devotion to Etta and Sonny Boy that it was almost a fait accompli that he should join the tightly knit Rickles team. "One day Mom just came out and said it. 'Ask Harry if he'd be willing to work for us. He's a gem. Hire Harry and, if we're lucky, he'll be with us forever,'" Don recalled. Harry spent the next forty-plus years as Don's dresser and man Friday. When Don and Etta moved into a bigger place at the Park Sunset apartment complex shortly thereafter, Harry helped Etta organize their pool parties. "Harry would lay out the food in an artful manner, displaying Etta's chopped liver like it was Beluga caviar," Don recalled, marveling at how his loquacious mother rounded up celebrities for the Rickles shindigs—including Jack Carter, Debbie Reynolds, Kirk Douglas, the Ritz Brothers, Frank Sinatra, and Milton Berle.

Don was in the Big Show now, and he was important enough to be invited to a surprise party for Hollywood bigwig Sam Briskin, the head of production for Columbia Pictures. It was set up like a gag: Don arrived at Chasen's restaurant posing as an important exhibitor who announced he was halting his distribution of Columbia's movies. It made the showbiz columns: "Sam had never seen Rickles, and almost had a stroke before catching on to the gag."[24]

Don's remarkable run at the Slate Brothers Club ended in the fall. He was scheduled to return the following year, in 1958. Jack, Henry, and Sid Slate worried that their customers, particularly the Hollywood insiders who flocked to be tongue-lashed by the "Sultan of Insult" (not as catchy as Don's later nicknames), would abandon the club once Don left in early November. "They think they've found the answer: Comedienne Pat Morrissey, from Chicago's Mister Kelly's plus the comedy team of Ralph Young and Sid Gould," noted one columnist. "Between the three the Slates hope to attract enough customers who like to pay to be insulted until Rickles returns." They did not.[25]

Don's departure from L.A. back to the East Coast in early 1958—he was set to open a run of shows in Miami Beach—fanned rumors that he was going to open his own nightclub in South Florida, on the site of the shuttered Gino's-Chez Paree. His partners were said to be musician/bandleader Bobby Sherwood and Mickey Hayes; Hayes had a financial stake with Patti Page and her manager, Jack Rael, in the President Madison Hotel on Collins Avenue. In the *Miami Herald* Hayes denied having any partnership with Don in a nightclub, saying only that he "just helped set it up."

The club was called the Riot Room, and Don opened there in early January, where he was joined by Bobby Sherwood and singer June Perry. Two weeks later, Herb Kelly's column in the *Miami News* noted that "singer Phyllis Dorne, fresh from *Bells Are Ringing*, makes her nightclub debut tonight in Don Rickles' Riot Room." Bawdy borscht belt comedienne Belle Barth was playing the El Patio that week, with Gene Krupa and his trio, over at the Golden Strand Hotel. Sherwood and Dorne were, Kelly wrote, in a "Hot Romance." Don was a guest on Jack Paar's *Tonight Show* in mid-January to promote the club, but the Riot Room was struggling. The local columnists liked Don and did their best to bolster business by writing flattering items about the Riot Room.

STARS ENJOY NEEDLING BY RICKLES HERE
By George Bourke
Herald Amusement Editor
Don Rickles is repeating his Hollywood film colony success here—all the crowned heads of show business are turning to his Riot Room club knowing full well they can expect to get "crowned" with the Rickles repartee. Betty Hutton, Lou Irwin, who manages the Ritz Brothers and others, Jack Rael, partner and manager of Patti Page and Billy Eckstine, were among those laughing at themselves on a recent night.

The publicity did not move the needle. A week later, on February 6, Kelly noted in his column in the *Miami Herald* that newsy items about the Riot Room are "now coming from two press agents.

And in addition there are the unsigned notes containing rumors about the room's bosses."

Kelly was not the only one hearing about the Riot Room and its "bosses." Word about the club and its internal operations landed on the desk of FBI director J. Edgar Hoover in a memorandum on the activities of the Miami underworld dated January 28, 1958.

The information pertaining to the Riot Room was provided by Herb Rau, who was recommend to the FBI as a possible PCI— agency-speak for "potential criminal informant." Rau was also the entertainment editor for the *Miami Daily News* and wrote a bylined column for the newspaper.

Subject: Miami Winter Season, 1957–58,
Criminal Section, Investigative Division.

NOTORIOUS PLACES OF AMUSEMENT

HERB RAU, PCI, advised that the Riot Room, a night club [*sic*] located in Miami Beach, allegedly is operated by one **DON RICKLES**, an entertainer at that establishment. He pointed out that he has known **RICKLES** for a number of years and knows from his personal knowledge that **RICKLES** does not have any money to finance the night club, and judging from the patrons of the night club, he is positive that the establishment is owned by hoodlums with **RICKLES** acting as a front. He, however, possesses no knowledge as to the identities of the hoodlums.

Rau also dished to the local FBI agents about other locals, including La Cosa Nostra member Norman Rothman—who "has a wife and child residing in Miami, as well as a common-law wife and child residing in Havana, Cuba."

Don was playing the Riot Room when *Life* magazine, one of the country's largest newsweeklies, with a circulation in the millions, ran a story that mentioned him, in its issue dated February 3, 1958, which featured Shirley Temple and her young daughter on the cover.

The article was headlined "New Little Clubs Light Up U.S. Night

Life" and touched on the resurgence of smaller clubs—the Crystal Palace in St. Louis, Mister Kelly's in Chicago, the Tree Club in Dallas, and the Slate Brothers Club in L.A.: "There, comedian Don Rickles shouts ad-libbed abuse at the film celebrities who frequently turn up in the audience. And they seem to take to it as easily as to adulation. 'Sure, I've insulted you,'Rickles ends up his abrasive act, 'but I sincerely believe I've insulted you with warmth." The article was accompanied by a full-page photograph showing Don's reflection in the mirror of the Slate Brothers Club, hectoring Frank Sinatra (looking downward, as if he was examining his fingernails) while Lauren Bacall, seated next to Frank, laughs it up.

Don's mirror-image national notoriety did not drive customers to the Riot Room in Miami Beach. Singer Julie Sands could not save the club, nor could Don himself, "an improved performer since he toned down the religious kick at the Riot Room" . . . and then kicker . . . "But the rest of the show is from bulimia. (He means it's from hunger!)" In mid-February, the *New York Daily News* reported that "Don Rickles, master of comic insult, has hauled his act into a hotel, the Seville, after a luckless adventure with his own club, the Riot Room."

Don played his final show at the Riot Room on a Tuesday night. Three days later, he opened at the Seville Hotel's Matador Room, its tables "squeezed closer to make the spot more intimate. Rickles is taking Bobby Sherwood with him. Jack Herman and Al Silverman will determine the Riot Room's new policy this week."

They did. They closed the place.

The Riot Room failure was a minor blip in Don's life. He enjoyed a successful run at the Seville, where he shared the bill with singer Delores Leigh and Pete Brady's orchestra (three shows a night). Joe E. Lewis came to catch the show. "You're an old-timer, Joe," Don barked. "Get outta the business!" So, too, did local hotel "character" Swifty Morgan: "I talked to the Old Folks' Home. They'll take you." *New York Post* columnist Earl Wilson was sitting ringside in the

Matador Room one night: "Laugh it up, Wilson. You're not that big." It brought the place down.

Don closed out his stint at the Seville and took the act back to the Slate Brothers Club in L.A., where Frank faithfully caught the show and, of course, got the Rickles treatment. "What a figure. I've seen this boy in shorts—and he's nothing!" Don roared. "And those old dames he goes with, I mean, I wouldn't trust him with my mother!" Lana Turner laughed it up with her "protégé," actor Michael Dante. Esther Williams was there, too, smiling through gritted teeth as Don barked at her. "Grease up and swim around the room!"

Later that year, he wowed them at the Black Orchid in Chicago—"Not responsible for what he says—but we enjoy it," ran the tagline advertising the show—and then it was back to Miami Beach to play the lounge at the Admiral Vee Motel on Biscayne Boulevard, a place owned by Edwin Seinfeld, a former shoe manufacturer who did well for himself. Jules Styne, the acclaimed Broadway songwriter who was working on *Gypsy* with Stephen Sondheim—it was scheduled to open in 1959 with star Ethel Merman—"winged into town" to see Don's show at the Admiral Vee. He and Don also discussed the possibility of Don starring in a Broadway show. The idea went nowhere.

In the midst of all of this activity, Don signed on for his second movie, a supporting role in a family drama from United Artists called *The Rabbit Trap*, starring Oscar winner Ernest Borgnine (*Marty*) in the title role and based on a 1955 episode of NBC's *Goodyear Television Playhouse*.

Run Silent, Run Deep, the movie Don filmed in Hollywood in 1957, opened in theaters nationwide on March 27, 1958. In the months leading up to its premiere, Don's hardworking manager, Joe Scandore, made sure the big showbiz columns ran photos of Don and *Run Silent, Run Deep* star Burt Lancaster, on the set, smiling for the camera. The plot of the World War II drama, based on Edward L. Beach's eponymous 1955 novel, centered on US Navy commander J. P. Richardson

(Clark Gable), who is intent on avenging a Japanese destroyer that sank four US submarines, including Richardson's former command, in the Bungo Straits off the Japanese islands of Kyushu and Shikoku. Richardson is ordered not to bring his USS *Nerka* anywhere near the Bungo Straits, but he does not heed the order—to the consternation of his second-in-command, Lieutenant Commander Jim Bledsoe (Lancaster), who also resents Richardson, convinced that he, and not Richardson, should be in command of the *Nerka*.

Among the movie's cast were Jack Warden, Brad Dexter, and Mary LaRoche, who played Richardson's wife, Laura. (The movie's title refers to the term "silent running," a stealth tactic used by submarines to avoid detection, such as shutting off their nonessential systems and slowing down significantly to eliminate noise from their propellers.)

Don played Quartermaster First Class Ruby, a role relegating him to a few scenes and precious little screen time, despite his billing in the movie's opening credits—directly underneath Warden and alongside Dexter. "A sunburned crew's a happy crew, sir. It's an old Navy axiom," a smiling Ruby says to Bledsoe in the movie's opening minutes. "That you just made up!" Bledsoe responds to laughter all around.

Run Silent, Run Deep opened to generally favorable reviews. "Gable and Lancaster are well-matched," Kate Cameron opined in the *New York Daily News*. "Jack Warden, Brad Dexter, Don Rickles, Nick Cravat, Joe Maross and Eddy Foy III respond well to Wise's deft direction."

Bosley Crowther, in the *New York Times*, called the movie "a straight tale of undersea adventure . . . Jack Warden, Don Rickles and Joe Maross are shipshape as members of the crew and Brad Dexter is credible as an officer whose mouth is a little too big."

The *Los Angeles Times*: "Brad Dexter, Jack Warden, Don Rickles, who supplies some comedy, and Joe Maross fill important supporting roles." (Cravat and Don would both appear later in separate episodes of *The Twilight Zone*, Don in the 1961 episode "Mr. Dingle, the

Strong" and Cravat in 1963, playing the furry gremlin menacing William Shatner's Nervous Nellie airplane passenger Bob Wilson in the classic episode "Nightmare at 20,000 Feet.")

Run Silent, Run Deep did not give Don the hoped-for boost, at least in terms of his movie career, but it did keep his name in the press and added an impressive acting credit to his résumé. For now, it was back to the clubs, and in the fall he returned to Ocean Boulevard in Brooklyn to open at Joe Scandore's Elegante: "Appearing Nightly "The Emperor" Returns!"

But the best was yet to come.

CHAPTER 7

J obbing comedians from any era of show business have stories about the quirks of life on the road, the offstage monotony of those endless days and nights in towns and cities that start to blend together, mile after mile, in a mélange of faceless hotel rooms—the meals eaten, often alone, passing the idle daytime hours doing something, anything, before the adrenaline kicks in and it is time to go on stage.

Don Rickles had been living the grinding-it-out comedian's lonely life for nearly a decade now. The national acclaim was great, but the hard work did not stop. Chicago was followed by L.A. was followed by Miami Beach and then on to New York City and points north: Montreal, the Great Lakes region, and on and on. His nomadic life allowed Don little time for romance or forming any sort of lasting connection. He dated and did what he did with whoever he did it with in the time he had to himself.

In later years, Don spoke of fleeting romances during his time as a bachelor, never naming names but letting it be known that he enjoyed female companionship when the opportunity afforded itself. Before his breakthrough at the Slate Brothers Club in the summer of 1957 there was no public mention of Don's romantic life. That changed when his name started to appear in the columns of powerful show business journalists, who, while praising the act (most of the time) also started to link the thirtysomething comedian to several different women.

In January 1959, "Hollywood's New Court Jester" returned to the West Coast for his third go-round at the Slate Brothers Club, this time a fifteen-week run taking him through early May. Don Rickles was back in town, and once again many of the big names flocked to the little club on La Cienega Boulevard to be insulted: Milton Berle, Victor Mature, Jack Benny, James Mason, Gary Crosby (Bing's son), Audrey Meadows, Red Buttons, Jill St. John, Harry Ritz, Gig Young, Johnny Mathis—a who's who of the showbiz elite, who sat through singer Peggy Sands and the musical stylings of saxophonist Vido Musso before the star of the show bounded onto the stage and ripped them all to shreds.

He was rarely billed as "The Emperor" anymore; now he was "The Merchant of Venom" or "The Insultin' Sultan," although the latter moniker never quite caught on, try as they might. "Mr. Warmth" would come later; "The Merchant of Menace" was tried out and quickly discarded. Don's growing popularity went hand-in-hand with the inevitable nuggets of gossip in the showbiz columns, those personal tidbits inserted between the ellipses or mentioned in a line or two before it was on to the next titillating tale about another hot-and-heavy romance or infidelity or divorce or public lovers' quarrel or whatever else they did in the "Look at me . . . please!" world of Hollywood.

If it was considered a badge of honor to be insulted by Don Rickles, the same held true for making it into Walter Winchell's column. Winchell was still pounding the column out in 1959, and though he was not nearly as powerful as he had been in the preceding decades— television and changing social mores took care of that—he still held sway. Don made his first appearance in the column that April. "Casa Cugat lark Peggy Sands gets all those long-kisstance calls from Don Rickles," Winchell wrote in his inimitable style. Two months later, he included another item about Don—sans Peggy Sands. "Don Rickles, 'The Merchant of Venom,' and Sandra Burns, dghtr [sic] of Burns & Allen, are serious. Prob'ly will blend" (Winchell-ese for "marry").

Sandra Burns, who was twenty-four in 1959, was the adopted daughter of George and Gracie and the older sister of her younger brother, Ronnie, who was also adopted. Sandra kept a relatively low profile in Hollywood, despite her parents' fame. She appeared intermittently on *The George Burns and Gracie Allen Show*, which had ended its eight-year run on CBS the previous year, most of the time in small supporting roles (a waitress, telephone operator, secretary, etc.). Ronnie Burns, a year younger than his sister, took the opposite tac; he joined his parents' television series, as himself, in 1955. (Ronnie also made a fondly remembered cameo appearance as a beatnik teenager opposite Jackie Gleason's Ralph Kramden in "Young at Heart," a classic 1956 episode of *The Honeymooners*.) In 1953, when Sandra was nineteen, she had eloped with Young Wilhoite III, the son of a Los Angeles clothing manufacturer. They were divorced five years later, in March 1958.

Don's romance with Sandra was still going strong in June, at least according to the breathless items in the gossip columns. "Funnyman Don Rickles has fallen hard for Blonde Sandra (Burns) Wilhoite, Gracie Allen's and George Burns' beautiful daughter," Hollywood doyenne Louella Parsons wrote. "Sandra and Rickles have been out together since Don's return from Las Vegas, chaperoned, of course, by Sandra's brother, Ronnie."

Parsons returned to the subject several weeks later. "If you think the romance between Sandra Burns Wilhoite (Gracie and George Burns' lovely daughter) and comic Don Rickles isn't serious listen to this: Don gifted Sandra with a bracelet of pearls and gold with a secret inscription on the gold heart attached." Don and Sandra, accompanied by Ronnie, then traveled to Las Vegas to support George Burns, who was closing at the Sahara—the first time he was working without Gracie by his side following her retirement in 1958. In late August, Sandra was at the Slate Brothers Club, "rooting for her boyfriend, comic Don Rickles."[1] And then, suddenly, it was over. Just like that.

In September, Sandra eloped, once again, with her second husband. He was not named Don Rickles. "If Don Rickles is torching over the elopement of Sandra Burns Wilhoit and director Rodney Amateu, he is covering it with the comedian's practiced smile," reported L.A.

showbiz columnist Harrison Carroll. " 'It was a complete surprise to me,' says Don, 'but I wish them both every happiness.'" Don added a final touch to Carroll's item and claimed that he called Sandra to say hello . . . on the very night she eloped with Amateu.

Dorothy Kilgallen, who would be one of Don's harshest critics in succeeding years, also got into the act. Sandra's elopement, she wrote, was "a blow to comedian Don Rickles, who regarded himself as her 'steady' beau and the only serious contender for her hand." Etta's reaction is not known, at least publicly. If Sonny Boy was hurt, she was hurt. It was that simple.

By mid-September, Don seemed to have recovered quickly from the Sandra Burns contretemps when he was spotted by Harrison Carroll in the bar at La Rue's in Vegas "with his old enthusiasm, singer Betsy Duncan. They had a ball. If anybody was sad, it was Betsy. Her apartment was robbed. Some no-good stole her French phone, some sofa pillows, some bric-a-brac."

Then, in October, Don was suddenly dating . . . *Peggy Lee?* "Saw them at Larue for dinner," Louella Parsons reported. "They were also at the Moulin Rouge and the Deb Star Ball—and when he opens at the Sahara in Las Vegas, Peggy is expected ringside."

The "romance" was, in all likelihood, a publicity stunt, something fun to gin up interest in Don's maiden run in Las Vegas. Walter Winchell: "Coasters can't figure out the connection, if any, between Peggy Lee and Don Rickles. She's so photogenic and he's so photo-pathetic." Ouch. Dorothy Kilgallen: "Peggy Lee, who has been rumored as a romance item with such contrasting types as comedian Don Rickles and Ingemar Johansson, firmly denies that she cares for either gentleman." By November it was over—if it had ever even started. The Peggy Lee–Don Rickles whatever-it-was was never mentioned again in any romantic context. (They would work together again, several times, over the years. In 1973, when they shared the bill at the Westbury Music Fair on Long Island, Don had Peggy's dressing room filled with flowers. The mercurial Lee was having none of it when she heard that Don wanted to stop in and say hello. "Why would I want to talk to that . . . second-rate comedian?" she snarled.)[2]

In December, Don told Harrison Carroll that "his favorite Las Vegas date was showgirl Joyce Beatty." Touché.

It had all led up to this. The big break. Las Vegas. By 1959, the once-quiet desert outpost was a bustling hub of gambling and entertainment, the place where the high rollers and average Joes alike flocked to win big, blow it all, or finish somewhere in between. They usually lost. That was part of the allure.

Mobster Benjamin "Bugsy" Siegel's Flamingo Hotel & Casino, the city's first legitimate taste of glitz and glamour, had opened in December 1946 with headliners Jimmy Durante and Xavier Cugat and a Hollywood crowd including George Raft and George Sanders. Little went right for the Flamingo at the beginning; bad weather and the incomplete hotel and grounds (construction was way behind schedule) cost Siegel and his underworld backers too much dough. By the time the Flamingo started to right itself, it was too late for Siegel. He met his maker in a hail of machine-gun bullets as he sat on a couch reading a newspaper in his girlfriend Virginia Hill's house in Beverly Hills. She was conveniently in Paris at the time.

But the Flamingo eventually turned a profit and opened the floodgates for other big-money hotels that followed: the Sands, the Tropicana, the Thunderbird, the New Frontier, the Riviera, the Dunes, the Fremont, and the Sahara had all opened in Vegas by 1957, bringing Hollywood, a short plane ride away, to the Nevada desert, where they performed, gambled, or did God-knows-what in those establishments.

In a short two-year span, the balding "Mouth That Roared" had conquered Miami Beach, Los Angeles, New York, Chicago, San Francisco, and so many forgettable points in between. His act caught the attention of the elite Vegas power brokers, the guys who ran the hotels, booked the acts, and knew a guy who knew a guy who knew how Don Rickles was knocking 'em dead in clubs. Now they wanted The Merchant of Venom to perform in their clubs and drive action to their windowless casinos illuminated by artificial lighting, which thrummed twenty-four-hours a day with the cacophony of one-armed bandits and loud dealers at the blackjack tables—all enveloped in a haze of cigarette smoke, sweat, and misery. The big-time entertainers had already played Vegas: Sinatra, George Burns, Liberace, Marlene Dietrich, Sammy Davis Jr., Bing Crosby, Mae West, Milton Berle, Betty Hutton, and so many more.

Now it was Don's turn.

In the early months of 1959, Stan Irwin at the Sahara and Jack Entratter at the Sands got in touch with Joe Scandore and told him how much Don Rickles would mean to their establishments in drawing the big late-night/early morning crowds looking for a release after gambling it all away or raking it in at their casinos. Irwin and Entratter were the biggest pursuers; Irwin went to see Don's act at the Slate Brothers Club in L.A. three times. In the end, he won out, signing Don to a three-year deal at the Sahara. The contract stipulated that Don perform a minimum of twelve weeks at the hotel and that he was free to perform elsewhere, wherever and whenever he so desired—and that he could use his Sahara salary as a negotiating chip in lining up other bookings.[3]

In early May, Don finished his fifteen-week run at the Slate Brothers Club, where he was on the bill with Stan Kenton's wife, singer Ann Richards, and then it was off to Sin City. "Don Rickles . . . tries his luck for the first time in Las Vegas when he opens next Tuesday at the Hotel Sahara," John L. Scott wrote in the *Los Angeles Times*. "Rickles will toss his caustic barbs across the bar in the Casbar Theater. He'll find a different type of audience and while he always fooled oddsmakers by getting away without being belted . . ."[4]

In the run-up to Don's big Vegas debut, Sinatra and his Rat Pack brethren—Sammy Davis Jr., Dean Martin, Joey Bishop, and Peter Lawford—razzed him from the stage of the Sands, where they convened each night for their largely improvised, anything-goes, loosey-goosey "Summit" show after spending the day shooting their new movie, *Ocean's Eleven*. Every little bit helped, and Frank took care of his best pals—Don included. He always would.

Don opened in the Casbar Lounge at the Sahara on Tuesday, May 5, 1959, sharing the bill with his friend saxophonist Vido Musso. They played three shows a night, at midnight, 2:30 a.m., and at 5:10 a.m.—the breakfast show for anyone still half-conscious at that ungodly hour. "I always figured it was going to be murder, but actually [the crowds] were good," Don recalled. "But it was a tough way to go. It was three shows a night in those days. But you were young and full of piss and vinegar, so who cared? If I did it today they'd have paramedics in the wings."[5]

On May 8, Don turned thirty-three, and Stan Irwin surprised him onstage. Gary Crosby, Bing's son, assisted in the festivities, presenting Don with a cake inscribed with the words "Happy Birthday Idiot" on the side in big letters so everyone could see the gag. Don cracked up. Vegas—what a gas! That same week at the Sahara, Marlene Dietrich began a four-week run with her cabaret act—in the big room, of course. "The fabled beauty and most colorful grandmother in show business again figures to startle the blasé city with new, provocative gowns and familiar husky-voiced singing," ran one report. "The Szonys, dance stars, will also be featured. Don Rickles has taken over the Sahara's lounge successfully."[6]

That was an understatement. The stars turned out in droves to see Don's show and receive their expected tongue lashings, even in the much-smaller Casbar Lounge. Don to bandleader Harry James: "Harry's trying to be casual—but Betty Grable's working in New York and he hasn't received his allowance yet." Don to actor Barry Sullivan: "Drink—let everyone know you're a big star. Caught your last TV show—embarrassing."

But there were the off nights, too. Dick Williams in the *Los Angeles Mirror News*, July 31, 1959:

Don Rickles had a jam-packed celebrity audience in the Sahara Lounge at 2:30 in the morning. Keely Smith, Red Skelton,

Carol Channing, Milton Berle and his wife, the four Crosbys, Jan Murray and Gloria DeHaven were wedged into the mob. So Don proceeded to blow it with the worst show I've ever seen him do. Perhaps he was trying too hard. But the "Emperor," who wowed 'em at the Slate Bros. went way overboard on the coarse talk. And this scarcely seems the place to work God and religion into the patter and cracks.

Louis Prima and his wife, Keely Smith, had been the stars-in-residence at the Sahara since 1954 by the time Don arrived. The excitement they generated on stage, backed by Sam Butera and the Witnesses, helped put the Las Vegas "lounge act" on the show business map. Prima, the ebullient New Orleans–born singer/entertainer, was a sharp contrast to Smith, who was eighteen years younger. But it worked, and then some. Prima and Smith recorded their album *Las Vegas Prima Style* in the Casbar Lounge in 1958. They worked the 10 p.m. to 11:30 p.m. show, with Don following the high-energy duo at midnight.

"The setup was strange," he remembered. "Right in front of the stage was a pit where the waiters and bartenders walked back and forth serving food and drinks." In Don's version of events, if the lounge was empty at the 5:10 a.m. show, he would run offstage and into the casino, climb up on a table and yell, "Hold down the noise! I'm trying to do a show in there!" Sahara Hotel boss Milton Prell eventually told him to knock it off.

Different acts would occasionally rotate with Prima and Smith in the slot before Don, including Freddie Bell and His Bellboys. Bell, who was from Philadelphia, recorded a version of "Big Mama" Thornton's "Hound Dog" in 1953—three years before Elvis Presley. "We outdrew the ballroom," he said. "There was a line waiting to come in the lounge. We walked out to a full room every show. The sunken bar in front of the stage was where everybody wanted to sit to be picked on by Rickles."[7]

Sometimes, even Don went too far. One night, he insulted a guy in the audience: "Hey, Dummy, this floozy is your latest thing? You

can do better than her, 'cause I've seen better legs on Sonny Liston."
The man was not amused, and as Don found out, he was a mobbed-up
guy who did not have much of a sense of humor—and did not appreciate his woman being attacked by "The Insultin' Sultan." He threatened to break both of Don's legs after the show. Don, scared half to
death, went to his friend singer Connie Francis, who was in Vegas at
the time, and asked for help. (Connie knew people who knew people.) "It was a mob guy's girlfriend and the mob guy said he was going
to break Don's legs," she recalled. "Don came up to my room and he
was sweating like a pig and he said, 'Connie, the guy's gonna break
my legs. I didn't know who he was.' So I called my uncle, who was
connected, and said, 'You've got to do something. He says he's going
to break Don Rickles's legs.' He said, 'I'll take care of it.'"

Don's legs were safe. For now.[8]

"There was a guy who came in one night and Don always did a
bit with people in the front row," recalled Don's longtime publicist
Paul Shefrin. "And the guy's wife is sitting next to him and he says,
'Is that the wife?' 'Yes.' He said, 'God, you married a moose!' Now
after the show, the guy comes back and said, 'So you think my wife
is a moose?' So Don calls Joe Scandore and Joe says, 'Don't worry,
sweetheart.' The next night the guy comes back in with his wife
again and they come backstage. He says to Don, 'Remember you
called my wife a moose? You're right—she is a moose.' Joe was the
fireman. If there was a problem, he would take care of it. He helped
build Don's career and believed in him from the early days when he
had him at the Elegante in Brooklyn."[9]

Jazz singer Billy Eckstine told the story about the time Don was
working the Casbar one night when a table was reserved for a Saudi
Arabian prince and his entourage. Don was told to lay off the prince
and his cronies. No one wanted an international incident. Don followed his marching orders . . . almost. After telling the prince
how honored he was to play for such royalty, he asked him to stand
up and, turning to the audience, yelled "Ready! Aim! Fire!" and
quickly ran off the stage.

How the prince and his entourage reacted is anyone's guess, but it could not have been too badly; after Don's final scheduled show at the Casbar, Sahara boss Milton Prell picked up his option for another seven weeks . . . at $4,500 per week.[10]

"He helped create the whole late-night civilization in Vegas," said George Schlatter. "We'd go and see Frank on stage and then go see Don. It was Don Rickles and Louis Prima from midnight until four or five in the morning and it was, 'Let's see Rickles.' It was always strange why people wanted to go see Rickles at 2 in the morning and pay for a table to go in and have Rickles abuse them. It's one of the mysteries of Las Vegas—why people would pay all that money to go into the Sahara Hotel and have Don Rickles beat up on them. That was one of the phenomena of show business. What was the appeal? The appeal was, if Rickles attacked you it meant that you were famous."[11]

The Rabbit Trap opened in early September while Don was playing the Slate Brothers Club in L.A. to packed crowds. It was his second movie role in a picture with a big star—Ernest Borgnine this time—and featured a good supporting cast (Bethel Leslie, Jeanette Nolan, Russell Collins). Borgnine played an Army veteran named Eddie Colt, a draftsman at a construction firm who has only taken three weeks off in ten years on the job. He and his wife Abby (Leslie) plan a two-week vacation with their young son (Kevin Corcoran), but Eddie is called back to work the very next day. Abby pleads with him to ignore work and enjoy his vacation. Don played one of Eddie's friends, Mike O'Halloran.

The movie, adapted from a television drama that aired in 1955, came and went quickly, most of the reviews failing to even mention Don. It did nothing for his Hollywood ambitions.

"I'll always keep my act but if Hollywood offers steady work, I'm an actor first, and a comic second," he told *Associated Press* entertainment writer James Bacon at the time. But not all was lost; that same month he signed a deal with producers William Perlberg and George Seaton for a top featured role in his third movie, *The Rat Race*, starring Tony Curtis and Debbie Reynolds.

Bill Perlberg came to see Don's act at the Slate Brothers Club and got the treatment. He told Don before the show that he "liked his face" and wanted to test him for the part of a producer who gets rough with the Debbie Reynolds character. Then Don took the stage. "Look at this crazy producer, laughing it up," he snarled. "Any producer who'd want me in his movie has gotta be out of his mind!" The role was his.

The Rat Race was a Paramount Studios production and was adapted from Garson Kanin's 1949 Broadway play starring Betty Field. Robert Mulligan was directing a cast featuring dependable big-screen veterans Jack Oakie and Kay Medford supporting Curtis and Reynolds. Oakie was returning to the big screen for the first time in a decade; Medford was starring on Broadway in *The Thurber Carnival*. Curtis was hot off of *Some Like It Hot* with Jack Lemmon and *Operation Petticoat* with Cary Grant. The score was by Elmer Bernstein. The movie had promise. "Everybody on the set was surprised I knew a little bit about acting," Don told James Bacon later that year.

We interrupt this biography to mention Don Rickles . . . the horse. Yep, he was a real horse, named after Don and owned by Milt and Eddie Seinfeld. Eddie owned the Admiral Vee Motel in Miami, where Don was a regular, and named his new horse, which he purchased for $3,500, after his favorite comedian. (Seinfeld also owned several other horses at the time, including Admiral Vee, Clear Road, Decimal, Vet's Boy, and Rough Note, all of which performed admirably. Admiral Vee ended his career with over $300,000 in winnings.) The Seinfelds do not appear to be related to future comedian Jerry Seinfeld, though the words "horse" and "Don Rickles" sound like a plotline from *Seinfeld*—"The Rye," a 1996 episode in which Kramer (Michael Richards) feeds the mare pulling his hansom cab in Central Park some Beef-a-Reeno, with predictably stinky results.

Don Rickles, the horse, was bred in Kentucky by one Harry

Heiman and was the three-year-old son of Quiet Step-Jacodema. He made his namesake proud, placing in the Bay Shore Handicap, the Bernard Baruch Stakes, and finishing third in the Travers Stakes. Don Rickles (the horse) finished his career with a record of eleven wins in eighty-one starts.[12] In April 1960, "The Hooved One" competed at the $75,000 Wood Memorial at Aqueduct Raceway and was a "strong contender"; his intended jockey, Panamanian rider Manuel Ycaza, was pulled from the race and suspended for ten days for "careless riding." Don Rickles did not win that race. The *New York Daily News*: "Merrick Stable's John William finished third, another two lengths back and 1¼ lengths ahead of Don Rickles, third choice in the machines back of the first two finishers."[13]

Sometimes, just the mention of Don Rickles (the horse) was unintentionally funny. "Yorktown had to stave off a foul claim lodged by Willie Shoemaker, who rode Don Rickles," the Associated Press noted in a story about a race at Aqueduct. "Reginald N. Webster's Count Amber, who set the pace for a mile, was no match for the thundering leader, but had scant difficulty taking second by four lengths from Edward Seinfeld's sluggish-moving Don Rickles."[14] The horse won nearly $90,000 throughout its career and set a precedent. Twenty years later saw the second coming of a horse called . . . Don Rickles. More on that later.

In the fall of 1959, Don and his insults moved from the Slate Brothers Club to the upstairs room, called the Interlude, at Gene Norman's Crescendo club on the Sunset Strip. There, "The Emperor" closed out the year with a five-week run, patrons shelling out $15 for a buffet dinner, drinks, and the show, which included George Matson and Buddy Freed. (Mort Sahl and Stan Kenton played the bigger room downstairs.)

This date at the Crescendo's Interlude room is important in Rickles lore. Don would always claim that it was Johnny Carson who anointed him "Mr. Warmth," the nickname he cherished the most, after his first appearances on *The Tonight Show*. But that was still six years in the future.

Harrison Carroll in the *Los Angeles Times*: "Introducing him, Milton Berle said, 'I give you Mr. Warmth, a young fellow who has parlayed a mental disturbance into a fortune. Before this, he was the house comic at Menninger's institute.'" In the audience for Don's opening at the Interlude were Nancy Sinatra with her date, Gary Crosby, one of Don's good friends in those days, and Gary's brother Phillip, there with his wife, Sandra. Other targets on the receiving end of Don's barbed tongue included Ernie Kovacs and his wife, Edie Adams; Zsa Zsa Gabor (again), who was there with her date Franchot Tone; Donald O'Connor; Monique Van Vooren; and Anna Maria Alberghetti. (To cowboy star Dale Robertson: "Sit down, you bum. If your fans could only see how you booze it up.")

Don appeared at the Interlude through January—and he always had time for the spare gig. Bing Crosby paid him handsomely to heckle the guests he assembled for his son Lindsay Crosby's twenty-second birthday party in Hollywood.

In February it was back to the Sahara in Vegas, where he lambasted Frank Sinatra for sending him a welcoming gift of a half-dozen Turkish towels: "I'd just like to say this about you in public, Frank. You're cheap." It was an inside joke between them.

Sinatra's friendship and his influence had cut a wide swath for Don since their tête-à-tête at Murray Franklin's in 1957. "Rickles was not really a star until he met Sinatra," said George Schlatter. "What made Don Rickles famous and desirable was his relationship with Sinatra. He really liked Don a lot . . . and once Don abused Sinatra, everybody wanted him."[15]

Don was already welcomed as a part-time member of Sinatra's Rat Pack, and now that he was a hit in Vegas he was initiated into the group. "I never received an official membership card but Frank made me feel part of the fun," he said.[16] When Frank, Dean, Sammy, Peter, and Joey were filming *Ocean's Eleven* on location in Vegas (including a few scenes at Don's professional home, the

Sahara), they were all over the town. One night, Frank, Sammy, and Dean showed up to watch Don's show at the Sahara, all three of them pretending to read newspapers as soon as he came on stage. (Don: "You guys will do anything to keep your names alive.") Frank extended Don the ultimate Rat Pack honor: inviting him to *schvitz* with the guys in the steam room at the Sands, where they relaxed between takes on *Ocean's Eleven* or after carousing all night, wolfing down hot dogs, talking shit, and ribbing each other mercilessly.

They all wore personalized bathrobes bearing the nicknames bestowed on them by the leader (Sinatra)—including the unfortunate moniker "Smokey" for Sammy during a time when that was still okay and no one thought twice about it (Sammy took a grin-and-bear-it approach, but it hurt, deeply). Don's robe was emblazoned with "Bullethead," Frank's pet name for him that he used for the rest of his life. Sometimes the fun got a bit out of hand, like the time that Frank grabbed Don, who was taking a shower in the steam room, and shoved him, stark naked, into the Sands swimming pool area. "I just stood there like a jerk," Don recalled. "I said I was a beach umbrella, and just waited until they let me back in."[17] All fun and games.

Vegas was a different town back then. "They called it the mob influence. Call it what you may, but there was always one guy you had to answer to. That was the boss," Don recalled. "You knew him personally. He was the guy that ran the place and that's what you had to worry about. It was much more catered to high rollers and people dressed up in furs and diamonds and it was not a family-oriented place and there were very few hotels, so it was very intimate. All the acts and the dealers, we all hung out together. Went to Lake Mead, water skiing. It was a different world. It was like a family."[18]

The steady work in Vegas, Miami Beach, New York, and Chicago paid the bills and kept Don's name in the public consciousness. The television offers were just not there yet. His next appearance on the small screen would be a supporting role in an episode of *The Twilight Zone*, Rod Serling's highly regarded CBS anthology series, which was slated to air during the 1960–61 season. Perhaps that would help turn some heads and mark his entrée into a medium that could turn someone into an overnight star. Even someone who was pushing thirty-four.

So it was steady club work for Don that spring: the Interlude—with Rowan and Martin downstairs at the Crescendo—where Don tore into Gary Cooper ("I finally caught your act in *High Noon*. Man, you can't act—you hung around that railroad station too long"). For a change of pace one night, he sang "Over the Rainbow" in a duet with Judy Garland as they sat on the edge of the Interlude stage. On his closing night there, his targets included Milton Berle, Tony Curtis, Kirk Douglas, and Walter Winchell, who was trying to keep his dying career afloat by verbally sparring with Don in the club and then writing about it in his column the next day.

Then he was back in Vegas at the Sahara in May. Victor Borge, who was appearing in the hotel's Congo Room, surprised Don for his birthday, and for Mother's Day, by flying Etta in from Miami Beach for a visit. She remained an integral part of Don's life, even at this stage of the game. On one occasion, Don was dating a chorus girl who worked at the Latin Quarter in New York. The young woman gifted him with a color photo of herself from a girlie magazine, which showed her wearing a tight pair of blue capri pants—and nothing else. Don figured he would pull a fast one on his mother and showed her the photo of "the girl I dated last night." She studied the bare-breasted woman with a frown on her face—and then delivered the punchline: "You know, Don, that's the color I wanted for the drapes!"[19]

"Don's mother was like a mother to everybody he ever met," recalled actor Don Murray, Don's friend and classmate from the American Academy of Dramatic Arts. "Everybody was taken in by her. She was just absolutely amazing. She knew everyone's career and she would compliment them and name specific scenes. It was quite remarkable to be around Don and his mother."[20] Etta traveled often with Don in those early years and kept an album of celebrity snapshots, including her Sonny Boy with Clark Gable on the set of

Run Silent, Run Deep. (Years later, someone broke into Etta's apartment in Miami Beach and stole most of those treasured photos.) The photo with Don and Gable was dated October 1957: "To Etta. It was a pleasure working with your talented son Don. Sincerely, Clark Gable."

Later in Don's career, if Etta was seated in the audience during one of his frequent visits to *The Tonight Show,* Johnny Carson would take a moment to introduce her on-camera. "She was unbelievable," Don's longtime business manager, Bill Braunstein, recalled. "She was very small and skinny and had red hair, and I never saw her without a cigarette in her hand, ever. She was very opinionated with Don, and he really loved her. She was very important in his career. No question about it. She supported Don and was behind him. She was an amazing woman . . . very old-time New York."[21]

Ernest Borgnine, too, fell into Etta's orbit. The Oscar-winning star of *Marty* went to see Don's act at the Slate Brothers Club in L.A., some time before they appeared together in *The Rabbit Trap,* and his less-than-leading-man visage was low-hanging fruit for The Merchant of Venom. Don turned to a woman in the audience: "There she is, ladies and gentlemen, the first runner-up in the Ernest Borgnine lookalike contest." The line got the expected laughs, and Borgnine loved the joke so much that he went to visit Don backstage after the show to say hello . . . and Etta gave him a bowl of soup. "Stand behind my Don because he's a good boy," she told him.[22]

"Don's mom was such a huge influence because she worshipped Don in the sense of a son. And he just adored her," Lorna Luft recalled. "And he had that part of his show when he would say, 'My darling Etta.' He was a really good son."[23]

Shecky Greene, who was not a big Don Rickles fan, had fond memories of Etta. "Etta was really a Jewish mother," he said. "She was strong. She was, 'My son is the best,' you know? As a matter of fact, the first time that I was with Don Rickles, he took me to his house, and his mother made potato pancakes. I took a bite out of the pancake and she said, 'Now, what do you do?' and I said, 'I'm a comedian.' She took the potato pancake back." Rim-shot! "But she was a nice lady," he added. "Two years after that, she gave me the other half of the potato pancake."

The Rat Race, the third movie in which Don appeared, opened nationwide in May 1960 to solid reviews. Don's role was small, but memorable, and he garnered a good measure of critical praise.

The Rat Race revolves around ambitious saxophone player Pete Hammond Jr. (Tony Curtis), who arrives in New York City from Minneapolis, and there meets and falls in love with dancer Peggy Brown (Debbie Reynolds). She works for sleazy dance hall owner Nellie Miller (Don). Pete and Peggy share quarters in a rooming house, and to save money (and to appear chaste—Dwight Eisenhower was still in the White House) they divide their cramped living space with a curtain. When a jazz trio (played by real-life musicians Joe Bushkin, Sam Butera, and Gerry Mulligan) steals Pete's saxophone, he gets a job on a cruise ship—but he's a man without a reed, so Peggy reluctantly agrees to ask Nellie for a loan. When Nellie makes advances on her, and she does not fulfill her end of the bargain, he strips Peggy of her dress and shoes to prove that he "owns her." Kay Medford plays penny-pinching landlady Soda Gallo, while Jack Oakie is Mac, a philosophical bartender who works at the joint across the street.

The *Philadelphia Inquirer*: "Don Rickles . . . drops comedy to play the sweaty, greasy dance palace proprietor." The *Boston Globe*: "Don Rickles portrays one of the meanest villains of the season."

The *New York Times*: "Don Rickles is a frighteningly porcine." The *New York Daily News*: "Don Rickles is a slimy villain you will want done away with." The *Los Angeles Times*: "Rickles, as the heavy, is positively repulsive . . . If he's ever tired of being the insult artist he's got a career as the double heavy waiting for him."

The two newspapers in Miami, the city in which Don had risen to stardom, gave him a split decision for his role in *The Rat Race*. "Don Rickles, [gives] an Academy Award nomination job with his role of the sleazy dance-hall operator who is fanatical about making Debbie step into the world's oldest profession," George Bourke enthused in the *Miami Herald*. The *Miami Times*, meanwhile, was more succinct: "Rickles . . . has little trouble playing the evil part well."

Don spent the summer of 1960 on the West Coast, playing the Riverside in Reno for the first time, where one wag dubbed him "The Insultin' Sultan of Verbal Swat" after catching Don's act in the hotel's Olympic Room. The nickname did not stick, for obvious reasons. Don was not only a hit at the Riverside, but he helped local casino lounge singer Frankie Fanelli grab a part in Clark Gable's next movie, *The Misfits*. (Don knew the film's coproducer, Tom Shaw, and recommended Fanelli, who appeared in a scene as a gambler in a bar.)

Around that same time, word broke in the press that Don and Jack E. Leonard would be performing that fall in New York at the same time—Fat Jack at the Blue Angel on East 55th Street and Don at Basin Street East seven blocks away on 48th Street. The news, such as it was, provided the columnists and show business press something to write about during the slow summer months, and they played along as they ginned up interest in the "showdown" between the two insult comics. Don's upcoming gig at Basin Street East did not please his longtime critic, Dorothy Kilgallen, who wrote, somewhat scathingly, that Don and his put-down act would tarnish the club. He was not one of its "tasteful performers" such as Peggy Lee and Benny Goodman, both of whom had recently been in residence. "An October package will star Billy Eckstine, Charlie Barnet and, for no accountable reason, 'insult comedian' Don Rickles," she wrote in her "Voice of Broadway" column. "All this means is that celebrities who love Billy Eckstine and think Charlie Barnet's band is great will stay away in droves, rather than risk being embarrassed by the very unfunny Mr. Rickles. It seems like a frightfully dumb parlay."[24]

Even Fat Jack got into the act. "Rickles is my road company," he said. "I'm going to open up a Don Rickles Charm School. Don is a very religious boy. Every Saturday he stays home and listens to Lenny

Bruce records."[25] Besides, he said, he was moving away from the insult humor. "There are a hundred road companies of me now, only they all go farther than I do. Don Rickles was a big sensation on the West Coast doing my act, only he's dirty." (Author's note: No, he was not. Maybe suggestive, but never dirty.)

Don flew from Reno to San Francisco, where he joined buxom Sandy Cherniss, "the 44-inch buster" (they were not subtle back then), at Fack's nightclub, in support of Duke Ellington, who was coming off a successful run in Vegas. He returned to the Crescendo several weeks later, sharing the bill with singer/pianist Frances Fay. Don was playing the bigger room now, with Lenny Bruce and singer Mavis Rivers upstairs in the smaller Interlude. It was a subtle change in his status, but an important notch in his nightclub belt.

He was back in the Nevada desert, at the Sahara, through August and September. Sid Caesar and his wife, in Vegas for the weekend, caught the show. "Look at Sid Caesar. He said to himself the other day, 'How's Sid?' Then he said, 'Oh, I forgot. *I'm* Sid!' Mrs. Caesar is sitting there laughing. She doesn't know she's out of the will." Caesar took the ribbing in stride and climbed up to the stage in mock anger to confront The Merchant of Venom. "I came here to hate you, I really did," he said, "and instead, I love you." Jack Lemmon was there, too. (Don: "I saw you in *The Apartment*—and you should have left the gas on.") So was Don's Rat Pack crony Dean Martin: "You're really great the way you smoke and drink on stage, and I hear a rumor tomorrow night you may even sing."

By now, the Rickles shows were a highlight of any trip to Vegas, as the Sahara patrons, gamblers, vacationers—whoever—entered the Casbar lion's den expecting (hoping?) to be targeted for the trademark Rickles treatment as he ran onto the stage, accompanied by his calling-card toreador music. Club owners, hip to the act, seated the badly dressed, the overweight, the yokels, the homely, and the minority patrons in Don's eyeline, in the first few rows— low-hanging fruit for the master of insults.

"You, sir, are you married?" "No." "And you never will be,

wearing that roller derby jacket. This is the kind of guy who told the captain of the *Titanic*, 'Captain, I think something may be wrong. My socks are wet.'" (Don used that *Titanic* joke frequently in those days—he barked the same line at Jack Carter during a show at the Slate Brothers Club.)[26] One raucous night, in all the excitement, he tripped and fell off the Casbar stage, sprained his back, and gashed his leg in several places. The mishap knocked him out of commission, but only for a day or two, before he was back sweating and riffing and prowling the stage scanning the audience for his next victim. It was, remarkably, completely ad-libbed; Don did not use writers, ever, but he did follow a routine before each show. Observers noted how, in his dressing room, he would fire off insults at whoever was around, even if they made no sense, to wind himself up like a tight spring for the hour ahead, to get the adrenaline coursing through his veins. He worked this way to the end of his performing career.

In mid-September Don was at MGM Studios in Culver City to film his part as an obnoxious barroom bully in "Mr. Dingle, the Strong," an episode of *The Twilight Zone* that aired the following spring. "It was a kick doing the heckling instead of blocking it," he reported from the set. The television doors were beginning to open just a little more. He signed on for an episode of Jackie Cooper's CBS Navy comedy *Hennesey*—Cooper played Navy physician Lt. Charles "Chick" Hennesey and Abby Dalton his love interest, Navy nurse Lt. Martha Hale—and was hired for an episode of the top-rated NBC series *Wagon Train*, in its fourth season on NBC. There were rumors that Don was in talks to star in a television version of the old radio show *It Pays to Be Ignorant*, which had aired on Mutual, NBC, and CBS from 1942 to 1951. Nothing ever came of it.

And then it was time for the mid-October showdown—a show business version of *High Noon*, only with the bustling, congested streets of New York City replacing a dusty town in Old West New Mexico and veteran gunslinger Jack E. Leonard at the Blue Angel staring down the new kid, Don Rickles, at Basin Street East seven city blocks away. The press revived stories of the alleged feud between Leonard and Rickles, but they were sorely disappointed; when the comics met at a celebrity event several weeks before their opening dates, Don and Fat Jack were "excessively polite" to each other. "Asked if he were still burned at Rickles," wrote *Chicago Tribune* columnist Herb Lyon, "Leonard snapped, 'Who feuds with a student?'"[27] Bob Hope was asked if he would attend their openings. "Nope, I'll stay home with the wife and kids and get insulted," he said (or, more likely, one of his stable of writers said it for him). Don Rickles the horse even reared his head again and got into the act. Someone noticed that he was running at Aqueduct . . . and that his jockey was named Jack Leonard. Fun stuff. He finished fourth in the race, but who cared? It was great publicity.

The drama, though, was nonexistent. Don opened at Basin Street East by lambasting Ethel Merman—"Sorry to yell louder than you do"—and "Ethel squealed happily," according to Earl Wilson. But did she? It was open to interpretation. "Some of those who were present for Don Rickles' opening at Basin Street East report that he 'lost' the audience when he attacked Ethel Merman—who was a great star before anybody heard of him and will still be a star when he's forgotten," Dorothy Kilgallen sneered. "To compound the felony, he stayed on and on and on far longer than his allotted time, which left Billy Eckstine pacing his dressing room waiting for his cue (unforgivable since Billy is the headliner) and made the audience audibly restless."

Kilgallen, though, was the anti-Rickles and delivered a minority report. Nearly every other columnist or reporter covering both Don and Fat Jack wrote glowing reviews of both performers. Over at the Blue Angel, Leonard "barbecued" his audience and the club, describing its narrow show room's décor as "Early Claustrophobia"; he described the air-conditioning (it was an unusually warm fall that year) as "being forced through a hot water bottle." Singer Johnnie Ray, he said, had a wonderful voice ("It's too bad it's in Vic Damone's throat"), while the United Nations, he barked, should be called "Chock full o'Nuts." He revealed his happiness over his newly signed two-year television deal: "The payments are very reasonable, too." Cue the rim shot. Don's mother, Etta, went to see Fat Jack at the Blue Angel, and when he spotted her in the audience, he did not waste time getting in a dig at her. Fat Jack: "Now that your son's a big man, ma'am, isn't it time you stopped wearing a rented mink coat?"[28]

Don matched Fat Jack insult for insult, and then some, and the stars continued to come to see his show and to be roasted on the Rickles spit: Doris Day, Jackie Gleason—who was no slouch himself in the insult department from his days at Club 18—Diahann Carroll, Audrey Hepburn ("looking as dazzling as Tiffany's diamonds"), Kirk Douglas, Stanley Donen, and on and on. Don's old friend and Sahara stablemate, Keely Smith, was there at Basin Street East for Don's opening night and took a ribbing; so, too, did actor Franchot Tone: "Hey, Franchot, watch the *Late Late Show* and make believe you are still working!" To radio disc jockey Alan Freed, who, the previous year, had been embroiled in a payola (pay-for-play) scandal Don barked, "Tell the truth, Alan, what'd you get—a car?" Keely Smith returned several more nights to show her support. "Laugh, you dum-dum Indian broad," he roared at her, "but Louis cut you out of the will!"

And then it was all over. If there were any bad feelings left between Don and Leonard, they kept them between themselves. Fat Jack even sponsored Don for a membership at the Friars Club.

Columbia Records recorded Don's act at Basin Street East with an eye toward releasing it as an album in the suddenly lucrative comedy genre. Bob Newhart's first album, *The Button-Down Mind of Bob Newhart,* had hit stores the previous February, reached number one in August, and remained in the top spot for fourteen weeks, an astonishing run for the young comedian just two years removed from an advertising job in Chicago. It was the first comedy album to reach that plateau and garnered Newhart two Grammy Awards, for Album of the Year and Best New Artist. By February 1961, talk of Columbia Records and a Don Rickles album had died down, according to obnoxious *New York Mirror* columnist Lee Mortimer, who was decidedly not a Don Rickles fan. "Guess Columbia's having trouble with the proposed Don Rickles (Ugh!) album which is making some of its executives as ill as he makes me,"[29] wrote Mortimer, who was also a true-crime author (*New York Confidential, Washington Confidential, Chicago Confidential*) and knew the ins and outs of the club world. (He was also the columnist Frank Sinatra infamously slugged at Ciro's in Hollywood in 1947 after he allegedly uttered an ethnic slur as Frank walked by. They settled out of court, but had several run-ins thereafter as Mortimer continued to document Sinatra's alleged ties to the Mafia and to the Communist Party.)

Don's romances continued to be fodder for the gossip columnists, though only he really knew if there was any truth to the rumors—and he never publicly commented on his love life, other than working the occasional line into his act. (Besides, it was free publicity, so why bother?) Walter Winchell, for one, linked him to "the doll of his heart," a Vegas showgirl named Mary Taylor, while, at the same time, he was said to be "dating pretty blond Ilene Lehrman," an actress who was seen earlier that year with cartoonist Charles Addams—and then with actor Sam Levene when they toured in summer stock in *Make a Million*. Following that flurry, neither woman was ever mentioned again in connection to The Merchant of Venom (perhaps Don or Joe Scandore planted the items in the first place). A few months later, Lee Mortimer reared his head again to repeat his opinion of Don's act in an elliptical mention of actress Selene Walters: "Never thought it would come to Selene Walters and Don Rickles, whose 'comedy' makes me ill."[30]

Don finished out the year at the Celebrity Room in Philadelphia, where he drew record crowds. From there, it was on to the Civic Playhouse in Las Palmas for something called *A Timid Evening with Don Rickles*. The show was the brainchild of local stage producers Zev Bufman and Stan Seiden. Don was, for the first time in ages, billed as "The Emperor" and he was booked for fifteen shows in a musical comedy revue that promised "a complete new repertoire of insults" through New Year's Day (two evening performances on Friday, Saturday, and Sunday). It was his first appearance in a legitimate theater.

He sold the place out in record time and prepared to appear in his fourth big-screen movie.

It was a Columbia Pictures service comedy called *Everything's Ducky* and starred Mickey Rooney, Jackie Cooper—with whom Don had worked on *Hennesey*—Buddy Hackett, singer/actress Joanie Sommers, and a talking duck (really), with Don, Red Buttons, and Jonathan Winters pegged for the supporting cast. For reasons unknown, but not unusual in the frenetic world of Hollywood dealmaking, Don was out of the picture by the time production began in early 1961, as were Buttons and Winters. Hackett generated whatever laughs were to be found and received second billing behind Rooney. To no one's surprise, *Everything's Ducky* sank without a trace. Don did not work with Joanie Sommers in that movie, but he was in the audience at the Crescendo in January when she opened for Mort Sahl.

CHAPTER 8

D on spent the early months of 1961 in the warmth of Miami Beach, where, in February, he opened for a two-month run at the Deauville Hotel on Collins Avenue and added yet another nickname to his growing list of monikers: "The Mad Emperor of Insult." He played the smaller Musketeer Lounge while Sophie Tucker wowed them in the hotel's spacious Casanova Room. Despite the attendant hoopla and the critical raves—"He throws the harpoon, pulls it back and sinks it into another customer"—he was not yet a marquee name. That, of course, would change over time, but for now the Don Rickles style of humor was, in the parlance of the time, considered "sick" and appealed to a niche audience that could not sustain him in the long run. "It doesn't seem reasonable that the 'I-hate-you-and-don't-give-a-hoot-if-you-hate-me' routine Mr. Rickles follows can stretch out from 30 to 50 years as have the careers of Durante, Lewis and Tucker," one wag opined. "I could be wrong, but that's the way it looks." He was wrong.

Don reunited with Murray Franklin while at the Deauville. It had been a long time coming. The two men had not spoken for five years, since Don's career-boosting splash at Murray's club—something along the lines of "He's gotten too big for his britches." There were hard feelings on both sides; when Don played a club in the Miami Beach area, he would not mention Murray's name in press interviews or during his act. He never dropped into the club to say hello. Murray, for his part, never hired Don again or uttered his name in public. The feud festered over time.

The Ritz Brothers, who followed Sophie Tucker in the Casanova

Room at the Deauville, were aware of the mutual cold shoulders, and teamed with a reporter from *Variety* to try to remedy the situation. Whatever they said to Don did the trick, and he began to speak favorably about Murray from the stage of the Musketeer Lounge. *Miami News* columnist Herb Kelly got into the act, and for Don's final show at the hotel, a 3:30 a.m. Sunday redeye, he drove Murray to the Deauville, where he sat at a front table. "Everything I am or have today I owe to one man—he's sitting at a table here. It's Murray Franklin," Don said. Murray stood up: "And that goes both ways." They shook hands and kidded each other and the past five frosty years between them melted away.[1]

The Twilight Zone was in its second season on CBS, and already a critical darling (if not a breakout ratings success), when "Mr. Dingle, the Strong," featuring Don in a supporting role, aired on Friday, March 3, 1961. The episode, filmed the previous September, was written by series creator Rod Serling. Burgess Meredith starred as the titular Luther Dingle, a meek vacuum-cleaner salesman and perennial loser. Luther is chosen by two visiting Martians (played by Douglas Spencer and Michael Fox) who conduct an experiment by endowing him with superhuman strength to see how he reacts to this miraculous change. Luther is in the neighborhood bar when he discovers his gift, which shocks his nemesis, loudmouth, cigar-chomping bookie Joseph J. Callahan (that's Don) "whose entire life," Serling intones in his inimitable opening narration, "is any sporting event with two sides and a set of odds."

Luther gets carried away with his newfound superpowers—he picks Callahan up, twirls him around in the air, and tosses him away like a piece of trash. Just as he is about to lift an entire building off its foundation, on live television, the two Martians sap Luther's strength, and he's back to being a laughingstock. As the aliens leave town, they run into two visiting Venusians (hey, it's *The Twilight Zone*)—and they, in turn, conduct an experiment of their own: endowing Luther with otherworldly intelligence. Fade out.

The *Twilight Zone* episode boosted Don's national profile, and television executives and casting agents took notice. He was asked to appear with Mort Sahl on *Here's Hollywood*, a half-hour celebrity interview show from Desilu Productions that aired weekday afternoons on NBC in most markets, with hosts Joanne Jordan and Dean Miller. Sahl talked about Don's "controversial" brand of humor, and Don explained how he earned the nickname of "Emperor." In March, he reportedly signed on for a role in the big-screen heist comedy *Sail a Crooked Ship* with stars Robert Wagner, Dolores Hart, Carolyn Jones, and Ernie Kovacs, but once again, the role did not come to fruition. In a sad coda, *Sail a Crooked Ship* marked Ernie Kovacs's final movie appearance. In January 1962, he was killed in a car crash in Beverly Hills.

Don was back in West Hollywood at the Crescendo in April, sharing the bill with singer Frances Faye. There, he eviscerated Bing's boys Phillip and Gary Crosby, actor Doug McClure, and talent manager Bullets Durgom, who handled Jackie Gleason and Mort Sahl, among others. As always, there was someone in the audience who was not in on the laugh; this time around, Don angered Vincent Price, apparently with a lethal insult that, unfortunately, was not recorded for posterity but was alluded to in the gossip columns. Everyone got the joke, though, when he opened for a short run at the Club Alamo in Detroit. "Rickles employs his rapier tongue with a deftness that keeps him just on the verge of being clobbered as he holds a finger and microphone under the chin of a red-faced listener," the *Detroit Free Press* reported. "This 'Sultan of Insults' is in his second week of jesting with the ringsiders and playing hob generally with celebrities. He has a good time, and so do his victims."[2] He tore through a young couple ("Do I knock you and your junkie boyfriend?"), ripped Southern segregationists ("Remember the wonderful old days in Mobile when we blew up the bus?"), and turned on a man sitting near the front row: "I know you from Poland. You hung my uncle."[3]

Don Rickles and the self-described "hillbilly singer" Kay Starr should, by any measure, have had very little in common. Don was a brash Jewish kid from Queens who was still very close to his mother and leading a peripatetic life of endless club dates and fleeting romances, both real and created for the press. Kay, four years Don's senior, was born Catherine Laverne Starks on a reservation in Oklahoma. Her father, Harry, was an Iroquois Native American; her mother, Annie, was part Native American and part Irish.

Kay broke into show business as a singer for big bands fronted by Bob Crosby (Bing's kid brother) and Glenn Miller. She rode her voice to the top of the charts throughout the 1950s with a string of hits including "Bonaparte's Retreat," "Oh! Babe," "Wheel of Fortune," and "Side by Side," but by the end of the decade her career was cooling off. At the age of thirty-nine, she'd been married and divorced four times (from Roy Davis, Harold Solomon, bandleader Vic Schoen, and publisher George Alfred Mellen) and had a fourteen-year-old daughter, Katherine (from Roy Davis). As far as anyone knew, Kay Starr and Don Rickles were passing acquaintances since meeting in Las Vegas when Don opened at the Sahara in 1959.

Two years later, shortly after celebrating his thirty-fifth birthday, Don returned to the Sahara, and to the Casbar Lounge, in May 1961. Kay Starr was there, too, entertaining patrons in the much larger Congo Room. Initially, Don's attentions, according to the gossip columns, appeared to be focused on romancing the "busty singer" Betty George ("the scenery in M. Berle's act"), with Kay nowhere on his radar. Alas, whatever it was he had with Betty George changed forever on the fateful night that she found out "The Emperor" had called singer Kiki Paige to whisper sweet nothings in her ear—right after dropping Betty off at the end of a date. Whoever fed that line to the gossip columnists left out the obvious question: How could Betty have known who Don called if she was already home?

In July, Sahara boss Milton Prell signed Don to a new three-year, $500,000 deal to headline at the Casbar for a minimum of twenty weeks each year. The deal included elevator-scale raises through June

1964. Don was now one of the highest-paid lounge acts in Vegas. Etta Rickles—not Don or his manager Joe Scandore—broke the news about his big new deal to the Miami papers. Mother knows best.

And then, suddenly, seemingly out of nowhere, Don Rickles and Kay Starr were a hot item. There was Kay in the audience in mid-July when Don, "who looks like a cross between Yul Brynner and Khrushchev," opened at Fack's nightclub in San Francisco with singer Mavis Rivers. Kay watched her new boyfriend tongue-lash Tony Martin, Cyd Charisse, Nat King Cole, former Dodgers pitcher Clem Labine (now with the Pittsburgh Pirates), San Francisco Giants owner Horace Stoneham, and former *Dragnet* costar Ben Alexander: "Remember the old days, Ben? When you were known?" He made sure to insult Kay, too, just to throw off the scent of anyone sniffing around their romance: "Be nice, Kay—you could blow your voice any minute."

Bing Crosby's oldest son, Gary—who, years later, wrote the book *Going My Own Way*, a scathing indictment of Dear Old Dad— was scheduled to follow Don at Fack's with his singing act. When he was forced to postpone the engagement amid ongoing emotional turmoil in his private life, the club's owner, George Andros, asked Don to stay on for another month to fill Crosby's slot. Don declined, citing other commitments, though it's unclear if one of those "commitments" was to Georgia Holden, the "44-D Girl" and a dancer at the Moulin Rouge and at Fack's. "She and the insulting Don Rickles seem to have struck up a warm mutual admiration," reported a wag at the *San Francisco Examiner*.[4] Enough said.

Don's relationship with Kay Starr continued throughout that summer, and by September, it was daily grist for the gossip mill. He flew from Las Vegas to Lake Tahoe "to romance" Kay while she was appearing at Harrah's. Walter Winchell, in his inimitable style, called it "truluv" and broached the possibility of Kay becoming Mrs. Don Rickles. Dorothy Kilgallen ('natch) weighed in with a reprimanding item: "Bad-taste comedian Don Rickles is supposed to be wooing Kay Star [sic], who is so charming and attractive. (Say it ain't so, Kay!)" Later that month, Kay flew to Europe—she traveled there

frequently—while Don opened at Basin St. East, and Kay, reportedly, "will fly here Oct. 8 to see boyfriend Don Rickles." Romantic
ardor did not defuse Don's edge at Basin Street East, where, in short
order, he ripped Harry Ritz ("Check with your brother Jimmy to see
what's funny before you laugh!"), insisted he "carried" Tony Curtis in
The Rat Race, and snarled to a patron in the front row: "Is this your
wife? Well, keep your chin up."

"He can insult ten people while you're lighting a cigarette," one columnist noted. "He'll insult you for your race, religion or shape of your
ears. If your wife is along, he'll insult her, too. Oddly nobody gets
sore."[5] Actor Gig Young did not seem to mind the ribbing. "Look at this
dumdum—still wearing his tuxedo. Can't believe he didn't win the
Academy Award!" Milton Berle guffawed when Don turned to him:
"Sure, you're laughing—while your wife's writing down my material.
Milton, hope and pray your act comes back."

Kay called Don from France to say hello and to let him know she
was flying into New York City (he told her he had been golfing with
Prince Rainier). Once she arrived, they reunited briefly before Kay
flew on to L.A., where Don joined her after closing at Basin Street East
in early November. "That was quite a love scene Kay Starr and Don
Rickles staged at International Airport!" Harrison Carroll reported
in the *Los Angeles Times.* "We're really serious," Don countered before
flying to Vegas for more performance dates at the Sahara. His ardor
dampened shortly thereafter when he cracked wise on stage about the
rash of guest-room burglaries plaguing the hotel and announced that
his room was open season, since he was covered by insurance. That
was all it took; a person or persons with a passkey promptly broke into
Don's suite at the hotel and robbed him of $100 in cash, a money clip,
and a gold, diamond-encrusted watch given to him by hotel owner,
Milton Prell. Two other wristwatches and several credit cards were
also stolen. The haul was estimated at $1,325.

By late November, the rumors began to surface: Don and Kay
had been secretly married. Don denied it in playful fashion when
he insulted Kay as she sat in the Casbar Lounge audience. "I can say

anything I want to about her," he joked, "she's not my wife." Their "marriage," as it turned out, was a practical joke played by a reporter in Las Vegas on one of his colleagues.

The Rickles-Starr romance continued, on and off, until the early part of 1962—when Kay was linked, suddenly, to "rich Texan" Jack Valenti, who was working for the Kennedy administration as a press liaison. (In 1966 Valenti was named the president of the Motion Picture Association of America.) In February, Kay and Don had dinner at the Beachcomber Hotel in Miami Beach and she drove him to the airport, telling him that she hoped to catch his act when he returned to the city to begin a run at the Deauville. "But, believe me, we have no wedding plans," she told a reporter. "He makes me laugh. I seem to stimulate him. We'll settle for that."[6] And then it was over. Just like that. Don was playing the Sahara in March when he tellingly invited actress Barbara Crane to opening night—while Kay performed in the Congo Room. It ended amicably between them; when Kay closed at the Sahara in April, Don made sure the stage was covered with twelve dozen American Beauty roses.

(In August 1962, Kay married her fifth husband, Earl Spencer Callicutt. She would divorce and remarry one final time before passing away in November 2016 at the age of ninety-four.)

Joe Scandore continued to manage Don's career. He was loyal and reliable and was always on the lookout for his top client, his number-one priority. He often traveled with Don on the road to make sure everything ran smoothly. (Etta no longer accompanied Don on tour.) Harry Goins was there, too, as Don's dresser, confidant, and right-hand man. Don signed with a new Hollywood agent, Jack Gilardi, who was with General Artists Corporation (later ICM). Gilardi had negotiated Don's guest-starring roles on *Hennesey* and *Wagon Train* and worked out a deal for his client to appear on *Cain's Hundred*, an NBC crime series starring Peter Mark Richman as a former mob lawyer who teams with the FBI to bring mobsters to justice after his fiancée is mistakenly killed. Gilardi, who was well-connected in showbiz circles, also landed Don a small part in an episode of *The Dick Powell Theatre*, which also aired on NBC.

Don's guest-starring role on the NBC Western *Wagon Train* was the first of these projects to hit the airwaves, in June 1961. The episode, "Wagon to Fort Anderson," featured Don as US Army soldier Joe Carder and Albert Salmi as Joe's brother, George. Joe and George, along with the Ellison sisters (Carol Rossen and Candy Moore)—one of them a deaf mute—are the only survivors of a Native American attack. Flint McCullough (series star Robert Horton) wants to lead the group to safety, but Joe has other ideas, and sees this as his chance to desert from the Army and look for gold. He tries to convince the Ellison sisters that Flint is an untrustworthy saddle tramp who is only pretending to help them. George, who is good-natured and a bit simple-minded, goes along with Joe's plan, if only to appease his older brother.

Five months later, on November 20, viewers could catch Don in prime time by tuning in to the CBS series *Hennesey*, which mixed comedy and drama. The episode that night, "Professional Sailor," was unique in its presentation; similar in structure to a one-act play, it featured only two actors, Don and series star Jackie Cooper (who also directed). Don played Chief Petty Officer Ernie Schmidt, who reports to Cooper's Dr. "Chick" Hennesey for a physical examination. Ernie has already served twenty-four years in the service but wants to reenlist for another six years. He is a gruff sort who does not take any bull, but Dr. Hennesey eventually wins him over and Ernie shares his life story and his reasons for wanting to continue to serve his country. "That's all there is, but Rickles the night club comic, is just right as the chief," wrote the *Philadelphia Daily News* television critic.[7]

Don't next prime-time role was his "special guest star" turn on *Cain's Hundred*. The episode, "Blood Money," aired in February 1962 and featured Ed Begley, Larry Blyden, Everett Sloane, and Don in support of star Peter Mark Richman as the titular Nicholas Cain. Don played gambling czar Dave Malloy, who makes a deal to support mayoral candidate Jay Adams (Blyden), who is running on a platform of citywide reform against crooked incumbent Tully Johnson (Begley). Johnson tells Adams's honest campaign manager, Sam Palmer (Sloane), about the deal, and there is a murder. Cain, with help from the FBI, finds the killer (of course) and cleans up the whole sordid mess. The episode aired to little fanfare, which was not surprising. The hour-long *Cain's Hundred* aired Tuesday night opposite the popular *Gary Moore Show* on CBS (with rising star Carol Burnett), which rang the NBC show's death knell after one season of thirty episodes.

Not long after his *Cain's Hundred* episode aired, Don was a guest on *The Tonight Show*—Jack Carter was subbing for Jack Paar that night—but for the next year all was quiet on the television front for The Merchant of Venom as he returned to the nightclub stage. He was contractually committed to twenty weeks a year at the Sahara, and it was there, in April 1962, that he was (good-naturedly) tackled on the stage by Tony Bennett and Sammy Davis Jr. after one too many insults lobbed in their direction. They ripped Don's trousers off in mock rage as he grabbed a tablecloth, wrapped it around himself, and bellowed to someone backstage, "Hey, Angelo, hurry up and get me a robe. I look like a butcher out here!" The crowd loved it. He squired Barbara Crane to his thirty-sixth birthday party in May, thrown by Jimmy Durante's producer, Jackie Barnett, at the same time the columns linked him to dancer Lori Lynn. Everyone, it seemed, wanted a piece of the hottest lounge act on the Vegas strip.

"He would attack people in the audience," recalled Carol Burnett. "I remember [that] one of the first times I ever saw him, I had been on *The Gary Moore Show* and had done very well on that show so I was kind of up-and-coming. I was in the audience in Las Vegas this one time, and he came out and he was doing his shtick and everything, and then he looked at me, and he said, 'Oh, there she is, folks, sitting around waiting for Lucy to die.' Oh God, the audience loved it and . . . I was so embarrassed. But that was the only time he ever did a bit on me. That was my first encounter with him."[8]

"I don't feel I insult or hurt anybody," Don told a columnist chronicling his rise through show business. "I never hit below the belt.

People will come into the club and they'll either hate me or love me. The majority of them are in my corner. If they weren't I'd be working on the docks. And I don't depend on celebrities to be in the audience. I can do as much with a butcher. Humor is humor. We should be able to laugh at ourselves."

In June, Don returned to the Slate Brothers Club for four nights, and the line to get in to see Rickles snaked around the block. Don ripped into Hollywood's A-list, everyone from Eddie Fisher, party-animal Los Angeles Angels pitcher Bo Belinsky, Connie Stevens (who was starring in the hit TV series *Hawaiian Eye*), Jack Warden, and Walter Winchell—who thought "his refreshing nonsense belongs on B'way, Mr. Merrick." Winchell's item was not the first report linking Don to the theatrical world in one form or another. The following April it was reported that he "may make his Broadway acting debut this fall," and around the same time there were rumors that Don would star in a Las Vegas–based version of the musical *Take Me Along*, as Sid Davis. Jackie Gleason had played the role on Broadway for over a year and won a Tony Award in 1960.

Don took most of that summer off, and the Rickles name, at least in newsprint, was replaced by mentions of his equine namesake, who ran in a handful of races throughout July and August of 1962. In the fall, Don was back in L.A., on the stage of the Slate Brothers Club, and then he returned to Las Vegas to open at the Flamingo Hotel—where Tony Bennett and Billy Eckstine "infuriated" him by talking loudly during his act (it was probably *part* of his act). He moved desert venues from Nevada to California to play a string of gigs at the Chi Chi club in Palm Springs, ending the year—where else?—at the Slate Brothers Club on La Cienega Boulevard, appearing on the bill with crooner Kaye Stevens and, one night, spying Loretta Young in the audience. "Loretta, quit oiling the doorknobs," he barked at her. "You're not on television anymore."

CHAPTER 9

The canon of Don Rickles lore is chock-full of colorful stories that were repeated, time after time, by Don and others in print and, most frequently, on late-night television talk shows. Indeed, this book opens with the oft-told tale of Don's breakthrough at Murray Franklin's in 1957, when he barked at Sinatra, "Make yourself comfortable, Frank, hit somebody." That story followed Don to the end of his life, and thereafter in his obituaries, as the touchstone of his bona fide start in show business.

There is another story involving Don and Frank Sinatra that was put through a sweaty workout over the years, particularly once Don Rickles became a household name. It is similar to the Murray Franklin's story in that its location often changes, but to keep matters simple, let us assume it happened in Las Vegas.

Here is the setup.

Don was having dinner with a young woman he was trying to impress. His goal: to knock her off her feet and into his bed later that evening. He knew that Sinatra would be eating in the same restaurant that night. So, as the story goes, Don asked Frank if he would stop by at his table on his way out to say hello. His date (who was never identified) would surely be gobsmacked by the sight of Old Blue Eyes in the flesh—and even more astonished that the world's most famous entertainer knew her balding, slightly paunchy dinner date. Frank loved a practical joke (when he was in the mood), so he cooperated and sidled up to Don's table as he was leaving the restaurant with his retinue. "Hi, Don," he said, "how are you?" Rickles looked up, annoyed: "What's the matter with you, Frank, can't you see that I'm eating?"

Frank retold the story with relish to Johnny Carson years later on *The Tonight Show*, on one of those nights in the seventies when Don waltzed in unannounced—he did that a lot in those days—and made himself at home, sitting on the couch next to Frank while Ed McMahon dutifully slid over until he was virtually out of camera range.

The story is funny and true, but what happened the following night, when Sinatra got even with Bullethead, is the true icing on the cake. Don's longtime business manager, Bill Braunstein, picks up the narrative. "So Rickles comes back with the girl to the restaurant, right? He is sitting in the booth. Frank tells his buddies, 'Listen, when Rickles comes in, I want you to take his table and the chairs and put them outside.' So Rickles comes in with the girl [and] they're sitting at the table. The waiters and everybody come over, they lift the table and the chairs, they bring them outside, and they put Rickles onto the street with the girl. And that's how Frank got him back."

As we have seen, Don did not need Frank Sinatra's help with the ladies. He dated quite a bit, and the more his star ascended the more frequently his dalliances with bold-faced names of the opposite sex landed in the gossip columns. Perhaps Don was buoyed by his recent weight loss. On doctor's orders he had dropped forty pounds and slimmed down to 160 pounds by adhering to a liquid diet. If anything, the weight loss sharpened Don's tongue; he ran into Lenny Kent one night at the Slate Brothers Club and noticed that the actor looked a bit heavier: "Look who's got my old body!" he snapped.

The steady parade of women to whom Don Rickles was romantically linked did not falter in the wake of his breakup with Kay Starr. Over the next year, "Don Rickles was seen with (fill-in-the-blank)" made the rounds of the gossip columns with increasing frequency.

There was Molly Bee, the country music singer ("I Saw Mommy Kissing Santa Claus") and the *Pinky Lee Show* sidekick. Molly, thirteen years Don's junior, was born Mollie Gene Beachboard—so no one blamed her for changing her name—and like Kay Starr, she was part Native American. Don and Molly's close encounters led to the inevitable hoary wordplay ("Don Rickles is begging to get stung by

Molly Bee") for a month or two, and then nothing more was heard of the romance. There were others, including singer Eileen Barton and the "exotic" hypnotist Pat Collins, who was dubbed "Steve Allen's favorite hypnoteuse" after appearing on his television show. "Don Rickles, incidentally, has been getting into Pat's act, both offstage and on . . ." Once that relationship ended, actress Susanne Sidney reportedly entered Don's life ("Doesn't she belong to Vic Damone?" one wag slyly noted). Don was also seen in the company of Sharon Dobkin at Tractons Restaurant, located just outside of San Diego . . . but, wait, he was seeing "Hungarian beauty" and actress Eva Six, right? Maybe; he was cagey about that one when asked. "She's beautiful and talented," he said. "I know, because she whispered in my ear, 'I'm beautiful and talented.'"

For a short period of time, Don and fellow comic Red Buttons were supposedly both "sharing the same curvy date" in Miami Beach, one Ethel Besher—who, it was said, broke up with Don in Las Vegas. "His mother always came first!" she complained. Don was spotted dining out, again at Tracton's near San Diego, with actress Sharon DeBord. The restaurant became one of his favorite haunts when he was in town; he also dined there with actress Alberta Nelson, who then "drove him to the airport to get a plane for Miami Beach and his opening at the Deauville." Their names were never again uttered in the same sentence. At times, the dating exploits of Don Rickles beggared the imagination: he was "romancing" Leslie Hall, the ex-wife of actor Huntz Hall; later, according to Earl Wilson, he was "calling Jo Ann Miller at the Westchester Dinner Theater" while he was dating . . . wait for it . . . Connie Francis.

Don and Connie knew each other, of course, from Vegas, and she had helped him that time by calling in a favor so Don would not have his legs broken by a mobbed-up thug after insulting his woman. They were pals, but was there more to the friendship? In early April of 1963, there was talk of Don "saving his flowery phrases" for Connie. Shortly thereafter, Walter Winchell reported that "they may be sealed. Intimates are not convinced."[1] In early May, gossip

columnist Sheila Graham threw hot water on their supposed "incip-
ient" romance. Connie, she wrote, told Don that he had to ask her
domineering father, George Franconero, for permission to escort his
daughter for a night out on the town. "I don't like your act," Mr.
Franconero supposedly told him. (This was the same man who, so
the story goes, chased Connie's former suitor, Bobby Darin, out of an
apartment building at gunpoint. He did not mince his words.)

"Every act in Vegas had been to see his show, except me. I was
working in the main room and Don was in the Casbar Lounge,"
Connie Francis recalled. "And I heard he was very dirty and he was
very vile. So I didn't go to see his show. And he felt very bad and
he told my Aunt Marie, who always traveled with me, and my hair-
dresser/secretary, Rico . . . he said, 'I can't understand why Connie
won't see my show.'

"Rico said to me, 'You have to see his show. He's not dirty, Connie, he doesn't have to be.' I said, 'What about the F word?' and he
said, 'No, he doesn't use that word. He doesn't use foul language.' I
was so naive. So I went to see his show and I wore a white gown and
I had my mink stole on, and I'm walking down the aisle and Don saw
me and he said, 'Who's that broad with the gravy stains all over her
dress!' He devoted the whole show to me, but he never mentioned my
name once. He called me 'The Great White Queen of Italy.'"

Don asked Connie out on a date shortly thereafter. "The first
time we went out we were going to a very classy movie house and
he rented a red Corvette to take me to this movie," she said. "And
when we pulled up, the valet said, 'Wow, Mr. Rickles, she's a
beauty,' and Don said, 'The car, dummy! The car!' He also bought
me a teddy bear. I said, 'I love stuffed animals, is it for me?' And
he said, 'No, it's for your Aunt Marie.' I thought that was very
sweet because everybody was always bringing me gifts and Don was
thinking of my Aunt Marie."[2]

The newspapers reported that Connie "broke appointments" to
drive Don to the airport (a familiar Rickles romantic trope); in the
fall, he escorted her to the Cocoanut Grove in L.A. for the opening

of singer James Darren's show. (Darren split the headlining bill with comedian Gary Morton, Lucille Ball's second husband.) Other celebrities in attendance included Joey Bishop, Laurence Harvey, Nancy Sinatra, Jack Benny, and Ethel Merman, who was rehearsing for *The Red Skelton Show* and rushed over to the Cocoanut Grove, arriving just in time for the show.

Don stuck to his modus operandi of never commenting on romances real or drummed up (possibly by Joe Scandore). Connie, however, addressed the gossip in November 1963. "I try to be sexy. It's quite a feat, it's ridiculous as a matter of fact," she said. "Because sexy is not part of my personality. In Las Vegas, Don Rickles kids about dating me. He says, 'Come on, honey, I'll take you on some of the rides.'

"One night as a gag at the Hotel Sahara, I put on a sexy gown and borrowed a mink stole I could drag. I put on false eyelashes and a lot of lipstick. I dragged the mink down the hall and knocked on the door to Rickles' room. When he opened the door I shifted my hips, and in the way Brigitte Bardot would say it, I said, 'Hello, darling.' Do you know what he said to me? He said: 'What is this—trick or treat?'"[3]

That did not stanch the talk about Don and Connie's romance. It carried over into the early part of 1964, when Connie flew to L.A. to see Don open at the Slate Brothers Club before she opened in Las Vegas. Two months later, in March, she was still denying that her relationship with Don went any further than a platonic friendship. "He's just a good friend and a lot of fun and I love the way he insults me," she said. "Don will tell me 'get under the table and play with your fire truck until I call' and I break up. He knows hip people. But marry him? No. I wouldn't marry another performer." In April, Don was reported to be back in the arms of Molly Bee; Connie had been relegated to being his "telephone pal." She had the last word when she ran into columnist Mike Connolly, who asked her about Don and whether they "are still duetting 'Love's Old Refrain.' Flashed she: 'I'm singing it solo these days and it includes no part of Don Rickles, not even the slimmed-down version!'"

"We dated for a couple of years but I was dating other people, too," Connie told the author. "His mother wanted us to marry. Etta said, 'Why aren't you marrying my Donald? He'd make a terrific husband.' I said, 'I love Don, Etta, but not in that way.' Etta was the best; she and Frank Sinatra's mother, Dolly, were my two favorite show business mothers. Etta cooked for the world; when I was doing a movie and I had a cold, she brought me chicken soup on the set. She was just the most amazing woman and Don loved her dearly. Everybody did."[4]

Meanwhile, Don's non-romantic professional pursuits were bearing more fruit—with the inevitable swings-and-misses along the way.

In early 1963, he signed a deal to costar in his fourth movie. It was another role as a heavy, in line with Nellie Miller in *The Rat Race*, and Don was costarring alongside long-ago Oscar winner Ray Milland, Harold Stone, and John Hoyt. The movie was a science-fiction thriller tentatively titled *X*; B-movie king Roger Corman was directing. (Don: "It's got the shortest title since the movie *M*.") Floyd Crosby, the father of future rock star David Crosby, was the cinematographer.

Frank Sinatra wanted Bullethead for a small role in his next semi–Rat Pack movie, *Robin and the Seven Hoods*. Joey Bishop and Peter Lawford were on the outs with Frank, but Sammy Davis Jr. and Dean Martin were along for the ride, as were Bing Crosby, Barbara Rush, and Peter Falk. Don's participation in it did not happen, for reasons unknown, but likely due to Don's commitment to Roger Corman. Sinatra was on the set filming *Robin and the Seven Hoods* on November 22, 1963, when word broke that President John F. Kennedy had been assassinated in Dallas. Sinatra, who had worked so hard to help get Kennedy elected, was shattered.

Next word on Don's career was that he would cut a record album in Las Vegas called *Three Years of Me and My Insults*. Sinatra promised to make a cameo appearance on the disc. That record fell by the wayside, as did a ninety-minute television project in which Don would play Babe Ruth—the "Insultin' Sultan" as the "Sultan of Swat."

One likely apocryphal newspaper report had Don "vooming" in from Vegas to pay a call on Alfred Hitchcock in L.A. to discuss acting roles. *That* would have been interesting. In another small nugget planted by another hard-charging publicist (or maybe by Joe Scandore, always on the lookout for Don), studio executives were trying to lure Don and Basil Rathbone to costar in a television pilot called *Hooray for Hollywood*. That cheer was ignored.

The strangest Don Rickles news splashed down in April, when word broke that The Merchant of Venom would be opening a club in New York City called the Gospel Truth—featuring, as its name implied, gospel singers. Had anyone cared to dig a little deeper, they would have discovered that Joe Scandore, in addition to managing Don and several others, was enjoying some success with his newest act, the Sweet Chariot Gospel Singers. It sounded like the Riot Room situation in Miami Beach all over again. This time, though, Scandore put Don's name out there as a stalking horse for his planned gospel club.

In May, Scandore opened his club, now called the Sweet Chariot club, in a cellar on West 46th Street in Times Square, and within a month, it was drawing a celebrity crowd (George Maharis, Tammy Grimes, Jack Cassidy, Eydie Gormé, Rex Harrison, Red Buttons, Nanette Fabray) with acts such as the Golden Chords from Philadelphia and the Herman Stevens Singers from Newark, New Jersey. The Sweet Chariot waitresses were called "Angels"; they wore wired halos, toy wings, and mesh tights. The headwaitress was the "Archangel," the doorman was the "Deacon," and the white table wine was labeled "Satan's Temptation." Of course it was. Scandore envisioned a string of Sweet Chariot clubs in other cities (including Chicago and L.A.) but scuttled those plans when the Times Square club sputtered in the fall after buckling to pressure from outraged Christian groups. "I wasn't aware they would offend anyone," Scandore said. Ya think?

For all of these phantom endeavors, there were deals that came to fruition. Don's agent, Jack Gilardi, was working hard behind the scenes to diversify his client's entertainment portfolio. He worked out a deal for Don to appear in an episode of the ABC television series *Burke's Law*—starring Gene Barry as millionaire L.A. homicide captain Amos Burke—and for Don to appear in a two-episode arc in Season 4 of *The Dick Van Dyke Show* on CBS, which aired on November 4 and 11, 1964. Don played Lyle Delp, a stickup man who, in the first flashback episode, robs Rob and a pregnant Laura (Van Dyke and Mary Tyler Moore) while all three of them are trapped in a malfunctioning elevator (it ends in a feel-good fashion). In the second episode, "The Alan Brady Show Goes to Jail," Rob and the *Alan Brady Show* gang are putting on a special show in the prison where Lyle is a trustee—giving Don, as Lyle, the chance to briefly heckle his fellow inmates: "That's why you guys are sitting here with the West Point cadet suits on, for being wise guys."

The television roles were starting to pick up, and Don found himself moving between the small-screen worlds of two of Sid Caesar's former writers as he segued from Carl Reiner (*The Dick Van Dyke Show*) to Neil Simon. He and veteran character actor Lou Jacobi were hired to costar as bickering New York City firefighters sharing a two-family house in *Kibbee Hates Fitch*, a CBS pilot written and created by Simon, plotting his return to television following his back-to-back successes on Broadway with *Come Blow Your Horn* and *Barefoot in the Park*. (Art Carney and Jim Backus were offered the costarring roles in *Kibbee Hates Fitch*. They both declined.)

In the meantime, Lucille Ball reached out to Jack Gilardi; she wanted Don for an episode of *The Lucy Show*, but he was forced to demure due to his busy schedule. (Ball was persistent; four years later, she finally snared Don for the series.) American International Pictures, the studio behind Don's upcoming movie *X*, was so pleased with his work that they signed him to play Jack Fanny (yep), the owner of a gym, in *Muscle Beach Party*, one of the studio's cookie-cutter schlockfest beach movies. It was scheduled to begin filming in early 1964 with stars Frankie Avalon, Annette Funicello, and Luciana Paluzzi, who was later to play an assassin stalking James Bond (Sean Connery) in *Thunderball*.

Somehow, Don managed to juggle his growing list of movie and television commitments with his club work throughout 1963. He played all the usual spots—Basin Street East (with Vic Damone), the Sahara, the Deauville in Miami Beach—and took no prisoners at the Slate Brothers Club in May. He turned thirty-seven, and on his closing night the club's owners presented him with a huge birthday cake to mark the occasion. It left Don all choked up and close to tears . . . but only after the show. Onstage he was his usual venomous self, hectoring Joey Bishop, Bob Hope, and Jackie Cooper, who had shown up to take their ribbings.

Back at Basin Street East, he ripped into a noisy woman heckler —"Lady, I couldn't warm up to you if we were cremated together!"— and insulted a prominent New York politician—"You've got to give that boy credit. There's a self-made nobody." He dissed *Dr. Kildare* star Richard Chamberlain—"Well, well, look who's here, Doctor Killjoy"—and even turned on Jules Podell, the feared tough-guy owner of the Copacabana—"You were great in that movie climbing the Empire State Building carrying Fay Wray!"

(Don knew that he could insult Podell and get away with it. He retold a story in later years of how Joe Scandore, trying to get him booked into the Copacabana, took Don to meet Podell in person at the club. Don sat next to the burly nightclub owner, but Podell never once looked at him. "Joe, I am never going to have that unfunny Jewish motherfucker guy ever play in my place. Never!" Scandore: "Jules, Jules, don't get upset. Everything will be okay. We will figure it out." Podell's veins were now poking out of his neck. "Never!" Don thought his career was over if he could not get booked into the Copa. Two weeks later, Joe Scandore calls Don. "Hey Don! You're working at Copacabana in two weeks!" Hey, it's who you know . . .)

In the summer, Frank Sinatra flew to Vegas to attend Don's open-ing night at the Sahara with his ex, Ava Gardner, in tow. (Even Don did not dare go *there*.) Frank then flew Etta Rickles in from Miami Beach on his private plane so she could see Sonny Boy's show and maybe take in Shelley Berman's show; Don's fellow "sick" comedian was playing the hotel's Congo Room with the Mills Brothers. The fall months found Don back on the West Coast, including a two-week run at the Holiday Inn in Oakland, where he did not waste time introducing himself to the locals: "Oakland? Man, where's Oakland? Even the grass is dead here. I'm out among the crickets. Why won't they let me play stateside?"

The title of the movie in which Don costarred with Ray Milland, formerly known as *X*, had been changed to *X: The Man with the X-ray Eyes* when it opened on September 18, 1963. It was shown in most theaters nationwide on a double-bill with AIP's *Dementia 13*, a gothic horror movie directed by twenty-four-year-old Francis Coppola (he added the "Ford" for his 1966 movie, *You're A Big Boy Now*). Don played Crane, a humorless carnival boss who exploits noble Dr. Xavier's (Milland) ability to see through everything (hence the "X-ray eyes") after a self-experiment goes horribly awry. The good doctor endures a series of hellish events, and when he ends up in a revival meeting in the movie's climax—he's now totally blind—he quotes a preacher, "When thine eye offends, pluck it out!" The movie's tagline said it all: *Suddenly . . . he could see thru clothes . . . flesh . . . and walls!* Don wasted no time in joking about his role. "I steal the picture from Milland. I'm the star whose name is 'X.' Milland plays some other unimportant letter of the alphabet."

The *New York Times* gave the movie a decent write-up. Ray Milland received wide praise for his "gripping" performance. Don's name was tough to find in any of the movie's reviews—and, if it was mentioned at all, it was in passing or relegated to the last few lines of a review . . . an afterthought for a role that was deemed too unimportant to merit any analytical comment. "There's a nice bit from Don Rickles as a vicious little con-man," the *Montreal Gazette* noted.

Corman cowrote the script with Ray Russell and recalled that he had Don in mind for the role of Crane from the outset. "I first saw Don in his act in Las Vegas and I was impressed, particularly about the way he could ad-lib; he could be working on one routine and somebody would say something and he would immediately switch to the other person and spontaneously improvise a whole new act.

"I thought this was an unusual talent, and when we were doing *The Man with the X-ray Eyes*, Ray Milland was the lead and there was this sort of carnival barker type of guy who was played dramatically but also for a kind of hard comedy within that dramatic area."

Before shooting began, Corman met with Don and told him not to be afraid to improvise "any time you want," as long as it fit within the framework of the script. "Don, of course, was known as this very tough, hard-hitting comedian, but to my great surprise he was a little bit nervous on the first day of shooting," Corman recalled. "He did pretty well on the first take but you could sense that he was nervous. So I said, 'Don, that's great, but I would like to see you improvise more' and so we went through two or three takes and he improved and lost his jitters. We did four takes for one scene, which was normally more than I do, and the picture was on a fifteen-day shooting schedule, so we had no time for multiple takes. But Don got better and better and I think I printed the fourth take. I thought he gave an outstanding performance in the picture because he stayed with the script and improvised when he felt it was necessary."[5]

The Man with the X-Ray Eyes did not exactly set the world on fire, but Don and Corman remained friendly for years afterward. "Don was a good guy," Corman said. "When our eldest child, Catherine, was applying to a private school here [in L.A.], John Thomas Dye, which was a notoriously difficult school to get into, I asked Don to write a letter of recommendation. I think they were pretty startled to get this letter from Don Rickles and my daughter got in. I wouldn't say it was totally on Don's recommendation, but it did help."[6]

The business of television works in mysterious ways. Don and Lou Jacobi experienced the industry's foibles once they began shooting the pilot episode of *Kibbee Hates Fitch* (it was alternately referred to as *The Neighbors* and was called an "audition film" in the quaint industry parlance of the day). The powers-that-be at CBS were not happy with the structure of the sitcom, which costarred Pert Kelton, Herb Edelman, Karleen Wiese, and William Ade. In late January 1964, parts of Neil Simon's script were jettisoned as hasty rewrites began and Don and Lou reshot their scenes under the direction of Stanley Prager (*The Patty Duke Show*). CBS was hoping to include the sitcom on its prime-time lineup in the fall.

The *Kibbee Hates Fitch* "audition film" was shot in black-and-white in the network's New York City studios and was burdened with a hyperactive laugh track and freeze-framing—not uncommon for the era of television productions. Russell Kibbee (Don) and Arthur Fitch (Jacobi) have been friends for twenty years and are both lieutenants in the New York City Fire Department (Hook & Ladder 23). They share a house together in Jackson Heights (a nod to Don). Fitch doubles as the landlord and lives downstairs with his wife, Marsha (Kelton), and their daughter, Nancy (Wiese). Kibbee lives upstairs with his wife, Selena (Nancy Andrews), and their son Kevin (Ade). Nancy and Kevin are in love with each other and have plans to marry.

The relationship between Kibbee and Fitch takes a cold turn when their captain retires; Kibbee replaces him on an interim basis and Fitch is angry—he does not want to take orders from his cohort. This plot point provides the hoped-for comedic friction between the two men. Back in Jackson Heights, they squabble over who should mow the lawn; in one scene, Kibbee throws hot water (literally) on the barbershop quartet that Fitch has organized among his coworkers. The situation grows so tense between them that they refuse to pass the ketchup to each other—gasp!—during a Kibbe-Fitch family barbecue in the backyard.

The pilot was a rare misfire by Neil Simon, and though CBS president James Aubrey called it "one of the funniest shows he's ever seen," that was for public consumption. Privately, CBS executives were not amused by the weak material. The network demonstrated its lack of faith in (or was it disdain for?) *Kibbee Hates Fitch* by waiting over a year to finally burn it off in August 1965 as an episode of *Summer Playhouse*—five months after Simon's latest Broadway smash, *The Odd Couple*, opened at the Plymouth Theatre on West 45th Street with stars Art Carney and Walter Matthau as Felix Unger and Oscar Madison. CBS did not give up the ghost of *Kibbee Hates Fitch*, though; nine years later, in 1974, the network gave the go-ahead for another *Kibbee Hates Fitch* pilot episode, this time with Michael Bell and Chuck McCann as Kibbee and Fitch. It failed. Again.

On February 7, 1964, the Beatles touched down at Kennedy Airport in New York City to mass hysteria, and the world seemed to tilt just a little on its axis. The "Four Moptops" from Liverpool—John Lennon, Paul McCartney, George Harrison, and Ringo Starr—arrived in America with a number-one single, "I Want to Hold Your Hand." Their live appearance two nights later on *The Ed Sullivan Show* generated the largest television audience in US history up to that point, with an estimated 73 million viewers tuning in. Beatlemania was born.

And Don Rickles got into the act.

"The Boys," as the enchanted press corps was already calling them, were booked for a follow-up performance on Sullivan's CBS variety show when it moved south to Miami Beach the following Sunday night, to the Deauville Hotel on Collins Avenue. Carol Lawrence and comedian Myron Cohen were playing the larger Casanova Room; Don (he was still "The Emperor") was in the smaller Musketeer Room with Mandy Campo ("Authentic Latin American Rhythm") and the Bobby Fields Trio. Tony Bennett and Lenny Kent caught Don's show at the Deauville; Milton Berle was over at the Eden Roc and swung by one night in early February. Don invited him onto the stage for a back-and-forth insult-fest. John, Paul, George, and Ringo were arriving at the hotel in a few days, and Don was hip to the scene. "I have something the Beatles don't have," he said, "a forehead!"

On Sunday, February 16, the Beatles took the stage at the Deauville and rocked and rolled and shook their heads to shrieks and
screams in a carbon-copy performance of their previous week's
appearance on *The Ed Sullivan Show*. Ed's guests this night included
Myron Cohen (it was a short walk from the Casanova Room), Mitzi
Gaynor, and the comedy team of Allen & Rossi (Marty and Steve).

Two nights before "the Big Shew," the Beatles and their retinue,
which included a local bodyguard, were ushered into the Musketeer
Lounge to catch Don's act. It did not go well for either camp. "He
was a vicious type of comedian," Ringo Starr recalled. "He would
say, 'Hello, lady, where are you from?' and she'd say, 'Oh, I'm from
Israel.' He'd go to another table, 'Where are you from?' They'd
say, 'Germany,' and it'd be: 'Nazi, get out! What the hell is this?'"
Don's humor, and his tommy-gun attack style, were unlike anything
the British lads had ever experienced. Several months before, back
in England as Beatlemania took hold, the Beatles had performed
on *Two of a Kind*, the popular ATV television show hosted by comedians Eric Morecambe and Ernie Wise—who gently kidded them
about their floppy hairstyles (goofy Eric donned a "Beatles wig")
and falsetto *oooohs*.

Don Rickles was something completely different.

"We were all at one table with our policeman buddy, our chaperone," Paul McCartney recalled. "We had this one bodyguard who
came everywhere with us; he was a good mate and we often went
back to his house—and he started on him: 'Hey, cop, get a job!
What's this? Looking after the Beatles? Great job you got, man, looking after the Beatles!' He went on, 'It's great. They just lie up there
on the ninth floor, in between satin sheets and every time they hear
the girls screaming, they go "Oooohh."' Very funny, we thought. We
were not amused, as I recall. Very cutting. I like him now, but at first
he was a bit of a shock."[7]

George Harrison recalled how the group was trying to keep a low
profile (as if that was possible), but Don insisted on needling them.
"He'd say, 'Nice people, these police. They're doing a great job.' Then

he'd turn around and snap, 'I hope your badge melts' . . . He turned out to not be cool, though. He blew it all at the very end because he started apologizing for everything he'd been saying, instead of just going off and leaving the buzz in the room."[8]

Harrison had a point, and he was not the only person critical of Don's closing remarks, the "I'm a nice guy" and "Can't we all get along?" spiel which came off, to many, as maudlin, sentimental, and above all, extremely phony following an hour in which he'd ripped anyone and everyone a new asshole. The night the Beatles saw his act, Don pulled his familiar shtick and asked the Jewish and Arab audience members to stand up and take a bow in the name of togetherness—and, as they rose up out of their seats, he dove to the floor and bellowed out the *rat-tat-tat* of machine-gun fire. It always got a laugh then—and in the years to come, when he recycled the joke hundreds of times.

"I have no set act," Don once explained. "If I like an ad-lib, I file it permanently in my mind and use it again the next time a similar incident occurs. Playing a lounge is more challenging than a nightclub because the patrons are just there to have a drink, and if they don't want to be entertained they let you know. In a club, there's a cover or a minimum and the patrons ante up the loot because they want a show. I've been in Vegas six years and I have a big following of regular customers, but there are always a few guests on hand . . . and they want to take on the fastest gun in the West. Of course I need those people or I wouldn't have an act."[9]

He was now closing his shows, after the apologies, with a song, "What Kind of Fool Am I?" Not everyone was buying what The Merchant of Venom was trying to sell. "As usual, at the close of his act he makes a tender speech like a kid apologizing for being a bad boy," the *Miami News* noted after Don opened for the first time at the Eden Roc and worked insults about "Protestants, Jews, Whites, Negroes, Puerto Ricans, Jesus, the confessional, doctors and Medicare" into the routine.[10]

Don's man Friday, Harry Goins, became part of the act, too. Harry noticed how much Don was sweating one night on stage at the

Eden Roc and brought him out a glass of water. Don introduced his reluctant aide-de-camp to the audience and spoke sentimentally of how he and Harry were from different backgrounds, "but stand on this stage as brothers," referring to the race riots breaking out across the country. Of course, Don being Don, he could not or would not let it go at that. "It's awful how stores are being looted," he proclaimed. "The burning, the rioting, the stealing. But if, God forbid, it does happen again—and I pray it doesn't—all I can say is, 'Harry, I could use a couch and a couple of end tables.'"[11]

In March, Don signed on for a costarring role in another questionable AIP movie, *Bikini Beach*, with Frankie Avalon and Annette Funicello once again in the lead roles. As that news sunk in, Don's manager and agent, Joe Scandore and Jack Gilardi, were working overtime planting items about Don in the newspapers. None of them came to fruition. There was talk that Don and Mickey Rooney were teaming up for a movie (plot not revealed) in which they would play all the roles. On the theatrical side of the showbiz ledger, Don's name was bandied about as a possible costar of *The Odd Couple*, still a year away from opening on Broadway; yet another item had him signing on to play Pseudolos, the role originated on Broadway in 1962 by Zero Mostel, in a stage production of *A Funny Thing Happened on the Way to the Forum*—not on the Great White Way this time, but in Las Vegas . . . at the Sahara Hotel. "He has been bugging his bosses at the Sahara on this project for the last year," it was reported, "and as of now it looks as if they've bought the idea." They did not.

Jackie Cooper reportedly signed Don to a five-year television contract. His first project under the new deal was to be a starring role in *The Bey of Turhan*, a series from Screen Gems about the Austrian-born actor Turhan Bey. Dubbed "The Turkish Delight," Bey enjoyed some success in Hollywood in the 1940s. Don, after all, had slimmed down to 151 pounds over the past ten months, so a role as a leading man was not so far-fetched. Wrong again. *The Bey of Turhan* idea disappeared, as did the plan "for a Mr.-and-Mrs. TV comedy series" starring Don and Judy Holliday. It likely had never existed in the first place. In December 1964, Don was supposedly booked for a trip to Italy to shoot a television series for Bing Crosby Enterprises called *Rome Sweet Rome*. Que sera, sera.

Don's profile in Hollywood was neither raised nor lowered when *Muscle Beach Party* was released in April, and his role as gymnasium owner Jack Fanny garnered the same mixed response as the movie itself. The *Chicago Tribune* called it "this little monstrosity . . . a stretch of beach and a cheaply constructed night club are the only sets. The plot is thin and ridiculous with a rich and man-eating female trying to buy Frankie Avalon, to the great indignation of his girl-friend, Annette Funicello. Buddy Hackett tries to be funny during all of this silliness, but he's wasting his time and talent. Don Rickles is extremely unfunny as a moron who runs a gym for muscle-men." (One of Jack Fanny's musclebound gym rats, "Mr. Galaxy" Flex Mar-tian, was played by Rock Stevens, the sometime screen name of body-building champ Peter Lupus. He would later star in the CBS series *Mission: Impossible* as Willy Armitage. Thirteen-year-old Stevie Won-der appeared on-screen in a *Muscle Beach Party* musical number. He was credited as "Little Stevie Wonder.")

The reviews were not all scathing; one critic called Don's part "another key comic role" and praised his performance as Jack Fanny: "a comic interpretation that will open new comedy avenues for the famed 'master of insult.'" Hardly. The *Philadelphia Inquirer* labeled the movie "jovial strife" and mentioned Don in passing ("screen and TV comedian Don Rickles"); another critic carped that the movie is "pure drivel . . . Of the males, I can say less—Frankie Avalon, John Ashley, Don Rickles (who really chilled me), Jody McCrea, Morey Amsterdam and Buddy Hackett."

Muscle Beach Party scored a bull's-eye with its teenage demo-graphic, the critics be damned, and the movie turned a nice profit for AIP. The studio was already shooting a sequel, *Bikini Beach*, this one directed by William Asher with returning stars Avalon, Funicello, and Don joined by Keenan Wynn, Martha Hyer, and Harvey Lem-beck (as recurring "beach movie" character Eric Von Zipper). *Bikini*

Beach was slated for a release in July. Peter Lorre, who had appeared briefly in *Muscle Beach Party*, agreed to make a cameo in *Bikini Beach*; he died in March at the age of fifty-nine. Boris Karloff replaced him in the small role of an art dealer. How far the once-mighty had fallen.

Bikini Beach, billed as "a fast-moving story of modern youth and their hobbies," opened near the end of July at drive-ins around the country with little fanfare and dismal reviews—not completely unexpected for a movie in which Frankie Avalon played two roles, one of them a ginger-haired, shaggy, Beatle-esque character named Potato Bug (with a really bad English accent). One of the movie's "costars" was a chimpanzee named Clyde who surfs and dances the Watusi (he was played by Hungarian actor/stuntman Janos Prohaska). 'Nuf said. "These films weren't exactly *Gone with the Wind*, but they were big box office," Don told David Ritz, who coauthored his jokey 2007 memoir, *Rickles' Book*.

In *Bikini Beach*, Don played Big Drag, the proprietor of a teen hangout called the Pit Stop. Big Drag also runs a drag-racing garage and announces the races at Bikini Beach Drag Strip. If you thought it might be hard for Don to top Jack Fanny, have no fear—Big Drag admits he was born as Jack Fanny but changed his name out of embarrassment. And so it goes. "Somehow, lesser performers such as Keenan Wynn, Martha Hyer, and Don Rickles have been forced upon us," wrote one sarcastic critic. Thankfully for Don and his *Bikini Beach* cohorts, reviews were few and far between; most of what was published was canned-hype fodder provided by the studio, AIP, which often ran as captions to stills from the movie. Don's adopted hometown paper, the *Miami Herald*, did him a solid in its review:

RICKLES A GREAT CHARACTER ACTOR

Don Rickles continues his screen comedy triumphs in "Bikini Beach," but don't let these dumb-bunny beach boy portrayals fool you. He's a great character actor.

Don certainly did, and he wondered when or if his dramatic training would ever pay off. While he was off playing Jack Fanny and Big Drag, Jason Robards Jr., his pal from the American Academy of Dramatic Arts, was knocking 'em dead on Broadway in *A Thousand Clowns* and *After the Fall*. This was not how Don's acting career was supposed to have unfolded. Nor was he supposed to still be single and unattached as he neared the age of forty. Etta was growing impatient at Sonny Boy's domestic situation, but he was unwilling, or unable to, "find the right girl" and settle down. Just ask Sandra Burns, Kay Starr, Connie Francis, et al. His dating exploits, though, were still landing him in the gossip columns on a semi-regular basis. Don was spotted at the Doll House outside of San Francisco celebrating a television deal with Canadian actress Gail Gilmore; another item had him in San Diego romancing jazz singer Betty Bennett at Tracton's; yet another report saw him squiring his "new girl," Marlene Spivy, a dancer at the Riviera Hotel in Vegas: "They like to cook together." Duly noted.

That was all about to change.

CHAPTER 10

D on returned to the Sahara in July for another long run
in the Nevada desert. Johnny Carson, at that time a passing
acquaintance who was two years into his run as the host of *The Tonight
Show*, was playing the Congo Room with January Jones and dancer
John Bubbles; Don was, of course, in the Casbar Lounge—the "Impre-
sario of Indignities" (another nickname that did not stick), sharing the
bill with several performers, including Freddy Bell, Roberta Linn,
and the Peter and Hank duo.

Disaster struck in August when a fire ripped through the Sahara's
casino and show lounge. Fifty firefighters from eighteen units
rushed hundreds of gamblers out of the casino and fought the
blaze for an hour. Miraculously, no one was injured. Firefighters
evacuated the hotel's original structure, located in the back of the
casino, as a precaution; guests in the new twenty-four-story tower
could remain in their rooms. As far as it could be determined, the
fire started in an attic above the original casino area, a faulty air-
conditioning unit the likely culprit. The restaurant on the main
floor sustained major smoke damage. The Casbar Lounge, Don's
home for the past five years, was completely destroyed, as was the
hotel's theater, so headliners Buddy Hackett and Buddy Greco were
temporarily unemployed. The damage was estimated to be in the
neighborhood of $1 million.

The cooler autumn weather brought better news. Don agreed to
make a cameo appearance (thank God!) as "Big Bang" the Martian
(do not ask) in his third silly AIP movie, *Pajama Party*. Don Weis was
directing stars Tommy Kirk (no Frankie Avalon this time) and good

soldier Annette Funicello. The majority of the "beach movie" regulars returned for the hilarity and hijinks; the supporting cast included Buster Keaton (as Chief Rotten Eagle), Dorothy Lamour, and Don's nemesis, Dorothy Kilgallen, who played herself. A year later, she was found dead in her Manhattan townhouse at the age of fifty-two from an overdose of alcohol and barbiturates.

The television work began to pick up. Don's announced guest shot on *The Bill Dana Show* playing a hotel detective never transpired, but Don Adams, as bumbling hotel dick Byron Glick, grabbed that bull by the horns and ran with it—incorporating several of Byron's catchphrases (including "Would you believe?") into his role as Maxwell Smart, Agent 86, on his NBC hit series *Get Smart*. (Don guest-starred in a two-part *Get Smart* episode four years later.) Meanwhile, our Don, Mr. Rickles, signed on for episodes of *The Munsters, Gomer Pyle: USMC, The Andy Griffith Show, F Troop*, and *The Beverly Hillbillies*, among others, marking an onslaught of sitcom roles taking him through the next half of the decade. In October, Don and Skip Homeier played a pair of spooked bank robbers in a Halloween episode of *The Addams Family*, which was in its first season on ABC; offstage, Don got up on the Slate Brothers Club stage to help boost singer/dancer Larry Kert and managed to insult an audience member—who promptly threw a glass at him (he missed). It was safer for Don to be working on a Hollywood set—and it led to a huge sea change in his personal life.

While Don was filming his cameo role in *Pajama Party*, the movie's star, Annette Funicello, was in a relationship with his agent, Jack Gilardi (they married in January 1965). Don was a frequent visitor to Gilardi's office in L.A. during that time as his bookings on television increased and he was required to be there to sign contracts, etc. It was in Gilardi's office that he met Jack's secretary, Barbara Sklar. Barbara, the daughter of Louis and Eleanor Sklar, was a nice Jewish girl from the Philadelphia suburbs. She was in her late twenties; several years before, she had moved to L.A. for a change of scenery, hoping the more temperate climate would help her skin condition (eczema).

Don was smitten at first sight; Barbara, initially, was having none of it. She refused to laugh at his jokes, and try as he might, Don could not break through her façade of indifference. "Barbara was different," Don recalled. "I couldn't get her out of my mind. She was poised, she was smart, she was the picture of elegance, she was everything I wanted in a woman."[1] He was in hot pursuit of Barbara but was getting nowhere fast since she repeatedly turned him down for dates. And then, serendipity . . . their relationship coalesced when Barbara and a friend went to see Don's show at the Sahara in Vegas. They were standing by the rope outside, waiting to get into the show, when Don saw them and had a word with someone at the front. They were seated immediately. "I put her in the front row and I started insulting her," he recalled. "I said, 'I never liked your boss, and if you work for him you ought to be put in an institution.' Then I took her to dinner to find out whether the boss was going to get me any jobs. I kept insulting her but she didn't notice it—she was too busy finding out if I was serious about her."

He was. In mid-November, Don announced that he and Barbara were engaged and were to be married four months later, in March 1965. "Don Rickles finally pleased his mother," wrote gossip columnist Rona Barrett. "He's marrying a nice, sweet girl from Philadelphia named Barbara Sklar. She's executive secretary to agent Jack Gilardi, who marries Mouseketeer Annette Funicello on January 9. Don and Barb do it in March, providing she hasn't dropped from exhaustion from carrying around that sparkler that almost makes the Hope Diamond look molecular."[2]

They were married on March 14, 1965, in Young Israel of Flatbush, an Orthodox synagogue in the Midwood section of Brooklyn. The reception was held at the place where it all started for Don: Joe Scandore's Elegante on Ocean Parkway. Don was thirty-eight, turning thirty-nine in May; Barbara was twenty-seven. Buddy Hackett, Jerry Vale and his wife, and Steve Lawrence and Eydie Gormé celebrated with the newlyweds. Steve and Eydie sang "More" for Don and Barbara ("More than the greatest love the world has known"). Don could not resist: "You sang beautifully, but I had no idea you'd ask for money." Sinatra was unable to make it; he and Joe E. Lewis sent a one-word telegram: "Why?"

"I was a bachelor until thirty-nine because all I met during my travels as an entertainer were women who were loose, unreliable," Don told one interviewer rather uncharitably. "I wanted somebody who was beautiful, with simplicity, someone who could command attention and respect. I found someone like that, and I married her."[3] Joe Scandore gifted the newlyweds with an all-expense-paid trip to Rome. (Joe Scandore sold the Elegante in the summer of 1966. It closed its doors for good later that year along with another Brooklyn nightclub staple, the Town & Country Club.)

Back in L.A. before the Big Event, Don's friends threw him a bachelor party. Carl Reiner emceed and they all turned out—Jerry Lewis, Jack Jones, Herkie Styles, Regis Philbin, Gene Barry, Jackie Cooper, and Larry Storch to name just a few. Etta was there, too, "looking very much like Red Buttons," to give Sonny Boy some motherly advice. Etta approved of Barbara. She was good enough for her son. The two women would enjoy a close relationship over the next twenty years.

"Barbara and Don were a unit. They were each other's best friend," recalled their friend Lorna Luft. "It was Barbara and Don. She supported him absolutely ten thousand percent, not only in his career, but in his life."[4]

"It was a special relationship," said Don's longtime publicist, Paul Shefrin. "On stage he would make jokes about his wife Barbara, 'I drowned her in the pool,' that sort of thing. But at home he was the most devoted, caring, loving husband you could imagine. So here he is, making a joke about Barbara and offstage he was always like, 'Barbara, how was the show? Was it good? Did you like it?' And they would go to dinner and sit and be social and then they would call it a night. It was never just Don. It was always Don and Barbara. He used to joke with me and say, 'The only reason I keep you around is because Barbara likes you.'"

In the late fall of 1964, Don began shooting his fourth AIP movie, *Beach Blanket Bingo*, at, where else?, Leo Carrillo Beach, located sixty miles from Hollywood in Malibu and named after the actor and conservationist (he died in 1961). Frankie Avalon was back, and so was Annette Funicello, and this time around Paul Lynde joined in the forced fun along with newcomer Linda Evans (subbing for Nancy Sinatra) and Deborah Walley. Buster Keaton was back, too; Earl Wilson, perhaps Don's biggest booster among the columnists, had a small role as a talent scout. "We are the 'dramatic talent,'" he wrote in a first-person account of life on the set. "All these young lovelies are in their teens or early 20s, and are making a packet for American-International which discovered that there's a big market for uncomplicated movies about surfers and other beach nuts."

The plot of *Beach Blanket Bingo* (does it really matter?) had Linda Evans playing a singer named Sugar Kane, who is being double-crossed for promotional purposes by her slimy manager, Bullets (Lynde). From there, it devolves into a string of farcical situations with many scenes of bikini-clad young women dancing and jiggling on the beach with the guys, and dancing and jiggling in a beachside nightclub. It ends with Ms. Kane tied up and ready to be sliced in half by a buzz-saw; once she is saved, there is more dancing and jiggling on the beach and in the nightclub. Fade out.

Don played Big Drop, the owner of Big Drop's Skydiving Club ("Just a nickname. They used to call me 'Big Droop,' but I had it shortened"). Big Drop hires out two skydiving surfers for a publicity stunt. Director William Asher let Don cut loose in a two-minute scene in the nightclub where Big Drop (who is wearing a zipped-up red sweatshirt with the words "BIG DROP" on the front, just in case) rips into the other characters as his assistant, Buster (Keaton), looks on, stone-faced. Who knew that Big Drop was also a comedian? Don was doing a version of his stage act, so it was easy, and he started in on his first target, Earl Wilson (sporting a crew cut). "Sitting in our audience, right here, one of the greats. So great, Earl, I get the chills every time I mention your name. One of the greatest writers of our time, a sweetheart of a fellow . . . you're great Earl, it's nice to see you, and I want to tell you something as a friend. Somebody tell you you're 11? Get rid of that hairdo, know what I mean? You don't need the crew-cut haircut. It's a little embarrassing, because at your age, believe me, you act as if you were in the sandbox and you flunked."

Then he moved over to Frankie and Annette (who were playing Frankie and Dee Dee): "Frankie and Dee Dee! Hi, Frankie! Hello, Dee Dee! You two forty-three-year-old yo-yos skipping around the house. Grow up! You're a man already, Frank, how long can you stand in the bathroom in front of the mirror going [mimes combing his hair]." And so on.

The movie opened in April, accompanied by a thirty-six-page *Beach Blanket Bingo* Dell comic book with cartoon versions of Frankie and Annette on the cover ("Fun-time beach adventure . . . with surfers, sky-divers and cycles!!"). The critics were not amused. "No one can blame Nicholson and Arkoff for continuing a pattern that has made them money, but this is ridiculous," *Variety* opined in its reference to producers James Nicholson and Samuel Arkoff. "Are teenagers responding to such drivel as good natured satire of themselves rather than identifying with it? Let's hope so."

The *Los Angeles Times* (singling out Earl Wilson): "Its teen-age inanities are not nearly so dull as its adult presumptuousness." The *New York Times*: "It's for morons." Ouch. Don escaped unscathed from the critical barbs. He was mentioned in passing, and nothing more. Still, he had had enough of the silliness and exited the franchise. The *Beach* series continued with *How to Stuff a Wild Bikini* (1965) and *Ghost in the Invisible Bikini* (1966) before exhausting itself, and its dwindling moviegoing audience, taking its regrettable place on the bottom rung of 1960s-era pop kitsch.

(An interesting sidelight: Don shot an "inside commentary" promotional movie while filming *Beach Blanket Bingo*, which he had done before on the set of *Bikini Beach*. Not everyone was pleased. The *New York Daily News*: "His first one, an exposé of studio goings-on during the filming of *Bikini Beach*, started several feuds and resulted in wholesale barring from the set of agents, managers and wives, many of whom wish Big Drop would Drop Dead.")

On Wednesday, February 3, 1965, Don made his first appearance with Johnny Carson on *The Tonight Show*. Johnny was doing the show that week from L.A. Carson, who was seven months older and worlds apart from Don—he was born and raised in Nebraska and resented his cold mother—was two-and-a-half years into his run on *The Tonight Show* and was already being hailed as "The King of Late Night." He opened every show with a witty, topical monologue—unlike his mercurial predecessor, Jack Paar—and celebrities jockeyed for an invitation from Johnny to appear on his show. A spot on Carson's *The Tonight Show* meant instant exposure to thirty million viewers and could make (or break) a career in one fell swoop. Carson had no competition, but he needed to fill ninety minutes of airtime, live, each weeknight at 11:30 from the show's NBC studios at Rockefeller Center in Manhattan. (*The Tonight Show* switched to an hour-long format in 1980, eight years after Carson moved the show to "Beautiful Downtown Burbank" to be closer to Hollywood's glitz and its steady supply of guests.)

Comedian Godfrey Cambridge appeared with Don on his first *Tonight Show* appearance. It marked not only a huge break in Don's career, but the start of a twenty-seven-year association with Carson in which Don would make over one hundred appearances on *The Tonight Show*—and guest-host for Johnny, on occasion—providing some of the most memorable moments in the history of late-night television. Such was Don's popularity as a guest that, like Bob Hope, he eventually had carte blanche to walk onto Johnny's show, unannounced, whenever he wanted.

That was further down the road, but Don struck late-night gold in his maiden appearance with Johnny. "Hello, dum-dum," he greeted Carson upon being introduced, and then let loose a barrage of insults as Johnny doubled over in laughter. "That's it, laugh it up. You're making fifty million dollars a year and your poor parents are back in Nebraska eating locusts for dinner." Johnny loved it and invited Don back eight months later—opening the door for Don's subsequent appearances on talk shows hosted by Merv Griffin, Mike Douglas, Joey Bishop, Dinah Shore, and others. (Carson also resuscitated a nickname for Don—"Mr. Warmth." Such was Johnny's popularity, and the power of his show, that the moniker stuck with Don for the rest of his life. He loved it.)

A few years later, in 1968, Don was the subject of the *Playboy* Interview. His replies to the questions were rarely serious, and at times were nonsensical—particularly when he offered his opinions on the current group of talk show hosts. *On Johnny Carson*: "A peachy guy. I had dinner at his home one night; he made us all sit on the floor and shuck corn. Those Midwestern guys never forget their taproots." *On Mike Douglas*: "Runs a real wholesome, family-type operation. I spent a day in his dressing room sewing name tags on his shorts so he could go to summer camp, and I gave him some animal crackers to eat on the train." *On Merv Griffin*: "Merv used to sit in a high chair above the Freddy Martin band, banging his spoon and screaming, 'I want my Farina, I want my Farina!' I'm generally forced to spend an hour with him before each show convincing him that he's tall."

Several nights after his first appearance with Johnny on *The Tonight Show*, ABC aired the episode of *Burke's Law* in which Don guest-starred. He joined Macdonald Carey, Diana Hyland, Martha Raye, and Billy De Wolfe in a tale about the murder of a multimillionaire financier who, in his younger days, traveled with a carnival (that's where Don's character entered the picture). It was one of several *Burke's Law* episodes in which Don appeared over a two-year period. His television work was shifting into high gear now. He played a dance hall operator on an episode of *The Munsters*, and followed that up the following week with a guest-starring turn on the top-rated

CBS sitcom *The Beverly Hillbillies*, in the episode "Jed's Temptation." He portrayed Fred, a betting man with a nagging wife (played by Iris Adrian) whom series star Buddy Ebsen (Jed Clampett) encounters at the racetrack.

In March, Don appeared on another CBS sitcom, *Gomer Pyle: USMC*, as Sergeant Mason, one of Sergeant Carter's (Frank Sutton) buddies from the Korean War, whose battle-hardened memories differ from Carter's—which confuses Gomer Pyle (Jim Nabors), who tries to stop them from comparing notes and ruining their friendship. A month later, Don popped up on *The Andy Griffith Show* playing an eccentric junk peddler named Newton Monroe, who unloads his wares on twitchy Deputy Barney Fife (Don Knotts). Barney and Andy (Griffith) find an excuse to lock Newton in a Mayberry jail cell in an attempt to get him to reform his sketchy ways. It does not go well. "Excellent characterization and dialogue in this one," noted a newspaper blurb. Frank Sinatra caught the episode (who knew?) and sent Don a telegram: "I stumbled on *The Andy Griffith Show* and I'm not worried about it."

Don was so ubiquitous on prime-time television during the 1965–66 season that, for the first time, he was the subject of several bigger newspaper and magazine profiles, in which he shared his philosophy on acting and his career. "I really flatter the stars and I make ordinary people important by insulting them, too," he said by way of explaining his aggressive nightclub approach to syndicated Hollywood columnist Erskine Johnson. "I had to win recognition in nightclubs before anyone would give me a chance to act. It would have to be a very unique part if I ever got the girl."[5]

"I never thought about it, but I really am a shy guy," he told another columnist. "It's funny how it comes back to me—I remember going with my mother on the subway in New York. My mother is a well-educated and cultured woman, but I remember she talked loudly. She said, 'Come on, we have to get off, this is 72nd Street.' She said it so loud I was embarrassed. And she knew it and she said, 'Don, you're fifteen and you should start to assert yourself.' And

I think that was the turning point. After that, I was always on at parties, telling jokes and imitating people."[6]

The flurry of movie and television work meant valuable time away from his bread-and-butter club dates, and in May, he returned to the Sahara for a months-long run—this time as the headliner in the Congo Room, while the Casbar Lounge underwent renovations following the fire the previous summer. (He moved back into the Casbar in August 1965.) Eddie Fisher, who had been divorced from Elizabeth Taylor the previous year, was in the audience one night—and he was easy bait for Don. "You don't need those Cleopatra broads. Settle down and marry a nice Jewish girl," he barked at Fisher. In July, Don began shooting an episode of *F Troop*, a new ABC series premiering in the fall with stars Forrest Tucker, Ken Berry, and Don's old friend Larry Storch. Don called it "a sort of 19th century burlesque of the cavalry." He flew from Vegas to the *F Troop* set on the Warner Bros. lot in L.A. each morning at 6:30, and left at 5 p.m. to fly back for that night's show at the Sahara. It was a brutal routine; Sinatra helped ease the burden by loaning Bullethead the use of his personal helicopter. Frank's pilot picked Don up at Los Angeles International Airport each morning, flew him to the studio, and then flew him back to LAX later in the afternoon. It paid to be friends with the most powerful man in show business.

Don opened in Lake Tahoe for the first time in August, a three-week engagement at the new Sahara-Tahoe Hotel and Casino on the South Shore, in its Aspen Grove Theatre. He was always nervous when he played in a new venue, always unsure if his verbal attacking style of humor would go over with the locals. "I just put people on—I rib them like you'd rib someone at a party," he told the *Reno Gazette-Journal* in a preemptive strike before his first show there. "I aim at a happy medium, not too far below the belt, and not too far above it." He need not have worried; his shows were standing-room-only from the first night through the entirety of his run. Turns out the gamblers and tourists in Lake Tahoe were just as amused as their counterparts in Las Vegas four hundred and fifty miles to the south.

Don managed to carve out a block of time that summer to shoot a special with Bob Hope for his NBC anthology series, *Bob Hope Presents the Chrysler Theatre*. Rickles to Hope on the set: "Don't just stand there. Make believe I'm a soldier and tell jokes." Don said he took the job over a role he was offered in a big-screen movie, *Easy Come, Easy Go*—which was canceled on the first day of shooting after an on-set train accident in Chatsworth injured the director Barry Shear, star Jan Berry (of Jan & Dean fame), and fifteen crew members. Don lucked out, but Jan Berry was not so fortunate; in April 1966, he was severely injured in a car accident in Beverly Hills. He was in a coma for two months and suffered brain damage and partial paralysis—injuries from which he never fully recovered. (The title *Easy Come, Easy Go* was revived in 1967 for a totally different Elvis Presley movie.)

In September, Don's television blitz paid off. NBC vice president Mort Werner announced that the network was signing him to an exclusive contract to star in a sitcom pilot that, if it worked out, was projected to join NBC's prime-time lineup for the 1966–67 season. The news was exciting, but this was already familiar territory for Don. When the dust settled, the pilot met the same fate as *Kibbee Hates Fitch*, with one caveat: it never saw the light of the TV screen.

The proposed series, which went through several title iterations—*Stone Walls Do Not, The Unpardonables,* and *Plotkin Prison, We Love You!*—was NBC's answer to *Hogan's Heroes*, a sitcom takeoff of the big-screen William Holden movie *Stalag 17. Hogan's Heroes* premiered in September on CBS, one week before Mort Werner's big announcement about Don's new deal with NBC. *Stone Walls Do Not* (we will stick with that title) was created by Jerry Belson and Garry Marshall, who wrote for *The Dick Van Dyke Show*, and revolved around a "zany" group of inmates who enjoy their stay in prison so much that they do not want to leave, hoping they will never be released. Cue the laugh track. Don played the prisoners' ringleader, Wilcox (his prison number was 51926, Don's birthday); Billy De Wolfe, Don's costar from *Burke's Law*, played the prison warden. The cast included Paul Stewart and Sterling Holloway. The pilot was produced by Barry Shear, the same Barry Shear injured in the *Easy Come, Easy Go* accident that summer. "Some may say it's a takeoff on *Hogan's Heroes*," Don said. "Well, maybe it is, but I think it will be a good show. I think the network will like it."

The episode was shot in October 1965 and reportedly cost $300,000, a record amount for a pilot. Frank Sinatra helped Bullethead again, this time by sneaking onto the soundstage while they were shooting a scene and doing a surprise walk-through as one of the convicts. It did not help the cause. "It's a funny business," Don said. "You never know what the heck's gonna sell. With *The Munsters* and all those other things that are on now, you just don't know what's funny anymore." NBC passed on the pilot and could not be bothered to burn it off somewhere down the road. In a twist of fate, Don brought his act to San Quentin State Prison shortly thereafter to put on a show for the inmates. "If I insult you," he told them, "just think of me as part of your punishment."

Billy De Wolfe, who had a terrific time shooting *Stone Walls Do Not*, was sorry to see their efforts go for naught (though he recalled Don's role differently). "We did nothing but laugh while making it," he recalled. "Don Rickles played the warden, a complete bungler. As the aristocrat among prisoners I was continually upset over his activities. 'Wilcox! What on Earth are you doing now?' I'd shout. It's a shame it didn't sell. I understand objections were raised about the way we pictured prison life. Now, isn't that silly—and in a half-hour comedy? What a pair Rickles and I made."[7]

The pilot did not fly, but America saw a lot of Don Rickles in prime time. His episode of *F Troop*, "The Return of Bald Eagle," aired in October. Don played the titular character, a strange, neurotic, barefoot, feather-wearing, arrow-carrying American Indian who will not work on his birthday. His big complaint? He is tired of the comparisons to his more famous cousin, Geronimo—who, to add insult to injury, earned higher marks than Bald Eagle in warrior school. *F Troop* was set in the fictional world of Fort Courage, somewhere in the West in the Civil War era. Clumsy Captain Parmenter (Ken Berry) commanded his troops at Fort Courage and worked alongside the Hekawi Indians and their chief, Wild Eagle (Frank DeKova). In the episode, we learn that Bald Eagle is Wild Eagle's son from a previous marriage ("His mother spoiled him rotten," says Wild Eagle, looking flustered). We also learn that not only did Geronimo best his cousin at warrior school, but that Bald Eagle failed miserably . . . because he was bad at scalping. Welcome to prime-time television in 1965, a land in which political correctness did not exist.

That fall marked Don's brief appearance opposite Bob Hope in *Chrysler Theatre Presents A Bob Hope Comedy Special*. The hour-long farce, supposedly based on an idea from Hope (more likely his team of writers), was subtitled "Russian Roulette," and revolved around a comedian, Les Haines (Hope), who takes an entertainment troupe to Russia as part of a cultural exchange program with the USSR. Don plays his agent, Linny, and Jill St. John is Janie Douglas, a secret agent who convinces Les to take her to Moscow so she can visit a downed U-2 pilot (Charles Walsh). He is in prison but has vital microfilm to hand over to Janie (which he passes to her via a long kiss). Victor Buono, Harold J. Stone, Leon Askin, and Leon Belasco joined in the forced fun.

The *Fort Worth Star-Telegram* reviewer gave the special a mediocre write-up but had some nice words to say about Don. "It wasn't a bad show. Hope got off some pretty good lines, and there were a couple of clever bits of business. But it wasn't a very good show either. The plot structure was just too casual, too sloppy in this age of exaggerated but carefully detailed super-spy stories . . . Don Rickles was around briefly as Hope's agent on his perilous mission to Moscow. The star probably was wise to limit Rickles' participation, because the insult ace from Las Vegas has developed into one of the craftiest scene stealers in the business."[8]

Don shot his role with Hope over three frenzied days of

back-and-forth trips between L.A. and Vegas that summer, much as he had done while filming his episode of *F Troop*. "I kidded Bob," he said. "I said, 'Would you believe you could do a show and not be on an aircraft carrier? Would it relax you if I pretended I was a soldier and you were entertaining me?'

"When we were alone, though, I found Bob to be a very warm, outgoing guy," he recalled. "Hope is more of a listener than a jokester. He gave me his undivided attention, more or less, as if I was bigger than Bob Hope." Hope invited Don over for lunch during the shoot. "It's like sending out for your own hanging," he said.

In mid-November, Don returned to the Sahara-Tahoe for a three-week engagement. He enjoyed the sellout crowds but not the frigid weather on the South Shore, which he joked about to the local press. "This country is great, especially if you are a bear. My wife and I spent most of our time at the trading post explaining to the Indians why we need the blankets. I won't say it's cold here, but we wonder why they hang meat in the lobby. Yesterday I went out of the hotel and listened to car chains on the highway."[9]

In December, Frank Sinatra reached out to Don in Lake Tahoe, inviting him to a Friars Club Testimonial Dinner at the Beverly Hilton Hotel in honor of Dean Martin. As the New Year turned over to 1966, Don was back at the Slate Brothers Club when he announced to the press that Barbara was pregnant with their first child. The baby was due in June, one month after Don's fortieth birthday.

CHAPTER 11

The Merchant of Venom charged into 1966 firing on all cylinders and preparing for his impending fatherhood.

Earl Wilson reported in his column that Don was flying into New York City from L.A. to meet with Broadway director and choreographer Jerome Robbins to discuss a role in his newest production, *The Office*, which counted among its cast Elaine May, Jack Weston, and Doris Roberts. Alas, it turned out to be one more phantom job for Don on the legitimate stage. He got lucky; *The Office* closed after ten performances and never made it to opening night. On the television front, Don appeared in an episode of *Run for Your Life* that aired in February. He played an assassin on the trail of Paul Ryan (Ben Gazzara), the doomed attorney with only eighteen months to live. The series, created by Roy Huggins (*The Fugitive*), was in its first season and was a modest hit that ran for a total of three seasons on NBC. It was a strong showcase for Don and a nice change from his corny sitcom roles.

Don was so grateful to Johnny Carson for giving him his first big shot on *The Tonight Show* that he did not think twice when he was asked to sub for Johnny, who walked away from a $40,000 nightclub gig in Miami Beach after two shows, due to a slew of technical glitches. Don filled in for Carson for one weekend and Wayne Newton followed the next week. The money was starting to roll in. Earlier in the year, Don had signed a new, $500,000 deal with the Sahara. Under the terms of the contract, he would play the Sahara for twenty-six weeks a year in 1966 and 1967; it also included unspecified "fringe benefits." He followed that by inking a new deal with the Eden Roc in Miami Beach—a five-year contract and they threw in a white Cadillac for good measure, a huge thank-you for all the sellouts . . . and for Don's onstage behavior. Don was on stage at the hotel, in the middle of his act one night, when Jackie Gleason, obviously drunk, walked in, plopped himself down on the stage, turned to him, and said, "Okay, Don, finish your act." It drew a few titters from the audience, but Don soldiered on. He was unnerved and angry at The Great One's intrusion, but he let it go. Gleason was too big of a star and it was not worth the aggravation. Don was not in the same league . . . yet.

In reality, Don Rickles made more television appearances on a weekly basis in the mid-1960s than did Jackie Gleason. On one Friday night in March 1966, for example, Don was on two different networks. He guest-starred on an episode of the CBS series *The Wild Wild West*, which was in its maiden season of serving up weekly doses of inventive, seriocomic sci-fi/Western—themed episodes set in the Victorian era. Four hours later, he was on *The Tonight Show* couch ribbing Johnny Carson, who had taken his show on the road to Hollywood that week.

Don's appearance on *The Wild Wild West* was in an episode entitled "The Night of the Druid's Blood," cast as the sinister magician Asmodeous, who wears a hood and a satanic-looking mustache and "is constantly flapping his cape and his mouth" (sounds like Don) in a plot about the violent deaths of many prominent scientists. He shared screen time with series stars Robert Conrad and Ross Martin—and later that night on *The Tonight Show* with fellow guests Bill Cosby and Rose Marie.

The guest-starring roles were great exposure, and they kept Don in the public eye. But a starring role in a series eluded him, and it was a running joke in the industry now and among his show-biz pals, who kidded him mercilessly about his unsuccessful ventures on that front. He was, obviously, an appealing draw for an episode or two—"There was hardly a sixties sitcom I didn't do," he recalled[1]—and the small doses of Rickles, with his acerbic nightclub persona in whatever role they expected him to play, scored with television viewers. That was the networks' party line. Most of all, he was dependable. His mercurial contemporary, Shecky Greene, lasted all of eight episodes in a costarring role on ABC's World War II drama *Combat!* before throwing in the towel and leaving the show. Shecky said he was *losing* money doing a weekly television series: the gigs in Vegas were more lucrative.

"They were never able to catch on with me, with my image," Don told the author fifty years later. "It was tough to write how I am. The dramatic stuff always went over big, but I never had luck with comedy. The people around me were great, but somebody said I was 'too strong' on TV—not with the language or what I said, but with my attitude. At that time I was comparatively young for TV . . . so it was difficult for me. I didn't feel that way, but that's the way it went."[2]

There were not many bigger stars in show business than Bob Hope, but even Hope, a self-professed Don Rickles fan, was wary of Mr. Warmth going off-script—perhaps because Hope was virtually unable to perform without cue cards (his "ad-libs" were written out for him in big, bold Magic Marker, out of camera range, of course, to keep up the charade). He seemed to think that Don was going to sabotage all the hard work, all the endless nightclub dates and television appearances, and blow it all in one fell swoop.

"I was with Bob Hope on a million shows, and he was always scared," Don recalled later, when he was a big enough star and did not need to curry favor with Old Ski Nose. "We'd be in rehearsal, I'd do something off the script, and everybody would fall on the floor. He'd look at me real serious and say, 'Is that the way you're going to do it?' And I'd go, 'Well, Bob, they're laughing, aren't they?' And he'd go, 'No, just read the card and do it the way I wrote it.' It got to the point where I'd say,' Good evening, Bob,' and he'd make a face. I'd have to go and sit in his office and practice '"Good evening, Bob," is that OK?' 'Try it again.' 'Hi, Bob.' 'That's a little better.' He treated me like a moron."[3]

Don now strapped himself in to copilot another proposed

television series for ABC called *The Pickled Brothers*. Don himself never mentioned this project. In June 1966, comedian Jackie Vernon ("The King of Deadpan") was in New York City, playing Basin Street East, when he told a reporter from the *Bergen Record* in Hackensack, New Jersey, that he was reading a script for *The Pickled Brothers*, in which he and Don were to play "mischievous siblings." Either the reporter or Vernon seemed to be confused; ABC was in the process of planning to shoot a pilot called *The Pickle Brothers* with the frenetic, madcap New York—based comedy team of Ron Prince, Michael Mislove, and Peter Lee. It never aired.

There was better news for Don on the movie front. The television roles were fine, but he considered himself a dramatic actor and was on the lookout for big-screen roles akin to Nelly Miller, the creepy lout he'd played in *The Rat Race* six years earlier. Jack Gilardi worked on Don's behalf in this regard, and in May, he steered Don to a small part in *Enter Laughing*, Bronx-born Carl Reiner's directorial debut which was based on his semiautobiographical comic novel about breaking into show business. The book had already spawned a 1963 Broadway show that ran for over a year with star Alan Arkin as protagonist David Kolowitz. That part would be played in Reiner's movie adaptation by newcomer Reni Santoni, with costars including Shelley Winters, José Ferrer, Janet Margolin, Jack Gilford, Richard Deacon (from *The Dick Van Dyke Show*), and Elaine May, who was making her big-screen debut.

Don was cast in a small role as one of David's friends, Harry Hamburger, a brash (of course he was) bachelor. *Enter Laughing* was not deep drama, but it was close enough, and it was beneficial for Don to be associated with actors (and a director) of the highest caliber. The movie opened in September 1967 to mostly favorable reviews. "*Enter Laughing* makes all the scheduled stops, but not without humor, grace and some good performances by an interesting company," wrote film critic Roger Ebert. "Reni Santoni, who plays our hero, is a young actor with just the right combination of spontaneity and desperation . . . Don Rickles, the mean-mouthed comedian of *Tonight Show* fame, is well cast as the big shot that is blackmailed into loaning his tuxedo, on the spot, to Santoni."⁴

"Don Rickles, in the minor role of Harry Hamburger, almost steals the show as a hat-industry executive whose devotion to a luscious blonde (Nancy Kovack) causes him to lose his pants," wrote the *Van Nuys Valley News* critic. "It's all very funny business and registers as the best American comedy of the year." Charles Champlin in *The Los Angeles Times* praised Don, "who has emerged as a very able character actor."

Don was playing his regular engagement at the Sahara in Las Vegas when he turned forty on May 8. He showed no signs of mellowing as he crossed the threshold into middle age, and picked on one of his favorite targets, his pal Ernest Borgnine, who was seated in the front row in the Casbar Lounge: "My gosh, Ernie, look at you! Was anyone hurt in the accident?" The Sahara threw Don a big birthday party and presented him with a huge cake—which "Big Mouth" Martha Raye playfully smashed into his face. Barbara was due to give birth around June 15 and was with Don in Vegas, but, as a precaution, she was ordered back to L.A. by her doctor toward the end of May. In early June, she gave birth to a healthy, six-pound, seven-ounce baby girl, Mindy Beth Rickles. Don and Barbara were over the moon, and Don posed for a staged photo in Cedars of Lebanon Hospital, with Barbara cradling the baby as he stood over her offering his newborn daughter a cigar in that hoariest of showbiz traditions. Joe Scandore's baby gift to Don and Barbara was generous: he would pay for part of Mindy's college tuition. Don later named his production company Mindy Beth Productions.

He was filming *Enter Laughing* at the time, and the columnists had him ready to "rocket off" with John Wayne on a three-week USO tour in late June to meet and entertain the troops in Vietnam. Don was not about to leave Barbara and Mindy so soon; he celebrated the baby's arrival by purchasing a thirty-five-foot sailboat from actor Leif

Erickson (who moonlighted as a part-time boat broker). He also used a portion of his earnings from *Enter Laughing* to buy himself a 1939 Rolls-Royce. Don and Barbara were fortunate—they could take the odd day off to relax, since they had a built-in babysitter: Etta Rickles lived in the apartment next door to them on Wilshire Boulevard and was more than happy to care for her granddaughter.

Don's maiden appearance on *The Ed Sullivan Show* finally arrived in July, a veritable small-screen reunion with his big-screen "Beach Movie" costars Annette Funicello and Frankie Avalon and Ray Milland from *X: The Man with the X-ray Eyes*. Ed's other guests that night included comic John Byner and Welsh singer Tom Jones. The remainder of that summer was devoted to nightclub work. Don returned to the Sahara-Tahoe for a four-week run, in its smaller venue; his *Ed Sullivan Show* spot was still not enough to land him in the hotel's glitzy, thousand-seat Sierra Theater, where Steve Allen and his wife, Jayne Meadows, were holding forth and selling out each night. Don had no trouble packing them into the Aspen Room, but he was not thrilled with needing to pace his act to appeal to the gamblers and vacationers at the resort. "It's a slow audience," he carped. "And so you have to start slow with them. They're mostly from small towns, not the hippies you get in Vegas. If I started this slow in Vegas, they'd kick me out of town."

The previous January, *Batman* had premiered on ABC. The campy quasi-comedy was an instant smash, with stars Adam West and Burt Ward as the Caped Crusader and his sidekick, Robin, cavorting in living color in prime time. One of the series' calling cards was the celebrities who popped up for cameos, or who guest-starred as villains (Frank Gorshin as The Riddler, Cesar Romero as The Joker, Otto Preminger as Mr. Freeze, Art Carney as The Archer, etc). As the series entered its second season in the fall of 1966, Don was thrown into the mix as just the man to play a new character, The Insulter, but, alas, it was not to be . . . or maybe it never was.[5] But not all was lost vis-à-vis Don Rickles and a comic book character, as we will see later in his story.

Bullethead's friendship with Frank Sinatra had played a minor role in April, when *Esquire* magazine published an article entitled "Frank Sinatra Has a Cold," an epic deconstruction of Old Blue Eyes that was written by Gay Talese—and is considered one of the finest pieces of magazine journalism ever printed. Sinatra, who had turned fifty in December 1965, would not grant Talese an interview, which was no surprise, given his stormy relationship with reporters. But Talese, undeterred, shadowed Sinatra for three months, took copious notes, and snared the occasional interview with a Sinatra insider who was willing to speak on the record about the Boss. In one section of "Frank Sinatra Has a Cold," Talese recounted how Frank and a group of buddies, including Dean Martin and Jilly Rizzo, caught one of Don's shows at the Sahara and were sitting at a table near the back of the room. Don cashed in big on his Merchant of Venom nickname that night; he insulted Eddie Fisher about his ex-wife, Elizabeth Taylor, and, when he spotted Frank, he went into overdrive on Jilly Rizzo ("How's it feel to be Frank's tractor?") and made sure everyone knew that Sinatra was wearing a toupee and that he was dating twenty-year-old actress Mia Farrow. Sinatra, Don said, was "washed up" as a singer, as he pointed to Joey Bishop, "who keeps checking with Frank to see what's funny."[6]

In the fall, Don made several more visits to *The Tonight Show*, and when the hard-partying Shecky Greene came down with a "sore throat," Don replaced him on Bob Hope's NBC comedy spy-caper special that featured fifteen comedians, among them Jack Carter, Bill Cosby, Milton Berle, Bill Dana, Dick Shawn, Rowan and Martin, and Jimmy Durante.

In his vignette on the Hope special, Don teamed with Red Buttons. They played the pilots of an airplane that was hijacked by Hope (after he borrowed Don Adams's shoe-phone from *Get Smart*, for which Agent 86 demanded a dime). Hope needed to hijack the plane in order to keep an appointment with a gangster (Wally Cox) at a Tijuana café (the sign outside read "Spies Welcome")—where Milton Berle was dressed in drag as a chanteuse (of course he was). When they taped the sketch, Hope was supposed to murder Don's airline pilot by lifting a gun to his head, pulling the trigger, and shouting "Take that!" The gun failed to make a sound and a hush fell over the studio audience. After a few moments of silence, Don turned to the stage crew. "Big man makes a thousand dollars an hour! A million dollars a week! And he's too cheap to buy caps for the gun!" Then he turned to Hope: "If you can't afford the caps, at least yell bang!" It broke the tension, Hope smiled faintly, and the show went on. "Nothing excites me more than watching a fresh young comic standing like an old pro," Hope said afterward. "And nothing gives me more pleasure than the company of old pros like Berle, or Red Buttons . . . I could even say the same for Don Rickles who, as I said, just destroys me."[7] Don teamed with Milton Berle again, in November, for a four-hour Friars Club event honoring George Jessel for starting the organization's West Coast branch in 1946 and to raise money for various charities.

Don was offered a role in the big-screen movie *Beach Red*, a World War II battle drama that was shooting in the Philippines and directed by actor Cornel Wilde. With the job came the use of a fifteen-room house, but it did not work out. No harm done; Don was busy enough on television, with roles that did not require him to fly halfway around the world and be away from Barbara and the baby.

In late November, he landed on *Gilligan's Island* as compulsive kidnapper Norbett Wiley, who makes a beeline for the wealthy Howells, Thurston and Lovey (Jim Backus and Natalie Schafer). He also signed on for two upcoming prime-time appearances—on *The Lucy Show* and an episode of *I Spy*, in its second season on NBC with stars Bill Cosby and Robert Culp. The Sahara made a slight concession for the demands on Don's time and all that flying back and forth from Vegas to L.A. for his television gigs. In December, the hotel announced that, going forward, Don would perform only twice-nightly (instead of three shows) on Sundays, Mondays, Tuesdays, and Wednesdays. Thursday was an off day, but he would still do three shows a night on Friday and Saturday nights. It was not much, but, hey, Don Rickles had the hottest lounge act going and the Sahara needed their cash cow to be at least a *little* more rested and ready. Don, though, never seemed to let the grueling schedule bother him, at least publicly; he was a good soldier who showed up on time, rarely failed to leave 'em laughing . . . and, always nattily dressed, looked good while on stage. He was named as one of the "10 Best Dressed Men in America" by the Custom Tailors Guild of America. Fellow entertainers Don Adams, Hugh O'Brian, Paul Newman, and Vic Damone also made the list. Somewhere, Don's dresser/valet/confidant Harry Goins smiled.

In mid-April of 1967, ABC launched *The Joey Bishop Show*, its first-ever late-night talk show. The network was hoping to give Johnny Carson and his *Tonight Show* the first serious run for its money. Bishop, dubbed "The Frown Prince of Comedy" was, by this time, out of favor with his Rat Pat patron Frank Sinatra. But he was still a marketable commodity. He had starred in his own NBC sitcom, *The Joey Bishop Show*, which ran from 1961 to 1964, and he was familiar to late-night audiences from his many appearances with Jack Paar on *The Tonight Show* and then with Carson, for whom he guest-hosted many times while Johnny was taking one of his frequent vacations. Joey was also a good conversationalist, and, unlike Johnny's his show was based in L.A., closer to the action, in a plush, multimillion-dollar studio into which perennial also-ran ABC pumped millions of dollars. It was a brilliant idea . . . on paper. NBC and Johnny—the undisputed King of Late Night—were not overly concerned about this new upstart. They knew, for starters, that ABC did not have nearly as many affiliate stations as did NBC, so fewer people in fewer television markets could watch *The Joey Bishop Show*. They were right.

Don's friendship with Joey Bishop dated back to Don's first days in Las Vegas. They enjoyed a comfortable rapport and did not feel threatened by each other's act. Don was, from the start of Bishop's late-night run, a welcome and frequent guest on Joey's couch, sitting alongside Bishop's sidekick, Regis Philbin. Like Carson, Joey knew enough to sit back and let Don fire away, unimpeded, to play straight man to The Merchant of Venom. "With Joey, you just attack, attack, attack," Don said. "He's beautiful."[8]

Joey's endorsement of Don, on paper, gave him a high-powered career boost—the power of a television appearance was unmatched in terms of cachet and visibility—but before too long *The Joey Bishop Show* started to wilt against the mighty Carson machine. It limped along until its death rattle on December 26, 1969, when Joey famously walked off the show just after finishing his opening monologue in a mic-drop moment—leaving an embarrassed Regis Philbin to finish the last episode and its replacement, *The Dick Cavett Show*, to pick up the pieces for ABC. (Perhaps the most memorable moment in the short history of *The Joey Bishop Show* was the night that comedian Redd Foxx broke down and cried on national television about the financial plight of his new comedy club, Redd's Place—which replaced the Slate Brothers Club on North La Cienega Boulevard.)

There were game shows, too, on Don's television résumé. He appeared several times as a "celebrity square" on *The Hollywood Squares* in its inaugural season on NBC with host Peter Marshall, and on the syndicated game show *PDQ*—"I threw the letters at [host] Dennis James. I told him I didn't want to play his stupid game. You should have seen the look on his face." He visited *Everybody's Talking*, a short-lived ABC series created by Jack Barry (whose name was kept off the show's credits due to his alleged involvement in the 1950s game-show scandals). "It's another world," Don said about daytime television. "Women doing the laundry and they don't know me from Lamont Cranston. I did a *PDQ* show with Zsa Zsa Gabor—you know Zsa Zsa, the last of the Ramon Novarro World. She thought I was from Mars."

Don was not choosy when it came to his television appearances; the quick-hit jobs were usually shot on a Sunday and the compensation was worth his time. In September 1966, he visited the afternoon series *The Dating Game* to help publicize the upcoming premiere of *Enter Laughing* and his appearance on *The Dean Martin Show*. Don was brought on to *The Dating Game* to help a young woman named Denise try to choose one of three "eligible bachelors" to escort her (and a chaperone) out on the town—and to grill them in trademark Don Rickles style. "Number One? Could he move his lips, say something. Charlie Dynamite behind the screen." "Number Three, could you move your arm? Anything? I got a dummy for Number Three." To host Jim Lange: "Just butt out and hope the jacket comes back in style." Don appeared ill at ease, but it was all over soon enough. Lange to Don: "One of them is going to be a date for Denise and I know you want to do your best for her, right?" Don: "I sure do, so we'll eliminate all three of them." (For the record, Don picked "Bachelor Number Two," a lanky Air Force officer named Richard Conley.) "I was supposed to ask those dumb questions for some girl in the viewing audience," he said. "Well, right off, I told No. 2 he was out of luck. He made the mistake of talking back to me, and I told him he might as well not say another word because he wasn't going out with anyone!"[9]

There were visits to other daytime series, including *The Pat Boone Show.* ("Mr. White Sneakers and Harry Vicious," Don said. "I taught Pat Boone how to drink, you know. Some drinker! Two vodka sours and he thinks his shoes are turning black.") In prime time, Don guest-starred on *The Lucy Show* as Eddie, an old prizefighter who wants to open a flower shop. Lucy (Lucille Ball) decides to manage his comeback in the ring, much to the chagrin of her boss at the bank, Mr. Mooney (Gale Gordon), who previously refused to give Eddie a loan. "The Ball-Rickles training sequences are fun, with Lucy working harder than her boxer, and Rickles scores right off the bat asking for a bank loan for a flower shop," one reviewer wrote. (Actor Bruce Mars, who played Sonny, Eddie's opponent in the ring, later quit show business and became a monk with the Self-Realization Fellowship in L.A.—changing his name to Brother Paramananda.)

In Don's episode of *I Spy*, which aired in March 1967, he played an egotistical comedian named Frank Bodie, who becomes a pawn in anti-American propaganda: "a clown onstage but a psychotic offstage." The episode was titled "Night Train to Madrid"; said one critic,

"Rickles, who's a competent actor, is quite good even though the role is overwritten and tends to weaken the effectiveness of the mystery."

Three years earlier, Don had been mentioned as a possible costar of *The Odd Couple* months before it opened on Broadway with Art Carney and Walter Matthau. Now it became a reality . . . sort of . . . and, in April 1967, nearly twenty years after graduating from the American Academy of Dramatic Arts, Don Rickles added his name to the school's list of alumni who acted on the legitimate stage.

But it was not on Broadway. Don was costarring in a West Coast production of *The Odd Couple* with Ernest Borgnine, one of his frequent nightclub targets (Ernie never took it the wrong way) and his costar in *The Rabbit Trap*. The success of *The Odd Couple* on Broadway—it was still doing big business at the Eugene O'Neill Theatre in Manhattan two years into its run—spurred numerous regional touring productions with a long laundry list of movie and television stars, including José Ferrer, Mickey Rooney, Phil Foster, and Henry Morgan, in the roles of slovenly sportswriter Oscar Madison and Felix Unger, the finicky, lint-picking neatnik who moves into Oscar's spacious Manhattan apartment after his wife kicks him out of the house. Borgnine played Oscar to Don's Felix.[10] "Actually, offstage, I'm very much like Felix," Don said. "I'm the neatest guy in town and I can't live or work in an atmosphere of disorder. I'm really compulsive about it. My wife could tell you, to her sorrow."[11]

The Odd Couple starring Borgnine and Rickles was scheduled for two separate two-week runs starting at the Circle Star Theater in San Carlos, twenty-five miles outside of San Francisco, before heading south for the Melodyland Theatre in Anaheim in Orange County. Neil Simon's brother, comedy writer Danny Simon—supposedly the real-life inspiration for Oscar Madison—was directing the production. Among the cast were a young actress named Loretta Swit, Lou Frizzell, Richard Latessa, and Cece Whitney. The ads promised "The Most Exciting Odd Couple Ever!"

Borgnine spoke fondly of Don in his memoir, *Ernie: The Autobiography*. "As cutting as he can be onstage, he's warm and loving in private.

I decided to take the job. I'd be playing the slob Oscar Madison, and he'd be the prissy Felix Unger. Perfect. And I figured, what the hell? Don had done a lot of acting, in TV shows like *F-Troop* and *Get Smart* . . . If nothing else, it would be a howl."

Don and Ernie rehearsed for the show in the playroom of Ernie's house in L.A.; when Don arrived for their first run-through of the script, he was unprepared for the stage production. He told Ernie he had "kind of" learned lines for his movie roles but that he also added a lot of improvisation for his short scenes. Ernie told him that that approach could never work for the stage, and that Don needed to learn the entire script by heart. He gave Don two pages of the script to recite; when Don returned to Ernie's house the following day, he still had not memorized the lines.

"I said, 'Listen, you've gotta work on these things. It's a show. You're going to perform it in front of people.' He said, 'Yeah, but I don't talk this way.' 'You've got to do it the way the author put it down on the page.' He thought about it a little and said, 'Okay, I'm going to go home, but I don't think I'm going to last. I don't want to do this.'"[12] Don learned the lines. Ernie Borgnine was a tough customer.

It was not a role on Broadway, but had not Don trained for this moment all those years ago? He yearned to be considered a "serious" actor, one who could play more than a neurotic Indian chief on *F Troop* or a flower-loving boxer on *The Lucy Show*. *The Odd Couple* was a comedy . . . but it was already one of the best-known comedies in theatrical history. Don got the message from Ernie's tough talk. "After a couple of weeks we had it down pretty pat," Borgnine said.

Don's premiere on the legitimate stage was not only a feather in his acting cap, but it caught the attention of Princess Grace of Monaco—Grace Kelly, who, all those years ago, had walked the halls of the American Academy of Dramatic Arts with Don Rickles from Queens. She sent him a telegram on opening night: "Class will tell. Our Class!"[13]

Opening night arrived at the Circle Star Theatre. Don was extremely nervous, and his entrance as Felix Unger nearly took a disastrous U-turn. "He walked onstage like a zombie," Ernie Borgnine recounted. "He didn't know where the hell he was going or what he was doing. He started coming straight across that round stage, instead of coming to the table. I thought, 'Oh God, I know it's wrong.' I tried to cover for him by going over and saying, 'Hey what's the matter, Felix?'

"It was like the bell sounding for a fighter. He was suddenly back in the game, and he gave the goddamndest performance that I've ever seen in my life. He just came across like a million bucks." Borgnine's investment in Don paid off. The rest of the run went off without a hitch, and it kept the critics happy in San Carlos and, two weeks later, in Anaheim. According to Borgnine, Neil Simon went backstage to say hello to Don after watching him in *The Odd Couple* and told him, "If you ever repeat what I'm about to tell you, I'll deny it. But you two are the first guys that ever did this show the way I had it written." Maybe so. We will never know, although acclaimed film director Robert Aldrich saw the show, too, and was effusive in his praise. "Jesus, I fell down on both knees," he told Ernie. "You are the funniest guys I've ever seen in my life!"[14] (Borgnine costarred in *The Dirty Dozen*, which Aldrich directed. It opened two months later in June and was an enormous hit.)

Ernie and Don's costar, Loretta Swit, recalled that Don tried to make her feel at home—in his own way. "The first couple of days of rehearsals, we were talking and getting to know each other and he said, 'What kind of a name is Swit?' and I said, 'Believe it or not, it's Polish,'" she recalled. "He said, 'What was it? Was it like Switovski or something?' and I said, 'No, isn't that interesting? People think that Polish names have to be a yard long and they need to end with *ski* and it's not necessarily true.'

"So he had all of my Polish information, and he started calling me 'Stanislavski' because we were both method, wonderful actors. Don was never given the true, deep appreciation for his acting ability. He was a wonderful actor. So I come running into rehearsal one day and he says 'Stanislavski is here.' But, oh God, I just adored him.

Working with him was an absolute, knock-out joy. He not only didn't vary from the script. You would think, 'He's a stand-up comedian, a genius, he's going to make the script better, he's going to put in jokes or whatever . . . but that man didn't change a comma. He was script-perfect from week one, from when we started rehearsing. He came in totally prepared and he was a joy. Now Ernie Borgnine was also wonderful [but] you expected him to be wonderful with or without his Oscar—and together, I have to tell you, to have worked with that very odd couple, they were wonderful, they were so wonderfully matched. Oh God, it was a tremendous experience. As actors say, you died and went to heaven with jobs like that. It's not a job. It is like going to a master class, working with people like that."[15]

Ernie Borgnine enjoyed working with Don so much that he talked about taking *The Odd Couple* to Australia, with the entire cast intact, after he finished shooting his next movie. "I'll never forget the comment that Don Rickles made about me when he was interviewed later in his room," he said. "Asked if I was good to work with, he answered: 'Yes, and if anybody says a bad word about the Guinea bastard, I'll kill 'em.' Every time that I have appeared somewhere with him or at his shows he has never spoken my name except with grace and gratitude. He's just one of the most marvelous guys I've ever known in my life.[16] He can cut you up and down and across, but you can still laugh about it. He doesn't do it to hurt you . . . I remember during the first day of rehearsal, things were all messed up, so Rickles goes over to the head man and says, 'There are 40,000 directors in California, and we get the dummy.'"[17]

Don celebrated his successful run in *The Odd Couple* by signing a new, four-year contract with the Sahara. The deal, which ran through 1971, was worth more than $1 million. It was almost cut short when, in mid-May 1967, when Don was performing in the Sahara's Casbar Lounge, and a man who checked in under the name "Thomas Jesen" left a homemade bomb in one of the rooms in the Sahara's tower complex along with a one-page, typewritten note demanding $75,000. "Jesen" claimed that other bombs were planted at two other hotels owned by Del Webb, the Mint in Las Vegas and the Sahara-Tahoe. People at both locations—as well as several other Del Webb–owned hotels in Arizona (and an apartment complex)—were evacuated by police. About one hundred people were asked to evacuate the Sahara tower complex in Vegas; Don finished his shows in the Casbar Lounge without incident. Connie Francis, who was headlining in the Congo Room, also finished her show safely but was moved to a different luxury suite. The unexploded bomb was eventually found in the closet of a room on the twelfth floor—two stories below her room. No injuries were reported.

Don returned to the Casbar after the incident and proceeded to rip Ed Sullivan ("Did you hear about Ed Sullivan? Two dogs died and they had to cancel the show."), Arnold Stang and Woody Allen (who "spend Sundays giving each other blood transfusions"), and Gary Crosby ("His father has 50 million and he goes on *The Joey Bishop Show* as a mercy case."). He was relentless.[18] Someone did the math, and calculated that Don, in the eight years since he opened at the Sahara, had insulted approximately sixty-five thousand visitors to Las Vegas.

We interrupt this book for a bit of social context vis-à-vis Mr. Don Rickles.

By the summer of 1967, Don was one of the most popular comedians in America. That fall, he attacked daytime and prime-time television with a blitz of appearances. There were the Rickles critics, though, and he did not get a free pass, despite his growing fame (or maybe in spite of it). Not everyone appreciated The Merchant of Venom's cutting, take-no-prisoners barbs aimed at all ethnic groups and people with exaggerated physical traits. Over and over, he took great pains to explain to anyone who would listen that his brand of humor leveled the playing field by targeting both celebrities and everyday people and celebrating (if that is the right word) the human condition. If we cannot laugh at ourselves, then shame on us. That was the Rickles credo.

"I have my own theory on humor," Don said in one of the many profiles of him published during this frenetic time in his career. "It's very simple—there's humor in everything, even the most sacred things. Even in the midst of the most profound grief, there is always something funny that happens. This is the saving grace of the human animal. If we couldn't laugh at life, we'd end up in a rest home . . . I never refer, of course, to deformity or illness. Then it would cease to be funny."[19]

"You take truths and exaggerate them for laughs. But you must never really sting anyone. You must always know where to draw the line."[20]

America, in 1967, was a country deep in the clutches of one of the most, if not the most, turbulent decade of the twentieth century. Civil rights legislation and the growing Women's Liberation Movement were at the forefront of social upheaval and change as race riots raged in cities across the country. War was raging in Southeast Asia, and as President Lyndon Johnson escalated the US military presence in Vietnam, the newscasts were recounting death, destruction, and body bags on a nightly basis as America sat down to dinner. There was growing dissention about the war on both sides—the hawks and the doves—and racism was thriving, particularly in the Jim Crow South, where states refused to change their segregation policies or just ignored federal civil rights mandates—despite the best attempts of Rev. Martin Luther King Jr. and President Johnson's "Great Society" legislation. Women were still decades away from achieving even a modicum of social and political parity.

Despite this conflagration of sociopolitical events, show business operated in its own strangely insular bubble, save for the few rebels—Lenny Bruce, Godfrey Cambridge, Mort Sahl, the Smothers Brothers—who dared buck the system. Don targeted Blacks, Hispanics, Asians, Jews, everyone, it seemed, and the public ate it up and saw nothing wrong or insensitive in his remarks. That is not a judgment but merely a sign of those times, when it was acceptable—and accepted.

"I remember you," Don cracked to Japanese American comic Pat Morita. "The day after Pearl Harbor you went around telling everyone you were Hawaiian—just before you pulled that grenade out of your navel." Or, to a couple sitting in the Casbar Lounge watching Don rip everyone to shreds: "I make fun of Negroes, but you should be proud of your race. A great Negro, Emerson Jones, said in Mobile, Alabama: 'All aboard!'" He barked at a German couple watching his stand-up act, "What is this, Munich? Forty million Jews in this country and I got four Nazis sitting here in front waiting for the rally to start." Like that.

"I make fun of everyone, including myself," he said, reflecting the tenor of the times. Mr. Warmth never worked dirty, never uttered profanity in his act. The manager of the clubs in which he worked made sure the ethnic-looking patrons, the middle-America out-of-towners, the obese, the homely, the people of color were seated directly in Don's eyesight—ripe for the picking. "I have a sixth sense. I know where the fine line is," he explained. "I, being a sensitive person, am careful not to come on too strong. I couldn't be as successful as I am if I didn't have that sixth sense; I'd just offend people. I wouldn't make them laugh."[21]

But not everyone was buying what Don was selling.

"The art of one Don Rickles eludes us; and we think some of the stars who retell on TV Rickles' blatant insolences to them in public places are managing to bury such humorless insults right in his back," read one editorial. "The Rickles performing style is insult for the sake of lippy insolence; only Jack E. Leonard seems able to remain the proper mini-distance short of arrogant stupidity while needling."

One of Earl Wilson's readers felt compelled to write Wilson a letter after reading his column in which he mentioned his neighbor, Fat Jack Leonard, walking his dog. "I hate to see Jack E. Leonard, period. He and Don Rickles are victims of megalomania. They try to take over, no matter whose shows they are on. I can't stand them."[22]

Dr. Samuel Livingston, the director of the Epilepsy Clinic at Johns Hopkins Hospital in Baltimore, expressed his displeasure with Don in a letter to the editor that was published in the *Baltimore Evening Sun.*

Just recently, on two shows on which he appeared as a guest comedian, Don Rickles, in his efforts to get laughs by imitating a tongue-tied, sputtering character, has attributed these grimaces and gestures to epilepsy—saying in one instance, 'they probably thought I had epilepsy'—and, in another, 'oh, he's an epileptic' . . . Gratuitous, tasteless remarks such as Mr. Rickles' are offensive and precautions against such comments should surely be included in the policy established by television networks and other media against jokes which poke fun at religious and racial groups.[23]

Don toned it down, of course, for his network television appearances. In late September he merited a write-up in *Newsweek* magazine. The article appeared in its TV-radio section under the headline "The Merchant of Venom" and noted how, "for a decade, the rubber-jowled comic has had to settle for an occasional guest shot on dramas or late-night talk shows" due mainly to his acerbic nightclub act that "made television producers squirm." The writer rattled off a string of Don's one-liners from a recent appearance at the Sahara, including "You're Italian, right? We need Italians. What-the-hell do we need Italians for? Oh, yeah, to keep the cops busy.

"His ethnocentric gags, squeezed off in staccato bursts as he sweats and bounces under the spotlight, are studied variations of the street-corner insult," the article noted. "But network TV—desperate for a funny new face—this season has finally turned to Rickles."[24]

The few notable women comics in the mid-1960s—Totie Fields, Joan Rivers, Phyllis Diller, Belle Barth—joked about their husbands or their weight or their looks or their inability to find a man. *Playboy* magazine thrived, and excused itself with a dash of literary legitimacy. The June Cleaver archetypes of 1950s television paved the way for Mary Tyler Moore (*The Dick Van Dyke Show*) or Elizabeth Montgomery (*Bewitched*) or Barbara Eden (*I Dream of Jeannie*) or Eva Gabor (*Green Acres*)—safe and predictable. Don Rickles was different. An acquired taste, maybe, but different. No one could argue otherwise.

In the meantime, Don switched up his management team, defecting from GAC and Jack Gilardi to the William Morris Agency. Loyal, hardworking Joe Scandore remained, of course, as Don's personal manager. Joe was branching out, too, and added comedians Bernie

Allen and Pat Henry to his roster of clients. Don was his top priority, and Joe would tell anyone within earshot (or who was writing about Don) that The Merchant of Venom was misunderstood.

"People who know Don just *love* him," he said in one interview. "In reality, there are two Don Rickles—the fellow that's acting, that's making caustic remarks and insulting people—and the real Don Rickles. The real Don Rickles is the one the public doesn't know—a loyal, affectionate, warm man, a good man, a man who's *loved*, absolutely *loved*, by his fellow performers." Thou dost protest too much? Perhaps. Johnny Carson, who popularized the "Mr. Warmth" nickname, had a simpler explanation: "I think he's doing something a lot of people would like to do—putting people down. He's getting all that hostility out."[25] Don agreed with Carson. "He doesn't mix much," he said of the late-night host. "But for some reason he regards me as a friend—and I can say anything to him and he laughs. And I'm not sure why. Maybe it's because he's a millionaire, you know, and he made his choice a long time ago about the way he was going to get there, but I think he'd really rather be doing my kind of material than what he's doing."[26]

In September, Don signed on for his second appearance on NBC's *Run for Your Life* opposite Ben Gazzara. In the Season 3 episode, "Down with Willy Hatch," Don played a once-famous comedian who's hit on hard times and is arrested for statutory rape in a small backwater town where he is performing. Teetering on the edge of a nervous breakdown, Willy calls his friend, lawyer Paul Bryan (Gazzara), who arrives on the scene to defend him. Don's role was offered to Milton Berle first, but he had to turn it down due to professional commitments. Don understood; he faced a similar situation when he was forced to decline an offer of $17,500 to appear with Judy Garland for one week at the newly opened Madison Square Garden in Manhattan because of his contracted dates at the Sahara.

He was ready, willing, and able to appear on television, though, which allowed for a bit more flexibility in working around his schedule. He spent a week on *The Hollywood Squares* with fellow "squares" Steve Allen, Jayne Meadows, Roddy McDowall, and Shelley Winters. "Comics like Don Rickles, who play the nightclubs, know the value of doing a game show like ours," said the show's coproducer, Merrill Heatter. "Fans see them playing tic-tac-toe on TV and then pay a tab to hear their jokes at a nightspot. We're a good showcase."[27]

In a touch of show business irony, Don was booked that fall to appear on both *The Dean Martin Show* and *The Jerry Lewis Show*. Martin and Lewis, the once-formidable comedy partners, had not spoken to each other in over a decade following their famously fractured breakup. Their shows, however, taped across the hall from each other at the huge NBC color studios complex on West Alameda Avenue in Burbank. It marked Don's second appearance with Dean Martin following his September visit to *The Dean Martin Show*, where he appeared in a Western saloon sketch with Dean and husband-and-wife team Roy Rogers and Dale Evans. (In a showbiz tale perhaps apocryphal—but oft-repeated—Don, while taping Dean's show, walked across the hall to the soundstage where Jerry Lewis was rehearsing his show. Counting the members of Jerry's orchestra, he said to a startled Lewis, "Gee, too bad, Jerry. Dean has forty musicians in his orchestra!")

Don's television schedule was crammed with appearances on many top-rated shows, and he was a wanted man, with Danny Thomas, Bob Hope, Mike Douglas, and Jackie Gleason lined up in the Rickles queue. His January calendar included turns on *The Kraft Music Hall* on NBC and, on CBS, *The Smothers Brothers Comedy Hour*. "I was surprised when I turned on the TV sermonette the other night," Johnny Carson cracked on *The Tonight Show*. "Don Rickles wasn't on it."

"To me, being a star is when the guy in the wheat field knows you," Don told a reporter. "That's my goal—I want the whole world to know Don Rickles. Right now they know me mostly from [*The Tonight Show Starring Johnny Carson*]. He gave me my first real chance to wail on TV. I remember once, I was on his show and I turned to the audience and said, 'This guy makes $50 million a year, and his folks are sitting on a porch in Nebraska, watching the locusts, and his sister's working in Philly, making waffles in a Harvey House.' Carson fell off his chair."[28]

Don Rickles was big enough now to spawn an imitator, some guy down in Miami named Bill Gallus, who advertised himself as "The Poor Man's Don Rickles" . . . and who vanished from the nightclub scene shortly thereafter. The real Don Rickles, meanwhile, signed a deal to headline the Eden Roc in Miami Beach in March 1968—finally graduating to the hotel's larger and fancier Pompeii Ballroom. It was all starting to come together.

Don padded his sitcom résumé in October with a visit to *I Dream of Jeannie* in an episode called "My Master the Weakling." He played Francis Kiski, a tough NASA training instructor who barks at astronauts Tony Nelson (series star Larry Hagman) and his pal Roger Healey (Bill Daily) as he puts them through their paces and tries to get them in shape. Don almost cost the production an extra day of shooting because he was continuously convulsing the cast and crew with his ad-libs. When Larry Hagman, who was the son of Broadway actress Mary Martin (*Peter Pan*), flubbed a line, Don was ready: "You do that again, dummy, and I'll have to cut the wire to Peter Pan!"

Barbara Eden and Don Rickles were casual acquaintances before he guest-starred on *I Dream of Jeannie.* "My husband at that time, Michael Ansara, and our friends, Charles Bronson and his wife, Harriet, would go to Vegas a lot, the four of us, just to see certain shows," Eden recalled. "We didn't gamble, we just went to see the shows. This one time, we went to see Don. If I remember correctly, there were a lot of actors in the audience at that time. Perhaps they were invited. I don't really remember. I just remember sitting there while he was very mean to everyone in the audience except me. It was almost like I wasn't there. He ignored me. And after the show, everyone was talking to Don, saying how wonderful he was. Don came over to me and he had tears in his eyes. And he said, 'I'm so sorry, Barbara. I tried to think of something to say, and I just can't insult you. I can't.'"

Don made his debut on *The Jerry Lewis Show* on October 28, alongside Dorothy Provine and Sergio Mendes (and his band, Brasil '66).

PARAMOUNT presents   TONY CURTIS   DEBBIE REYNOLDS   in   THE RAT RACE ⓐ

Don as creepy Nelly Miller, harassing naive Peggy Brown (Debbie Reynolds) in *The Rat Race*, 1960. *(Photo courtesy Alamy)*

The Merchant of Venom in action onstage at the Mill Run Playhouse near Chicago, 1975. *(Photo courtesy Alamy)*

Don and wife, Barbara, 1979.
(Photo courtesy Alamy)

Dr. Steven Mitchell (Richard Lewis) and his blowhard father Al (Don) in the short-lived Fox sitcom *Daddy Dearest*. *(Photo courtesy Alamy)*

Don and Robert De Niro in a scene from *Casino*, 1995. *(Photo courtesy Alamy)*

Near the end: Don's battle with necrotizing fasciitis in his leg left him unable to stand on stage — but he still kept 'em laughing. *(Photo courtesy Alamy)*

The proud father and his son, Larry, with their Emmy Award for *Mr. Warmth: The Don Rickles Project*, 2008. *(Photo courtesy Associated Press)*

Don toured with his old friend Regis Philbin in his final years. Here they are at the Bellagio in Las Vegas in 2014. *(Photo courtesy Associated Press)*

Chomp on that: Don harassing Burgess Meredith in *The Twilight Zone* episode "Mr. Dingle the Strong," 1961. *(Photo courtesy of Getty Images)*

Don guest-starred on a dizzying array of '60s-era sitcoms, including this 1964 appearance on *The Addams Family*, with Skip Homeier (left) and Jackie Coogan as Uncle Fester. *(Photo courtesy of Getty Images)*

"Marco Mongononzo was hurt" — Don rips into Frank Sinatra in a classic appearance on *The Tonight Show Starring Johnny Carson* in 1976.
(Photo courtesy of Getty Images)

Face time: John Wayne was game for a laugh on Don's 1975 CBS special.
(Photo courtesy of Getty Images)

Not so groovy: Pat McCormick,
Don, and Don Adams cut loose
on *The Don Rickles Show*,
a short-lived disaster on ABC, 1968.
(Photo courtesy of Getty Images)

The Young Hopeful in 1960,
shortly after taking Las Vegas by storm.
(Photo courtesy Photofest)

Don and Ray Millar in a scene from Roger Corman's *The Man with the X-ray Eyes* (1963). It killed at the drive-ins. *(Photo courtesy Photofest)*

Muscle Beach Party, 1964. 'Nuf said. *(Photo courtesy Photofest)*

...n as Harry Hamburger in
...rl Reiner's *Enter Laughing*
...th Nancy Kovack and
...ni Santoni, 1967.
...hoto courtesy Photofest)

The two Dons, Adams and Rickles,
on "The Little Black Book,"
a two-part episode of *Get Smart*, 1968.
(Photo courtesy Photofest)

Don and Frank on the Academy Awards telecast (1969).
Don went over his allotted time, annoying Mel Brooks. *(Photo courtesy Photofest)*

Kelly (Clint Eastwood) has some words for Crapgame (Don) in *Kelly's Heroes*, 1970.
(Photo courtesy Photofest)

Miscast as family man Don Robinson in *The Don Rickles Show*
with costars Louise Sorel and Erin Moran. It lasted one season on CBS.
(Photo courtesy Photofest)

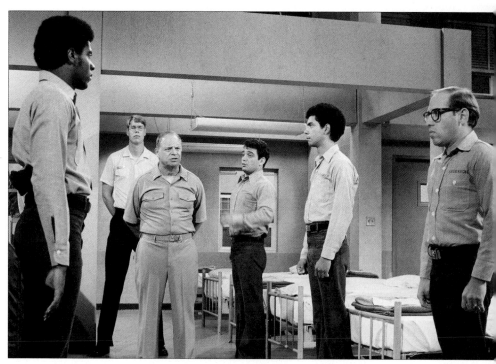

Don, who served in the Navy during World War II, tasted moderate prime-time success as Chief Petty Officer Otto Sharkey in *C.P.O. Sharkey*, which ran for two seasons on NBC. That's Peter Isacksen as Seaman Lester Pruitt standing behind him.
(Photo courtesy Photofest)

Don was a regular on T*he Dean Martin Celebrity Roast* specials. He always closed the show. "No one could follow him," said fellow comedian Tom Dreesen. *(Photo courtesy Photofest)*

Don backstage, holding his Emmy for *Mr. Warmth: The Don Rickles Project.*
(Photo courtesy Photofest)

The very next night, NBC aired his *Run for Your Life* episode. The *Oakland Tribune* television critic weighed in with a glowing review of his desperate comedian Willy Hatch. "Rickles had an actor's field day, compulsively doing bits and impressions, desperately submerging his anxiety in gags and horseplay, panicking when left alone, giving way to childish blubbering, staring in bewilderment at the people who no longer laughed, and finally giving up his tenuous hold on reality. It was a smashing performance, and the nightclub scene was so devastating it was almost too cruel to watch."[29]

Dean Martin was one of Don's go-to targets on the nights he sat ringside at Casbar Lounge or at the Slate Brothers Club. They were good friends, and Dean, good-natured and perpetually unruffled, loved the needling. "The more Rickles loves you, the more he insults you," Martin said. "I hope he always insults me."[30] Both men circled Sinatra's orbit, of course, and Don's honorary membership in Frank's Rat Pack ensured him a good camaraderie, not only with Dean but with Sammy Davis Jr. and Joey Bishop. While Joey was no longer part of Frank's world, he was close to Sammy and Dean, and his open-door policy toward Don vis-à-vis *The Joey Bishop Show* helped keep Don in the television spotlight.

Dean, too, had his own television show, albeit in prime time. *The Dean Martin Show* premiered on NBC in 1965 and was a steady Friday-night ratings-grabber for the network despite viewership traditionally a little lighter with the approaching weekend. Dean's producer, Greg Garrison, knew Don from the Slate Brothers Club and was a big Rickles fan.

Don's second appearance on *The Dean Martin Show*—taped in mid-October for an airdate in late November—broke down the walls of conventional television wisdom. Garrison, with NBC's approval, devoted an astonishing seventeen minutes of airtime to The Merchant of Venom. It was an unheard of breach of prime-time tradition, but Garrison knew what he wanted. The producer choreographed Don's segment as if he was in his natural habitat—a nightclub setting—with the viewers at home sitting ringside for the action. Garrison invited over twenty celebrities—including the Andrews Sisters (minus Laverne, who had died earlier in the year), Lena Horne, Ricardo Montalban, Debbie Reynolds, Jackie Cooper, Rose Marie, Danny Thomas, Don Adams, Pat Boone, Ernest Borgnine, and Polly Bergen—and seated them at tables in front of the show's stage. The studio audience was blacked-out behind them. Dean Martin, in his standard tuxedo and adopting his best lush-life attitude, walked out and introduced Don, who walked up to the stage blowing kisses and then let loose.

To wit:

"Dean Martin has been a friend of many, many years. Dean, I say this from my heart, really—I've never liked you. Never. I mean, where is a man going with [singing drunkenly] *Volare*."

"Isn't this fun, Pat? You're staying up late and everything. You can put on your pajamas and run around the room playing dump truck."

To Ricardo Montalban: "Here's some mud. Finish your hut."

To Danny Thomas: "You ever see his nose? When he breathes the lip gets sucked right up. You're not Lebanese, you're a hawk."

"Take a look at what Ross Martin married. Looks like a real mercy mission. Throw a stick on the floor, see if she brings it back."

"One of the great stammering idiots of our day, Bob Newhart."

"Dom DeLuise . . . have you ever heard of cottage cheese? Looks like a hard-boiled egg that didn't break on the dish."

And on and on. Don, sweating profusely, his sparse hair tousled, closed the act and de-clawed his preceding cutting remarks by invoking his "I'm really a nice guy" shtick. He did not sing—this time—but, accompanied by a tinkling piano, he was suddenly serious: "I speak of all faiths, creeds, and colors, and why not? Because when our time's up, we will be on one team, so why do we need bigotry and nonsense?" He repeated Will Rogers's famous quote about "only picking on big people . . . May I say to you fellow performers, and you folks way in the back, you are pretty big, and I thank you for making me feel important."

"That was difficult to do," Don said afterward, "because it was total ad-lib with the cameras going. I knew some of the people, of course, but they didn't tell me who was going to be there."[31]

Don's centerpiece on *The Dean Martin Show* aired November 30, and the episode garnered solid viewership numbers for NBC. Viewers coast-to-coast, who might never see Don's act live in Vegas or in Miami Beach or at the Copa in New York, were given an up-close-and-personal taste of The Merchant of Venom at work in his sandbox. Greg Garrison's gamble paid handsome dividends, and it planted a seed in the producer's mind. He knew all about those ribald, no-holds-barred Friars Club roasts. (Don was due to be turned on the spit in a few months.) Rickles kept it just clean enough for middle America and the NBC censors, and the audience at home ate it up. Garrison had the inkling of an idea: Why not tame and tailor the roast into a one-hour special?

Bob Hope was also one of Don's targets that night on *The Dean Martin Show* when, as was his wont, he walked in late and took a seat at a table in the back. "Look who's here. The war must be over," Don cracked and everyone laughed. Hope was across the hall taping his next NBC special, *Shoot-in at NBC*, a Western-themed mishmash of nonsense for which Old Ski Nose had recruited a group of comics and actors for support, including Rickles, Larry Storch, Jack Carter, Steve Allen, Don Adams, and Bill Dana. The special aired in early November and was roundly panned by the critics. "There were so many bodies on the stage that nobody had a chance to be funny. Any three of the comics could have done a funnier show. Paul Lynde, who can be hilarious, didn't stand a chance with his three lines. Wally Cox popped a few sorrowful one-liners and retiring (*sic*) looking chagrined. Don Rickles mugged a little and gave up . . . It was a colossal mess, and a very big waste of talent, including Hope's."[32]

Don did not fare much better on *The Danny Thomas Hour*, which shot an entire episode on location at SeaWorld in San Diego. The hour was dubbed a "cheap-in" with "an abysmally bad script, over-enthusiastic laugh machine and a couple of guest performers." In the final sketch, Don and Danny Thomas dressed in drag and danced a hula with a group of Polynesian women. "That's the sort of show it was," sniped one critic.[33]

The bad reviews hardly dented Don's popularity—he was only a guest star, after all, not the main attraction—and he rode out the year on a high note. In December, he presented Joe Scandore with the 1939 Rolls-Royce he had purchased a year earlier—a bonus for all of Joe's hard work, loyalty, and friendship. And . . . *would you believe?* . . . he filmed an episode of *Get Smart* starring his pal Don Adams.

It was entitled "The Little Black Book." Don played CONTROL agent Maxwell Smart's Army buddy, Sid Krimm. Sid stumbles upon a KAOS black book with the names of its agents and, no rocket scientist he, assumes that the book belongs to Max. So, as one does, Sid proceeds to line up a double-date for himself and Max with two KAOS agents (played by Arlene Golonka and Ann Prentiss). The episode was intended as a one-off, but Don (Rickles) could not help himself during the production and ad-libbed mercilessly. In one take, while he was shooting a close-up scene, Don was annoyed by the sound of a studio carpenter sawing away in the background. "Would someone tell that guy in the back to build his house at home?" he snapped in true Rickles fashion. "Every time I get a close-up, somebody has to start up with the Tinker Toys."

The executives at NBC figured that it was cheaper to use the additional footage generated by Don's antics than to leave it on the cutting room floor, so they added a second episode and aired the two-part "The Little Black Book" on consecutive weeks (January 27 and February 3, 1968). Bernie Koppel, who played Max's enemy, German KAOS chief Siegfried ("Shtarker! This is KAOS! Ve don't *pffffttt* here!"), recalled the atmosphere on the set during Don's visit to the show. "He and Don Adams were great friends from the stand-up times and they would fart around like it was nobody's business," he recalled. "I spent some time with Don Rickles. A delightful, gentle, caring, considerate human being . . . Fat Jack E. Leonard said, 'Don Rickles stole my act! Don Rickles stole my act!' Well, Don Rickles did not steal his act. He got his act from his father, but he amplified it."[34]

Get Smart director James Komack recalled that the only way to get Don to follow the script was to allow him room to improvise (those bits could be cut later). "Rickles' energy is so high he literally talked us into a four-day shooting," he said. The two Dons, Adams and Rickles, convinced Komack to make a cameo appearance in "The Little Black Book," as a killer.

On Friday, December 12, Don made his first appearance as a sub-stitute host for Johnny Carson on *The Tonight Show*, welcoming guests Sammy Davis Jr., Connie Francis, and Robert Culp. Meanwhile, in that familiar "here we go again" refrain, Don reportedly was close to signing a deal to star in another pilot for a series, this one to be called *Rome, Sweet Rome*, in which he would portray the Emperor Nero in modern times. (Don't ask.) "The big interest for the industry is that it will be produced on tape, not film, hopefully accounting for a 50 percent saving," the *San Francisco Examiner* reported. "The taping experiment will be conducted at CBS Television City in Hollywood within two weeks." There is no record of whether the taping of *Rome, Sweet Rome* materialized. Let us keep a good thought and assume that Don Rickles as a modern-day Emperor Nero was simply a misguided notion on the part of well-meaning network executives.

CHAPTER 12

D on Rickles continued to plant his ubiquitous flag into the prime-time television landscape as the calendar turned to 1968. On the night of January 14, he visited *The Smothers Brothers Comedy Hour*. The variety show, in its second season, with hosts Tom and Dick Smothers, was the bane of the CBS censors for its liberal take on politics and the siblings' not-so-subtle criticism of the ongoing war in Vietnam. *The Comedy Hour* skewed to a younger, hipper audience and showcased many musical acts considered too radical for a more mainstream series; in 1967, British rockers the Who (mostly) lip-synched to their hit "My Generation" before the group's whirling-dervish drummer, Keith Moon, set off a high-powered cherry bomb hidden in his drum set. The resulting explosion reportedly caused guest Bette Davis to faint in the wings and seriously damaged guitarist Pete Townshend's hearing.

Don was a lifelong Democrat; in public, he kept his politics to himself, occasionally zinging California governor Ronald Reagan (with whom he shared a close friendship) or President Lyndon Johnson (with whom he did not). On *The Smothers Brothers Comedy Hour*, he skirted any perceived controversy and appeared in a sketch with Tom and Dick that started with Don shaking a tambourine before hectoring them about guest stars booked on shows without any regard to their true talents. It was inoffensive . . . and yet it still roiled some viewers.

Robert Sylvester, writing in the *New York Daily News*, criticized Tom and Dick Smothers for "rapping the government and being otherwise coy" and then turned his attention to Don. "On the program they had their buddy [*author's note: not quite*] the 'insult comedian' Don Rickles. He's all over TV, these days, like Joey Bishop. You know what I'm gonna do? I'm gonna watch and watch Rickles and Bishop until one of them eventually says or does something funny." Ouch.[1] Don, for his part, said afterward that he did not enjoy his appearance on *The Smothers Brothers Comedy Hour*: "I've done a lot of guest shots this year, and of all the shows I've done, let's just say the *Smothers Brothers* was not one of my favorites."[2]

Later that month, Don stepped in for Art Carney, who was battling the flu, to host a *Kraft Music Hall* special called "Physical Phitness" on NBC. He had been booked as a guest on the show prior to Carney's illness, so it worked out, and he joined Joe Garagiola, Pat O'Brien, George Plimpton, Red Sox slugger Carl Yastrzemski, and NFL star Roosevelt Grier in an hour-long spoof of sports and physical fitness—homing in on Yastrzemski: "the Polish kid."

"If the show sometimes resembled a dress rehearsal gone wrong, everyone had a lot of fun," said one critic,[3] while another opined that "even Rickles, a notably hard man to discomfit, was looking glassy-eyed long before the end of 'Physical Phitness.'"[4] The special was, apparently, slapped together without much thought. Perhaps Art Carney knew something.

On January 24, Don was roasted by the Friars Club at a stag luncheon in Manhattan. It was the largest turnout for the event in recent memory, and as usual, it was blue and bawdy, with unprintable jokes and wisecracks. Jack E. Leonard emceed the event: "Not only has he been doing my act for twelve years, but he also stole my head. I am here to make a citizen's arrest." Ed Sullivan, Norm Crosby, Flip Wilson, Bernie Allen (Joe Scandore's client), Cab Calloway, Pat Paulsen, Johnny Carson, Jackie Vernon, and others showed up to spit some venom back at The Merchant.

Jack E. Leonard said that he hoped Don's appearances on *The Tonight Show* would be a stepping-stone for him and when Carson got up to the podium he took his best shot: "I've seen Don entertain fifty times and I've always enjoyed the joke." Jackie Vernon recounted how Don addressed him in the Casbar Lounge audience one night in Vegas: "We have a baby hippo here, let's give the little slob a hand." Vernon got even: "I never thought I'd see the day the Friars would honor a lounge act."[5]

As was the Friars Club custom, Don, as the star being roasted, got in the last word—but his closing remarks that afternoon were far from vicious. "Ed Sullivan, you are not a well person. I was supposed to be on your show once but my bear died. I've had a lot of wonderful afternoons but this one will not go into my scrapbook." Not the stuff of epic put-downs. Nevertheless, the crowd sent him off with a ten-minute standing ovation.

There was talk, again, of putting Don in a Broadway show, this time to play W. C. Fields in a musical version of the comedian's life. "We hope Don, an enormous Las Vegas favorite, turns it down because it's definitely not his cup of tea," wrote prescient Las Vegas columnist Ralph Pearl. Nothing more was heard about the project. Besides, where would Don find the time? He opened with Lainie Kazan for a ten-night run in the Cafe Pompeii at the Eden Roc in Miami Beach, where Ed Sullivan introduced him. Eden Roc owner Morris Landsberg reported that between four hundred and five hundred people were being turned away each night trying to get in to see the Rickles show. In March, Don was among the celebrities and industry insiders invited to a black-tie soiree to help Milton Berle celebrate his twenty-year anniversary in television. Carl Reiner emceed the affair.

There were more visits to Carson's *Tonight Show* when Johnny took the show to Hollywood . . . again. (Don: "Hey, Ed, do something. Move your lips so we know you're alive!") The Rickles comedy train made its usual stops: Merv Griffin, Joey Bishop, Pat Boone, and Mike Douglas—who taped his show in Philadelphia (Don paid a call on his mother-in-law there). In one memorable appearance on *The Mike Douglas Show*, Don was an "usher" who brought a candelabra onstage for Liberace—and then stayed to heckle the flamboyant pianist for a minute or two.

He filled in for pal Don Adams on *The Jerry Lewis Show* and ad-libbed the whole shebang, only because he could: he had a stipulation built into his contract that, when he subbed for another performer, he did not have to learn the script and could wing it after being briefed on the setup.[6] Someone who crunched the numbers calculated that Don made an astounding sixty-two network television appearances in 1967—and had already racked up sixteen small-screen visits in the first two months of 1968. And he was just getting started.

The *Chicago Daily News Service*, February 25, 1968: "To many viewers, the idea of a man who made his reputation by insulting people publicly receiving this much recognition is appalling, and we have been told by producers who use Rickles that their mail indicates some people react by tuning out the show." Letter to the Editor, the *Chicago Tribune*, March 5, 1968: "I recently saw Don Rickles on the *Smothers Brothers Comedy Hour*, and I just want to tell you how disgusted I am with him. Every time I see him on TV, he is criticizing someone, and although he thinks of it as a joke, he always seems to be slapping someone for something. I really don't think the stars appreciate this. I know a lot of people who feel the same way about him."

"It's funny," Don said at the time. "All those years I couldn't get on, and then all of a sudden everyone wants me. Getting the exposure is one thing, sure, but the timing has to be right if you're going to be invited back. And, now, I guess a lot more people are ready for my humor . . . A psychiatrist wrote me a while ago telling me that what I do is a healthy thing. It's like a safety valve. It brings a lot of things out into the open, releases a lot of the pressures, lets out a lot of the steam that people feel."[7]

But Don still had a lot to learn about the vagaries of the television business.

In March 1968, ABC announced seven new series for its fall prime-time schedule, including *The Don Rickles Show*. The series was described as a hybrid comedy-game show. After all the failed pilots and rumored pilots and hoped-for series, The Merchant of Venom was finally starring in his own television showcase. Details regarding the format for *The Don Rickles Show* were slim to none or, at worst, extremely vague; when they announced the series, ABC executives were not quite sure just *what* to do with Don Rickles. It was not uncommon, though, for network executives to fiddle with a series during its development: changing costars, hiring and firing writers, and altering its format before the Big Reveal in the fall. Don was about to experience the backstage machinations that went into constructing a network television show . . . including one that was not very good.

The Don Rickles Show was scheduled to air on Friday nights at 9 and would be produced in ABC's Hollywood studios. Each week, Don would welcome three celebrity guests who would, in turn, pose questions to contestants playing the game. The contestants, in turn, "must judge the star's veracity," whatever that meant (it was murky). "It'll be a takeoff on his café act, which deals with slashing away at the stars in the audience," one reporter wrote. "Only this time Don would be speculating with his star-studded audience. He'll have the celeb planted in the room."

Don played the good soldier; he was working at the Sahara when the show was announced, and he took a day off to fly to Chicago to glad-hand executives from ABC and its national affiliates, whose numbers paled in comparison to CBS and NBC. Don performed at the dog and pony show, and he was joined by Wayne Newton, Carol Channing, and Joey Bishop, whose ballyhooed late-night ABC talk show ended abruptly the following year. *The Don Rickles Show* began taping in New York in early May; Eden Roc owner Morris Landsberg and his wife, Jean, flew up from Miami Beach to watch their favorite comedian shoot his maiden episode.

Don, meanwhile, had somehow found the time in mid-1967 to appear in his tenth movie and to record a live album for Warner Bros. at—where else?—the Sahara.

The movie was *The Money Jungle*, a drama directed by Francis D.

Lyon, who worked mostly in television (he directed four episodes of *Perry Mason* in 1962). The film revolved around five competing oil companies each vying for offshore drilling rights in California—and the troubleshooter, Blake Heller (John Ericson), sent in to investigate the deadly chicanery, including the murders of four geologists. Lola Albright and Leslie Parrish played Heller's romantic interests, and Nehemiah Persoff was the dogged police lieutenant. Don played a stock market expert named Harry Darkwater, who assists Heller in his investigation. The role was small and untaxing; *The Money Jungle* opened in the summer of 1968 to little fanfare, mostly at drive-in theaters, and promptly disappeared without a trace.

The album was called *Hello, Dummy!* after the usual Rickles salutation to whoever was about to be cut by Don's verbal lance (or maybe it was a term of endearment—you decide). Advance word on the album was building and the buzz was promising: Warner Bros. claimed there was already an advance order of one hundred thousand copies of *Hello, Dummy!* and made sure this promotional nugget found its way into newspaper columns and the industry trades. Cary Grant reportedly called Warner Bros. to ask for a few copies; Don's mother, Etta, mailed over two thousand letters to Don's "celebrity friends" telling them to buy Sonny Boy's album—oh, and if they were visiting Miami, they were always welcome to drop into her apartment for a plate of her famous stuffed cabbage.

Future stand-up comedian and *Tonight Show* host Jay Leno was sixteen years old when *Hello, Dummy!* was released, and he was immediately entranced by the album, particularly by the reaction of Don's audience at the Sahara. "I had a tape recorder," he recalled, and "I would tell a joke in the tape recorder and drop the needle on the part of the record where Don was getting applause and laughter, and so when you played it back, I was telling the joke. I played it for my parents and my father said, 'Do you want to do a show somewhere?' 'I go, 'Yeah, Pop.'"

Decades later, when he was hosting *The Tonight Show* and Don was a guest on the program, Leno told him the story. "He thought that was pretty funny," he said.[8]

Don was a well-established star at this point and did not need *Hello, Dummy!* to be a monster hit, as had his good friend Bob Newhart when he shot to overnight stardom with his first album, *The Button-Down Mind of Bob Newhart*, recorded at a small nightclub in Houston and released in 1960 (also on Warner Bros.), then shooting to number one on the charts and winning a 1961 Grammy Award as Best New Album (Newhart was named Best New Artist). Still, it would be nice to have that same validation for *Hello, Dummy!* And, if the album was successful, it would be terrific publicity leading into the premiere of *The Don Rickles Show* in September. Warner Bros. pulled out all the stops and waged a campaign of promotional saturation in support of the album. Don agreed to do several interviews for its release—none of them with any hint of seriousness or reflection. They read like snippets from his nightclub act. (Question: "Is there any reason you always wear a tuxedo when you're performing in Las Vegas?" Answer: "My uncle is a caterer, and I like to be near the business in case things get bad.")[9]

Don and his zingers were sorely needed at the Emmy Awards that year. The telecast, which celebrated the ceremony's twentieth anniversary, aired May 19 on NBC. Frank Sinatra and Dick Van Dyke hosted the split broadcast, Sinatra in Hollywood and Van Dyke in New York. The show turned into a coast-to-coast fiasco, particularly for Van Dyke, who was bedeviled by technical glitches in New York and who took the brunt of the criticism the next day. Sinatra's track record on television was sketchy at best, but he opened with a song and a strong monologue, while Van Dyke floundered three thousand miles away and laughed at his own jokes—which did not help his cause.

Don came to the rescue as the night dragged on (some things never change) when he presented an award with Sally Field, starring as *The Flying Nun*, in its first season on ABC. "But it was Rickles, a comedian with an instinct for attacking the jugular, who put the whole Emmy system into its proper perspective, and in its place. He was up there, with Sally Field, to present awards for writing achievements in music or variety shows . . . 'I'm fed up with all these guys,' he cracked, and the place broke up. Everybody knew he had hit at the heart of the matter as only a fine humorist can."[10]

It did not end there; when Field opened the envelope to read out the winner, Don said what everyone else was thinking: "Who cares?" (The ten-member writing staff of *Rowan & Martin's Laugh-In* cared—they won the award.) Frank invited Don over to schmooze, and, as expected, he turned on Sinatra: "With your kind of money, couldn't you chip in and buy a tie? Dick Haymes in his heyday was better than you . . . You will never marry my mother."[11] Frank cracked up. Bullethead always did know how to thread that sensitive Sinatra needle. (The Dick Haymes barb was not new. Don used it so often on Sinatra—including in later years, when Haymes was unknown to younger audiences—that Rickles aficionados almost expected to hear it whenever the two men were together.)

Don made the first of many visits to *The Carol Burnett Show* on CBS in 1968, appearing in comedy sketches with Burnett and her stellar supporting cast (Harvey Korman, Vicki Lawrence, Lyle Waggoner, and, only occasionally in those early days, Tim Conway). *The Carol Burnett Show* players were known to break each other up via flubs or moments of improvisation—and the unplanned fun included the show's guests. "I remember a scene in one show which called for Rickles to rip my clothes off," Harvey Korman recalled. "Just as he did it, I said one word almost under my breath. 'Savage!' But Rickles heard it. He came back and completely destroyed me with ad-libs of his own."[12]

"He was the total opposite of what he was on stage," Burnett recalled. "He was a pussycat . . . and he was a great audience. There was one sketch we did that I remember; it was a musical takeoff of Tin Pan Alley, the music industry in the early 1900s. It was Mel Tormé, Don, and Nanette Fabray. And he was a music publisher in the sketch. I wish you could see it. He was so funny. And a really good actor, so he didn't really go off-script. But he really took off after Harvey and also Nanette—then he went off-script. But he didn't [do that] in the little musical takeoff we did. He was right in character."[13]

Don's work schedule that summer included a ten-week engagement at the Sahara; in his free time, he was busy with preproduction work for the imminent debut of *The Don Rickles Show*. Don warmed up for his opening at the Sahara with a fifteen-night run at the Sherman House, a landmark hotel in Chicago, where he raked in a cool $45,000 in total (two shows each night). The Rickles train was charging down its tracks so powerfully that Phyllis Diller, who was playing elsewhere in Chicago while Don was at the Sherman House, was forced to cancel all of her second shows on Monday and Thursday nights—she was losing business to The Merchant of Venom. There were no hard feelings, though; she booked Don to appear on her new NBC sitcom, *The Beautiful Phyllis Diller Show* because, she said, "I'm absolutely crazy about the man." *The Beautiful Phyllis Diller Show* premiered in September. It was canceled three months later.

Everyone wanted Don Rickles in their club or on their television show, or they wanted to see Don's act live—including the Copa's famously scary owner, Jules Podell. He finally relented and, in October, booked "that unfunny Jewish motherfucker" into his legendary New York nightclub. Before he opened, Don got the lay of the land by sitting in the Copa audience several times. He was spotted there one night and invited up to the stage to do a few minutes. "Just spring training for my debut here," he said.

The Don Rickles Show, meanwhile, was going through that painful birthing process of trying to figure out what worked and what fell flat. There were conflicting opinions on the creative side regarding the show's format—a problem that was still there when the series premiered. That was never a good sign for continued success.

Actor/writer Pat McCormick, a year younger than Don, was hired to be the show's head writer, announcer, and foil. McCormick was a huge man who clocked in at six-foot-seven and weighed around 250 pounds. His writing credits included *The Tonight Show*,

The Danny Kaye Show, The Andy Griffith Show, and *Get Smart.* He wrote for Jonathan Winters when Winters guest-hosted for Jack Paar for a week on NBC, and as an actor, McCormick made appearances on *The Merv Griffin Show* and elsewhere. He was, among his industry peers, considered to be a genius-level comedic performer/writer, and he cut Don down to size when they met for the first time in person: "I didn't know you were so small. I'm going to have you bronzed and hang you from my rearview mirror." He was a man after Mr. Warmth's own sneering heart.

McCormick, in turn, hired his friend and sometime performing partner actor/writer Jack Riley, to provide material for *The Don Rickles Show.* (Riley would go on to play the irascible Mr. Carlin on *The Bob Newhart Show.*) Frank Ray and Eddie Rider rounded out the writers' room. Johnny Carson's younger brother, thirty-nine-year-old Dick Carson, a veteran of *The Tonight Show,* jumped to ABC to direct Don's new series. What could possibly go wrong?

The comedy-game show format was dumped over the summer. It was a relief to everyone involved. "It's not a game show at all," Don explained. "I open the show with a comedy monologue and then interview members of the studio audience. What they say will trigger me to kid them." The three-celebrities-a-week idea was also scrapped; now, only one star would visit Don every Friday night. Frank Sinatra and Ed Sullivan were tentatively lined up, and Don wanted Johnny Carson as his opening-night guest. "The show will be pretty loose," he said. "I may have five guests from 'right off the street': people with a funny story to tell. In the run-through, I had a guy who had fifty canaries in his house, all flying around outside of cages. 'You are alone a lot,' was my remark to him when he told me what he did. He laughed and the audience loved it."[14]

"We're competing with the CBS movies and NBC's *The Name of the Game,* and that makes me the underdog," Don said. "Have mercy on me. Tell viewers to turn on the show and use it as a night-light if nothing else. I've got to make some kind of showing in the ratings." Those were not the words of a very confident man.

His album *Hello, Dummy!* was released in mid-June to favorable reviews. It gave people who might never see Don's act in Las Vegas (or anywhere else) a thirty-five-minute taste of what all the fuss was about. "A lot of people can't come to nightclubs and get insulted in person," he told Earl Wilson. "This way I make house calls." On the album, he made fun of Mexicans ("You never fool around with the wife, right? You're too busy laying on the floor fixing the mud so it don't cave in"); Polish people ("Me Polack. Push car for Jew and get quarter"); Blacks ("Ever since the war, they don't say 'Negroes' . . . 'Hawaiians'"). He also poked fun at *Get Smart* star Don Adams, who was in the Sahara audience that night ("A real weirdo, talks into his shoe. Gonna put him in a sanitarium. He's starting to get answers"); Mormons ("You Mormons never laugh, do you? Just sit there with your Pilgrim hat waiting for your duck to die"); Arabs ("I've met you before, haven't I? That's right, you hung my uncle."); spending his day off with Ed Sullivan ("You know how exciting that is? It's [like] watching a casket warp."); Italians ("We need the Italians. For what? Oh yeah. 'My shoes ready?'"); and Jews ("Gotta be like the Jews. Just sit around in your house in your underwear: 'Put on the TV, Shirley.'"). And there was more . . . much more.[15]

"Don Rickles has made a name for himself insulting people, and his *Hello, Dummy!* album demonstrates with much more clarity than his television appearances how well he has refined this act," one critic wrote. "From personalities to races to sex he's about as insulting as can be. But he never goes beyond the bounds of decency . . . There's a lot of laughs in this album, and with Rickles in sharp form you have to be alert to catch them."[16]

Within a month of its release, *Hello, Dummy!* had sold over 100,000 copies, and when all was said and done, it charted as high as number 54 on the *Billboard* 200 music chart. "In *Hello, Dummy*, Don Rickles displays the audacity that has resulted in his being given his own television show for the coming season . . . Rickles is a master of the irreverent wisecrack and has a seemingly bottomless bag of funny insults. The strong laughter of the Sahara's audience is indispensable to the album. If Rickles gets a similar reaction on his television show, he is a cinch to emerge as the comedy sensation of the year."[17]

If only it were that easy. Hint: it was not.

The Don Rickles Show continued its bumpy journey throughout the summer of 1968. Formats were adapted and then quickly tossed away; cooler heads searched for and argued about how best to fit the Don Rickles persona into that small box, how to take The Merchant of Venom's recipe and make it tasty enough for him to be welcomed into America's living rooms week after week. Nobody had a clue.

"They wanted Rickles to be like Groucho. They wanted to do *You Bet Your Life*, and he couldn't do it," writer Jack Riley recalled. "He took twenty minutes to say hello. So they decided to make it a variety show, with a game-show budget, and we had people come in . . . we did it every Sunday . . . we had David Janssen, we had Jimmy Durante, [he] later fell out, we had Mickey Rooney. Rickles was hilarious. He's a comedy animal, you know? Lorne Greene came in; Rickles was in a cowboy suit and he pulls up Lorne Greene's shirt and starts biting him on the stomach and says, 'This is the prairie!' It was really a variety show on the cheap."[18]

There were other internal issues as production on *The Don Rickles Show* rolled in to opening night. Harris Katleman, the show's executive producer, recalled that "well into production Don started to veer away from the show's format." Katleman placed the blame for Don's U-turn squarely on the shoulders of his pals Frank Sinatra, Joey Bishop, and Dean Martin. "They teased him relentlessly for doing a lowbrow quiz show, and it apparently got under his skin," recalled Katleman, who was on the receiving end of an angry phone call from ABC president Elton Rule: Don was going off-script. Something needed to be done. Katleman called a crisis meeting with Joe Scandore, whom he did not much care for. Scandore, he said, "got ahead in business by tricking gullible Hollywood executives into thinking he played an instrumental role in the Italian mob." In Katleman's version of events, Scandore told him, "It's a variety show now. I suggest you knuckle under if you know what's good for you." Katleman proceeded to call his cousin, Beldon Katleman, who owned the El Rancho Vegas hotel and casino and who "ate hacks like Joe Scandore for breakfast." Beldon Katleman approached Scandore, who folded— and said nothing further about the show's format.[19]

The Don Rickles Show producers, game-show veterans Mark Goodson and Bill Todman, hired Vic Mizzy to be the musical director; Mizzy wrote the music for sitcoms *Green Acres* and *The Addams Family* (including the finger-snapping theme), among others. He was an industry veteran who knew what he was doing. "That was not a good thing," he recalled about the situation behind the scenes. "What happened was there was a big fight as to who was going to score [the show], because Goodson-Todman produced it and Joe Scandore, who was Don's manager . . . there was an argument. But I happened to live in the same hotel as Don Rickles, and I liked Don and he liked me and his mom used to make us brisket sandwiches all the time. There were a lot of arguments. They tried to get a formula, they had a good orchestra and [they had] a good theme."

Don was being pulled elsewhere and could not be in three places at once. That was yet another fly in the ointment. He was simultaneously taping a *Kraft Music Hall* special with Alan King, Eddy Arnold, Bobby Gentry, Sugar Ray Robinson, Joe Louis, and Rocky Graziano (Don was a lifelong boxing fan). "Rickles, in the process of being occasionally funny, put in what must have been the most exhausting performance of his career," one critic opined. "Perspiration rolled down his bald head in rivulets in a sketch. He has his own show starting soon on ABC-TV and if it takes that much out of him every week, he won't last until Christmas."[20]

Don signed on for a second *Kraft Music Hall* hour, this one slated to air September 18, ten days before the premiere of *The Don Rickles Show*. It was called *Don Rickles' Brooklyn*—never mind that he was born and raised in Queens—and featured Brooklynites Steve Lawrence, Robert Merrill, and Joan Rivers. Barbra Streisand appeared live on the special, at the Broadway world premiere of her first movie, *Funny Girl*, and introduced a clip from the film in which she belted out *Don't Rain on My Parade.* The producers flew Etta in from Miami Beach and she surprised Don when he opened a door during a comedy sketch to scream "Mother, Mother!"—and there she was, in all her glory. Don broke up.

In early September, he guested on *The Beautiful Phyllis Diller Show* along with Johnny Carson and Sonny and Cher and paid a visit to *That Show,* a half-hour comedy/talk show hosted by Joan Rivers. In the press, he announced his role as a Las Vegas casino dealer in the upcoming 1969 movie *Where It's At* and played the Concord Hotel in the Borscht Belt, earning $10,000 for a night's work in the Catskills.

Don and his new television director, the taciturn Dick Carson, were Johnny's guests on *The Tonight Show* the week before *The Don Rickles Show* premiere, Johnny lending his kid brother and top-tier guest a hand in drumming up interest in their series. (Liberace was the other guest that night, and veteran radio announcer Harry von Zell filled in for Ed McMahon.) Don puffed on a cigar throughout the interview and mentioned that Johnny was going to be an upcoming guest, "which we're thrilled about," since Johnny gave him his big break in late-night television. "I also have passage on the *Andrea Doria,* big deal," Johnny replied. (The sinking-ship metaphor proved to be prescient.) Dick Carson sat back and let Don and Johnny banter for most of the interview, looking as if he wanted to be somewhere—anywhere—else. Two nights before his show's premiere, Don dropped by *The Joey Bishop Show* on his home network, ABC.

The Don Rickles Show hit the airwaves on September 27, 1968. Danny Thomas was Don's first guest. He told Don he was there to help—which did not help—and the two men exchanged compliments, Don saying that Thomas "is the type of guy who takes his family to an apple pie factory and raises the American flag." "Between them, they did everything but send up [Pat] McCormick as a burnt offering attempting to induce a laugh," once critic wrote. "Like nothing happened." McCormick laughed at everything in Ed McMahon–type fashion. And why not, since he wrote most of those lines himself. His deft touch, this time around, failed him.

Thomas appeared later in the episode in a sketch in which he transformed from his nice-guy persona into a version of The Merchant of Venom. The laughs were few and far between. Later, Don picked on a fat gentleman in the audience, and he hectored Vic Mizzy and the guys in his band; when he learned that Mizzy's singer, Greta Winter, was German, that was all he needed: "Get a rope—I'll bet during the war your daddy was a ski instructor." Then he broke into a goose step.

The best lines in the premiere came during a taped bit in which Johnny Carson, Joey Bishop, Dean Martin, Jonathan Winters, Jimmy Durante, Don Adams, and others gave their reactions to Don's new show. "What do you think of Don Rickles?" Martin was asked. "I don't think of him," he said. "Why should I think of him when I can think of Raquel Welch!" Ba-dum-bum.

The Don Rickles Show stumbled badly in its opening night. Or did it? The reviews ran the gamut from appreciative to snarky. Middle America hated the show. New York and Los Angeles loved it—or at least their critics lapped it up. *The Hollywood Reporter* liked what it saw, and gave the show a solid write-up: "Cut-down comedian Don Rickles threw out his barbed lances over the ABC network in a program which can best be described loosely as a host and a guest format interspersed with insult skits and film clips, 'all for fun,' as the star explained . . . The show was quick-moving with zingers emanating from Rickles. Producer Mark Goodson has put Rickles in a format in which he is well suited."

Other reviews were brutal. The *Minneapolis Star Tribune*: "Everybody familiar with Rickles' work expected it to be embarrassingly bad, and it was."[21] The *Rochester Democrat and Chronicle*: "It is really that bad . . . this one is unbelievably terrible."[22] The *Indianapolis News*: "The premiere of his half-hour show on ABC last night was an embarrassment, a struggle with desperation. Desperation won."[23] The *San Francisco Examiner*: "The enthusiastically awaited 'Don Rickles Show' premiered Friday night. It was a calamity. Just dreadful . . . It was like a very bad last half-hour on an off night of the Johnny Carson show."[24]

As mentioned, it was not all doom and gloom. The *Los Angeles Times* called the show "fast, furious and funny" and singled out Pat McCormick for making a good foil for Don—though it pointedly criticized Don's penchant for closing his show as if he were doing his nightclub act, with the sappy sentimentality vis-à-vis his Will Rogers "I never picked on a little guy, only big guys" quote.[25] The *New York Daily News* thought the show "the funniest television show of the season. If ABC-TV doesn't shift him to Monday nights at 8, to hammer away at Laugh-In's ratings, then I don't know network thinking."[26]

Don's reservations about his show's time slot were quickly confirmed once the ratings came in for the premiere: *The Don Rickles Show* did not stand a chance against the formidable CBS and NBC lineups. The show finished in seventy-second place that week, sandwiched between *The High Chaparral* and his own network's painfully dumb sitcom, *The Ugliest Girl in Town*. Its time-slot competition, *The CBS Friday Night Movie* (*Sex and the Single Girl* aired that week) and NBC's *The Name of the Game*, did just fine, thank you. It did not help that ABC lacked the affiliate firepower of its rivals; in Philadelphia, *The Don Rickles Show* aired on Sunday, opposite NFL football. In Johnny Carson's hometown of Lincoln, Nebraska, it aired Saturday night at 9:30, opposite the popular *Mannix* on CBS. It was the same situation in Moline, Illinois, where it aired at 9:30 p.m. on Saturday night; the ABC affiliate in that market opted to program a movie on Fridays at 9 p.m. *The Don Rickles Show* aired on a total of 118 ABC stations nationwide—chicken feed compared to NBC and CBS—and was saddled with a per-episode budget of a paltry $53,000.[27] There was no way it could compete with the big boys.

The show soldiered on, but the writing was on the wall. Johnny Carson guested on the second episode and shot an apple off of Don's head using a bow and arrow. It was a fun bit that few people saw, Johnny's popularity notwithstanding. Don looked out into his studio audience and spotted Ed Sullivan and his wife, and Dodgers pitcher Don Drysdale, each of whom came in for some ribbing. But no one cared. The second show finished even further down the ratings chart, in eighty-third place. "All in all, a step up in laughs from last week's opener, but the show is a matter of taste," wrote a critic. Subsequent visits from A-list guests including Carol Burnett, Don Adams, Kirk Douglas, Agnes Moorehead, Jimmy Durante, Debbie Reynolds, Bob Hope, Jim Nabors, and Andy Griffith did nothing to right the ratings ship.

Don, and everyone behind the scenes, was keenly aware that *The Don Rickles Show* was fighting a losing battle. By early November, Don was reportedly "telling chums he wants out"; the show was blasted as "pathetic" and "embarrassingly bad"—and worse— and the death watch began. ABC pulled the plug on November 12, two months into its run. The network allowed Don the courtesy of announcing his own cancellation on *The Tonight Show*, where, in that sometimes cruel showbiz fashion, his fellow couch mates were starring on thriving shows—Dan Blocker (*Bonanza*), Don Adams (*Get Smart*), and Kaye Ballard (*The Mothers-in-Law*, canceled in the spring)—and, of course, there was Johnny. Don was resigned to his fate but did not seem too bothered, and he graciously thanked ABC for the missed opportunity. That same night, his network stablemate and friend Joey Bishop ripped ABC on *The Joey Bishop Show* for not giving Don more time to establish himself and the series. (Joey and his sidekick, Regis Philbin, appeared in a later episode of *The Don Rickles Show*. Joey played his mandolin.)

The show limped along until the end of January. It was replaced by an evening edition of *Let's Make a Deal* in the 9 p.m. slot on Friday night. The final episode was an all-comedians special: Morey Amsterdam, Jack Carter, Joey Forman, Jan Murray, and Rose Marie all came on to pay their respects to Don. ABC also canceled *The Beautiful Phyllis Diller Show*, *The Ugliest Girl in Town*, *Journey to the Unknown*, *Felony Squad*, and *Operation: Entertainment*.

For all of the I told-you-so finger-wagging among the pundits, there was also some bile and veiled dog whistles directed at *The Don Rickles Show*. An angry columnist writing for the *Courier* in Waterloo, Iowa, commented on the show's cancellation and called out "a certain sort of person, invading the Sodom and Gomorrhas of New York and Burbank to seek entertainment in a TV studio audience"—read between the lines—and then later, in the same column, referred to "the half-world of the drug addicts, hippies and homos" seen on television of late. 'Nuf said.

Ben Gross, writing in the *New York Daily News*, took a more mature, levelheaded, analytical approach to the show's cancellation. Don and Jack E. Leonard, he said, were the two funniest insult comics and also did well on someone else's show (e.g., Johnny Carson, Merv Griffin, Joey Bishop). "But the fact is that neither Leonard, Rickles or their predecessors have ever been able to please a nationwide broadcast audience with a regularly scheduled weekly series"[28]—a quandary that plagued Don for the rest of his career.

He kept up a brave front. He knew deep down, almost from the very beginning, that *The Don Rickles Show* was a nonstarter. That did not mean, however, that he was not stung by its cancellation. "Four million people saw me," he said. "Those who didn't like me tuned out. Those who liked me continued to do so. And at least a few who never saw me before became fans." It was already being reported that ABC was still in Don's corner and was hunting for another starring vehicle for The Merchant of Venom. Somehow, it made sense in the makes-no-sense world of television. "It may be a spinoff series on ABC, and that's where I had my 'failure'!" Don said.

There were a few career highlights for Don that fall. On October 24, he opened for a two-week engagement at Jules Podell's Copacabana at East 60th St. He was taping *The Don Rickles Show* at the Vine Street Theater in Hollywood, so he flew into New York City for the shows. The lines to get into the Copa to see Don's act snaked around the block. Those who wanted to get in to see the 8 p.m. dinner show started lining up at 6 p.m.; for the midnight show, the queues began forming three hours earlier. Don was in top form, despite the bad news on the television front. "There's Jack Cassidy," he said one night. "He once confided to me in Hollywood, 'I'm handsome.' His wife Shirley Jones couldn't be here—she's in Eydie Gormé's dressing room cutting up Eydie's gowns." And another night: "I'd like to introduce Jerry Vale and his nurse, Rita." And: "[*Ben Casey* star] Vince Edwards is running around here asking people how to spell 'doctor.'"

Johnny Carson, *I Dream of Jeannie* star Barbara Eden, Ed Sullivan ("Is this too fast for you, Ed? You have to learn to move your neck."), Jack Jones, Godfrey Cambridge, and columnist Earl Wilson came to see the Rickles show, and all were ripped to shreds. (Johnny fought back: when Don walked out, he stood up and shouted, "Waiter! Check Please!") Don, in his equal opportunity offender fashion, did not only pick on the stars. He referred to one woman sitting ringside as "The one with the fat under the arms" and walked around the stage flapping his arms and grunting and groaning. He said to another woman "You look like a hooker!"—and her husband laughed uproariously. Etta Rickles was there, too, every night, beaming as Sonny Boy lit up the room. On Don's closing night, the Copa captains and waiters carried him off the stage and gave him a cigarette case for all the business he'd brought into the club. He was the first Copa entertainer to be honored in this fashion. Best of all, he beat his nemesis to the punch: Fat Jack Leonard would not play the Copa until two months later, in January.

Sandwiched in-between taping *The Don Rickles Show* and his Copa gig, Don filmed his cameo role in *Where It's At* as a Vegas card dealer who is caught cheating by hotel/casino owner A. C. Smith (David Janssen). He earned $20,000 for two days of work and appeared in only one scene in the movie, which was filmed on location at Caesars Palace and opened in May 1969. "I play a Las Vegas dealer," Don said. "When the director said to me, 'Deal the cards,' I said, 'I can't. I never dealt cards.' They had to get a double to do my dealing."

Don's costar in *Where It's At*, Brenda Vaccaro, recalled Don as being "so adorable with me. One time, we were at a table and they were going to start to shoot there, so out of politeness, they would say to the people at the tables, 'OK, anybody who doesn't want to be in this shot, you have time to move your stuff from the scene, it's going to be on film.' And people would look up and they were looking around nervously like there were cops or something. Nobody wanted to be in the shot, so Don says, 'You got to get off now!' He took that and rolled around in that and made it such a comedy. For a half hour we were dying laughing. What was it that Jack E. Leonard said? 'You can't be funny unless you're hostile'? Comedy is hostile. Sometimes the truth turns into a comic twist—dangerous, but hysterical. It's a great way to tell the truth sometimes."[29]

The movie, and Don's performance (or what little there was of it), were universally panned. "Don Rickles has a minor supporting role, probably because he was handy on location—heaven knows there could be no other reason—and that's about it," wrote one critic; another journalistic sniper called him "simply embarrassing." In the gossip columns, Desi Arnaz was talking to Don about playing a murderer in a whodunit film. The project was never mentioned again after *Where It's At* opened nationwide and disappeared quickly, relegated mostly to drive-in theaters that summer.

The movie's failure was a small blip on Don's radar. The Friars Club roasted him, again, at a dinner that drew two thousand people, with Joey Bishop, Shecky Greene, Jack E. Leonard, Jackie Mason, and Bob Newhart taking turns turning the spit. Don closed out the year with a New Year's Eve performance at the Sahara.

His prime-time flop did little to damage his reputation or his credibility. The New Year's Eve show was his last gig at the Sahara as a lounge act. He opened there in February 1969 headlining in the larger Congo Showroom and doubled his nightly salary from $17,500 to $35,000 (or $40,000, depending on the source).

CHAPTER 13

The year ahead promised to be a busy one for Don Rickles. He was like the showbiz equivalent of a shark, always moving, always working, afraid to slow down lest he cut the oxygen powering his career. All of his hard work, and even the failures, paid handsome dividends in terms of Don's bank account. He was earning nearly $1 million a year now, a far cry from playing the Wayne Room in D.C. in the mid-1950s for twenty-five bucks a night.

Ed Sullivan was a frequent target of Don's barbs and professed to be a big fan. He devoted a lot of ink to Don in his newspaper column, introduced him when he opened at the Copa. Sullivan, though, never asked Don to be a guest on his CBS showcase, *The Ed Sullivan Show*. Perhaps Sullivan and his producers thought that Don's super-charged persona was too much for middle America—although the irreverent Jackie Mason was a frequent *Sullivan Show* guest throughout the 1960s, even after Ed mistakenly thought he had flipped him the bird during a 1964 appearance.

Sullivan finally rectified the situation by booking Don on *The Ed Sullivan Show* as a special guest when it aired "live and in color" (that was still a big deal) from the new Circus Circus hotel and casino in Las Vegas on January 12, 1969. Don appeared on Ed's stage with Gina Lollobrigida and Jerry Vale; it marked the first time that Lollobrigida, the Italian bombshell actress, sang and danced on television.

In his memoir, *Rickles' Book*, Don recalled how, when Sullivan started the show that night by introducing "the famous Brasini Monkeys," he ran out on stage. "I think you're making a big mistake with those monkeys, Ed. The lead monkey is William Morris' hottest client and is demanding more money." Sullivan, seemingly caught off-guard, changed the subject. "Do me a favor. Go home," he said to Don.[1]

Don eventually did his usual insult act, which appeared to go over well with the Circus Circus audience. After the show aired, however, Sullivan's producer and son-in-law, Bob Precht, publicly apologized to Mexican Americans for a crack Don made about them.[2] Sullivan, for his part, said to Don when the show ended, "We were dynamite together, weren't we, Don?"

Don returned to *The Ed Sullivan Show* in late June. It was, once again, airing "live and in color" from Circus Circus. Don to Sullivan: "I tell you as a friend—Sylvia's leaving you." "By the way, you oughta get the teeth scraped, Ed." "Once in a while, Ed, move your body. They'll throw dirt on ya." Then to the audience: "That's his wonderful wife Sylvia. She used to be a cocktail waitress, used to hang around in San Diego by the ships going, 'Hi, Navy!'"[3]

There was another appearance on NBC's *The Kraft Music Hall*. This time around, Don cohosted with Don Adams, and they poked fun at the laid-back California lifestyle with guests Kaye Ballard, Joseph Cotten, and the Beach Boys. Shortly thereafter, Don and Phyllis Diller cohosted ABC's Saturday-night variety show *The Hollywood Palace*, where they joked about their short-lived shows in a sketch: "Two grandchildren—thirteen weeks old and already they've been canceled by ABC!" Don also dropped by groovy *Rowan & Martin's Laugh-In*, in one sketch playing a schoolteacher who deals with a problem student (*Laugh-In* trouper Arte Johnson).

"Don was famous for his relationship with Frank Sinatra, but my favorite thing was when we'd have him come to *Laugh-In*," recalled the show's creator/producer, George Schlatter. "The whole cast just attacked him. Don Rickles on *Laugh-In* was some of his best moments because he was the victim. The tables were turned. Everyone was kind of afraid of Rickles but not on *Laugh-In*. We'd have him come in, [the cast members] would do one line, and leave. Don would just stand there. It was interesting; Don could attack anybody, but when he came on our show he was vulnerable. He was helpless."

In one visit to the show, Schlatter and the writers came up with a big production number featuring Don—knowing that he would not be able to handle all the elements of the sketch, which included singing and dancing. "He had no sense of rhythm or melody or time, musically, so we put him in this production number that was very difficult and was impossible for him to do," Schlatter recalled. "We kept running clips of him blowing it. Don Rickles in a musical production number was one of my favorite things we did with him. It was impossible to feel sorry for Don—but we came close to it."[4]

In March, Don played himself in an episode of *The Mothers-in-Law*, which was in its final season on NBC with stars Kaye Ballard and Eve Arden (it ended the following month). The plot in "Show Business Is No Business" was an homage to Lucille Ball and series creator Desi Arnaz. Don, it turns out, belongs to the same lodge as Herb (Herbert Rudley) and Roger (Richard Deacon). He is in town to emcee a charity benefit for the lodge, at no charge, and spends the night at Herb and Eve's (Arden) house. "Is that all the luggage you have, Mr. Rickles?" Eve's best friend, Kaye (Ballard), asks Don. "That's right, Don got off the plane, but his luggage didn't," Herb says. Don fires back: "I have one other suit packed, but it's probably on its way to Cuba, like everything else these days." Don wants to do more than emcee the show, however—he wants to perform. The setup: Eve and Kaye vie to assist him on stage. Cue the laugh track.

Don's first comedy album, *Hello, Dummy!*, sold over 200,000 copies. Warner Bros. was pleased with those sales figures, and Don signed on to record his second album for them. *Don Rickles Speaks!* was released in February 1969. The format, this time, was different. It was not, by definition, a live album; Don was introduced by *Laugh-In* announcer Gary Owens (in his best "official" voice), and he answered seemingly innocent (and scripted) questions from a panel of inquisitors: writer

Rosalind Ross, popular Southern California DJ Dick Whittington, Pat McCormick, and Warner Bros. recording executive Joe Smith. The venue was a nightclub-type setting, and Don riffed spontaneously in answering the questions posed to him.

Over the course of the forty-minute album, Don lacerated Frank Sinatra ("He's definitely finished . . . the man's voice is gone, his looks are bad . . ."); Sammy Davis Jr. ("He's great. You can't get help like that anymore. To have a guy sing and dance and dust?"); Dean Martin ("He has no voice or humor and makes a great deal of money"); Barbra Streisand and Carol Burnett ("Between Streisand's nose and Carol's mouth, if they were put together, you could have a deadly animal on your hands"); and others, including Doris Day, Jordan's King Hussein, Ronald Reagan, and Johnny Carson. *Don Rickles Speaks!* was a hit-or-miss affair. Some of Don's ripostes fell flat; others hit their intended target. Either way, each answer was accompanied by hearty guffaws from the panelists. It could have passed for a typical Rickles performance at the Sahara.

"I believe it was a project fostered by Joe Smith," recalled Dick Whittington. "I got a call and he said, 'What we would like you to do is just sit in the studio with Don Rickles—don't do any prep—just ask him questions regarding anything, from world politics to baseball.' We met in Beverly Hills at a very small studio; I was surprised because I thought it would be over at Warner Bros., and it was just Don, myself, and the engineer, who I never saw.

"I was surprised, like so many who had seen him work," he said. "He was very subdued and very polite, not just to me but to everyone. I didn't think we would get anything going, he was that quiet, and I sat across from him in maybe a six-by-ten studio, one light between us, and I would just pepper him with questions. I had no idea what Warner Bros. had in mind, but I knew in my experience that it's not going to be Don Rickles as we know Don Rickles. But no matter what I threw at him, he came up with some very good stuff, but I was his only audience . . . At the end of the hour, he looked at me and gave me that Don Rickles side look. I don't think he was too thrilled."

Whittington recalled that the rest of the album was pieced together in similar fashion, with Don's answers from each panelist edited together into the final product. "I do not think that it was a great album, but I don't think it was his fault," he said. "Don Rickles needed an audience, he loved his audience, and the audience spurred him on. He was fascinating to watch—his eyes cast down and his lips pursed, almost going into a process, another world that he had in that marvelous brain of his, and he came up with some marvelous ad-libs. But I think, of all the work he did, that [album] was the weakest link."[5]

The forty-first Academy Awards aired on ABC on April 14. It was the first time the Oscars ceremony was held at the Dorothy Chandler Pavilion in L.A., and the first time in eleven years it did not have an official host.

Don was there, onstage with Frank Sinatra, to heckle and joke with Old Blue Eyes while Frank was presenting one of several awards he handed out that night. (Don: "I was in the back watching Burt Lancaster's chest move!") "When you get old you start to slip," he said to Sinatra. "Later on we're gonna buy a Dick Haymes album and see what's wrong with your career." Sinatra convulsed with laughter, but Don, as was his wont, did not know when to stop and proceeded to jump way over the top. When a thrilled Mel Brooks bounced onstage to accept his Oscar for writing *The Producers*, Don could not leave well enough alone. "Best of luck, Mel, he said, hugging Brooks. "Do me a favor, huh?" He did not finish the sentence. Brooks, visibly annoyed, abruptly cut him off. "You did twenty minutes," he said. "You killed my whole thing already."

The Rickles-Sinatra Oscar-night show was called "a cheap interruption convulsing only themselves—amateur night in a second-rate neighborhood,"[6] while Don was called "the evening's vulgar intruder" in reference to his Mel Brooks moment. Sinatra even took some heat in the Jewish community for cracking on the telecast that "Hadassah is plural for yenta."

Johnny Carson was now the undisputed King of Late Night as

ABC's *The Joey Bishop Show* sank deeper into the ratings morass. He was minting money at NBC and, with his newfound power, was taking a lot of vacations. In mid-May, Don guest-hosted *The Tonight Show* in Johnny's absence; Peter Lawford, Carl Reiner, and Bob Newhart had preceded him that month. After fulfilling his obligation, he took Barbara and three-year-old Mindy for a weeklong vacation at the Eden Roc in Miami Beach. In July, just days before Neil Armstrong and Buzz Aldrin touched down on the moon, Don Rickles took his own giant leap—flying to Yugoslavia for a four-month shoot on his twelfth movie. By his estimation, he was losing $500,000 in future nightclub work, but it was worth the risk for a chance at the big-screen respectability that had, thus far, mostly eluded him. He took some solace—he was booked into the Sahara for a one-week, $40,000 payday when he returned to the States.

The movie was called *The Warriors*. It was a big-budget World War II ensemble buddy comedy produced by MGM. Two of its costars, Clint Eastwood and Donald Sutherland, were hot items in Hollywood, and the studio was banking on their names to draw some attention to the film and generate some early buzz. Clint Eastwood was four years removed from his television role as Rowdy Yates on the CBS Western series *Rawhide*. The spaghetti Western phase of his career was over and he had scored two successive box-office hits with *Paint Your Wagon* and *Where Eagles Dare*. Eastwood's pal, Don Siegel, who directed him in *Two Mules for Sister Sara*—which was already in the can—was signed by MGM to helm *The Warriors*, but had to pull out of the project when he ran into post-production problems with *Two Mules*. He was replaced by relative newcomer Brian Hutton, who had directed Eastwood and Richard Burton in the World War II action flick *Where Eagles Dare*. Hutton wanted to shoot *The Warriors* in Northern California but was overruled by the studio. Thirty-four-year-old Donald Sutherland was engendering early praise for his performance as the offbeat Captain Benjamin Franklin "Hawkeye" Pierce Jr. in *M*A*S*H*, director Robert Altman's satirical take on a mobile army surgical hospital during the

Korean War. It was scheduled to premiere in 1970. *The Warriors* also counted among its cast television veterans and future CBS stars Carroll O'Connor (*All in the Family*), Gavin MacLeod (*The Mary Tyler Moore Show*), and Telly Savalas (*Kojak*).

The movie was set in France but was filmed in and around the small Yugoslavian (now Croatian) village of Viznada, since it was a US-Yugoslav coproduction and, more importantly, Yugoslavia was one of the few countries in Europe that had fully functioning World War II—era mechanical equipment (tanks, etc.), which helped for authenticity. Screenwriter Troy Kennedy Martin based the plot of *The Warriors* on a *Guinness Book of World Records* entry, "The Greatest Robbery on Record," which briefly recounted how, in 1945, during the waning days of the war, a combination of US military personnel and German civilians joined forces to rob the German National Gold Reserves in Bavaria. The Reichsbank had transported over $2 billion worth of gold and currency there as the Russian and American forces drew their noose around Berlin. Fifteen years after the movie's release, authors Ian Sayer and Douglas Botting recounted the tale in their book, *Nazi Gold: The Sensational Story of the World's Greatest Robbery—and the Greatest Criminal Cover-Up.*

Don arrived in Yugoslavia in late July and settled in as filming got underway. MGM paid for Barbara and Mindy to join him in Yugoslavia for a few weeks. Eastwood played the taciturn Kelly, a former lieutenant busted down to private after taking the blame for a botched infantry assault. He learns about the Reichsbank loot from a drunk Wehrmacht officer he's interrogating near the French town of Nancy, and hatches a plan to stage the robbery. Kelly recruits Crapgame (Don), a wisecracking supply sergeant, to "finance" the plan and collect the necessary equipment needed to break into the bank vault in the town of Claremont, behind enemy lines. "He's . . . a supply sergeant who has a fist in every pie," Don said. "He insults everyone but no one belts him. Instead, they do business with him. And in the end they like him. I knew a guy like this in the Navy."

Kelly also convinces tough-guy sergeant "Big Joe" (Savalas) to join the caper, and the plan is overheard by spaced-out tank platoon commander "Oddball" (Sutherland), who offers his services along with around twenty-seven other GIs.

The shoot was long and grueling and kept Don out of the public eye for the rest of the summer, his name mentioned only in newspaper listings of one of his old movies or television appearances. *The Warriors* was scheduled to wrap in late October, but the usual production snags and delays kept its cast in Yugoslavia until mid-December; many members of the crew remained there for another three months. Location filming took all of them throughout the country, from north of Belgrade to near the Italian border to Novi Sad and the coast south of Trieste. "I'm not going to dwell on how rough it was," Don said upon his return. "But stumbling around the woods in Yugoslavia isn't my idea of a picnic, despite the modern conveniences of an American movie outfit on location." In the movie's original script, Crapgame was killed off, but Don's performance was so strong that his part was rewritten and Crapgame was wounded but alive.

"Just waiting around for the cameras to be set up, I must have gone through enough material for four specials," Don recalled. He kept everyone on the set loose by joking around. "What do I do here?" he asked a reporter visiting the Yugoslavian location. "I sit around my hotel room and watch the moths die . . . Savalas? He sits around watching old movies and hoping he's in one of them . . . Eastwood? He sits around all day and plays with his ducks. I'm the star here." Back in L.A., Savalas settled the score when he was asked about working with Don: "I'm finally in a picture with a guy who makes me look like Paul Newman."

A recently unearthed promotional film shot during a press junket for the movie by a crew from KTRK, the ABC affiliate in Houston, shows Don joking around with Eastwood on the set and reducing his costar to gales of laughter. "Clint, we've been on the picture with you for about two days and I want to say, on behalf of the whole cast, Clint, we're fed up . . . and standing next to you I get the feeling you're a building and I'm a bad Fiat car or something . . . I read the script and you read the script and now that we've read it, let's get on a plane and go home—'cause I think it's bad."

Don to a Filipino reporter asking him about Vegas: "First of all, Joe, it's good to have you here. I thank you so much—the shirts came back just the way I asked. I'll tell you the truth, though, the brown rice you gotta work on." To a reporter from Canada: "All dummies up there. But we need Canada, so we can go across the border and stay out of the Army." To a reporter from Boston: "Boston's a lot of fun. I was there on a Sunday once and saw a truck go by."[7]

John Landis was working on the movie, as an eighteen-year-old gofer (known now as the more elegantly titled "production assistant"). The future director of *Kentucky Fried Movie*, *Animal House*, *The Twilight Zone*, and *Trading Places*—and the director/coproducer of the 2007 Emmy-winning documentary, *Mr. Warmth: The Don Rickles Project*—recalled how The Merchant of Venom kept the cast and crew in high spirits, often in very trying situations.

"I was one of the few people who knew who he was, because the Brits, the French, the Yugoslavs . . . Don Rickles, who the fuck is that?" he recalled. "He's a very American comedian. He's not known anywhere else. He was so funny. They'd do a scene and Clint would finish and Don would go, 'Brian, you gonna print that? You're gonna walk away? That's it? What, are you gonna animate over Eastwood?'"

Landis recalled how the movie's props department made a fiberglass reproduction of a 50-caliber machine gun that Don's character, Crapgame, had to carry in a scene after the men were strafed by an Allied plane. Director Brian Hutton ordered him to put the heavy reproduction in his trailer; it turned out Don really was "shlepping around" an actual 50-caliber gun, which weighed roughly three hundred pounds, Landis recalled. "In the movie you can see [Crapgame] complaining about it . . . and everyone thought that was so funny."[8]

Shortly after arriving back home in L.A., Don entered Cedars of Lebanon Hospital to undergo surgery to remove a quarter-sized metal fragment embedded in his left thigh—collateral damage from filming a battle scene during the movie. Before leaving Yugoslavia, he and Clint Eastwood bought $2,000 worth of toys and gave them out to the local youngsters. Eastwood described the standard of living there as "so low that it's unbelievable to the average American" and said that the atmosphere in the country was "quite depressing. Most people slug away and work hard every day without much hope that tomorrow's going to be any better."[9] In late January 1970, MGM announced it was changing the movie's title from *The Warriors* to *Kelly's Warriors*—and then promptly changed it again to *Kelly's Heroes* in time for its premiere in June. (Eastwood was unhappy with the title change; he felt it sounded too close to *Hogan's Heroes*, the *Stalag 17*–inspired CBS sitcom starring Bob Crane that was still on the air—and would be for another year.)

Don returned to the clubs and to his busy television schedule after recovering from his thigh surgery. In early January he opened at the Sahara with Bobby Vinton for a three-week run and was one of a handful of comics (among them Mike Nichols and Elaine May, Godfrey Cambridge, Mort Sahl, Allan Sherman, and Carol Burnett) who guest-starred in Bob Newhart's special *A Last Laugh*, which looked back at the world of comedy in the 1960s.

He performed, along with Sammy Davis. Jr., at a Democratic Party fundraiser in Miami Beach—to help the party pay off its multimillion-dollar campaign debt after losing the 1968 presidential election—and had a scare while playing the Eden Roc in early February. A fire broke out in the kitchen just as Don started his opening-night 10 p.m. show in the Pompeii Ballroom. ("That foul stuff blowing all around me had to be smoke, or I was in Los Angeles on a very bad day," he said.) No one was injured and the hotel was evacuated; Don refused to go on for the 10 p.m. show once it was deemed safe to do so. He went upstairs, retrieved Barbara, three-year-old Mindy and her nurse, and sat it out in the lobby before returning for his midnight show. It was no laughing matter; Barbara was pregnant with their second child, who was expected to arrive in the fall.

Don's act, most notably his midnight show, was getting a bit coarser. A *Miami News* columnist counted forty-three times that

Don used "that three-letter word" (it was "ass") during a show at the Eden Roc ("He's dethroned Buddy Hackett") while ripping everyone in sight: "Jews, Catholics, Arabs, Negroes, Puerto Ricans were his favorite targets."

Joe Scandore's growing stable of clients now included singer Sue Raney, who opened for Don at the Sahara, in the Borscht Belt, and in Wildwood, New Jersey. She joined him on the bill at the Eden Roc for his two-week run at the hotel.

"When I was at the Eden Roc, there was a fire in the kitchen," she recalled. "I was on stage, opening for Don of course, so he came out and tapped me on the shoulder. And the first thing that I thought of in the middle of my song, I thought, 'Is this how they tell you that you've stayed on too long?' Don said, 'I should've been up there, I could've made a big deal out of it. Why was it you?' He thought [the fire] would have been great for his type of comedy."

Raney segued from working with Don to opening for Bob Newhart. "Sometimes, I thought that the people who really loved Don, I was a little bit . . . more sensitive and soft-spoken, and I think when he started with Marilyn Michaels [as his opening act] after that, she was a little better for him than I was," she recalled. "I always thought that. I was more conducive to Bob Newhart's personality. I think that Bob and I were a better duo than were Don and I, in a way. I never really got to know Don. I really didn't. I do feel that I got to know Bob Newhart, and even when I ran into Ginny and Bob Newhart, I always felt that I knew him better than Don. I had this respect for people who were in an echelon that I was not in yet. You are not only aware of them, but you respect where they've come from and where they've been and where they've gotten to. You don't feel a camaraderie because of that respect."[10]

In late February, Don joined Don Adams and singer Edie Adams, Ernie Kovacs's widow, for a CBS special called *Hooray for Hollywood*. As its title implied, the two Dons and Edie, each a bona fide movie buff, spoofed the big-screen classics—everything from Charlie Chaplin to *Gone With the Wind* (with our Don as Rhett Butler) to recent

Oscar winner *Midnight Cowboy*. The special was shot over a six-day period, and Don Adams, who was also producing, talked Charlton Heston into narrating the proceedings (he also had to deal with CBS over script and budget issues). The two Dons, who had worked so well together on the two-part *Get Smart* episode in 1968, had a long, shared history steeped in the drudgery of the nightclub circuit. And they genuinely liked each other. "We were both playing burlesque joints in Washington, D.C., when I first met him," Adams recalled. "We went out for coffee after he caught my act. We sat down and he said, 'Don, I'm speaking as someone who doesn't know you all that well—you're rotten, kid. Take my advice and get out of the business.'" Classic Rickles.

The special aired in late February; Don played a variety of roles, Adams did his best Humphrey Bogart and Marlon Brando impersonations, and Edie Adams broke out her old impression of Marilyn Monroe (for the first time since Monroe's death nearly eight years before) and played a chorus girl in the Follies. The special aired to positive reviews. "Rickles as the High Lama in *Lost Horizon*, Rickles as an exhausted Astaire who forgets to stay on his diet and Rickles as Nelson Eddy losing Jeanette MacDonald over a cliff showed more versatility than we thought he possessed and quite stole the show."[11] Critics lauded the special's use of makeup and set design, the attention to detail, which hewed closely to the original movies spoofed throughout the hour.

Hooray for Hollywood went on to win an Emmy for Outstanding Achievement in Makeup and went a long way toward proving that Don, given the right creative material, could excel on television outside of his Merchant of Venom persona. If only the television executives could understand that. There were mitigating factors, though; when Don had played it close to the insult vest in a visit to *The Jim Nabors Hour* earlier in the year, outraged viewers inundated CBS with angry letters. Cast member Ronnie Schell recalled that Don "took our script, which bombed in rehearsal, and tore it up! Then, he came back and just fired out lines without hesitation. What a mind!" CBS officials ignored the hate mail and invited Don back for a return appearance with Jim Nabors in the fall. Meanwhile, the executives at ABC had very short memories; they were now talking about Rickles shooting another sitcom pilot, in which he would play a harried advertising executive, but shades of the disastrous *Don Rickles Show* cast a shadow over the idea . . . for now.

Don returned in March to the Copa, where he was introduced by Johnny Carson and did not take long to sling arrows at the celebrities in the audience. "You were a hit when Dane Clark was around," he barked at actor Robert Alda, and then turned on the club's tough-guy owner. "May I pay my respects to Mr. Jules Podell . . . who had great faith in me and said to me, 'You'll never work here!'" He riffed on his *Kelly's Heroes* costar Clint Eastwood—"You ever spend five months just watching flies cross his eyes?"—and turned his Mr. Warmth charm on other targets, including Jerry Vale, Phyllis Diller, Pat Henry, and Rodney Dangerfield ("Get back in your kennel!"). He brought out his valet, Harry Goins; they reminisced about how, in the old days, Don sometimes feared he would not be paid for a nightclub gig: "How we gonna get it? We're gonna roll him!"

Don and Barbara had been living in a high-rise apartment in L.A. since their marriage in 1965. Mindy was approaching her fourth birthday, and with another child on the way, Don purchased a house in Hollywood. On May 12, four days after Don turned forty-four, Barbara gave birth to a healthy six-pound, seven-ounce boy at Cedars of Lebanon Hospital. They named him Lawrence Corey.

"Rickles, to his dying day, constantly reminded me that when his son was born, I went to a sports store and bought every piece of sporting equipment you could think of. I mean, literally everything," recalled actor James Caan, who met Don through Don Adams and struck up a lifelong friendship with The Merchant of Venom. "The baseball crap, the hockey stuff . . . there were two big boxes and I handed them to him and I said, 'This is to make sure the kid grows up straight.' He never forgot it. Twenty years later he would still bring it up."[12]

Don was over the moon at the birth of his son. Flush with hap-piness (and cash), he celebrated Larry's arrival and joined Buddy Hackett, Don Adams, and Woody Allen as an investor in Kings Castle, a plush new $20 million resort/casino in Lake Tahoe. On paper, it was a solid business model; the four comics would per-form at the casino in a loose rotation, insuring big crowds and, ostensibly, bigger profits for the establishment. (Don opened an eleven-night run at Kings Castle's Camelot Theater in August.) At a press conference to discuss the business venture, Adams joked about the difficulty of traveling to the resort. "You make a nine-hour drive to a trading post where you pick up an Indian guide and a canoe. You portage the canoe over mountains and down some rapids—and, if you live, Rickles becomes your partner."[13]

Buddy Hackett, whose ego was growing to obnoxious propor-tions, said he thought that what Kings Castle needed was "three more Buddy Hacketts"—and ripped his new business partners in the press, which was not what anyone had had in mind. "None of the others can do any good here," he said. "Why? 'Cause they're not funny. The only one who has half a chance is Woody Allen." What about Don Rickles? someone asked Buddy. "He'll never be great until he makes audiences stop hating him," he said. "I can remember when I used to be a wise guy on stage, before I made people love me." Not everyone loved Buddy, especially the night that the roly-poly comic interrupted his opening act, Teresa Graves, by prancing around the Kings Castle casino stage in nothing but a G-string. Graves called in sick the next night.

Buddy Hackett was wrong—none of the comics made a differ-ence in the fortunes of Kings Castle. In the fall, Don applied to the state of Nevada to license him as a part owner of the resort with a 1.6 percent stake. But the big guns of comedy could not move the hotel's needle into the black. Its promotional department did what it could, including launching an "Insult Don Rickles" contest in which peo-ple mailed in their insults leveled at The Merchant of Venom. Susan Reynolds from Taos, New Mexico, won the grand prize: "Dear Don,

I despise myself and have absolutely no regard for myself as a person. Marry me!" She was flown to Lake Tahoe to see Don perform and to meet him afterward. "I'd really like to take you up on your offer to marry you," he said to her, "but I have a low tolerance for boredom." "Does that mean you never rehearse your act?" she snapped back. (At least that was the "official" version.)

Don lost a chunk of money when Kings Castle shut down two years later, in 1972, a victim of poor planning, internal issues, and labor problems. It briefly reopened in 1974, then was sold off, in 1975, to Hyatt, which still runs the Hyatt Regency at Incline-Village (as it is now called).

Kelly's Heroes opened in late June. It was a crowded field that year in the big-screen war genre; *M*A*S*H* (January), *Patton* (February), *Catch-22* (June), and *Tora! Tora! Tora!* (September) all premiered in 1970 and all trod different contextual ground. Critical reception for *Kelly's Heroes*, and for Don's performance, was mixed. By its third week in release, though, the movie had passed the $1 million mark in box-office receipts, no mean feat when the average ticket price to see a movie was $1.55. The *New York Daily News* called *Kelly's Heroes* "a noisy World War II contrived comedy" but singled out Don, as Crapgame, for providing "his own brand of insult humor to comic effect . . . By punctuating his film with continued bombings and skirmishes, director Brian Hutton has insured himself a wide-awake audience, even though the war theme is tiresome."[14]

"*Kelly's Heroes* is hereby nominated as the dumb-dumb movie of the year," the *Philadelphia Daily News* critic thought. "It's a confused and confusing action comedy that has all the symptoms of a bad case of 'box office fever' . . . Savalas is always a lot of fun to watch in action and Rickles generates some laughs with unused portions of his nightclub act."[15] Other critics weighed in with various degrees of harshness. The *Pittsburgh Press* critic opined that "Rickles and Savalas make up for what Clint Eastwood lacks in acting ability; they're both great and provide a number of laughs." The *New York Times*, which, up to this point, had provided scant coverage of his career, published a photo of Don and Clint Eastwood in a scene from *Kelly's Heroes* to accompany its review, which reduced Don's contribution to "samples of stand-up comedy." The *Cincinnati Enquirer* scolded the movie for an unlikely scenario "that bears any semblance to the truth . . ."

When all was said and done, *Kelly's Heroes* grossed a modest $5.2 million in the US and turned a $1.2 million profit for MGM. It clocked in as the year's thirty-third highest-grossing movie, right behind John Wayne's *Chisum*.

Kelly's Heroes was not the "big break" movie for which Don had hoped, and he knew that, as he entered middle age, the window was slamming shut on any chance he had to forge a second career as a serious actor. If it had not happened by now, it never would—and it never did . . . at least not in a way he could have imagined as the new decade kicked into gear.

Money was not part of the equation. Don was a millionaire now, with a tasteful house in Hollywood (nothing too garish) and a steady income from his nightclub work. He drove a Rolls-Royce. He was one of the highest-paid entertainers in Las Vegas and in Miami Beach; one unnamed hotel in Vegas reportedly offered him an eight-year deal: $100,000 a week for ten weeks a year, or $8 million in total over the ten years. He continued to tour the country, with stops including the Westbury Music Fair on Long Island (where he grossed $135,000 over six nights in September), the Latin Casino in Philadelphia, and north of the border in Montreal and Quebec.

Johnny Carson's NBC Orchestra had started playing Don's entrances onto *The Tonight Show* stage with "*La Virgen de la Macarena*," "The Bullfighter's Song" in English, which he adopted as his introductory theme music for his live shows. Not everyone appreciated the ironic bravado. For every rave about Don's act, there was a naysayer who thought that his insults and his treacly "Can't we all just get along" talk was growing moldy around the edges. The times they were a-changing: the Black Power and Women's Liberation movements were gaining momentum . . . and Don's critics were vocal in their disdain for his act.

"The only minority group Don Rickles fails to insult is that of aging, sweaty comics whose material has worn thin thru overuse," wrote one Chicago critic, reviewing Don's weeklong run at the Mill Run Playhouse. "It's hard to figure out why Rickles is so popular, except to use one of his dummy-from-the-audience comments: 'I don't know what he's doing, but look at his crowd!' . . . Always, between insults, he slips in his justifying message: 'We got to love one another, gang! It's all part of life' . . . His audience is in the mood for blood and would be more interested in seeing dancing bears or a race riot as a warm-up for the Confrontation."[16] The critics be damned; Don earned $90,000 for his efforts.

Singer/comedian Marilyn Michaels, who had starred in the national touring company of Funny Girl, opened for Don at the Mill Run Playhouse. She was a recent addition to Joe Scandore's client list, and he teamed Marilyn and Don in venues around the country, including the Sahara. "Joe Scandore saw me perform. He was a very sweet kind of godfather," Michaels recalled. "He decided to use me as an opening act for Don. It was kind of good at that time because it was going to be in Las Vegas and he decided he would handle me. They didn't pay me very much. I did very well, and I was not doing a lot of comedy at the time—mostly improvisation and thinking on my feet, which was okay, because all of the comics that I worked with were the most insecure people in the world. They would breathe down your neck to see if you were getting laughs, and if you were getting laughs at something they did, you had to take it out.

"I was doing mainly singing and vocal impressions of the famous ladies. I was the perfect act for Don. Every time he was in Vegas, I was always there. Don called me 'Tina Robin.' Let me explain what that means. Tina Robin was an attractive little girl singer, who sang well, a little blonde person who then disappeared. So no one wanted to be called Tina Robin. He knew I wasn't that. But he knew just what to say to be annoying, you know?"[17]

Don was keenly aware of his critics, and he tried to play to both sides of the aisle, ramping up his "I'm a nice guy" and "Can't we all just get along?" shtick at the end of each show. That often failed to do the trick, even for longtime Rickles fans and admirers, including syndicated columnist Harvey Pack. "I recently caught Don Rickles' act in Las Vegas and I think Mr. Warmth—one of my favorite entertainers—has gone overboard with his finale apology for all his barbs," he wrote. "The cop-out is not a put-on, for Rickles, basically a shy and gentle man, does it because—like all comedians—he wants to be loved . . . Once he has told you he's sorry and please love him . . . how can he possibly expect people to laugh at the next insult?"[18]

Noted comic book and television writer Mark Evanier, who entered Don's outer orbit in 1971, caught his act at the Sahara around this time and was put off by the ways in which The Merchant of Venom went out of his way to prove he was a nice guy—and how it struck a disingenuous chord with him. "It was the dinner show at the Sahara Hotel and he had a girl singer opening for him who I never heard of before or after," he recalled. "He came out and he spent the whole act doing two things: he did impressions of Jimmy Cagney singing *Yankee Doodle Dandy*, and he lectured the audience about how they didn't appreciate Frank Sinatra enough.

"It was on and on about how, 'You people who aren't in show business cannot possibly understand what a great man Frank Sinatra is' and I'm turning to my friend saying, 'Did Frank Sinatra cure cancer?' There were no Rickles insults that night. At one point he was standing on the stage and he looked over and there's an older Black man standing in the wings with a pitcher of ice water. He goes, 'Oh my God, this is my dresser! What are you doing here, Harry?' And Harry said, 'Oh, Mr. Rickles, I saw how hard you were working to entertain this audience and I thought you might need a glass of ice water.' And Rickles was all broken up, like he didn't expect this. And he goes over and hugs Harry and asked everyone to thank Harry, and I remember thinking, 'Harry is standing there with a pitcher of ice water and no glass and he left without giving Rickles any water.' It was this little moment of what a great guy Don Rickles was and that an old Black guy loved him and it was schmaltz and it was so phony. I thought it was just awful."[19]

Don was scorched for his "anachronistic vulgarisms" by *San Francisco Examiner* critic Philip Elwood, who caught Don's show at the Circle Star Theater in San Carlos (he shared the bill with crooner Jerry Vale). "His rib-ticklers about 'colored folks' and 'Japs' and 'Polacks' are just what every bigot in America must love to hear. And his comments about the Roman Catholics and Mexicans and Puerto Ricans and Jews must leave some people positively limp from laughing. 'I laugh at our heritage and I'm proud of it,' is a typical Rickles cop-out. Like others of his trade who have confused disgraceful insults with well-turned satire, Rickles pretends that because he is Jewish he can be offensive about his own . . . He is a distressingly unorganized, nervous and gropingly repetitive monologist who even brings a Black lackey [*author's note: Harry Goins*] onto the stage (while shouting 'Water Boy!') and insults him with blatantly racist and condescending remarks in the name of 'good fun.'"

Ed Sullivan, who was spending more time in Las Vegas now that his namesake television show was history (CBS canceled *The Ed Sullivan Show* in 1971), reported in his column that Don was pulling down $65,000 a week in Vegas, putting him in the same Sin City earnings league as Sammy Davis Jr., Danny Thomas, Wayne Newton, and Leslie Caron. There were rumors that Don would not renew his long-standing contract with the Sahara when it expired in the spring—and that he would be scooped up by a competitor (translation: to be paid a lot more). He reportedly asked the Sahara for a raise to $100,000 a week and was turned down.

In April 1971, Don defected to the Riviera Hotel on South Las Vegas Boulevard, signing a four-year, multimillion-dollar contract to start there in December. He would earn $80,000 a week under the new deal[20]—not the $100,000 he had hoped for but a nice raise from the $65,000 a week he was currently pulling down at the Sahara.

Don headed into the fall to finish his twelve-year association with the hotel that had put him on the Las Vegas showbiz map and burnished his name into the city's lore. In early November, he gave his final performance at the Sahara, in the Congo Room. Ed Sullivan in the *New York Daily News*[21]: "The night was unforgettable. Rickles, really a warm person, experienced mixed emotions leaving the Sahara, because he started in the Lounge as an unknown and left as a superstar. He switches to Vegas Riviera Dec. 9. Buddy Hackett, who followed Rickles into Congo Room, was a smash hit." Sullivan was off by one day; Don followed Dean Martin at the Riviera and opened for a six-night run on December 10.

CHAPTER 14

The television exposure once so elusive to Don Rickles was a faint memory now. He was always welcomed by Johnny Carson, Merv Griffin, and Mike Douglas, and when *The Joey Bishop Show* went belly-up in late 1969, he segued flawlessly onto *The Dick Cavett Show*, Joey's late-night successor on ABC. There were visits to *The Glen Campbell Goodtime Hour*, *The Sonny and Cher Comedy Hour*, *The Flip Wilson Show*, *The Carol Burnett Show*, and more *Kraft Music Hall* appearances on NBC, including a special called *Locker-Room Follies*, a sports-themed hour with boxer Joe Frazier, baseball players Tony Conigliaro and Boog Powell, NFL star Alex Karras, and New York Rangers star Vic Hadfield. His frenzied guest-starring sitcom spree of the mid-to-late sixties was not necessary anymore, and his guest shots on *The Hollywood Squares* and other daytime and early evening game shows were drawing to a close. He was a late-night and prime-time performer now.

In September, he hosted an ABC comedy special, *The Many Sides of Don Rickles*, with guests Harvey Korman, Don Adams, and Robert Goulet, and followed that with a return to *Laugh-In*. He was the brunt of yet another Friars Roast, which aired on *The Kraft Music Hall* on NBC and was emceed by Johnny Carson. (Roaster Dick Cavett: "You really have come a long way since those days as a paperhanger in Munich.") Don was roasted so many times he could be forgiven if he felt charred.

There was talk . . . again . . . of Don playing an advertising executive in a sitcom pilot. ABC was no longer interested in the idea, but CBS was in the game. Television veterans Sheldon Leonard and Sam

Denoff, who between them produced hits including *The Dick Van Dyke Show*, *The Danny Thomas Show*, *The Andy Griffith Show*, and *That Girl*, were attached to the project. Denoff wrote the pilot script, which would be shot on the Paramount lot.

Denoff and his longtime writing collaborator, Bill Persky, knew Don from back in the Elegante days, when they were on the staff of New York radio station WNEW writing jokes for local comics. "It was owned by the mob, as most nightclubs were," Denoff recalled about the Elegante. "But there was a graveyard next door. So any time you would write for a comic you would go there and they would sit you next to the comic's manager who was also a wiseguy, and he'd say, 'I think this needs some fixing.'"[1]

Details on the nascent sitcom were vague. In December, Louise Sorel was signed to play Don's on-screen wife. Sorel, a Broadway veteran (*Take Her, She's Mine*, starring Art Carney, and the short-lived *Man and Boy*, starring Charles Boyer), was fourteen years younger than Don. Singer Vicki Carr reportedly turned the role down; Janis Hansen, who was later to play Gloria, the ex-wife of Felix Unger (Tony Randall), on *The Odd Couple*, auditioned but did not get the part—nor did Marilyn Michaels, Don's opening act in Vegas and points in-between.

"I remember that I had a terrible cold sore on my lip. Don was going to have his own series and I was Joe Scandore's client. So they were, for sure, going to get me in there to be one of the six gals who was auditioning for Sheldon Leonard," she recalled. "It was a scene with his wife, and I wore this beautiful negligee and I was twenty pounds lighter. I was young. But I was wondering how I was going to cover up the damn cold sore. I've never said this to anyone else before, but I found that Don was attracted to me. It's not anything he said, but you feel these things. I felt it like crazy. But he was married and didn't go there. And when I played the part of his wife, at the end of the scene, with the other actresses he would go and embrace them, but with me, they just stopped it. And I realized that he didn't feel comfortable going there because he maybe wanted to go there."[2]

Joe Scandore himself "wanted to go there" with Marilyn, and made a half-hearted attempt at a tryst. Don's success had made Joe a wealthy man, and he bought a large ranch house in the L.A. suburb of Chatsworth, in the San Fernando Valley. "I stayed there with Joe Scandore and they had horses and everything," Marilyn Michaels recalled. "It was quite an interesting setup there, because I never messed with anybody that I worked with and this followed through with anybody at all.

"Joe had two mistresses and they both had the same name, let's say 'Big Linda' and 'Little Linda'—they were beautiful, and one was petite and the other was, you know, a bigger gal. She was staying in the house there, and I had my own room, too, but nobody messed with me. I was the opening act and you didn't mess with me. And . . . I think Joe was handling Pat Morita. His wife was the housekeeper of this big ranch where I stayed. Anytime I did *The Tonight Show* or something, I would stay at the ranch.

"I remember one time Joe came into my room and he was sitting on the bed and he sort of, in a very gentle manner, propositioned me. I mean, why not add something to the mix, you know? I told him 'No, you have enough to tide you over,' so that was it."

(Don spent some time at the Chatsworth ranch and, as a gift, bought a horse and a saddle that were delivered to Scandore there. He included a note: "I'd have sent this sooner, but I had trouble finding a horse that resembled you.")

Don was always available to the press—Joe Scandore and Don's publicist, Gene Shefrin (Paul's father), saw to that—and he was good for a quick zinger or a pithy line, those two best friends of a busy showbiz columnist or entertainment writer on deadline. It is a good bet that many of those lines and zingers were dreamt up by Shefrin or by Joe Scandore—anything to keep their client's name in circulation.

The Merchant of Venom persona was so ingrained into pop culture that Don Rickles, or a reasonable facsimile thereof, entered the

DC Comics universe, where he was supposed to meet—and, yes, insult—Superman. That never happened—cue Maxwell Smart's "Missed it by *that* much"—but, in 1971, Don and his comic book alter-ego, Goody Rickels (purposely spelled differently), were featured in two issues of *Superman's Pal, The New Jimmy Olsen*. The resulting story line sprung from the fertile mind of legendary comic book artist/writer/editor Jack Kirby.

The idea to feature Don in the comic book had been brought to Kirby by his assistants, Mark Evanier and Steve Sherman. "I'd seen Rickles a couple of times in Vegas, though I never met the man," Evanier recalled. "Rickles used this line, 'I never pick on the little guy, I only pick on the big guys,' and we were doing the Jimmy Olsen comic book for Jack, and he was asking us to come up with ideas for it.

"Steve and I thought, 'Wouldn't it be funny if Don Rickles insults Superman?' We wrote a page of Don Rickles insults for Superman and Jack loved them. Jack was a fan of Don Rickles. There are places on the Internet that will tell you that Don and Jack were friends, that they were neighbors. That was not true. They never met and they didn't live anywhere near each other."[3]

Kirby told Evanier and Sherman to get permission from the Rickles camp to use Don's name and likeness in the comic book, so they drove to Gene Shefrin's office and explained to him what they had in mind. "He said, 'Fine,' and gave us a letter giving us permission to do it," Evanier said. "It was going to be two pages, tops, a little cameo . . . but when Jack told DC Comics what he was doing, the publicist, who was the kind of publicist who couldn't get the president's name in the newspaper, said, 'This is great—why don't you make it two issues and we'll put him on the cover?' They somehow had it in their heads that they would do this and . . . that Rickles would take [the comic books] on *The Johnny Carson Show* and show them off, and that would be great publicity—which was never going to happen.

"So Jack came up with this story. Steve and I had very little to do with the comic itself; we actually wrote some of the sequences that did not involve Don Rickles or Goody Rickels. And Jack wrote these two issues and we put Don Rickles on the cover. Gene Shefrin gave us a pile of publicity photos of Don and we used those photos on the covers. The reaction was amazing—some people hated them and some people thought they were the funniest, greatest comics ever done . . . The Jimmy Olsen comic had been very dormant. Sales were plunging; it was a stupid comic that nobody liked, and Jack was trying to throw everything into it to make it get attention—and it got attention."

The Don Rickles/Goody Rickels story line played out in Issues #139 and #141 of *Superman's Pal, The New Jimmy Olsen*, which were published in May and July of 1971. (Issue #140, sandwiched in-between, was a reprint of old Jimmy Olsen stories.)

In the world of *Superman's Pal*, Don and Goody were not related, but they looked remarkably alike. Goody wore granny glasses and his patter was similar to Don's wiseass style ("And you! You Hockey-Puck! Can't you read signs? They say 'No Smoking in this car.' I can smell you, man!") Don was Don—or as close as Jack Kirby could get in conjuring up insults for Mr. Warmth: "Get off me, you runaway locomotive! Go out and sit on the Chicago Bears!" In one panel, Don eyes a pretty secretary and barks out "Get yourself a bikini and start a chain of heart attacks at a garden party!" The lines were not half-bad.

"Don was in the stories also, he played himself, and oddly enough Jack never got around to having Don Rickles meet Superman," Mark Evanier recalled. "There is no point in the two issues where Don Rickles met Superman and insulted him the way we had intended him to. There's something very appealing to some of us about Jack Kirby wildly improvising and free-associating and it doesn't always have to make sense . . . so the stories have a kinetic energy to them. They don't make a lot of sense, but we're talking about superhero comics—they don't *make* a lot of sense—so the stories are, to this day, controversial."

Don was not the first celebrity to be featured in the world of DC Comics. The precedent dated back to 1950 and Bob Hope (his comic book series ran for eighteen years), Jackie Gleason (for *The Honey-mooners*), Jerry Lewis, and for a brief time, Phil Silvers (for his Sgt. Ernie Bilko character from *The Phil Silvers Show*). "I think Jack had it in his mind that, 'Well, maybe it will do so well that we'll do a Rickles comic, that Goody Rickels would be a character, that they would license the right to do this from Don, but that Goody Rickels could be more malleable and change," Evanier said. "Instead of depicting Rickles the nightclub comedian, the guy who plays Vegas, he could make him into a funny superhero who talked like Don Rickles. It was easier that way."

The real Don Rickles was not pleased with the end result. "There was an episode of Conan O'Brien's show where Rickles was a guest and Conan pulled these comics out and asked him about it and he said, 'Put that away! I had nothing to do with that,'" Evanier recalled. "I gather he was not pleased by it, like, 'We okayed a little cameo with Superman and all of the sudden I'm on the cover of two issues.'"

Don shot the pilot for his CBS sitcom in January 1971. If the network liked what it saw, it would order a series. (Norman Lear's "new and controversial satire," *All in the Family*, which premiered that month on CBS, had been judged a "maybe" to make it to the fall.) In April, while Don was headlining at the Copa, CBS made it official—the still-unnamed comedy would start shooting in October as a midseason replacement premiering in January 1972.

CBS president Robert Wood showed good faith (and a sense of humor) when he came to Don's opening at the Copa, where he was duly insulted by his newest employee. "He's here trying to figure out how he got the job," Don barked at Wood. "He's the fellow who said *Hee Haw* was funny." Wood, to his benefit, sucked it up and returned for closing night. "Nice of you to be here," Don shouted at him. "I know how busy you are—trying to find out whether you're still president." Don did not let Wood forget about his previous series debacle on ABC. "I was on TV once but unfortunately my show failed, because we had other shows against us." Yikes. He was a bit more reflective shortly thereafter in talking with a reporter about the ABC flop. "Nobody knew what the format was until we actually started to tape it," he said. "It was nobody's fault, but it just didn't work."[4] Perhaps this time his luck would change.

Don was in top form during his two-week run at the Copa. He sold out every night to the delight of owner Jules Podell and lobbed a steady arsenal of zingers at the stars who turned up to be insulted—including Victor Borge, Shelley Winters, Morty Gunty, Corbett Monica ("He's the guy who runs in front of Joey Bishop's car to make sure there are no road mines"), and Ed Sullivan, still mourning the loss of his beloved variety show after twenty-four seasons. Don did not care about that. "You had to go off the air just when I got a dog act!" he said to Sullivan, who was sitting with his wife, Sylvia. They had to leave early, Don explained to his audience, "because Sylvia's jewelry is turning brown." Ed loved it; he jumped up on the Copa stage, embraced Don, and beamed.[5] He had a sense of humor, after all.

Don was riding high with the new television show, and in June, he sent his loyal and hard-working manager, Joe Scandore, a notarized letter naming him "My personal manager for the rest of our lives." They had been together for fifteen years, through thick and thin, tied to each other without a contract. Now it was time to make it official. "I remember Joe saying at one time . . . he was talking about Don and Don was so very successful at the time . . . he said, 'We have to be careful, and we have to make the right choices, because you never know when they will stop laughing,'" Marilyn Michaels recalled. "I remember Joe telling me that. They always lived in fear that it would all vanish."[6] There were a few hiccups for the Rickles-Scandore team along the way—Don's stuck-in-neutral movie career and the ABC disaster chief among them—but, overall, they had a solid showbiz batting average.

If only they could hit the curveballs that would be thrown at them in the coming months. Don opened for a short run at Kings Castle in

Reno in July. He was playing tennis there one morning when he rup-
tured his right Achilles tendon and crumpled to the court in agony.
His remaining Kings Castle gigs were canceled—Robert Goulet and
Bob Melvin were recruited as last-minute substitutes—and Don
returned home to L.A., where he underwent surgery and remained
hospitalized for a few days. Johnny Unitas, the famed Baltimore Colts
quarterback, had suffered a similar injury playing paddle tennis three
months earlier. He sent Don a note: "It couldn't have happened to a
nicer heel."

The peripatetic Mr. Warmth was ordered to stay off his feet for
six to eight weeks, and he returned home from the hospital wearing
a hip-to-toe cast that weighed forty pounds. He could not perform,
obviously, but while he recuperated quietly at home, the August
issue of *Golf Digest* magazine hit the newsstands. Within its covers was an interview with Don, who was a decent golfer, and who
did not disappoint his fans in lambasting the golfing greats. "They
ought to put a cord on his backside and make him a cannon," he said
of Jack Nicklaus (the imagery was priceless). "His idea of fun is to
sit home on Saturday night with a glass of hot cocoa singing Ohio
State fight songs." He also took a chip shot at Arnold Palmer: "He
is fantastic if you like to see a guy try on slacks all day. I call him
Harry Hitch. I can't figure out whether he's looking for his belt or
has trouble finding pants that fit."

Joe Scandore added the title of executive producer of Don's fledgling
sitcom, which began taping in November at CBS Television City in
Hollywood. The network was calling the new series . . . wait for
it . . . *The Don Rickles Show*, its ABC predecessor be damned. In January, it would join the CBS prime-time lineup along with *The Sonny and
Cher Comedy Hour*, coming off a strong summer run, and the unfortunately titled sitcom *Me and the Chimp*, starring Ted Bessell from *That
Girl*. The three midseason entries were replacing *The Bearcats*, *Chicago
Teddy Bears*, and *Funny Face*, a promising new series starring Sandy

Duncan that discontinued production when she underwent surgery to have a tumor removed (leaving her blind in her left eye). Duncan did return to CBS, in the fall of 1972, with *The Sandy Duncan Show*. It lasted half a season.

The Don Rickles Show posited the wiseass celebrity slayer from Queens as homogenized everyman Don Robinson, an advertising executive who lived on Long Island (in Great Neck) with his wife, Barbara (Louise Sorel), and their young daughter, Janie, played by eleven-year-old Erin Moran, who two years later found stardom playing kid sister Joanie Cunningham on *Happy Days*, opposite Ron Howard and Henry Winkler. *The Don Rickles Show*'s supporting cast featured Robert Hogan, Joyce Van Patten, Barry Gordon, and Judith Cassmore.

In *The Don Rickles Show* 2.0, the star would not be dishing out the insults and barbs but was at the receiving end of life's slings and arrows, both at home and in the Manhattan office of his advertising agency, Kingston, Cohen and Vanderpool. He was the underdog . . . which early on was cause for alarm. Don talked up his new series in the months leading into the January premiere. "It will show the human side that I have when I'm home," he said in one interview. "You know, when I get up in the morning I don't get up and say 'Shut up! Isn't that a funny line?' Our message is, 'Hey, don't pick on the little guy.' I'll take a great deal of abuse, which is a switch, and sympathy is on my side for a change."[7] Don Rickles as a toothless pit bull was not an appetizing course on prime-time's menu.

CBS knew all about Don's previous series but was willing to gamble that it would be different this time around. Network president Bob Wood was a Don Rickles fan dating back to the late 1950s and early 1960s, when he was the station manager of CBS affiliate KNXT in L.A. He saw Don perform at the Slate Brothers Club on North La Cienega many times, and when Sheldon Leonard signed a deal with CBS in 1970 to develop programming for the network, Wood made sure everyone knew how he felt about The Merchant of Venom. "I had a meeting with the CBS executives to discuss some ideas, when somebody said, rather wistfully, 'We wish you could come up with something for Don Rickles,'" Leonard recalled. He said he was "astounded" at the suggestion until he was apprised of Wood's infatuation with Don. "You don't argue with network presidents' tastes in comics, so I asked them what they had considered as a format for Don before that." Leonard recalled, "They said they had investigated everything, but it turned out that all the ideas had been some form of a variety show. I said, 'But that's all wrong. You can't channel that nightclub caricature into a TV series. You have to capture what Don does best—the shriveling invective, the spontaneous combustion—into a kind of Donald Duck fury against the things that bug all of us.'"[8]

So what happened?

The Don Rickles Show taped on Stage 19 at CBS Studio Center. In November, two months before the premiere, Don was sitting backstage with Joe Scandore, Sheldon Leonard, director Hy Averback, and several others when Ralph Edwards walked up with his big blue book to tell Don he was about to get the *This Is Your Life* treatment. For once, The Merchant of Venom was speechless.

Edwards was hosting a new syndicated version of *This Is Your Life*, which followed the blueprint of its long-in-the-tooth predecessor by surprising famous personalities (entertainers, cultural figures) with on-air reunions and sentimental reminiscences from people in their lives. A studio audience watched it all unfold. There were tears. *This Is Your Life* had started on NBC radio in 1948 (with Edwards hosting) and moved to television four years later, airing through 1961. Edwards had inside help in setting up his marks in order to keep the element of surprise from the honoree. Joe Scandore, Hy Averback, et al. had known that Edwards was lurking just outside of the room. Don was completely in the dark. He was wearing an orange sports shirt and a white baseball cap to read through a scene from *The Don Rickles Show*.

"Don Rickles, I know you're supposed to be rehearsing your script for your new television show," Edwards announced. "But I have here a script you've been rehearsing for all your life—as a matter of fact, you have the leading role in it . . . because, Don Rickles, *This Is Your Life!*"

Don had time to change before the cameras rolled again, and he returned in a suit with a wide tie and sporting a bad comb-over. He was greeted with hearty applause from the studio audience. Ralph Edwards escorted him onto the stage, such as it was, where he sat at a small round table adorned with a blue tablecloth. For the next twenty minutes or so, Don was greeted by Don Adams, Joe Scandore, Jack Carter, Jan Murray, Dick Martin, Red Buttons, Milton Berle, Ricardo Montalban, Danny Thomas, Ed Sullivan, his shy wife Barbara ("Mrs. Warmth" as Edwards called her), Carroll O'Connor, Kirk Douglas, and of course, Etta Rickles (who was on tape from Florida). They each paid their respects and took some benign (badly scripted) digs at the Man of the Hour. The comments from Milton Berle, Ricardo Montalban, Danny Thomas, and Etta Rickles did not make it into the telecast when it aired two months later in the run-up to the premiere of *The Don Rickles Show*. As Don recalled it, Etta said, "Don, dear, I have chopped liver waiting on the table for you, Ralph Edwards, and all your friends."[9] That sounds about right.

The rest of the fall was devoted to taping *The Don Rickles Show* and to a return to Vegas, where Don opened at the Riviera, in the Versailles Room. He was brought on stage by Dean Martin, who had preceded him at the Riviera (and who owned a piece of the hotel). "Introducing Rickles is the low point of my career," he told the audience. "However, I'll say this for Don. He likes pets. I often see him out walking his rat."[10]

An air of defeat permeated the atmosphere on Stage 19 at CBS as *The Don Rickles Show* was taping. The show was not very funny and Don was unconvincing as a put-upon schlemiel. "I remember there was a smell of 'This is never going to go' on the set," recalled Mark Evanier, who was in the studio audience for a taping of an episode.

"Sheldon Leonard did the warm-up himself, and he was basically threatening us, gangster-style: 'If you people don't give us an audible response, there's no point in bringing you in here, because it's expensive.' It was like, 'Laugh, or I'll throw you out.' Rickles did not look like a happy camper."[11]

Sam Denoff, who created the series, acknowledged the uphill climb in transforming Don Rickles from an insult comic into an everyman/family man, albeit with a slight edge, for whom America could root week after week. "Trying to sell Don Rickles as a regular person was not easy," he recalled. "With that image he had, it was crazy—but there was no more dedicated and diligent an actor and he was sweet to everybody on the set, and so careful about [hurting someone's] feelings and all that."[12]

TV Guide sent a reporter to the set of *The Don Rickles Show* to spend some time with its star, Joe Scandore, Hy Averback, Sheldon Leonard, and the other cast and crew members as they prepared for the show's premiere. The accompanying four-page article, "Mr. Warmth Spreads a Little Joy Around: A Few Venomous Days with Don Rickles," featured a photograph of Don lying on a couch with his head propped up by a pillow—looking exhausted, annoyed, and bored. The words that followed did not paint a flattering picture of life on the set.

"Between takes and in story conferences the old Rickles continues to snarl, hurl invective, utter exotic curses and indulge in wild, stream-of-consciousness slander. With his small, once-fat body bouncing up and down like an evil gnome's, he does brilliant bits of impromptu pantomime and outrageous but accurate impersonations of other stars." Don, the article noted, insulted his costars and even that week's guest star, Mary Jane Croft ("You're an old lady, Mary. I don't want you around me. You're starting to mildew."). When Robert Hogan, who played Don Robinson's friend Tyler Benedict, asked Hy Averback a question about a scene, Don snarled at him: "Your job is not to interview the director. Your job is to say your lines, wash up, collect your money and get out." During a story conference, Don turned to script consultant Richard Baer. "This is one show where I can't contribute," he said. "I only deal in humor and I can't find any here."[13]

In many of the print interviews he did to promote the show, Don was frequently lying on that same backstage couch featured in the *TV Guide* photograph, with his head resting on a pillow. "Writers never forget that other flop," he said to one interviewer, referring to the 1967 version of *The Don Rickles Show*. "It was a farce. We went on the air without a format to speak of, and tried to work something out as we went along." This time, he said, "There's been plenty of time to build a well-planned story line for me . . . You won't be seeing the aggressive, crazy-go-lucky guy I appear to be on stage. Occasionally, the Don Rickles sense of humor will shine through, but softened down a bit."[14]

That proved to be the show's main problem during its short run. Deconstructing Don's abrasive nightclub persona and repurposing him as harried suburban dad Don Robinson—"an advertising executive and family man who fights a continuing battle against the annoyances, frustrations and aggravations that plague the average American man"—was a huge misfire. "The guy in Kansas doesn't want to tune in and see me playing Hitler's kid," he reasoned. "If people believed my reputation, they expect me to be walking around with a machine gun under my arm."[15] But his image was too strong to overcome within the framework of a twenty-two-minute television sitcom embellished with all the usual tired bells and whistles. He never did find that happy medium as the star of a scripted prime-time series.

Publicly, Don said all the right things about his new series—what else could he do?—but he emanated a sense of gloom as he patiently answered the same old questions about his checkered television career. "I hope the public will have the predicament of deciding who is the real Don Rickles—the guy in the show or the guy in the nightclub," he told reporters gathered for a press conference in Las Vegas. "I think it's my personality that's going to make or break this show," he told another reporter. "People will say either

'Hooray' or 'Let's watch a different parade.'" Those are not the words of a confident man.

He pointed out to anyone listening that the role of Don Robinson was the first time that Don Rickles ever showed emotion to a woman on a screen either big or small . . . and, as he neared his forty-sixth birthday, he vented his disappointment at not succeeding as a movie actor—while flogging *The Don Rickles Show.* "My image is so strong that it's hard to cast me," he said. "Producers just can't see me as anything else . . . They're not willing to help me break the image . . . But I want people to be able to say, 'Look, Don Rickles can cry.' We're all just human people." Therein lay the rub.

The Don Rickles Show premiered on Friday, January 14, 1972, at 10:30 p.m., an unenviable time slot on the week's least-watched night of television. (Don: "Ten-thirty is the time they'd pick for a sneak attack on Pearl Harbor. It's the time when TV antennas wrap themselves up and fold up in the house.") Don's close friend and CBS stablemate, *All in the Family* star Carroll O'Connor, sent him a wire on opening night: "Being rated second didn't hurt Avis."

That same night, across the dial, NBC launched its new sitcom *Sanford and Son*, starring Redd Foxx as a junkman living with his son in the L.A. neighborhood of Watts, which had been rocked by race riots in 1965. It was symmetric poetry, television style: Don Rickles, the comedian who came of age at the Slate Brothers Club, and Redd Foxx, who fought his way up the stand-up comic food chain on the segregated Chitlin' Circuit and bought the Slate Brothers Club a decade later, renaming it Redd's Place. Don and Redd came from distinctly different ethnic, racial, geographic, and comedic backgrounds. And now here they were, each headlining a network television sitcom seen by millions of viewers.

That is where any similarities, poetic or otherwise, skidded to a halt. *Sanford and Son* grew in popularity and shot to the top of the television heap, battling *All in the Family* for ratings supremacy and transforming Redd Foxx into a major star. *The Don Rickles Show* opened with a whimper—and limped along with no momentum whatsoever.

The opening-night reviews were not all doom and gloom. In *The Don Rickles Show* premiere, written by Arthur Julian, Don Robinson suffers a case of nervous tension while shilling Moo Cow Milk for his ad agency. That, in turn, leads his wife, Barbara, to reminisce—cue the flashback scene—to a decade before, when Don suffers a bout of nerves before a big job interview just as she is about to give birth to their daughter, Janie. That, in turn, triggers a cascade of catastrophic hijinks when Don has an allergic reaction to a pill—and has to drive Barbara to the hospital. He ends up with his leg broken and his pride wounded.

"Rickles in this series is neither the insult comic of his professional act nor the sobbing sentimentalist of his talk-show appearances," read one of the kinder reviews. "He is a bit of both and almost plausible as a middle-aged family man [with a rather young wife] who is driven up the wall by such irritations as crooked auto mechanics but who does not hesitate to strike back."[16] "It was far from great but it was not lousy," Don's hometown paper, the *New York Daily News*, offered as a backhanded compliment. "Rickles is a very funny man, talented in heaping abuse on everybody and everything. But trying to make him a family man in a situation comedy is a problem."[17] The reviewer pointed out that Don was, on the night of his show's premiere, also a guest on the CBS special *The Entertainer of the Year Awards*, hosted by Ed Sullivan: "There he seemed more in character. Turning to Sullivan, Rickles said, 'I spoke to the wax museum. They're accepting you Friday." Another critic thought that *The Don Rickles Show* "had some funny lines scattered through it and generally seemed to be the best of the new crop of programs. "Don Rickles' insult humor has been muted, which helps too."[18]

The *Baltimore Sun* ran two reviews—one the day after the show's premiere and another on the following Monday—"Don Rickles . . . has now been converted into a neo-Dagwood Bumstead bore . . . The basic trouble is the inadvisability of presenting the star as a semi-lovable figure . . . The glove won't fit, nor does the material on the opener."[19] Cleveland Amory, the influential critic for *TV Guide*, devoted his entire column to parsing *The Don Rickles Show.* "Mr. Rickles was . . . hog-tied," he noted. "As a result, trying to make something out of nothing everything was overdone. From start to finish, it not only bombed, it depth-charged."[20]

The Don Rickles Show did not sink immediately, despite the widespread criticism. Its premiere episode ranked an unspectacular thirty-fourth place that week, well ahead of its CBS midseason stablemate, *Me and the Chimp*, which tanked at number fifty-six. *The Don Rickles Show* would, eventually, sink to that very number when all was said and done. Over on NBC, meanwhile, *Sanford and Son* finished in fifth place. The following week's episode of Don's show, "Greetings from Uncle Sam," finished eight spots lower at forty-two—and, from there, it was a freefall down the ratings ladder.

"The time slot wasn't good and [CBS] didn't get behind it the way they said they would," Don's on-screen wife, Louise Sorel, recalled. "Whenever we had a scene and I would go over to him and have to touch him or put my hands around him or sit on his lap, he would yell 'Barbara!' because that's who he was, a husband. My feeling was [that] they put him in a role that was not him. He would never be a Madison Avenue guy. That put him in a role that was not Don Rickles, which, in a way, I thought might be interesting to put him in a totally different situation to bring out his vulnerability. But he was like a constant explosion of energy.

"A couple of times we would go and watch the dailies and I was so touched by him," she said. "He had a vulnerability that, when it was allowed to peek out, you could just weep. It was so sweet. I said to him a couple of times, 'Oh my God, Don, you just broke my heart.' There were little quiet moments where he became really vulnerable, and I thought it would have been really great to see more of that."

Before the show premiered, Joe Scandore invited Louise Sorel to Las Vegas so she could see Don's show at the Riviera and experience the other, freewheeling side of her costar. "I had never been to Vegas . . . so they flew me there and I was picked up from the plane by four guys and taken to the hotel," she recalled. "I had the funniest experience. As much as everybody loved Don, and he was hilariously funny, having experienced him as an actor and doing scenes with him where I saw his vulnerability, all of the sudden I wasn't laughing. What I saw was a man who really wanted to be home and who did this [act] because it was important for him and people wanted to see him. I knew that underneath, he wanted to be accepted as an actor, but the act worked for him."[21]

(Louise slipped out to the restroom during Don's act. He spied her as she walked back to her table, and the spotlight swung around and caught her in its glare. "Here comes the girl who's going to play my wife," he snarled, "and she's just been to the bathroom.")

"Don was sweeter, because, obviously on a sitcom, you have to be sympathetic," recalled Barry Gordon, the former child actor who had worked with Jackie Gleason, George Burns, and Jason Robards (in both the Broadway and movie versions of *A Thousand Clowns*). Gordon appeared in several episodes of *The Don Rickles Show* as Conrad Musk, an avant-garde director of commercials who shoots an ad for Moo Cow Milk in Don and Barbara Robinson's kitchen starring their young daughter, Janie. "He wasn't the insult comic. But I thought that the show fit him very well," Gordon recalled.

"I remember just how much fun it was and how warm Don was. He had this persona on the nightclub stage, but he was one of the warmest people I have ever worked with. He was absolutely delightful and an incredible comic, so you were able to bounce off him in a way that just made the entire experience pleasurable and brought out the best in me as an actor.

"It was an interesting experience for me because, up until then, I had been basically playing nerdy roles," he said. "I kind of got plugged into that, and Conrad Musk was a complete departure because he was this flamboyant crazy man. To put a flamboyant crazy man with Don Rickles, and to see his reactions to that character, was just so much fun because he pulled that energy out of me. I don't even know if I had, at that point, realized that I had that energy, and he made it a very special experience. I actually loved that show. I thought it was very well-written [and] a very funny show."

Gordon's time on *The Don Rickles Show* was short-lived, but it paid off in other ways. "I never thought I would get that role because it was just so out there, so flamboyant and a little hippie-ish and . . . I had not played that before, so I wore longer hair," he said. "In fact, a weird thing happened—not on the show, but because of that show. I got my first on-camera commercial, for Royal Crown Cola, because they wanted a character that was exactly like Conrad Musk and they saw me on TV."[22]

The Don Rickles Show plodded along as January turned into February turned into March. In one episode, Don becomes his own defense attorney when he is accused of stealing a Takashamata television/stereo console; in another episode, he buys a fancy sports car and treats it with kid gloves—until a garage mechanic (played by John Byner) tells him the car was once in a major accident. In another story line, Don gets a draft notice, which is obviously a major mix-up, but he still has to go through the entire induction process, which includes an interview with a psychiatrist who thinks he is a nutcase. (This was shot as the pilot episode but aired out of order.)

Don Rickles' best friend, Bob Newhart, guest-starred in an episode as Don Robinson's brother-in-law/attorney, who convinces Don he should be preparing his will. "They couldn't get through a scene," Louise Sorel recalled about Don and Bob Newhart. "They couldn't look at each other. It was hysterical." It was not funny enough for viewers, though—and the episode, entitled "Where There's Will," barely moved the ratings needle. Out of desperation, and hoping to make a promotional splash, Don or Joe Scandore, or someone in the Rickles camp, floated the story that Don was hoping to corral his *Kelly's Heroes* costars Clint Eastwood and Carroll O'Connor as guest stars on Season 2 of *The Don Rickles Show*. Call it wishful thinking.

By mid-February, a month into its run, *The Don Rickles Show* had been written off as "unlikely" to be renewed for a second season, its prospects "dubious" at best. It did not help matters that NBC surrendered the 10:30 p.m. Friday-night time slot to its local affil-iates, which padded the show's ratings on CBS, since its compe-tition was nearly nonexistent. (ABC's hour-long anthology series *Love, American Style*, aired from 10 to 11 p.m. on Fridays opposite *The Don Rickles Show* and was not much of a threat—though it did enjoy a five-season run.)

Several weeks later, *The Don Rickles Show* stumbled further down the prime-time ratings hill to number fifty-two. Don and the cast were in the midst of shooting their thirteenth episode. Despite the sitcom's lame-duck status, movie theaters around the country still screening *Kelly's Heroes*, two years after its premiere, promoted the movie by showcasing two of its costars: "Carroll O'Connor from *All in the Family* and Don Rickles from *The Don Rickles Show*." You do what you can.

The Merchant of Venom fretted over the state of his series. "They call me up and say I got a 32 [rating] in Des Moines and I ask them what that means and they say it means I don't have anything to worry about and I say I wasn't worried until they called up," he said. "Then someone else calls up and says I got a 13 [rating] in San Diego and I ask what that means and they say it means I better start to worry. Meanwhile, the boss, Sheldon Leonard, is making plans for a trip to Europe and he says it'll be either a celebration or a wake. I'm home sitting on the potty sweating and he's in Venice making a left turn on some canal saying, 'I wonder if they've flushed 'The Kid' down the toilet yet?'"[23]

The state of his television show, however, did not impact his nightclub career. Don returned to the Riviera in Vegas in mid-March. He sold out every night. In early April, he opened for a two-week run at the Copa in New York City, followed by two weeks at the Westbury Music Fair on Long Island. Peggy Lee shared the bill. He returned to the Circle Star Theater outside of San Francisco. A year before, his act there had been ripped by *San Francisco Exami-ner* critic Phil Elwood, who blasted the "ethnic" tone of Don's act. Don had a long memory, and he now responded in kind—calling

Elwood a "slob" after taking the stage on opening night. "You'd think a nationally known star would have shrugged it off long ago," Elwood's newspaper noted. They had a point.

(Carroll O'Connor, firmly entrenched in American pop culture as *All in the Family* bigot Archie Bunker, decided now to try his hand as a nightclub act. He opened at Harrah's in Reno, telling jokes as his Archie Bunker alter-ego and singing a few songs from the 1930s. Why, O'Connor was asked, was he doing this? "Don Rickles said I couldn't do it," he answered. "I don't intend to make this a career . . . but at least I can tell Rickles I did it." O'Connor played the Riviera in July; the following week, Don opened there with singer Barbara McNair.)[24]

The Don Rickles Show received its expected visit from television's Grim Reaper in late March, when CBS mercifully pulled the plug, a little over two months after its premiere. By this time it had slid down to fifty-sixth place in prime time, a notch below *Alias Smith and Jones*, which was renewed by ABC (the third-place network needed all the help it could get). But despite the bad news, *The Don Rickles Show*, unlike its ABC predecessor, was not an abject failure. It even had a few supporters in the press who went out of their way to praise the show's writing and who eventually warmed up to the star's comic timing. (One of the show's guest stars was ten-year-old Jodie Foster, who made an early on-screen television appearance in an episode centering around a birthday party for Don Robinson's daughter, Janie.)

There were other factors in the show's demise, first and foremost its 10:30 Friday-night time slot. It was obvious, though, that *The Don Rickles Show* never caught America's fancy chiefly because what fired the engine of Don Rickles, nightclub comedian, could not be bottled into a twenty-two-minute show with a laugh track. Don was just too strongly identified with his Merchant of Venom persona—no matter how much it was diluted for the masses. *The Don Rickles Show* was not alone in being thrown into the television graveyard: CBS also canceled *My Three Sons* (after twelve seasons), *Me and the Chimp* (no shocker there), *O'Hara, US Treasury*, starring David Janssen (unable to replicate his success from *The Fugitive*), *Cade County*, *Arnie* (a sitcom starring Herschel Bernardi), and *The Glen Campbell Goodtime Hour*.

The Don Rickles Show was replaced on the CBS schedule with reruns of the sitcom *The Governor and J.J.* starring Dan Dailey—which had ended its original run two-and-a-half years earlier, in December 1970. Ouch. Everything old is new again in the unforgiving world of prime-time television.

Even CBS president Bob Wood, who, as previously noted, was a Don Rickles booster, was not impressed with the show. "It had a great big fertile opportunity" in its Friday-night time slot, he said and, pointing to Don's competition, reasoned that *The Don Rickles Show* should have earned at least a 45 percent share of all the television sets on during that time. Stiffer competition might have translated to a 35 percent share for *The Don Rickles Show*—but it hovered in the 30 percent range for the duration of its run.

In the "adding insult to injury" department, Don's best friend, Bob Newhart, and his sitcom were replacing him in the fall on CBS with *The Bob Newhart Show*. "That's what you get for being a nice guy," Alan King cracked when he heard the news. *The Bob Newhart Show*, which taped on the same soundstage as *The Don Rickles Show*, ran for six seasons in a better time slot—it aired on Saturdays at 9:30 p.m. for its first four seasons, sandwiched between *The Mary Tyler Moore Show* and *The Carol Burnett Show*. It is widely considered to be one of the best sitcoms in television history. Newhart played to type. Don Rickles did not.

CBS, though, was not done with The Merchant of Venom. Bob Wood was disappointed in the show's failure, but he was Don's personal friend in addition to being his boss. He was hell-bent on finding something, *anything*, for Don Rickles, an enormous talent, he said, who had yet to find a format suited to his distinct personality. Ya think? "He's a genius," Wood said, a month after dropping the hammer on *The Don Rickles Show*. "I wanted that show of his to be a big success as bad as I ever wanted anything. I had to say, 'Don, pal,' and tell him his show was canceled.

"Oh, and he's an absolute and total pro," he continued. "He started right in doing jokes about it. He said, 'You don't know what you've done for me. Getting fired is going to give me a half-hour's material for my nightclub act.' The guy is one of the quickest minds in the business. His mind is like a Polaroid camera [*author's note: this was 1972*]. He gets those instant pictures in his mind and down on his tongue and spits them out so fast. And on top of that, he's a pussycat.

"How can I ever give up on the guy?"[25]

There was talk of Don hosting a series of prime-time specials for CBS in the fall or (gasp!) starring in another sitcom. This one would be set behind prison walls and sounded suspiciously like a recycled version of *The Unpardonables*, the NBC pilot he shot in the fall of 1965 with Billy De Wolfe as the warden and Don as the smart-ass inmate. The *New York Daily News* reported that "a comedy is now being readied" for the 1973 television season in which Don would play "a madcap golfer who swings with more insults than a club." It never happened, but Rodney Dangerfield epitomized the role eight years later in the big-screen comedy *Caddyshack*.

The cancellation hurt. Don, to his credit, did not mention it when he opened at the Copa on April 6. He hoped to stay on CBS's radar, and slamming them would not help his cause; he also sent a birthday cake to network president Bob Wood (born April 17) to show him that there were no hard feelings. Don was however, still smarting from the 1968 version of *The Don Rickles Show* and took several shots at ABC during his Copa run. Bob Wood was nowhere to be seen in the club, but Ed Sullivan was there, and he was easy bait (Don: "He passed away and wasn't noticed"). Other celebrities got the Rickles treatment: Phyllis McGuire, Anthony Quinn (whose ABC series, *The Man and the City*, had also been canceled), Jerry Orbach, Jack Weston, David Steinberg, and comedian Morty Gunty. So did a woman sitting ringside wearing a sleeveless, off-the-shoulder blouse: "You're old. Stop wearing sun suits."

Mobster Joseph "Crazy Joe" Gallo was also there to see Don's opening at the Copa. Crazy Joe was celebrating his forty-third birthday and was, he claimed, a reformed man who was retired from the mob and working on his memoirs. He was enjoying his freedom, having been released from prison in April 1971 after serving nearly ten years on extortion charges. That night, Gallo was at the Copa with his sister; his wife of two weeks, Sina; and another female friend. Etta Rickles was there, too, and before the show she approached Crazy Joe and his entourage. "Joey, darling, tell your boys to put their guns on the table," she said. "I don't want my sonny boy to talk unless I can see the guns. Thank you, darling."[26]

Gallo and his party laughed along with everyone else at Don's insults—sadly, there is no record of Don zinging Crazy Joe—and, after the show ended, they headed over to Umberto's Clam House in Little Italy for Crazy Joe's big birthday party. At around 4:30 a.m., as Gallo sat at his table, a middle-aged gunman calmly walked up and pumped two bullets into him before escaping in a getaway car. Crazy Joe, mortally wounded, staggered after him before collapsing in the street. The gangland slaying triggered a bloody mob war that lasted two years.

Lorna Luft, who was at the Copa that night, credits Don with saving her life. "I went into his dressing room after the show to say hi," she recalled. "He knew I was in the audience. And there were about five guys with their wives, and there was a young kid. I didn't catch any of their names, but I knew who they were. And one of them said to Don, 'It's so-and-so's birthday, we're going downtown, will you come with us?' And Don said, 'No, I've got an early call tomorrow, thank you so much, it's been great.' Don didn't go out after the show. He always went home with Barbara. So one of the guys said, 'Lorna, do you want to go?' And I said, 'Oh, you know that would be . . . ' And Don elbowed me like, 'No, you don't want to go.' And I said, 'I have an early call,' and the next morning I woke up and looked at the New York Post and saw that Joe Gallo got whacked."[27]

CHAPTER 15

In the spring of 1972, Johnny Carson and *The Tonight Show* moved permanently from the NBC studios in Rockefeller Center to "Beautiful Downtown Burbank." Carson had, for years, been schlepping the production for weeklong visits to L.A.; now he and his show were planted in Hollywood's backyard, a stone's throw from its glitz and glamour. It only added to Carson's mystique.

The Tonight Show made its West Coast premiere on May 1. Carson chose Don Rickles, Bob Newhart, Raquel Welch, and Nancy Reagan (Ronald Reagan was six years into his run as the governor of California) as his inaugural guests in Burbank. It was a big honor for Don, as these things go; if America did not allow Mr. Warmth into their living rooms once a week for a half hour, he was still welcomed by Carson for adrenaline-shot doses of late-night riffing. Merv Griffin followed suit on his daytime show; in late-June, he launched a new syndicated version of *The Merv Griffin Show* airing in the late-afternoon hours in most markets. Don also continued to visit *The Mike Douglas Show* in Philadelphia and often stopped by to visit Barbara's mother, Eleanor Sklar, when he was in the city.

In June, the *Los Angeles Times* ran a three-page Sunday profile of Don with the headline "A Day in the Mouth of Don Rickles." The article captured a snapshot of Don's life—playing golf with a few pals, including Bob Newhart, relaxing at home in Beverly Hills with Barbara and the kids (whom the photographers were not allowed to shoot), and in Las Vegas before, during, and after two manic, sweat-drenched shows at the Riviera, both of which he performed with a splitting headache. The article was written before *The Don Rickles Show* was canceled.

Harry Goins was there, too, offering Don a pill for his headache, bringing him his tuxedo, holding his pants off the dressing-room carpet so they would not get dirty—doing whatever was needed to keep his boss comfortable. (Don: "He dressed me in alleys. He can have almost anything I have.") Don talked about his wealth ("I know I'm a big star. I know I make big dough. I don't need more money. I'll take it but I don't need it.") and about his state of being: "Am I happy? Hell, yes, I'm happy, because I got good friends . . . I'm blessed. I do what I do and I'm successful at it so I can pay my bills and do what I want in life. But without friends, it wouldn't be worth anything. What the hell is there in life if you're alone?"

He could always rely on his semi-regular television appearances to keep him in the public eye. In one week in June, he subbed for Johnny Carson on *The Tonight Show* and cohosted *The Mike Douglas Show* (pretaped in Philadelphia). Maybe he was too ubiquitous; the *Philadelphia Inquirer* reported that "Don Rickles won't be substituting for Johnny Carson again. Too many people who were on the show complained about Rickles' monopolization of the conversation (with his favorite subject, Don Rickles). And those insult jokes are a little worn around the teeth these days." Maybe . . . but Don did return to guest-host for Johnny many times in subsequent years.

"Don came on *The Tonight Show* one night, and in one spot he did a stand-up," the show's bandleader, Doc Severinsen, recalled. "And he looks over at the trumpet section and one of the guys happened to be a very dear friend of mine, Snooky Young, who was Black. He was like a brother to me. Don forgot that he wasn't in a club on 52nd Street and he made some remark and started walking toward the bandstand and Snooky stood up, waited until Don got to the trumpet section, and he reached into his pocket and he pulled out a knife, one of those switchblades, and that stopped Don dead in his tracks. And he very quickly got back and finished what he was doing.

"Snooky wasn't taking any real offense to it. He had heard a lot worse than that. It's hard to explain it to anybody who wasn't there at the time. You talk about it now and you say, 'Wow, they really didn't like each other.' But you couldn't do that nowadays. Let's face it, there was a lot of racial strife and religious things that people didn't really talk about, right there under the surface. Don did a lot more good than harm. He just put it right out there and talked about it and at the end of it all you said, 'I like that guy.' That's how it seemed to me."[1]

By the early 1970s, *The Dean Martin Show* was losing steam after nine seasons on the air. It was, for the majority of its run, a top-rated franchise player for NBC. Its dwindling ratings were not attributed so much to its host, Dean Martin, but to the show's format. With few exceptions, including *The Sonny and Cher Comedy Hour* and *The Carol Burnett Show*, both on CBS, variety shows were a vestige of television's past—replaced now in prime time by sharp, topical sitcoms (*All in the Family*, *Sanford and Son*, *Maude*, *Good Times*) and dramas. It was time for *The Dean Martin Show* to change it up.

Martin's producer, Greg Garrison, had not forgotten Don's groundbreaking appearance on *The Dean Martin Show* in 1967, when The Merchant of Venom spent an unprecedented seventeen minutes of airtime insulting an invited gaggle of celebrities in a watered-down version of a Friars Club roast. He and Dean Martin decided to rejigger the show's format to reflect the ambience of that night, and convinced NBC, which did not want to lose one of its biggest stars, to buy into the new plan.

Garrison said he was inspired by "The Friars Club Man of the Hour," an episode of Ed Sullivan's *The Toast of the Town* series that aired on CBS in 1958 with Sullivan as the guest of honor being roasted by, among others, Joey Bishop, Jack E. Leonard, Morey Amsterdam, Polly Bergen, and Jack Carter. The episode was the brainchild of acclaimed comedy writer/creator Nat Hiken, the man behind *The Phil Silvers Show* and *Car 54, Where Are You?*

In the fall of 1973, *The Dean Martin Show* entered its final season, and Garrison introduced a roast-type segment that borrowed its name from its 1958 forebearer. The "Man of the Hour" was, basically, an updated version of Don's zinger-filled attack six years earlier. California governor Ronald Reagan was the first person on the spit; he was followed, over the course of the season, by Kirk Douglas, Johnny Carson, Bette Davis, Joe Namath, Truman Capote, and Jack Benny. Don was, of course, frequently on the dais slinging insults; his turn to be roasted on *The Dean Martin Show* arrived in February 1974 when Joey Bishop, Foster Brooks, Carol Channing, Phyllis Diller, Kirk Douglas, Jack Klugman, Rich Little, Bob Newhart, Dan Rowan, and his "Kelly's Heroes" costar Telly Savalas took their (scripted) best shots.

"Every single line was written . . . there was not one ad-lib with the exception of two people," Garrison recalled. "One, of course, was Johnny [Jonathan Winters] and the other was Don Rickles."[2]

The segments were a hit with viewers. In the spring of 1974, NBC canceled *The Dean Martin Show* and brought Martin back in the fall to host *The Dean Martin Celebrity Roast*, which aired as a series of Thursday-night specials. The roasts were taped at the MGM Grand Hotel in Las Vegas. "It was a paste job, making Dean look good, but he really didn't have a chance to perform," Garrison said. Dean was perfectly happy to open the show and introduce the guests (the less work for him and more time to play golf the better). Garrison warmed up the audience of three thousand who were seated at tables in the hotel's ballroom. (The celebrity roasters were not paid very much, but MGM picked up their tabs at the hotel.)

Garrison corralled all the big guns for the roasts: Don, Red Buttons (and his "Never got a dinner" shtick), Jonathan Winters, Nipsey Russell, Jack Benny, Jack E. Leonard, Milton Berle, Joey Bishop, Phyllis Diller, Mort Sahl, Donald O'Connor, Rich Little, Slappy White, Foster Brooks (doing his drunk routine) . . . and on and on.

"I think I did twenty-four *Dean Martin Celebrity Roasts* and Don did about twenty-two," Rich Little recalled. "I would meet him after the roasts and we would talk and I would go see him when he was in Vegas. I knew him fairly well, but not personally. I think Don was the funniest comedian I've ever seen. I mean, he just was in a class by himself. He had an incredible mind. Someone that would come close to him would be Robin Williams. Don was like a machine gun. And when he was saying something funny, as he was talking, he was already thinking of what he was going to say next, and maybe beyond that. Robin Williams was the same way. They just run at one hundred miles per hour and they could just pull things out of the air so fast it absolutely amazed you."[3]

NBC aired six to seven *Dean Martin Celebrity Roast* specials each season. Garrison employed up to sixteen writers who were tasked with coming up with lines not only for the comedians on the dais— no mean feat—but for non-showbiz celebrities including astronauts (Neil Armstrong, Eugene Cernan), politicians (Ronald Reagan, Senator Lowell Weicker), athletes (Mickey Mantle, Willie Mays, Floyd Patterson), and even health food advocate and Post Grape Nuts pitchman Euell Gibbons. "Don was always the one to close the roasts," comedian Tom Dreesen recalled, "because no one could follow him."

The roasts were a Thursday-night staple on NBC for the next decade; fifty-four *Dean Martin Celebrity Roasts* aired through 1984. Martin hosted all but one of them. When it was his turn to turn on the spit, in February 1976, Don hosted the show—and, of course, insulted Dean as he sat on the dais at the MGM Grand.

The roasts often ran two hours or longer and were heavily edited into their hour-long format on NBC. It was a challenging and, for Garrison and his production staff, frenzied process of piecing the episodes together. At times, a celebrity's appearance was edited down to one line that made it onto the air. Some stars taped their bits either before or after the actual event if there was a scheduling issue—and they were edited into the episode. Garrison et al. could also mix and match the telecasts (and the talent) if there was a line from another roast that was better suited for that week's honoree.

"The running joke in the business was, 'Let's tune into the Dean

Martin roast and we can watch his hair change color,' because they used to intercut those things beyond belief," comedy writer/producer Bob Booker recalled. "There could be six roasts and you would end up with nine of them. If they had an act that didn't work, they would take [a celebrity] out and replace them with someone from another roast."[4]

One of Don's friends recalled how he accompanied Don to the big MGM Grand ballroom to watch him tape a roast. "He would grab me by the arm and say, 'Do you want to see how you make ten grand in five minutes?' And he would throw a tuxedo on and walk across a bare stage, all shoulders and above, and he would say, 'Who is it?' And they would go, let's say, 'Foster Brooks!' And he would do five minutes, walk off, and say, 'That's how you do it.'"

"If you watch Rickles on the Dean Martin roasts, he is having more fun than anybody," Jay Leno observed. "He is pounding the table. He is really laughing and enjoying it as opposed to a lot of the other comics who are just waiting for the other guy to finish so they can talk. Don really enjoyed hearing the other people. And nobody did what Don did, really. He had no real competition."[5]

CBS president Robert Wood made good on his promise to keep Don on his network after canceling *The Don Rickles Show*. Contractually, CBS had an option on Don until March 1973, and it was not going to waste a valuable asset. Don's first CBS special, *Alive and Kicking*, was set to air December 12, and Don was under no illusions that it would lead to something bigger for him. "CBS is referring to it as a TV special pilot," he told syndicated columnist Marilyn Beck. "Me? I'm just considering it a one-time program. I've had my hopes raised too many times in the past—only to have those hopes come crashing down to the ground." He told Beck that, if CBS did exercise his option and give him a series, he would need to play a controversial personality along the lines of Carroll O'Connor's Archie Bunker—and that the network would need to give the series time to grow, as it had done with *All in the Family*. "I have a cult, a following," he said, "a fantastically loyal following, but I won't be able to win over the masses overnight."[6]

The masses were a fickle lot when it came to Don Rickles— as were several of his show business brethren, including Groucho Marx, now eighty-two, whose early criticism of Don and his act intensified over the years. "Don Rickles once told me he stole my act," he told a reporter in 1972. "That's not true. I never worked like Rickles, just insulting people. Anyhow, Rickles is ugly." There were the members of the press who never warmed up to The Merchant of Venom, who had a long memory for being slighted or criticized. Marilyn Beck wrote a column lambasting Don's abrasive onstage personality and his brand of humor. He did not forget, and whenever he and Beck crossed paths thereafter, he was quick to remind her that her words were hurtful, and would go out of his way to prove to her that she was wrong—by demonstrating how sweet of a guy he was offstage. (Which he was, by most estimates. There was nary a bad word about Don's private life as a husband, a father, and a grown man who still doted on his mother.)

In the run-up to the premiere of his CBS special, Don guested, in October, on *The Julie Andrews Hour* on ABC. Marilyn Beck met with him for an interview at the Polo Lounge in Beverly Hills. She noted how obsequious he was when they sat down—and right off the bat, how he addressed her stinging words, telling her the criticism shook him to his core. "I think they should hold seminar sessions or something, so that writers can get to know a personality well before they analyze his act," Don said. "To me, the idea of pure heaven would be waking up one morning and finding out that every reviewer in the world said he loved me." It was a strange dichotomy uttered by the man known as The Merchant of Venom, The Fastest Mouth in the West, The Insultin' Sultan, etc.—but he was obviously sensitive to the criticism. "Of course, taking into account what's brought me fame and fortune, if that morning ever dawns that will be when my mother has to give up her fancy apartment in

Florida and go back to her old job as a short order cook at the deli."
(He just could not help himself.)

"I really want the world to love me," he said. "I'm a guy who hurts over rejections. I'm a guy who needs a lot of love."[7]

CBS reteamed Don with director Hy Averback from *The Don Rickles Show* for *Alive and Kicking*, which aired, as scheduled, in December (Joe Scandore was the executive producer). Johnny Carson crossed over into enemy territory to appear in the opening, and the special showcased a series of sketches teaming Don with his buddies Don Adams and Bob Newhart, the network's top star Carroll O'Connor, Anne Meara, and Harvey Korman (moonlighting from *The Carol Burnett Show*). It featured a meta sketch in which Don and Meara played newlyweds attending a Don Rickles show at the Riviera in Las Vegas and bearing the brunt of Don's insults. Singer and dancer Juliet Prowse belted out three numbers and was joined by Don in two of them. There was a five-minute segment in which Don, microphone in hand and in nightclub mode, left the stage to saunter into the studio audience and razz anyone who caught his eye—a young man with long hair and a beard; an elderly couple married forty-five years; a middle-aged couple from Ohio named Winger (easy pickings, although Vern Winger did not look pleased); and CBS stars Tim Conway and McLean Stevenson from *The Carol Burnett Show* and *M*A*S*H*, who were there to support their network stablemate and take one for the network team.

The critics were pleased, to a point, with *Alive and Kicking*: "good but not great . . . his versatility was impressive to one who never gave him that much credit" (*Cincinnati Inquirer*); "had some amusing moments but not nearly enough . . . Rickles wasn't in particularly good form, and, let's face it, even when Rickles is in great form he's a marginal risk for prolonged exposure as a variety frontman" (*Fort Worth Star-Telegram*); "some of his Neanderthal mumbling, as in a UN sketch . . . we can live without . . . but it was all in good fun, provided you like Rickles" (*New York Daily News*); "just fair part of the time, with a couple of moments of greatness . . . skits are funny, but a bit too long" (*TV Scout*).

The special averaged a respectable 36 percent share at 10 p.m., and Don's biggest supporter at CBS, network president Robert Wood, gushed about his star . . . but tiptoed around the question of whether Don Rickles would star in another weekly series. "I've often felt that if we could wire Rickles from the moment he wakes up till the time he goes to bed, we could get enough material for a show," he said, noting the special's decent ratings. "I'm wondering if the rejection [of Don on TV] is eroding."

Don would not headline his own CBS special for another two years.

He sprinted into 1973 by signing a new four-year deal with the Riviera and joining Bob Hope, again, on one of his ho-hum, by-the-numbers NBC specials—notable mainly for Hope's obvious reliance on cue cards. Jack Benny, Tony Randall, Jerry Colonna, Red Buttons, Jack Carter, and Jan Murray joined Don on *The Bob Hope Special* (catchy title). It came and went quickly in early February and Don kick-started his nightclub schedule: the Copa, the Riviera, Harrah's in Lake Tahoe, the Mill Run Playhouse outside of Chicago, the Latin Quarter in Philadelphia . . . and many points in between. He was a whirling dervish who kept a punishing schedule, but he somehow found the time to appear, almost daily it seemed, on television.

Several years before, Dinah Shore had reentered the talk show arena with *Dinah's Place*, and Don added frequent visits to her pleasant series to his rotating roster of daytime appearances on *The Mike Douglas Show*, *The Merv Griffin Show*, and even *The Vin Scully Show*, a short-lived afternoon talk show on CBS hosted by the veteran Los Angeles Dodgers announcer (Don was a devoted Dodgers fan; he switched allegiances from the Giants after moving to L.A.). *The Hollywood Squares* beckoned in the early evening hours on occasion, and in prime time, there were appearances on *The Dean Martin Celebrity Roast* and visits to *Laugh-In*, where he yukked it up with Arte

Johnson, Ruth Buzzi and the crew. Late night was reserved for *The Tonight Show*—both as a guest on Johnny's couch and as a substitute host when Johnny took yet another vacation. A spinoff series on CBS was not in the cards, and his name was conspicuously absent when CBS announced its fall slate in February. Don was in good company. The hopes of Lily Tomlin and Mariette Hartley to launch shows in September on the network were likewise dashed.

Don and Barbara joined their closest friends, Bob and Ginny Newhart, on a two-week vacation to Italy in April. "Wherever we went, Don's first question was 'Did they bomb here?' He even says that in Hawaii," Newhart recalled. "He's quite a linguist in Italian with two phrases, 'Prego' (please or thank you) and 'Did they bomb here?'"

After Don returned from Europe, his name surfaced in the press when a twenty-six-year-old German immigrant was arrested for trying to extort $250,000 from Johnny Carson. "I heard Don Rickles announce on Mr. Carson's show how much money he had," he wrote to the judge. "I did not discover where Mr. Carson lived until Mr. Rickles gave the indication that he lived in Bel-Air when he appeared again on Mr. Carson's show."[8] Carson insiders said that Don's running commentary on Johnny's swollen bank account stuck in his craw.

(In his 1989 biography of Carson, *King of the Night*, author Laurence Leamer told the story of Don and Barbara visiting Johnny and his then wife Joanne's newly renovated high-rise apartment in Manhattan. Johnny was showing them around the place when he slid open a door to a room housing what Leamer described as "a bizarre accumulation of boxes, bric-a-brac, and junk." Don took a step back. "Hey, Barbara, come here, you have to see this room! It's unbelievable! Johnny Carson. He makes a million bucks a minute. And he hires George Shearing to decorate his apartment."[9])

Don turned forty-seven on May 6. Four days later, Jack E. Leonard died at Mount Sinai Hospital in New York. He was sixty-three. In late March, Leonard, a diabetic, had collapsed after performing at the Rainbow Grill in Rockefeller Center and undergone immediate open-heart surgery, which was followed by a second heart operation a few days before his death. Don did not respond publicly to the news of Fat Jack's death.

Later that month, Don appeared on the Emmy Awards, which were, once again, hosted by Johnny Carson. Don was there to explain the Television Academy's rules and procedures regarding its voting process (Don: "Three guys and an old broad from Encino locked in a small room"). He took some flak from the press and from his peers for stretching his allotted four minutes of airtime into ten minutes, ending his running commentary by telling everyone that he was "fed up" with the Academy and, for good measure, adding that "Mike Douglas is a yo-yo." Why? No one knew. "Don would have been funnier in half the time," cracked Bob Newhart.

"Why does Don Rickles think the phrases 'hockey puck' and 'rubber ducks' are so funny he cliches them endlessly?" mused Ricklesbashing columnist Jack O'Brian. (He could have also included the word "cookie," as in "Give him a cookie and he'll go home," a line Don used often.) It was not an unfair question to ask, even from O'Brian. Don began working the "hockey puck" line into the act sometime in the mid-1960s, and there it remained to the end of his life, part of the Rickles lore. He thought "hockey puck" sounded funny, and it did, to a point; it became his calling card in a business where a catchphrase set comedians apart from the crowded pack (Henny Youngman's "Take my wife . . . please" and Rodney Dangerfield's "no respect" are two of the more prominent examples). Don's lightning-quick rat-tat-tat delivery often disguised that he was talking in gibberish. "If you listen to what Don Rickles actually says, it doesn't make any sense," recalled Mark Evanier. "One time, on my blog, I transcribed a speech he gave to Jerry Lewis on the [muscular dystrophy] telethon one year and it was so incoherent. It was funny when he said it, but when you actually transcribed it—'Go sit in a hot tub and watch a duck sink while you sip sap out of a rubber tree'—it doesn't make any sense. I remember there was a Dean Martin roast where Rowan and Martin got up and just read Don's insults like they were poetry. And who can forget, 'Why don't you drop your pants and fire a rocket!'?"[10] The failures of *The Don Rickles Show* on ABC and CBS left NBC as the last network standing in Don's quest for a prime-time series. His friend Don Adams was not having much luck on the small screen, either, since NBC canceled his landmark sitcom, *Get Smart*, in 1970. Now the network dangled that elusive series carrot in front of Rickles and Adams in announcing *A Couple of Dons*, an hour-long comedy/variety special constructed around sketches, monologues, and songs.

The special, which aired September 8, was taped in Burbank before a star-studded studio audience of thirty-one, including Bob Newhart. Dons Adams and Rickles were, supposedly, surprised by their celebrity-packed crowd, but with Joe Scandore as the executive producer, that was likely not the case. The two Dons were joined by the Jackson Sisters, a singing group, and by actress Sally Kellerman. "Oh yes, we're definitely interested in a series," Don (Rickles) said in the run-up to the telecast. "We're most anxious to work together. But we have to wait for all the votes to come in . . . The show really does have a new look. It's two non-partners together for a variety show. There's chemistry there. And it's also a new approach." Don did fifty-five minutes of his nightclub act for the studio audience, which was edited down to seven minutes for the telecast. *A Couple of Dons* premiered to warm reviews, but NBC did not take the series idea any further—although Rickles and Adams returned to the network in October for *NBC Follies*, joining Sammy Davis Jr., Michele Lee, and Frankie Avalon.

Don was in Chicago several weeks later when his room at the Ambassador East hotel was among seven that were robbed; burglars used a pass key (it was an inside job) to gain access. Don reported that he lost an estimated $5,000 worth of jewelry, most of it belonging to Barbara. He talked about the robbery on *The Tonight Show*, and three weeks later, two of the valuable baubles, one of them a gold, diamond-encrusted bracelet engraved with the names of their children, Mindy and Lawrence, were returned in an envelope . . . to Don's mother, Etta, in Miami Beach. She found the envelope on her front doorstep.

Etta had, long ago, taken a backseat as Don reached the heights of stardom, but her name popped up in public every now and then. In April 1974, when Don was roasted by the Friars as Entertainer of the Year, she was the punchline to Milton Berle's joke that Don, the family man, bought his beloved mother a swimming pool in Miami Beach—stocked with a shark. Johnny Carson emceed the $100-a-plate dinner, which drew a crowd of several thousand in New York while the Tony Awards aired live on ABC just blocks away. (Carson: "Will somebody kindly wake Ed Sullivan up?") Ed, always an easy mark due to his perpetually wooden demeanor, died six months later in October, at the age of seventy-three, from esophageal cancer of which he was unaware (his family kept it a secret from him—he thought he was in pain from his gastric ulcers). Ed had never recovered from the death of his beloved wife, Sylvia, the year before—and, to a lesser extent, from the cancellation of *The Ed Sullivan Show.*

Don returned to the Emmy Awards in May, which were emceed by Johnny Carson, and insulted a few celebrities in the course of delivering a (brief) history of the awards. A young stand-up comedian named Gabe Kaplan, soon to find television stardom on the sitcom *Welcome Back, Kotter,* impersonated a drunk Ed Sullivan telling everyone off on the final telecast of *The Ed Sullivan Show.*

The Don Rickles publicity and management teams were firing on all cylinders, always on the lookout for new opportunities that paid handsomely. In 1974, Don entered the lucrative world of television commercials and print advertisements. He starred in a thirty-second deodorant commercial for Right Guard—"My act is making people sweat, but how can I make you sweat if you're always using Right Guard antiperspirant?"—and posed in a print ad for National Car Rental, which "dared Don Rickles to try to criticize their weekend deal. But how could he criticize National's low rate of

$8.50 a day and 14 cents a mile . . . It's so good all Don could say was, 'These people are trying to go broke!'"

The commercial work was nice, and something new, but Don was laser-focused on that elusive network series. He figured, by now, that he was out of options, after NBC passed on *A Couple of Dons*. But then, Robert Wood, his biggest fan in network television, came riding in on his white horse. In August, he signed Don to a CBS development deal for up to four prime-time specials—and, if one of them showed promise, it would be considered for a prime-time series. "Rickles, to me, is a very unique and gifted comedian," Wood said of his prized pupil, ignoring Don's well-documented television failures. "He's been one of the most successful nightclub entertainers in the past dozen years. He's a broad talent who can do any number of things. No one has found the right formula for him on television yet, but everything he does is a hard-ticket sell, and he sells out. Obviously, there are a lot of people out there who agree with me." ("Just not television viewers," he might have added.) He did admit that "there is a very elusive essence that we're missing" in Don Rickles, and that "it is very difficult and frustrating trying to capture it. A lot of work will be put into developing the specials with the thought of going to series."

CBS paired Don with former *Laugh-In* producer Paul Keyes for the specials, which were envisioned as a variety show, a sitcom, and a late-night show (format unknown). Don was, simultaneously, negotiating with NBC to guest-host *The Tonight Show* for the entire month of October while Johnny was on vacation. (Don: "I keep failing and they keep saying, hey, let's give him another job.") The success was tangible, as was Don's underlying insecurity as a performer, as the wannabe dramatic actor who found fame and fortune as an insult comic and would be forever pigeonholed as such. That theme wove itself throughout interview after interview as Don vacillated between shaky bravado and admitting that he needed to be loved by everyone. He wore his emotions on his sleeve. "I believe I'm one of a kind, I really do. I don't think there'll ever be another Don Rickles," he told

Newsday. "Oh, I think there'll be copycats, but I don't think, with my personality and what I do, there will ever be another one. And I think to be one of a kind is a great accomplishment.

"I'm on a kick now in my life—it's so hard, the bigger you get—which is dumb, that's my thing—the more concerned I am about being loved. Now when I was a smaller guy, did what I did and I said, 'I don't care' [about the critics] . . . As you get bigger, you want more people to say, 'Isn't he marvelous?' Because as you get older, you say, gee, I've got a family. I want the littlest guy on the littlest paper to like me. Never will it be that way, but you strive for that." He added, for good measure, that Larry Gelbart, who adapted the big-screen movie *M*A*S*H* for CBS, was writing a television movie for Don "which shows me as a guy with a family." The project never saw the light of a camera.[11]

The first of his CBS specials, *The Don Rickles Show* (there's that title again), aired in January 1975 with A-lister guests John Wayne, Bob Newhart, Dean Martin, Jack Klugman, and *M*A*S*H* star Loretta Swit. "For the first half hour, it was a funny show," a critic noted. "Unfortunately it lasted an hour and slowly sank to Rickles' usual nightclub forte—insult humor and rapid fire racial and ethnic slurs. (All in good fun, of course, he kept telling his victims)."

In one four-minute sketch, Don wore the garb of an Indian chief, complete with feathers and headdress, and met with children at an elementary school who thought they were in the presence of the real thing. In another bit, Don did his familiar imitation of Clark Gable as Rhett Butler and ad-libbed his way through a *Gone With the Wind* soap opera parody with Swit, Newhart, and Klugman. The punchline? Rhett returns to Atlanta for Miss Scarlett . . . the Black maid. One part of the special featured a sketch about "the situation comedy that couldn't be done," in which Don has an out-of-the-closet transvestite brother: "If God intended man to dress up like a woman, He never would have made John Wayne." (Producer Paul Keyes said he and cowriter Mark London had pitched the "sitcom that couldn't be done" idea to CBS two years before and were told, "Never on CBS." They threw it in anyway and got away with it.)

John Wayne was there, dressed in his best movie-cowboy attire and wearing a black mask to disguise himself as his alter-ego, the comedian "Mr. Dynamite," regaling Don with corny jokes. (Sample: "I said, 'Doc, I have a sore foot.' He said, 'Don't worry I'll have you walking in an hour.' He did, he stole my car.")

Don sang his "I'm a Nice Guy" song just after insulting various members of the studio audience—including Frank Sinatra, who got up and walked out in a faux huff after spending seven minutes bantering with Don on camera. "They all recognize you, old-timer," Don said to Frank, who, obviously reading off cue cards, retorted with "That's the most applause I heard since Dean Martin left Jeannie and his kids." Hey, you read what they write. Frank: "They applaud anybody who can get you to stop singing, that's what they were really trying to tell you, buddy." Ba-dum-bum. Don: "I got relatives living in Jersey." Frank: "Not for long." Like that.

And . . . the N-word was dropped . . . twice. It had been used the night before by George Jefferson (Sherman Hemsley) on an episode of *The Jeffersons* (also on CBS), so it was apparently okay for *The Don Rickles Show* to follow suit—although it aired at 7:30 p.m., in the so-called "family hour" when the kiddies were still awake.

Years later, author/archivist Paul Brownstein received a call from a CBS tape operator who found a box that contained the rough-cut, unedited *Don Rickles Show* special. "He said, 'You might want to see this,'" Brownstein recalled. "CBS kept the air master from New York and L.A. of every show . . . and this was the unedited studio reels for that Don Rickles special. There was also a piece that wasn't in the final show. When the Sinatra bit began with Frank in the audience and he gets up and he comes on stage . . . Rickles was doing twenty minutes of the act that never made the show. He had this Black kid get up, a sailor, and he says, 'Sailor,' and gives him a hug—and then Rickles looks at the camera and rubs his cheek and says 'Did any come off on me?' I found out from two of the technicians that, through the years, because it was Don, he got away with it, but the Black audience was always offended when he did that. They just couldn't say anything because it was Don. But there was a lot of resentment."

Brownstein included the segment with Don working the crowd in the Time/Life DVD collection *Mr. Warmth! Don Rickles—The Ultimate TV Collection.* "I sat with Don and showed him this stuff on my laptop. He couldn't believe I had this shit," he recalled. "More importantly, when I got to the audience segment bit, he said, 'Holy shit, I was good, wasn't I?'"[12]

Etta Rickles thought so. Although she had not yet seen the special, she sent a letter to newspaper editors—or, let us say, sent a letter she supposedly wrote herself—imploring their readers to support her son's television endeavor. "On Sunday, Jan. 19, those nice people at CBS are showing a special that my son Donald is starring in," she wrote. "As you know Donald is a wonderful boy who makes friends wherever he goes and some of them, like Frank Sinatra, John Wayne, Bob Newhart are going to be with him. I know my son would love to have you watch the show, but he's really too shy to ask, so I'm asking for him. After all, what's a mother for? If the show is not a big hit, you may have to help pay for my apartment in Miami Beach."[13] Always the kidder.

The second of Don's four CBS specials aired ten months later, in November. The guests on *Rickles* featured returning guests Jack Klugman and Loretta Swit, James Caan, José Ferrer, Elliott Gould, Don Adams, and Michele Lee. CBS executives saw nothing in either telecast that would warrant a spin-off series; two months later, in January 1976, word was leaked to the press that Don's next pilot "will have him playing a WWII Navy veteran back in today's Navy."

Exit CBS.

Enter NBC . . . and Don's next series.

CHAPTER 16

The show was originally titled *Oh Captain! My Captain.* It was the brainchild of Aaron Ruben, an industry veteran and esteemed writer whose television résumé dated back over twenty years and included Sid Caesar's sequel to *Your Show of Shows, Caesar's Hour,* and *The Phil Silvers Show.* Ruben had gone on to create a string of hits— *The Andy Griffith Show, Gomer Pyle: USMC,* and, most recently, *Sanford and Son*—and he knew Don through their show business connections. "There was no in-between about Don—either you loved him or you didn't," he recalled. "I thought this would make a good setup for Don, where he plays a chief petty officer in the Navy and I surround him with the targets that he usually uses in his club act: a Jewish kid, a Puerto Rican kid, a Black kid, a Polish kid. Not that he would be making ethnic or racial jokes, but those little snappers that he had . . . as a CPO, those guys do a lot of yelling, a lot of insulting, and that's Don at his best."[1]

NBC okayed a pilot for the proposed series early in 1976. In March, Don guest-starred on an episode of the hit series *Medical Center* opposite Ruth Buzzi, the pair playing two depressives who meet and fall in love in the hospital. It was his final commitment to CBS and, shortly thereafter, Don shot the pilot for Aaron Ruben's naval sitcom. NBC executives liked the finished product. The show's title was changed to *CPO Sharkey,* and it was slated to premiere toward the end of the year. Don hoped his third prime-time series would be the charm, and this one had a real chance: he was, after all, a Navy veteran who served in World War II—just like his on-screen character, CPO Otto Sharkey.

"In the other shows I was yelling at everyone for no reason," Don said before the show hit the airwaves. "Sharkey is a chief petty officer who is a natural barker. All CPOs are. I have some characteristics in common with Sharkey, including the same sense of humor. He ribs people because he likes them and protects them in his own way. I see him as a lovable guy. When he tells the sailors they're yo-yos or hockey pucks they know he means it." Then he got to the crux of the matter. "I'll tell you why I'm doing *Sharkey*. I want to prove to myself I can succeed at a weekly comedy show." Don, anticipating the comparison, emphasized that Otto Sharkey was different from Ernie Bilko, the scheming sergeant played by Phil Silvers in *The Phil Silvers Show* (for which Ruben had written). Sharkey, he said, "has a tough time getting broads" and "has his sentimental moments."[2]

Ruben stuck to his original plan and surrounded Sharkey with an ethnic smorgasbord of stereotypical characters who were the recruits under Sharkey's supervision at a San Diego naval base: Seaman Lester Pruitt (Peter Isacksen), a dim-bulb Southerner given to long-winded stories who was Sharkey's chief comic foil; Kowalski (Aaron Ruben's son, Tom Ruben), who was Polish; the Jewish New Yorker, Skolnick (played by Don's cousin, David Landsberg); Daniels (Jeff Hollis), who was Black; the Italian recruit Mignone (Barry Pearl); the Puerto Rican Rodriguez (Richard Beauchamp); and Shimokawa (Evan Kim), a Japanese immigrant.

Harrison Page played Sharkey's best friend and fellow CPO, Dave Robinson; Elizabeth Allen was cast as their boss (and Sharkey's nemesis), Captain Quinlan. Sharkey was a stereotypical male chauvinist, and early in the show's run, he locked horns with Captain Quinlan. That plotline eventually tapered off, until Captain Quinlan was written off the show and replaced by veteran television actor Richard X. Slattery as Captain Buckner.

Peter Isacksen was a fresh-faced, extremely tall twenty-two-year-old from Fullerton, California, a newcomer to acting whose previous experience was a small role in Ron Howard's big-screen directorial debut, *Eat My Dust*. Peter and Ron Howard had grown friendly, and

Ron invited Peter to lunch one day at the Paramount lot. Ron was running late, so he told Peter about two casting directors he should see while he was there since—who knows?—they might have some work. "I walked in and I was this six-foot-six skinny character guy and they said, 'Well, we don't have much, but Ron never sends anybody over, and we're doing this pilot called *CPO Sharkey*. Why don't you read for it?'" Isacksen recalled. "They liked me, so they sent me to NBC and I met with Aaron Ruben and he went, 'Yeah, that's great, thanks for the audition, we'll let you know.'"

Peter was deflated and, figuring he'd blown the audition, decided to hitch a ride with his father, a garment salesman, who was driving to Arkansas on business. "We got to Fayetteville and my mom called us in the hotel room and said, 'NBC wants to see you tomorrow.'" In his first audition for Ruben, he had played Lester Pruitt without an accent. When he arrived at the Fayetteville airport for his flight back to L.A., he met a man with a Southern accent. "Aaron Ruben said, 'You did a great job last time. We're just looking for something different.' I said, 'Well, what about this?' and I did the guy from the Fayetteville airport and everyone started to laugh. Aaron said, 'You start Monday.'"[3]

Isacksen was already awestruck when he arrived at the NBC studios in Burbank and noticed the first three parking spaces in the lot, reserved for Johnny Carson, Ed McMahon,[4] and Doc Severinsen. "I had to go to a rehearsal hall and didn't know a soul. I didn't know anyone in Hollywood other than Ron Howard and a few other actors," he recalled. "And I see Rehearsal Hall 4 and it's a big door and I have to bend, and I look through the window and there's a long table . . . and there's Don. And my heart dropped. I went, Holy shit! It's really Don Rickles! I had memorized *Hello, Dummy!* and I was such a huge fan. I walked in and I went up to him and I said, 'Hi, Mr. Rickles,' and he said, 'Sit down, you big dumb moose!' And that was how we started this relationship and this show. I laughed for two-and-a-half years."

CPO Sharkey premiered on December 1, 1976, on NBC, along with *The McLean Stevenson Show* and *Sirota's Court*, starring Michael

Constantine. The triumvirate replaced *The Blue Knight, The Tony Orlando and Dawn Rainbow Hour,* and the Wednesday night movie on the network's prime-time schedule.

Aaron Ruben wrote the show's opening episode, which aired at 8 p.m. under the original title of the series, *Oh Captain! My Captain.* Don, as Otto Sharkey, was introduced in the opening credits as he marched out onto the deck of a Navy ship in his full CPO regalia, to brassy, military-style musical accompaniment. He strode on the deck, walked down a flight of stairs, hopped on a bicycle, and rode away (message: he's a fun guy, too!). In the twenty-two minutes that follow, Sharkey reenlists in the Navy, where he has spent twenty-four years of his life ("The Navy is my life. That's probably why I never got married. You might say I'm married to the Navy"). He also complains about how easy the modern naval recruit has it these days—"It's like a regular Caribbean cruise. The only thing missing is shuffleboard, rhumba lessons, and Tony Martin." It sounded like a line fired off by Don Rickles in one of his nightclub routines.

Sharkey tells Dave Robinson, who's Black, "Let's face it, man, you people do make the best drum and bugle corps" and, in the setup for his meeting with Captain Quinlan, vows that he will never work for a woman "because broads are trouble. Did ya ever look at dried makeup on a sink? Eyelashes with nobody in 'em?" Sharkey meets the recruits of Company 144—"I'm gonna keep an eye on you" he tells them— and writes a letter of resignation after his first encounter with Captain Quinlan (he cannot take orders from a woman). He has a heart-to-heart conversation with a seventeen-year-old homesick recruit, Fletcher (see, he *does* have a heart of gold!) and rescinds his resignation—after Quinlan calls him to her office to tell him how proud she is after hearing about his talk with Fletcher. He is a valuable asset to the US Navy, she tells him. He feels wanted and needed . . . and he can work with a woman boss, after all. Cue the closing credits.

The critical reaction to *CPO Sharkey* was mixed.

"It's unlikely that many will debate the failure of last week's NBC show, *C.P.O. Sharkey* . . . it is an injection of lameness," wrote

Miami Herald critic Bill Cosford. "Though dealing with the one comic who turned audience hecklers from opportunities to threats, *Sharkey*'s writers conspired to put the man in situations as saccharine as possible. Outside of dismissing a few random objects as 'hockey pucks,' Rickles . . . dispenses no more vitriol than kind-hearted wisdom. Everyone knows he doesn't do well with others' material in situations of others' design, but no one ever remembers when it comes to series time."[5]

The *Washington Post*: "Don Rickles last night appeared to finally have been cast in a role that allows him to fully exploit his genius at put-down humor . . . Cast in the role of a chief petty officer at the San Diego Naval Training Center, Rickles is allowed to use his talents as a put-down artist in much the same way that Phil Silvers' image as the con man so brilliantly exploited Sgt. Bilko . . . Though there is a very touching scene where Sharkey lies to a recruit about his first days in the Navy in an effort to cheer up the young man, the other material is pretty much vintage Rickles sarcasm."[6]

CPO Sharkey taped directly across the hall from *The Tonight Show* in Burbank. Don's proximity to Carson proved to be the fuel for one of the most memorable bits in *The Tonight Show*'s storied history—and in the short shelf life of *CPO Sharkey*. Carson made sure to include the moment in his annual montage each time he celebrated another banner year on NBC.

Here is the setup: On December 12, 1975, Don was a guest on *The Tonight Show*. Bob Newhart was subbing for Johnny that night, and Don broke into a bit about singer/songwriter/actor Anthony Newley, who was seated next to him on the couch. He then turned on Newhart, mocking his background as an accountant and telling Bob he "could now go to Mexico." (It made no sense, in that Rickles stream-of-consciousness style, but it got a laugh.) Don grabbed the wooden cigarette box that Johnny kept on his desk, broke into a stereotypical Mexican accent, and used the box to forcefully "stamp" some papers that Newhart had in front of him, in the fashion of a customs official—and broke the cigarette box in the process.

"Carson's cigarette box!" he shouted. "Oh my God, I broke Carson's cigarette box! I broke Johnny's box!"

Carson was back behind his desk the next night. In the opening segment following the monologue, he was chatting with bandleader Doc Severinsen (Ed McMahon was off) when he noticed the broken cigarette box. (He knew about it beforehand, but it made for better television to act surprised.) "What the hell happened to this?" he asked Severinsen, holding the box. "You know how long I've had this cigarette box? I brought this out from New York." Carson said he had seen Don before the show in the makeup room, getting ready to tape "that *FPO Harkey* show." He got up from behind the desk, and as a camera crew followed him, he marched out of his studio and across the hall (passing Carson regular Pat McCormick on the way). He opened the door to the *CPO Sharkey* soundstage and barged in. Don and Harrison Page were taping a scene for the show as Sharkey and Robinson. Everyone but Don was in on the joke.

"Johnny was a good enough actor that everyone thought, 'Oh, geez, is he pissed off,'" Doc Severinsen recalled. "And he got up behind the desk and went across the hall and the camera followed him the whole way."[7]

"Rickles! Rickles! Stop the taping, somebody broke my cigarette box!" Carson yelled. Don froze in his tracks and was speechless as Johnny confronted him. "Hey, a Black man!" Carson yelled in Rickles-type fashion, walking over to Page to slap his hand. When in Rome. Don quickly recovered his snarky mojo. "That's a darn shame," he said as Johnny showed him the broken box, "I'd give it to Tony Randall as a wedding gift." Johnny turned to Page again. "I hope you get the cotton mill down South," he said. "If this show goes like the others you're out of work come January."

Don warmed up the studio audience before every taping of *CPO Sharkey*. It helped him to round into fighting form as snarling Otto Sharkey. The stars of other NBC shows taping on the Burbank lot would often drop by to watch the proceedings. "Don was a fantastic actor, but he felt more comfortable in the warm-up," recalled costar Peter Isacksen. "He would come out a half hour before the show and just do thirty minutes. It was the greatest. So you would see people in the audience—Redd Foxx would come, Slappy White would come, Dean Martin was in the audience one night, Rowan and Martin were there another night. They just wanted to see a half hour of Rickles. He would say to people in the front row, 'Excuse me, can I speak to the Black man? You're lucky you're in the front row—don't make me move you.'"

Peter Isacksen grew close to Don during the show's run, and The Merchant of Venom took him under his wing. Peter's father and mother would often drive to Burbank to watch their son taping the show. Don got to know both of them. "Somewhere during his half-hour warm-up, he would say, unprompted, 'Where's Eddie? Is Eddie here? And it was my dad!" Isacksen recalled. "And my dad never had a light shined on him in his entire life, and he would raise his hand and Don would say, 'Eddie, listen, after the show, Chivas, you and I, the dressing room. Not with the big dumb one.' My dad lived for that." Peter's parents drove to Burbank even after Eddie Isacksen was diagnosed with stomach cancer. "They would come up and stay, and my dad would put his game face on—and when I tell you that Don Rickles kept my dad alive for another eight months, that is the absolute truth. My dad knew it. Don knew it. It's what my dad lived for. After he died, Don kind of stepped up and became my mentor, my second father."

CPO Sharkey and McLean Stevenson's widely derided sitcom survived into the new year. NBC dumped Sirota's Court—considered by most critics to be the best of the network's three new fall shows—and replaced it with Dan Haggerty and The Life and Times of Grizzly Adams. So much for television justice.

CPO Sharkey skirted the programming purge, but there was no guarantee it would make it to the fall. By early March, the sitcom was on the cancellation block and headed for the television graveyard, another Don Rickles one-season flop. In a Hail Mary move,

NBC programmed back-to-back episodes of *Sharkey* on March 23, opposite the time slot champ, ABC's *Baretta*, starring Robert Blake. The viewer response to an hour of Otto Sharkey was unexpectedly enthusiastic and saved the series from the prime-time dustbin. NBC executives changed their minds about canceling the show and, in a down-to-the-wire decision, renewed *CPO Sharkey* for a second season of twenty-two episodes that were slotted to air in a new Friday-night time slot in October.

"We've nurtured *Sharkey* along," network vice president John J. McMahan explained; everyone else just scratched their heads and wondered about NBC's programming acumen. It went a long way toward explaining the network's third-place finish that season behind CBS—which, in turn, was knocked off its longtime number-one perch by—wonder of wonders—perennial also-ran ABC, fueled by hits including *Laverne & Shirley*, *The Bionic Woman*, and *Welcome Back, Kotter*. Don toyed with taking out an ad in the trades: "I would like to thank NBC for the pickup for a second year but unfortunately I have to refuse the pickup because I don't know how to handle a second year." Yes, Don, be careful what you wish for.

NBC needed content for the fall. It had lost two of its biggest series personalities with the tragic death, in January, of twenty-two-year-old *Chico and the Man* star Freddie Prinze—who shot himself in the head—and the defection of Redd Foxx from *Sanford and Son* to ABC, which paid him a boatload of money to host a variety show (which quickly devolved into a chaotic mess). *CPO Sharkey* could, at the very least, act as a placeholder on NBC's schedule for the backup bench of midseason replacements waiting in the wings to take over from one of the network's inevitable fall failures.

Don and the *CPO Sharkey* cast and crew celebrated the renewal with a party on the set. He had made it. Finally. Don Rickles was now a prime-time series graduate, promoted to sophomore status at the age of fifty-one after all the unsold pilots and the two glaring series failures. So what if it was tenuous? Money was not an issue; his nightclub career was going great guns in all the established venues, and Don signed a two-year, $2 million deal to return to the Sahara in Las Vegas, to where it had all started for him eighteen long years ago. The new contract called for Don to perform a minimum of eight weeks a year; the Sahara would accommodate his traveling between Vegas and L.A. to shoot his NBC series. He continued to appear in ads for National Car Rental both on television and in print. The company, though, was starting to phase him out of its long-term plans. "Whether you like him or hate him, people know [Rickles] is there," said company president Joe James. "But you can only use one device so long."

In March, after *CPO Sharkey* was renewed, Barry Pearl, who played Italian American recruit Mignone (who was named after Don's bodyguard, Michael Mignone), learned that he was being dropped from the series . . . on his birthday. Pearl's screen time diminished over the course of the first season as Mignone faded into the background and was supplanted by Rodriguez, the Puerto Rican recruit played by Richard Beauchamp. Pearl recalled how the wear and tear of a weekly series was taking its toll on Don—who was in nearly every scene. The pressure was enormous.

"We would sit in the audience and Don would sit in the telescope director's chair on the stage and we would get notes," Pearl recalled. "And Don's aide-de-camp, Harry, would go into the prop cabinet and mix him up a martini that he would put in one of those 1950s tumblers. And we all knew what it was, but they couldn't put it in a martini glass.

"Don was uncomfortable because he was confined to a particular script and memorizing was tough for him," Pearl said. "He would get past it, but he was a nervous wreck. His freeform [style] was just that, he had it down to a T, and he was very comfortable, but not so much within the confines of scripted material. He would make it his own, but he was just shy of being the kind of brilliant performer that he was when he was extemporaneous. I think Don felt a bit like a fish out of water sometimes. He studied, he had done some dramatic roles, but he really soared as a nightclub comic and that's what he was known for. So I think that he felt penned in."[8]

The warning signs were there, and were exacerbated when Season 2 of *CPO Sharkey* premiered on Friday, October 21, at 8 p.m.—and was steamrolled by *Donny and Marie* over on the suddenly all-powerful ABC. The show's weak opening had the pundits predicting that it would be gone by December if its numbers did not improve. Besides, it was already living on borrowed time.

"At the end of the day, Aaron [Ruben] would give us notes and Don's valet would bring him a nice cooler of something that would make him feel better, and I believe he was a vodka guy," recalled Peter Isacksen, echoing Barry Pearl's assessment of the situation on the set of *CPO Sharkey*. "Aaron would start the notes process and you could see Don just drift away, and he would have one sip and another sip and he would go."[9]

Don tried not to let the stress and pressure of carrying a prime-time series affect the cast and crew, but the atmosphere was tense. He particularly enjoyed ribbing Isacksen, the show's goofy breakout star. He was profiled in *TV Guide*, sharing the cover with Don, as Otto Sharkey, standing on a box so he could scowl directly into Lester Pruitt's golly-gee face.

"Aaron Ruben came down to the stage one night, on a tape night, and Don was particularly tough on me because he's poking me and knows that if he pokes me, I'm going to laugh and he's not going to get in trouble," Isacksen recalled. "Aaron came down and said, 'Okay, I know you're a young actor. I want to give you some advice.' He said, 'When you look at Don, he is going to die in two weeks. Do anything you can so you don't laugh at this man.' Like that could have helped me. It was Don's playground. It was his show. He would turn to all of us and say, 'Sorry, I'm going across the hall to talk to Johnny.' We taped twenty feet away from *The Tonight Show,* just through a hallway."

Isacksen crossed that hallway himself when he was invited onto *The Tonight Show* shortly thereafter—and spent seven awkward minutes on Johnny Carson's couch. "I followed Andy Kaufman and there were no laughs left," he recalled. "It was too much for me. It was my first time on the show. And Rickles, about nine months later, came over to me in the corner and said, 'Monday night, I'm guest-hosting Carson. You're doing it.' I said, 'Really?' And he said, 'Yeah, don't screw it up and don't try to be funny. I'm going to make it right for you because nobody can live their whole life doing the Carson show that you did.' That night, on the show, he said, 'Here's my buddy, he's on my show give him a big hand.' I came on and did much better. That's my man."

CPO Sharkey was losing steam, quickly, and the series was pre-empted several times. The Friday-night time slot did not help, with *Donny and Marie* trouncing it in the ratings week after week. "The peo-ple who were writing it couldn't write funny for Don Rickles, CPO Sharkey," recalled comedy writer Ron Friedman. "If they just said, 'Okay, you're the noncommissioned officer and you're Don Rickles, do it,' that would have worked. But the people doing it had no idea what a stand-up comic was about. Nobody connected with the show had ever written stand-up or done stand-up. So they were fearful. They didn't know what to do, so they went the traditional route. 'Oh, you can't say that, that's nasty.' Horseshit, that's what it's all about. I saw Don once at NBC while I was doing a pilot that I had written and was producing and he was moping in the cafeteria. I said, 'What's the matter, Don?' He said, 'This show . . . they won't let me be me.'"[10]

As the calendar turned to 1978, Don found himself defending the show. The prime-time prognosticators were already focused on the networks' fall schedules—and on what would survive or die. "*CPO Sharkey* is a show that I believe in because it's the closest thing to what Don Rickles is about," he told a group of television critics in January. "And I was delighted to find that last week was the first time we had tied our time slot with a 27 share . . . against *Donny & Marie*, which the world seems to be watching. We only have 170 stations—we do have two more if there's a storm in Indiana and you put a wet wire on your *tuchus*. Then it lights up!"[11] He mentioned that the series was further hampered by airing on a delayed basis in fourteen markets—and that it had not aired in Miami Beach, home to Etta Rickles, for "seven or eight weeks," throwing in, for comedic effect that "if you've never been there, there's one dead gentile on the highway with an arrow in his neck and three Black guys going 'Shoot da Jew and win a prize.'" It made sense in the mind of Don Rickles—and he could not help himself when it came to his nightclub shtick. An audience was an audience.

Fred Silverman, the wunderkind programming chief who worked miracles at ABC, shocked the television industry by defecting to third-place NBC in early 1978. The forty-one-year-old "genius" was intent on putting his stamp on his new network home. He let *CPO Sharkey* run its course—its ratings did not improve in the winter months leading into its final scheduled episode. In May, he canceled the series. Silverman had the distinction of having run all three networks, and now Don Rickles had failed on all three networks—albeit with, at the very least, a two-season run on NBC.

"When they canceled it, much to my surprise, it had an excellent rating," series creator Aaron Ruben recalled, conveniently forgetting its weak Friday-night viewership. "There was somebody at NBC that didn't like Don. I really believe it. It's that simple." Ruben recalled that he saw Fred Silverman while on vacation in Paris, before *CPO Sharkey* was officially canceled. "He loved the *Sharkey* show. He said, 'I hear you're on some [fall] schedules and not on some others—you mean there's a doubt [that the series wouldn't be renewed]?' I thought we were doing so well. As a CPO, those guys do a lot of yelling, a lot of insulting, and that's Don at his best."[12]

Or not. Don did not publicly address the cancellation; there was talk NBC wanted to keep him on the payroll, so he kept his mouth shut. He was a semi-regular on two of the network's shows: *The Tonight Show*—both as a guest and as one of Johnny's rotating roster of celebrity guest hosts—and he could be counted on to deliver five minutes of insults on *The Dean Martin Celebrity Roast*. It was better that he did not criticize NBC.

He did not return to the prime-time series game for the next fifteen years.

Decades later, in *Rickles' Book*, Don barely mentioned *CPO Sharkey*, but in the wake of the show's cancellation, he joked about his latest television failure in his indefatigable talk-show appearances—but there were signs he took this latest setback particularly hard. Friends who saw him backstage before a nightclub performance noticed that he was taking more than a belt or two; one night, his faithful manservant, Harry Goins, felt the wrath of the frayed Rickles temper.

In August 1976, in Toronto to perform at a nightclub there, Don was having dinner with Joe Scandore, Joe's secretary, and Harry Goins. He was friendly to the locals who came over to the table to say hello, ask for an autograph, and banter with the famous comedian. Then, while Don ate his steak, he asked Harry for two packets of Sweet 'n Low so he could "tip" two waiters hovering nearby (shtick he pulled often in restaurants). Harry reached into the leather bag he carried around with him, but could only find one packet of the sweetener—sending Don into a mini-rage. "That's your job—I want you to go out tomorrow and buy two boxes. Do you hear me? That's your job!" he yelled, pointing his finger at Harry. "Get lots of stuff. Are you listening to what I'm saying?" The waiter refilled Don's coffee cup, and he continued his tirade after Harry fumbled through his bag and found another packet of Sweet 'n Low. "You're damn lucky, buddy," he said. "I was just waiting for you to say you couldn't find one. I was hoping you couldn't."[13]

In September, he was a guest on *The Tonight Show* (along with Bob Newhart and Dr. Joyce Brothers) and took the insults over the top. Two of the other guests that night were singers Marilyn McCoo and Billy Davis Jr., and The Merchant of Venom turned on them without warning. "Either he's Black," he said, nodding toward Davis, "or two cufflinks are coming toward me." Davis, simmering, did not crack a smile or say a word. "C'mon," Don persisted. "You're free now. Laugh. Either laugh or go pick me up a TV set." The studio audience tittered. Davis was not amused.

It was a harbinger of things to come.

CHAPTER 17

In 1977, New Jersey legalized gambling in Atlantic City, hoping to revitalize the now-decrepit oceanside metropolis, once home to a thriving nightclub scene, including Paul "Skinny" D'Amato's 500 Club, which helped launch Frank Sinatra and Martin and Lewis into orbit. (The club burned down in 1973.) Sinatra was back playing Atlantic City now, and Don, too, began performing there, at Resorts International, which opened its doors in May 1978 as the East Coast gambling mecca's first hotel/casino.

He was not headlining his own network series anymore, but he kept his name circulating in prime time, albeit in smaller roles. In 1980, he appeared in a forgettable television movie comedy called *For the Love of It*—something to do with a young couple (Jeff Conaway and Deborah Raffin) who come into the possession of top-secret Russian documents—and, two years later, he guest-starred opposite his close friend Carroll O'Connor on an episode of *Archie Bunker's Place*, a spinoff from *All in the Family* in which Archie continued to run the now-renamed bar he'd bought late in the run of *All in the Family*. He had a Jewish partner, Murray Klein (Martin Balsam) in a bid to show that Archie's views had evolved.

In early 1984, NBC was launching a new/old series called *TV's Bloopers & Practical Jokes*. It was an extension of several specials dating back to 1980 that highlighted "bloopers," mistakes made by actors and actresses while filming a series (fluffed or forgotten lines, missed cues, unintentional laughter—sometimes peppered with expletives). The show, hosted by Ed McMahon and Dick Clark, also included a *Candid Camera*–type segment of practical jokes played on unsuspecting everyday people.

The series had been a ratings success in its past iterations, and ABC girded itself for battle by ordering its own knockoff version of the show (ABC was legally forbidden to use the term "blooper"). The network called on executive producer Bob Booker to come up with something similar. Booker, an industry veteran, had cowritten and coproduced the 1962 JFK-spoof album *The First Family* with Earle Doud. The album was a smash it, selling 7 million copies and winning the Grammy Award for Album of the Year in 1963. (It was pulled from circulation following President John F. Kennedy's assassination; impersonator Vaughn Meader, who became a national celebrity after playing JFK on the album, slipped into obscurity.) Since then, Booker had coproduced *NBC Follies* starring Sammy Davis Jr. (on which Don appeared), worked on television specials with Charo and Paul Lynde, and written a 1978 episode of *CPO Sharkey* ("The Used Car Caper"). He knew Don from way back in the Murray Franklin days in Miami Beach.

"There was no host for the ABC series and we were still working on it," Booker recalled. "I read that Don and Steve Lawrence had done an act together up in Reno, I think, just fooling around. It sounded very funny and I knew both of them for years. So I said, 'Rickles and Lawrence would be a good idea.'

"I took Lew Erlicht, who was the president of ABC at the time, up to Vegas to see Don. Well, Lew had never seen Rickles. So we got on a plane and went to see him at the Sahara. I mean, I've never seen Lew laugh more in my life. He was standing on the table applauding and screaming. As we're walking out I said, 'So?' He said, 'Yeah, get him.' And he stopped for a moment and said, 'But don't let him do any of that,' which was Rickles' problem on television. All the guys would go see him, fall on the floor, and say, 'I love him. Hire him. But don't let him do any of that.' Well, to do 'any of that' is Rickles."

Steve Lawrence signed on for the project, and they shot the pilot a week later in L.A. "I took it over to Lew and we sat and looked at it.

He never smiled. Never," Booker said. "But the reason the show got on the air was . . . they liked the idea, they wanted it, and they needed this damn show to fill a spot." (It replaced *Just Our Luck*, a short-lived sitcom that premiered in the fall of 1983.) "I looked at Lew and I said, 'What do you think?' He said, 'It's the worst piece of shit I've ever seen in my life.' But they needed it a week from Monday."

Erlicht and his ABC programming executives told Booker there was "too much Rickles" in the pilot episode, so he edited Don out of a few segments. "Steve [Lawrence] was very bothered by that," he said. "He said, 'How dare they do that to Don!' But we changed some pieces. It was the same show, we just took Don's lines and gave them to Steve. Don was aware of it. He was being nice. He said, 'They're calling me to do the news.' I'll never forget that."

The show was now called *Foul-Ups, Bleeps & Blunders* and premiered as a midseason replacement in early January 1984, competing at 8 p.m. Tuesdays against *The A-Team* on NBC, the number two show on television. As promised, it highlighted outtakes from television shows, movies, and commercials, and as on its NBC rival, there was a hidden-camera segment and dropping-by celebrities (Don Adams, Bob Newhart, Sally Struthers, Leslie Nielsen, Madeline Kahn). "Capitalizing on a current fad of airing celebrity mistakes, ABC has sifted through material from cutting room floors to air its own outtakes series," one critic wrote. "Insulting Don Rickles and Nice Guy Steve Lawrence host, an odd pairing that doesn't work. TV audiences can take only so many flubbed lines and misfired props before the novelty wears off. Couple this with an identical series on NBC and you've got a blooper overdose."[1] Another critic described the hosts as "surprisingly inadequate." Some wags, fed up with the onslaught of outtake shows, labeled the format "Blooper Scoopers"—alluding to laws enforcing the retrieval of dog waste.

But a funny thing happened on the way to cancellation bin— *Foul-Ups, Bleeps & Blunders* was a modest hit out of the starting gate. It finished thirteenth in its premiere week (*TV's Bloopers & Practical Jokes* finished fifth), and by early February the prognosticators predicted it would be renewed for a second season. "I broke my neck studying and working as an actor and here I am presenting some yo-yo on top of a mountain falling into a bowl of fish and it becomes 25th in the country," Don joked.[2] In a testament to its popularity, producers of television shows were said to be staging bloopers in an attempt to get them onto *Foul-Ups* or *TV's Bloopers* and generate some publicity. Whatever works. Don's taping schedule allowed him the luxury of continuing his nightclub work nearly nonstop, including runs that winter at Resorts International in Atlantic City and a return engagement at Harrah's in Lake Tahoe. He continued to appear semi-regularly on *The Dean Martin Celebrity Roast*, which was winding down its ten-year run and aired its final episode in December.

Don was having his best run on television since the cancellation of *CPO Sharkey* six years earlier. On January 28, he hosted *Saturday Night Live*, NBC's vaunted late-night sketch/comedy series, with rocker Billy Idol joining him as that week's musical guest. *SNL* was in its ninth season and going through one of its transitional periods. Lorne Michaels, its first executive producer, had left the show in 1980 and didn't return until 1985, and its middling ensemble cast lacked the star power of the original "Not Ready for Prime Time Players" John Belushi, Dan Aykroyd, Bill Murray, Gilda Radner, Jane Curtin, et al. Its latest darling, Eddie Murphy, had left the show three months after Don's appearance.

Don opened his first and only time hosting *Saturday Night Live* with a vintage ten-minute version of his nightclub act: "Wayne Newton's not here—he's in Las Vegas on a ladder trying to make his letters bigger" . . . "I was up in Harlem the other night and said [drops the mic] 'Just the wallet! Just the wallet!'" . . . "I make jokes about Black people and why not? Because I'm not one" . . . "Are you Italian? No . . . the one with the flies around him" . . . "I'm gonna get a paper, you start" [Jews making love] . . . "They're laughing and one of their guys is up in my room now taking my jewelry" [Hispanics] . . . "There's a new thing out called cottage cheese" [to an overweight man] . . . "Can I grab you by the legs? I wanna dust" [to a young woman with her hair brushed way up on her head] . . . "We gotta make a fuss over them otherwise they burn the shirts" [Chinese people]. Former NFL coach turned CBS sportscaster John Madden and NBC president Brandon Tartikoff were there, and came in for some razzing as Don wandered off the stage and waded into the studio audience. He ad-libbed his way through sketches, breaking up *SNL* cast member Joe Piscopo in a "Witness Relocation" bit in which he played a schlub who crossed the mob—then followed that up with Piscopo when they appeared later in a "Romeo and Juliet" sketch in which he played Friar Don ("I hope Eddie Murphy robs your house!").

ABC, meanwhile, renewed *Foul-Ups, Bleeps & Blunders*, and it returned in the fall with Don and Steve Lawrence—but its premise, as some had predicted, was wearing thin and the ratings sagged. The show sunk to fiftieth in the prime-time ratings; ABC yanked it as a regularly scheduled series and aired it only sporadically thereafter through the end of the year. It returned in the spring of 1985 in a weekly time slot but didn't fare much better. ABC was having a lousy season—it wound up finishing third for the first time in a decade—and it cleaned house, axing *Foul-Ups, Bleeps & Blunders* along with fifteen other shows, including *T.J. Hooker* (starring William Shatner), *Matt Houston*, and *MacGruder and Loud*.

Don was vacationing in Hawaii with Barbara and the kids in January 1985 when he got a call from Frank Sinatra telling him—ordering him, really—that he needed "Bullethead" in Washington, D.C., in two days to perform at President Ronald Regan's second inauguration. No one turned down Sinatra, and if they did, they were iced out of his circle for a length of time or banished completely. Don packed his bags. He knew Reagan from way back, had roasted him on *The Dean Martin Show*, and was thrilled at the opportunity to appear on the nationally televised special airing January 19 on ABC. (Reagan was officially sworn in as president at the Capitol's rotunda on January 21.)

Sinatra sang, of course, as did Mac Davis, the Beach Boys, and Donna Summer. Rich Little did his Reagan impression, and Pearl Bailey, Merv Griffin, Mr. T, and Tom Selleck were there to introduce the acts. Don was welcomed on the stage by Emmanuel Lewis, the diminutive fourteen-year-old star of ABC's hit series *Webster*. "The inspired interlude was a visitation from Don Rickles, so much more audacious than Bob Hope would have been," Tom Shales wrote in the *Washington Post*. "'Is this too fast, Ronnie?' he asked Reagan at one point. 'Now you're big—and you're getting on my nerves,' Rickles said to the president. His hair white and his girth stockier, Rickles looked like a prankish Khrushchev."[3]

Don's relationship with the new president continued once Reagan was in office. One night, Don, Barbara, Bob Booker and his wife Barbara, and Dodgers manager Tommy Lasorda went out for dinner to The Palm, a steakhouse in L.A. "Gigi was the maître d' there and was a very good friend of Don's," Booker recalled. "So we all get out of the limo, and as you walk into the restaurant, there's a giant bar on the left and a door to the kitchen in the front and the maître d' stands to the right. The crazy thing about Rickles was [that] if he was going to do something, he never told you. He was not a Jerry Lewis who said, 'Watch this.' You never heard that from Don. It just happened. So we walk into the restaurant and Don pulls out of his pocket one of those stars that you get from the police, a card in case you ever get stopped. It looks very official. So he walks into the kitchen, holds up the card, and screams 'Immigration!' They were going out the windows and the doors. Nobody in that kitchen knew who the hell he was.

"So we're back at the table and Gigi says to Don, 'Ronnie is in the back.' That's all I heard. Well, you know what that is. And Don says, 'Don't tell him I'm here.' It was insane. We're sitting at the table and he never mentioned it. And up from behind Rickles walks the President of the United States. Ronnie comes up and taps him on the shoulder, and Rickles turns around and says, 'You again? Can't you see we're eating? Can't you see I'm with people?' And of course nobody laughed more than Reagan."

Etta would have been so proud of her Sonny Boy performing for the President of the United States. She died in September 1984 at the age of eighty-three in Mount Sinai Medical Center in Miami Beach after suffering from emphysema. "She was a legend, one of the most beloved mothers in show business," Don's publicist, Gene Shefrin, said in a statement. "She was befriended by every star—Frank Sinatra, Richard Burton. She used to make chicken soup for them and send food to their dressing rooms . . . Although Max Rickles tried to dissuade his son from seeking a show business career after World War II, Etta Rickles was supportive of Don's ambition to be an actor and comedian."

Etta's death was widely reported—as was the fact that Don had closed every show, for years, by saluting his mother: "Good night, Etta darling, wherever you are."

Don's popularity with the country's commander in chief continued with Ronald Reagan's successor, George H. W. Bush, who invited Don to the White House for a state dinner. Don recalled sitting next to first lady Barbara Bush, who told him that she followed his career and reeled off parts of his acting résumé (*The Twilight Zone*, *Run Silent, Run Deep*) before getting to the crux of the matter: "Were things so bad that you had to do *Bikini Beach* and *Beach Blanket Bingo*?"[4]

CHAPTER 18

Earlier in this book you met the horse named Don Rickles. A decade after he faded into oblivion, his successor, also named Don Rickles, began to race. This Don Rickles was bred in Kentucky, was purchased as a colt in 1982 by Ted Sabarese for $105,000, and was trained by Joe Scandore's "nephew," John Parisella, whose clients included James Caan, Jack Klugman, and Don Adams. Don Rickles 2.0 ran from 1983 to 1985, winning eighteen races, including the Nashua Stakes (Angel Cordero Jr. was the jockey that afternoon).[1]

One bright, sunny day in L.A., Don Adams, an inveterate gambler, took Don Rickles (the human) out to the Hollywood Park racetrack to see Don Rickles (the horse)—who finished fourth in his race. Adams took Don to the winner's circle, borrowed the flowery garland from the triumphant horse, and placed it around Don's equine namesake. "Don Rickles, stand next to Don Rickles." He snapped a photo. "Don Rickles, now you're the winner."[2]

Don turned sixty in May 1986, and the next few years flew by in a steady blur of nightclub dates, late-night television appearances, and the occasional guest-starring turn in prime time or a small movie role—including a 1989 episode of *Newhart*, Bob Newhart's successful follow-up to *The Bob Newhart Show*, and *Keaton's Cop*, a low-budget feature starring Lee Majors and Abe Vigoda.

Financially, Don was set for life and, in 1989 he shelled out over $2 million for a new four-bedroom, five-bathroom, 5,600-square-foot Mediterranean-style house in L.A.'s exclusive gated community

260

Century Woods Estates. The house featured a two-story entry with a sweeping staircase, a large living room with a hand-carved stone fireplace (imported from Europe), an elevator, and an "owner's suite" that included a private outdoor patio, dual baths, and roomy walk-in closets.[3] He and Barbara tooled around town in a $35,000 1988 Jaguar XJS; in March 1989, on their twenty-fourth wedding anniversary, they drove to daughter Mindy's apartment in West L.A. in the afternoon and parked on Fountain Avenue nearby. As they exited the car, they were held up at gunpoint by a man who pointed a gun at Barbara's chest, demanded her purse, then hopped in the Jaguar and drove off. Neither Don nor Barbara was injured, and despite being badly shaken, they continued on to dinner to celebrate their anniversary.

Don had exhausted the possibilities for a new series at ABC, CBS, and NBC, but cable television was a major player now, and Don was no stranger to the upstart platform. In 1982, he and Don Adams hosted a Showtime special called *Two Top Bananas*—which was heavy on burlesque and risqué humor—and four years later, he returned to the network.

In the spring of 1986, Bob Booker, the executive producer of *Foul-Ups, Bleeps & Blunders*, pitched Don to the executives at the cable network for a one-off special, and they bought the idea for *Don Rickles: Rickles on the Loose*, which aired in August. It interspersed clips of Don performing at the Sahara in Las Vegas ("Is that your wife? You should put her on a hook in a butcher shop") with comedy bits and sketches—including Don acting as the best man and marriage counselor for four couples who were getting married in the Sahara's main showroom before an audience of over a thousand people. The couples were brought to the hotel from a nearby wedding chapel after agreeing to be on the show.

"Investigative reporters were very hot at the time, and I wanted to do an investigation of all the things going wrong in the country, with Rickles as the investigator," Booker recalled. "And we actually set it up as a pilot. We went to ABC, unannounced. Don was the only man in the world who could do it, because there was no script. Nothing. We walked into ABC—it was two cameras, an audio man, Rickles, and me—and we walked into Lew Erlicht's office and Don said, 'Where's Lew?' The guy who was the head of comedy at the time saw Don asking for Lew and ran in and closed his door. Then we walked into the middle of a meeting and Don said, 'Okay, which one's Lew? Oh, that kid in the corner, right?' And he did twenty minutes with it. We never aired it. Lew said to me as we were leaving, 'Bob, if I ever see that on the show, you'll never do another series here—by the way, can you get me a copy of it and send it to the house?' In the second sketch, we walked into Nielsen, the ratings company, and every single person ran out of the building."[4]

Don Rickles: Rickles on the Loose featured The Merchant of Venom patrolling a Hollywood tour bus, barging in on a taping of *The Merv Griffin Show*, prowling Gold's Gym to harass the people exercising there, mingling with a group of Hell's Angels, ribbing Dodgers manager Tommy Lasorda and players Bill Russell and Steve Garvey, and paying a visit to the Department of Motor Vehicles. "Don said to one guy, 'Are you Jewish?' He was obviously a Hispanic man," Booker said. "He said, 'No,' and Don says, 'Get out of the way and let this Jew in.' He was lining up the crowd and he filed for a new driver's license. He had his chauffeur and he said, 'I'm too rich to drive.' It was crazy because it was just off the top of Don's head. You would tape thirty minutes and get maybe seven or eight minutes of really good footage." Bob Newhart made a cameo appearance in a bit featuring Don in a park; Ann Jillian, Jerry Lewis, and Frank Sinatra Jr. also briefly appeared.

The segments of the special featuring Don doing his nightclub act were trickier to shoot. "Don never wanted the act taped," Booker recalled. "He didn't want the act to be out there. I don't blame him. So I said, 'We'll put a couple of people in with you and you can do thirty minutes in the afternoon in the [Sahara] nightclub. I will let you be the judge of when you're finished.'" It took Booker and his crew about a month to film *Don Rickles: Rickles on the Loose* since they needed to work around his schedule. "I said to Joe Scandore, 'Would you like a check?' He said, 'Well, Don's not through with the job. When he finishes the job and you're happy with the job, then you pay him. You don't pay him up front,'" Booker said. "I never heard that before in my life."

Don's friendship with President Ronald Reagan came into play during the shooting of the special, but viewers never saw what transpired. One of the planned bits had Don meeting with Reagan when he stopped in Las Vegas in late June to campaign for Republican Senate candidate Jim Santini. "The producers wanted me to meet the president when he got off the plane," Don said. "Can you imagine that? But the White House said it would be too much security to clear. The president found out about it and called me. We arranged to meet in a parking garage after his speech. There we were, eighty-eight security people checking me out, dogs sniffing me. Can you believe it? It looked like Deep Throat. He's saying 'How's the wife and kids?' I'm saying 'How's Nancy?' He apologized for all the security and said he was sorry he couldn't be on Showtime. Can you believe that? The president apologizing because he can't be on Showtime? I told him to forget about it. I told him if he ran for re-election, me and the wife were gonna vote for him."[5]

Don Rickles: Rickles on the Loose came and went without much fanfare. The *New York Daily News* called it "a disaster . . . As for Rickles, he'd be lost without an insult. To a Black couple in the audience, he says, 'You look like you fell into a barrel of M&Ms.' And speaking to a Jewish man, he makes a rude comment about his nose. Nothing subtle about Rickles . . . It's the same old tired insult comedy."[6]

Maybe, but the shopworn shtick never got old, at least to gamblers and tourists who flocked to see Don in Las Vegas. Word broke in the fall of 1986 that he was leaving the Sahara—again—and taking his act to the Golden Nugget for eight weeks a year beginning in February. He was still under a long-term deal with Harrah's for its hotels in Reno and Lake Tahoe, and he continued to take his act on the road elsewhere, crisscrossing the country and always available to stop by *The Tonight Show.*

(He didn't dare appear on *The Late Show* starring Joan Rivers, which launched on the new Fox network in October 1986. Don and Joan were friendly with each other—that wasn't the problem—but Don was loyal to Johnny Carson, who never forgave Rivers for taking the Fox job without telling him and never spoke to her again. Rivers was fired by Fox in May 1987 after a turbulent seven-month late-night run.)

Don's longtime manager, Joe Scandore, died in L.A. toward the end of 1992 after battling emphysema—collateral damage from a heavy smoking habit. He was in his late sixties and had been a reassuring, guiding, collaborative, and powerful presence in Don's career for thirty-five years, since the old Elegante days in Brooklyn. "He was old-school show biz," Don recalled. "Like any savvy promoter who came up in the thirties and forties, Joe had connections outside formal show business. That was the way of the world. Without those connections, you never left the dock; with them, you sailed."[7]

In 1991, when he was in an L.A. hospital being treated for emphysema, Scandore called Frank Sinatra's manager, Eliot Weisman, in New York, and asked him to fly out for a face-to-face meeting. "He was having trouble breathing. Still, the first thing he said when I walked in was, 'I'm dying for a cigarette.' I laughed along with him but knew it wasn't a good sign," Weisman recalled in his book, *The Way It Was: My Life with Frank Sinatra.* "'I'm not going to be around much longer,' he said, speaking between labored breaths. 'I want you to take over for Rickles when I die.'" Weisman, in turn, told Scandore that his request should come from Don, and in a three-way call several days later Don did just that, and Weisman agreed to work with him when the time arrived.

As Weisman recalled in *The Way It Was*, he was in his office in South Florida on the day of Scandore's funeral, when Don called him, shaken and panicky. He was apparently calling from the funeral home (Weisman wasn't sure, but he heard muffled voices in the background). "'These guys are all over me," he said in a low voice. 'They're telling me now that Joe is dead, I get 40 percent of my income and they get 60 percent. What am I going do to?'" Weisman told Don that he would set up a meeting with a well-known entertainment lawyer, Harvey Silbert, and would fly to L.A. to meet him at Silbert's office. Barbara accompanied Don to the meeting and brought along his contract with Scandore. "The way the contract was written, now that Scandore was dead, Rickles didn't have any further financial obligations to him or his heirs. He didn't even have to pay Scandore's family the commission on the future work Scandore had booked," Weisman wrote—but he made it a condition of working with Don that he pay Scandore's estate 15 percent on all the remaining bookings Joe made before he died. When all was said and done, that amounted to a nearly one-year period in which Weisman received no commissions on the Scandore bookings. Don agreed with Weisman, who called a fixer whose name and number Sinatra had given him a decade before, telling him to call the guy if he ever had a problem. The wiseguys from Scandore's funeral quickly backed down and changed their tune. Don never heard from them again.

That same year, Weisman and Tony Oppedisano paired Don and Frank together on the same bill at Kirk Kerkorian's MGM Desert Inn in Vegas to celebrate Sinatra's seventy-seventh birthday. The Brooklyn-born Oppedisano, or "Tony O.," as everyone called him, was working full-time as Sinatra's road manager in 1992 after first meeting Frank twenty years earlier at Jilly's, the fabled watering hole on West 52nd Street in Manhattan owned by Jilly Rizzo. Tony O. had entered show business as a singer, and his ties to Don ran deeper than Don's friendship with Sinatra; in 1980, he and his group were performing in the Stateline Cabaret room at Harrah's in Lake Tahoe while Don headlined in the main room with Patti LaBelle.

"On my night off, I went in to see Rickles," he recalled. "I had seen him once before at the Copacabana in New York when I was bouncing around and working clubs. So here I am in Tahoe, sitting at the entertainers' table, and the entertainment director gave Don my name, because I was under contract and they were trying to promote my career. There was a spot in the show where Don used to introduce people in the audience." When he got to Tony, he looked down at the piece of paper in his hand. "He's going, 'We have a young performer in the audience who is making a lot of noise, ladies and gentlemen . . . Tony . . . Hop in the sauna?' And he says, 'How do you pronounce that?' I said, 'Oppedisano, sir.' He said, 'Is that Italian?' I said, 'It's Sicilian.' So he drops the microphone and throws up his hands in the air like he is being robbed. And he gets the band to do the same thing. He said, 'Where are you from?' and I said, 'Brooklyn' and he drops the microphone again. At that point, I had already known Sinatra for eight years and through conversation backstage, when he found that out, all of a sudden we became fast friends."[8]

Tony O. recalled that Sinatra wanted Don on the bill with him at the Desert Inn for the big shindig. "They were flying in all of the magazine shows and celebrities, Gregory Peck, Kirk Douglas, and all of Frank's friends. And I said, 'Who do you want to have on the show with you?' and he says, 'I don't want polite humor. I got an idea. How about Bullethead?" There was a fly in the ointment, however: Don was under contract at the Golden Nugget. "Frank said, 'You asked me who I wanted and I told you. Make it happen.' Long story short, Steve Wynn bought Don out of his contract so he literally got paid not to appear, so that Steve could close the show down earlier and save all that money. So Don was on the bill with Frank. And they billed it as 'The Voice and the Mouth.'"

Sinatra enjoyed working with Don, but his enthusiasm turned to irritation one night when Don began to sing, which he had been doing in his act for years. "Sinatra made a face," Weisman recalled in *The Way It Was*. "'Since when did he become a crooner? Tell him to tell jokes . . . People come to hear him tell jokes, not sing.'" When Don left the stage, Weisman went to his dressing room to relay Sinatra's sentiments. Don was not a happy camper, and while he agreed to cut down on his singing, he did not remove it from his act altogether. Sinatra was pissed off, and cut Don's act down from thirty minutes to seventeen minutes. "The tension was becoming too much and I couldn't wait for that gig to be over," Weisman recalled.[9]

Sinatra and Don ended their engagement at the Desert Inn in December. Shortly thereafter, Don reached out to Tony O. "He had no [full-time] management at this point," he recalled. "He calls and says, 'Listen, I know that Frank comes first' and I jokingly said, 'First, second, and third.' He said, 'How do you guys feel about handling me, too?' I said, 'Are you kidding? We'd be thrilled.' So he signed, and for the first two years or so I wasn't going on the road with him because, again, I was up to my eyeballs with Sinatra. But I was taking care of stuff on the phone, and he had his Guy Friday, Harry Goins. So he really didn't need someone to hold his hand.

"At the end of Frank's performing career, there were quite a few gigs where I put them together. We opened the MGM Grand, Don and Frank together, and we opened the Kiel Center in St. Louis [in 1994] and then flew to Chicago and opened the United Center together." When Sinatra retired in 1995, Tony O. began working with Don full-time as his personal manager and road manager. Eliot Weisman continued to represent Don at William Morris until they severed their connection in 2014.

Don's legions of fans extended to his fellow comics, particularly among a set of younger comedians who were coming of age in the 1970s and 1980s amid the boom in comedy clubs and a more edgy type of humor. Among them was Richard Lewis, whose neuroses and self-deprecation fueled a stand-up act and hip, indelible persona that propelled him into that rarefied air: selling out around the country, knockout appearances on *The Tonight Show* and *Late Night with David Letterman*, a slew of HBO comedy specials, and a four-season run opposite Jamie Lee Curtis on the ABC sitcom *Anything But Love*.

"To me, Don was the most fearless guy," Lewis said. "Nothing was sacred. Anyone loved to be ripped by him. No one else could be that authentic in what he did. When Don was on a talk show, particularly Johnny, it was an event. He is one of the great stand-up comedians ever. As someone who can not only destroy you person- ally with his humor, but also destroy an audience, there are very few who were as good."

Lewis had a production deal with Fox, and after *Anything But Love* was canceled in 1992, he got in touch with *Anything But Love* writ- ing teammates Billy Van Zandt and Jane Milmore, whose résumés included a long laundry list of prime-time series including *Newhart*, *Martin* (on Fox), and *Sydney*, starring Valerie Bertinelli. Van Zandt and Milmore were also playwrights (they wrote twenty-three published plays) and Van Zandt—who was married at the time to *Maude* costar Adrienne Barbeau—acted as well. He was a regular on Season 2 of *Anything But Love* (as Harold) and guest-starred on *Sydney*.

Lewis and his writing partner, Richard Dimitri, had an idea for a sitcom about an older, politically incorrect father who moves in with his son (played by Lewis) after separating from his wife. "Rich- ard asked us to write the show and we said, yes, we'd love to do it," Van Zandt recalled. Following a series of phone calls and meetings, Don agreed to play the father—taking his fourth stab at a prime- time series, albeit this time as a costar, at the age of sixty-seven (Lewis was forty-six). Fox gave the green light to shoot a pilot for the series, *My Son the Bastard*, though no one really expected that title to find its way onto the airwaves.

"I'm really excited about it," Don told a reporter backstage at the Desert Inn, his new Las Vegas home after signing a two-year deal with the hotel/casino. "I play a used Cadillac salesman and Richard plays my son. He's a psychiatrist and we're the ultimate odd cou- ple. The chemistry between us is great." He said he hoped it lasted longer than *Innocent Blood*, a 1992 comedy-horror-vampire movie, directed by onetime *Kelley's Heroes* gofer John Landis, in which he played a sleazy Mafia attorney named Manny Bergman: "It came out and twenty minutes later it was on Pay TV."[10]

Van Zandt and Milmore already knew Don from his 1989 guest-starring role on *Newhart*, when he played (what else?) an insult comic who was hired to host a late-night show—with Newhart's Dick Loudon as his sidekick. Fox flew them to Las Vegas, anyway, to see Don in action at the Desert Inn. "It was exactly what I expected. It was him on *The Tonight Show* all over again," Van Zandt said. "But it was always funny to me. He was the sweetest man you ever met. Then he'd turn on the 'other' Rickles, the onstage guy, and this was the Don Rickles people loved. But when you were with him one-on-one, he didn't do that stuff.

"Don only had one stipulation, which was 'Don't do what they did to me in *CPO Sharkey*' and we said, 'What was that?' and he said, 'The script would say, "Don enters" and that's all it would say, and then I would have to make up stuff to insult people that were in the scene with me. Don't do that to me.' So we didn't."

The pilot was shot in the spring of 1993—delayed for two weeks while Lewis recovered from an illness—and got off to an inauspicious start when Renee Taylor, who was hired to play Don's wife on the show, was late to the first read-through of the script after missing her flight. (Joan Rivers, Polly Bergen, and Brett Somers had been considered for the role.) Van Zandt wrote in his showbiz memoir, *Get in the Car, Jane!* that on the night the pilot was taped, one of the young actors playing Lewis's "morbidly obese" nephew vomited in the alley outside the studio right before airtime—after eating a bowl of bananas in under two minutes. Don used the breaks in filming to go after the studio audience members with his usual racial and ethnic insults.

The executives at Fox were pleased with the edited pilot episode and shortly thereafter announced that *Daddy Dearest* would join its schedule in the fall, with Don playing obnoxious, Archie Bunker–like Al Mitchell—who's thrown out of his house by his wife, Helen (Taylor) after losing their retirement money, and moves in with his son Steven (Lewis)—a divorced shrink with a young son who discovers Dear Old Dad in bed in his house just as he's about to have sex

(Al: "She looked like a screamer, and we both need our sleep"). The series premiered September 5 at 9:30 p.m., right after Fox's big hit, *Married . . . with Children* and opposite *The ABC Sunday Night Movie*, *The CBS Sunday Movie*, and *The NBC Sunday Night Movie*.

The critics hated it: "Horrifically unfunny" (Associated Press); "The worst new show of the fall TV season . . . Rickles is almost comically obsolete. His bullying persona comes across like a musty exhibit from the Shecky Greene Punch Line Museum" (Knight-Ridder); "Al is merely a vehicle for Rickles' jibes, most of them pointless or pathetic" (*Minneapolis Star-Tribune*); "Too loud, coarse and nasty even for Fox . . . 'Maybe you're retarded,' dad bellows at son. 'You always had an awful big head when you were a kid.' That should give you some idea" (*Washington Post*).

"In the writers' room we were making fun of everybody and coming up with jokes that you know can't possibly go into the script, that were so over the line or vulgar . . . and suddenly all those lines were going into the script," Van Zandt recalled. "People would look at me like, 'You've got to be kidding. You're putting that in?' I said, 'Yeah, we're putting that in! Maybe we can top it.' Richard was mostly reacting through the entire thing, but that actually made him funnier.

Despite all the negative publicity, the ratings for the *Daddy Dearest* premiere were not horrible: it finished forty-seventh out of eighty-nine prime-time shows ranked by Nielsen. Its fellow Fox freshman series, *Townsend Television*, finished dead-last, but before long, *Daddy Dearest* wasn't far behind.

A sense of doom and gloom pervaded the cast and crew as successive episodes faltered and fell further and further into the ratings abyss. Lewis felt that part of the problem was having two established comics as series leads. "My voice disappeared," he said. "And I'm not saying that I was angry. I just felt like, 'Well, this was a mistake as a comedian.' Hardly anyone could costar with Don Rickles and not just be bludgeoned comedically in terms of his persona and presence. I started to think, 'I'm like a ghost on the show,' and it was very disheartening."

Van Zandt: "Don was supposed to have a smaller role on the show, and his popularity with the audience just pushed it. It was supposed to be Richard's show and Don was going to be like Estelle Getty on *Golden Girls*. But it was equal parts insane and equal parts just the most fun you had in your life. Everybody was crazy. Every word that came out of Renee's mouth was a home run."

And then there was Don's inability—or, more likely, reluctance— to learn his lines.

"Don didn't enjoy getting scripts every night and rewrites. He wasn't used to memorizing lines . . . it really made it a very difficult show because he was unhappy," Lewis said. "He would do a couple of lines and then he would forget and he would stop and look at the camera and go, 'You see?' It was like twenty seconds. And then he would just rip everybody to shreds. The audience would go wild. He wasn't ill or anything. It just wasn't his bag. After so many decades of psychoanalysis, to me, I understood. 'He doesn't want to be here. He wants to be hanging out at the MGM Grand with Sinatra.'"

Before too long, outtakes from *Daddy Dearest* started airing over the show's closing credits—which turned out to be the best part of the show. "Don should have been Larry David on his own *Curb Your Enthusiasm* with actors who could act with him and rein him in and he could say whatever he wanted," said Lewis, a regular on Larry David's HBO series. "When you watch that outtake reel, it's so hysterical. It's his own voice in those outtake reels. Plus he didn't act like a comedian when it wasn't his real 'voice.'

"No one learned their lesson that you cannot tame a raging comic pro like him—he's just too powerful."

By mid-November, *Daddy Dearest* had sunk to eighty-first place (out of ninety-seven prime-time series). Frank Sinatra made an appearance on the series as a last-minute favor to Don—Angie Dickinson also dropped by—with Fox hoping both A-listers would push *Daddy Dearest* over the hump. It did not work. In early December Fox officially dropped the axe, replacing it with *The George Carlin Show*, which premiered in January with the comedian playing an opinionated part-time cabdriver. Fox also canceled Chevy Chase's late-night talk show—the successor to *The Late Show* starring Joan Rivers—which had proved even more disastrous than its predecessor and lasted only five weeks on the air. Don was booked as a guest on *The Chevy Chase Show* to promote *Daddy Dearest* before both shows went down in flames.

"I was glad, and Don was relieved, when we were canceled," Lewis recalled. "There were too many showrunners, and Don just didn't enjoy the process of a rewritten script every night, so it was a blessing. But [Fox] and the media put a lot of pressure on us because, at that time, Fox's big shows were *Married . . . with Children*, which was a giant hit, and *The X-Files*. They bring in Rickles and Lewis, so the pressure was huge, and the first couple of episodes the critics hated it, and that's a bad start.

"But everybody was in awe of Don—the cameramen, the guys who would run out with his script and show him the lines, the wardrobe people. It was impossible not to be in love with him. He was just too great a voice in the history of comedy."

"The problem with *Daddy Dearest* was that it hit at the beginning of the height of political correctness," Van Zandt said. "In hindsight, I wouldn't have changed the show. I thought it did exactly what I wanted it to do, and Don Rickles fans loved it. The ratings were actually pretty good—but the critics just hated us. Every other week we would be fighting the network."

Daddy Dearest was strike four for Don, and never again would he attempt, or be tempted, to carry a prime-time network series. He was in his late sixties now and did not need that kind of pressure or the aggravation, not for a job from which he derived little pleasure.

Don's television star shined brightest in the late-night arena, where a visit from Rickles was an event, even if he dropped in unannounced, as he so often did on *The Tonight Show*. Johnny Carson, who was nearly a year older than Don, retired in May 1992 at the age of sixty-six, and NBC handed *The Tonight Show* franchise over to comedian Jay Leno, a familiar face and one of Carson's regular substitute hosts. The network's decision to go with Leno angered Carson's handpicked successor, fellow Hoosier David Letterman— who jumped to CBS and, in August 1993, launched *Late Show with David Letterman* to great fanfare (and, in those early days, a bigger audience than Leno's *Tonight Show*, which floundered before finding its footing when Leno grilled Hugh Grant about his dalliance with a hooker: "What-the-hell were you thinking?")

But it was a 1991 appearance on *Later with Bob Costas,* which aired in the wee hours of the morning on NBC that, in hindsight, launched the next phase of Don's career following the cancellation of *Daddy Dearest.*

Costas, the popular NBC sportscaster, began hosting *Later* in 1988. The talk show aired at 1:30 a.m., four nights a week, following *Late Night with David Letterman*, on which Costas appeared semi-regularly as a guest and in comic bits. *Later* eschewed the usual late-night staples—monologue, sketches, a house band—in favor of a more conversational tone, with Costas and his one guest chatting face-to-face for thirty minutes.

In May of 1991, Costas welcomed Don to *Later.* Their interview aired over several nights. Don, who was turning sixty-five was, by turns, intense, funny, revealing, and nostalgic in reminiscing about his life and career, in a comfortable setting in which he didn't feel the need to constantly be "on." *Later* was customarily shot at the NBC studios in Burbank, without a studio audience. That changed when word got out around that Rickles was on the lot.

"When Mel Brooks was on, he was a guest multiple times, and what happened with him also happened with Rickles," Costas recalled. "You start out basically with the crew—three cameramen, the stage manager—and by the time the taping with Rickles began, there were like fifty people on the set. The receptionists were coming over on their lunch break. People were just coming over to watch Rickles. So, by the time he was done, he had an audience."

Costas and Don were not total strangers; they had met several times before, usually when Don was in the company of his pal, Los Angeles Dodgers manager Tommy Lasorda, and Costas was working the baseball game. "So I think he arrived with a favorable feeling," Costas said. "And he was very funny. There were moments that were comedy gold. But, mixed in, was this reflective side of him—about how he didn't get married until he was almost forty years old and he lived at home with his mom—he always referred to her with 'rest her soul'—and how he was awkward and unsure of himself in social situations and how, early on, how he was trying to make it as an actor and then he hit upon the insult routine.

"At one point he goes, 'Even at 1:30 a.m., here I am struggling. I gotta park Johnny Carson's car and some kid from St. Louis gets hot in the business.' To be insulted by Rickles is one of the great honors of all time. All his stuff was so politically incorrect. But when you think about it, some of the stuff that we laughed at from these guys—Rickles, Rodney Dangerfield, Johnny Carson doing Art Fern in the 'Tea Time Movie' with Carol Wayne—there was no balance in any of that and you couldn't do any of it today, even with that level of stardom. Rickles and Dangerfield were grandfathered in, and so they continued to do it."[11]

Don was celebrating his thirty-fifth year as a performer in Las Vegas when, in the summer of 1994, he was approached by film director Martin Scorsese about appearing in his upcoming movie, *Casino*. The mob drama, starring Robert De Niro, Sharon Stone, and Joe Pesci, would be shot on location in Vegas, mostly at night, with the Riviera subbing for the movie's fictional Tangiers casino. The movie, written by Nicholas Pileggi, was based on his nonfiction book, *Casino: Love and Honor in Las Vegas*. The book chronicled Chicago mobsters Frank "Lefty" Rosenthal (De Niro as Sam "Ace" Rothstein) and his friend and partner, the explosive Anthony "Tony the Ant" Spilotro (Pesci as Nicky Santoro), who controlled part of Vegas in the 1970s and '80s (Lefty, a prominent sports bettor, secretly ran the Stardust Hotel, changed to the Tangiers for the movie). Stone played Ace's loose-cannon wife, Ginger McKenna (Geri McGee in real life), who comes between Lefty and Tony—with deadly consequences. Authenticity was important: Alan King was cast as an organized crime figure named Andy Stone; Frankie Avalon, Jayne Meadows, Steve Allen, and Jerry Vale played themselves in cameo appearances.

Scorsese, who was the final guest on *Later with Bob Costas* in February 1994, was, at the time, in a relationship with actress Illeana Douglas. She remembered Don's appearance on *Later with Bob Costas* three years earlier, and the proverbial lightbulb went off. "Growing up, I was always kind of obsessed with comedians. My grandfather [actor Melvyn Douglas] had ties to several comedians," she recalled. "He produced a Broadway show called *Call Me Mister*, and he discovered Buddy Hackett and Carl Reiner, and comedy was a major part of my childhood. For some reason, I was just always obsessed with comedians. Growing up in an Italian household, my grandparents listened to Pat Cooper and Jackie Vernon. I always loved Don Rickles, even as he began to go really out of favor and out of style."

During the *Casino* casting process, Douglas recommended Melissa Prophet for the role of Nicky's wife, Jennifer Santoro, and suggested to Scorsese that he consider James Woods to play greasy, loser con artist Lester Diamond, who is involved with ex-prostitute Ginger. He was hired.

Douglas was also a huge Bob Costas fan which, in turn, eventually led to Don's involvement in the movie.

"Bob's late-night talk show got me through the 1980s," she said. "I became obsessed with his show. He would have people on, Norman Lear, for example, who weren't particularly promoting a film, and it was absolutely fascinating. He had Rickles on . . . each night it got wilder and wilder. Eventually, in one of those shows, Bob Costas laughs so hard he actually falls back in his big chair and is nearly on the ground laughing. I had never seen Don Rickles so informal. He would go on *The Tonight Show* and tell his jokes, but this was an interview that had a lot of depth. He was talking about his early days in Vegas and his wanting to be an actor and I just saw a different side of him.

"So when they were casting *Casino*, I said to Marty, 'You know who you should put in the film? Don Rickles.' He kind of thought about it—it wasn't like, 'Oh my God, brilliant idea!'—and he didn't seem convinced, like he was about some of the other people. But I said, 'I'm telling you, you've got to see these Bob Costas interviews. Once you see them, you will see the character' . . . and once Marty got hold of the videotapes and watched them, I think from that point on it became, 'Okay, that's an idea.' It wasn't stunt casting. This guy was really there."[12]

It was announced in September, as filming began on *Casino*, that Don was joining the cast as Billy Sherbert, who manages the Tangiers casino for his old friend Sam Rothstein. "Big deal for me: De Niro runs the casino and I'm his number-one man. I'm with him night and day," Don recalled in *Rickles' Book*. "I was excited to be working with all these Academy Award winners. No one does gangster films better than Scorsese."[13]

The eighteen-week shooting schedule was tedious, time-consuming, and exhausting. The days and nights on the set sometimes ran fourteen hours or longer, and Barbara tried to arrange her schedule around Don's workday, joining him for "lunch" at 4 a.m. "It was kind of horrendous," Don recalled. "But my wife saved my life. We're very good friends besides our marriage."[14] Don kept the cast and crew alert by doing what he did best—joking around on the set and keeping everyone on their toes by poking fun at De Niro's mumbling acting style and Scorsese's height ("When you direct me, Marty, could you stand on a chair so I can see you?"[15]). Scorsese took the ribbing in stride. He knew what to expect and was "doubled over with laughter" on the set. "You had to stay out of Don's line of vision once you finished a take," he recalled. "Otherwise, he'd go off on you."[16]

Don received fifth billing in the opening credits (one ahead of Alan King), although his role was relatively minor and Billy didn't have much dialogue (he mostly scowled). In Don's one memorable scene, Nicky—who is losing hand-over-fist at the blackjack table—brutally beats Billy over the head with a pay telephone, sending the older man sprawling to the casino floor.

(Don and Joe Pesci reunited sixteen years later, in 2011, for a surreal Snickers commercial for the candy bar's "You're not you when you're hungry" campaign. You can watch it on YouTube—describing it here would not do it justice.)

Casino opened in theaters in late November and fared well at the box office, grossing nearly $70 million combined in the US and worldwide over the next year. The critical reception was, overall, very good, although Scorsese was criticized in some quarters for treading familiar mobster ground he had already covered in *Mean Streets* (1973, starring De Niro) and in *Goodfellas* (1990, starring De Niro and Pesci). Don was generally given a passing grade if he was mentioned at all, since the focus was squarely on the Big Guns: Scorsese, De Niro, Pesci, and Sharon Stone, who garnered an Oscar nomination for her portrayal of Ginger (Susan Sarandon won that year for *Dead Man Walking*).

CHAPTER 19

*C*asino **premiered on November 22, 1995,** on the same day as *Toy Story*, the first feature film to be animated completely by computers using CGI technology. The movie was produced by Pixar Animation Studios in collaboration with Walt Disney Studios and reportedly cost in the neighborhood of $100 million. It was directed by animation wizard John Lasseter and revolved around a group of living toys and their adventures. The all-star cast was headed by back-to-back Oscar winner Tom Hanks (*Philadelphia*, *Forrest Gump*) as Sheriff Woody, sitcom star Tim Allen (ABC's *Home Improvement*) as astronaut Buzz Lightyear ("Not a flying toy"), and . . . Don Rickles, venturing into the on-screen animation genre for the first time at the age of sixty-nine. He played bowler-hat-wearing, mustachioed, and grouchy Mr. Potato Head—who was already familiar to a generation of kids since being introduced by Hasbro in 1952—the first toy ever to be advertised on television (on *The Jackie Gleason Show*). Lasseter called Don's participation "the casting of the century," and the movie's writers, not to be outdone, had Mr. Potato Head, in true Don Rickles fashion, insult a hockey puck by calling it . . . wait for it . . . a "hockey puck."

"John Lasseter came out to Don's beach house," Tony O. recalled. "He held up Mr. Potato Head, and he says, 'When I look at this, the only voice I can hear coming out of it is yours.' And he made his pitch, and after he left, I stayed to have dinner with Don, and he said, 'What am I going to do with a friggin' cartoon?' I said, 'Don, look what it's done for Mel Blanc. That's an annuity, are you kidding me?' He considered it and he finally did it."

The hush-hush project, which also featured television stars John Ratzenberger (*Cheers*) and Annie Potts (*Designing Women*), gave Don his first bona fide movie hit nearly forty years after his inaugural big-screen role in *Run Silent, Run Deep*. Clark Gable had nothing on Mr. Potato Head.

"I didn't want to do Popeye, Olive Oyl stuff," Don said. "But this is very mature. It's done with a different style than most. So I said OK, 'I'll take an adventure.' John came down to my beach house and asked if I would be Mr. Potato Head. I said, 'Leave me alone.'" He said he "threw myself in a pot of boiling water to relax . . . If I had to make a living at it, I'd have to go twenty years to pay off the car. But I figured if Tom Hanks took a cut from $8 billion to do this, so could I."[1]

Hasbro was thrilled with the frenzied run on Mr. Potato Head toys in the wake of the movie's holiday release, not only in stores but at Burger King restaurants nationwide, where Mr. Potato Head and the other *Toy Story* characters were included in meals as part of a promotional tie-in to the movie.

Production on *Toy Story* began in January 1993, and Don recorded his role, on and off, for the next two years in five or six studio sessions. "Every time it came up, I said, 'Oh yeah, I'm doin' that thing,'" he recalled. "Then everyone started talking about it, sweatshirts came out, advertising started, so that's when I said, 'Ooh, gee, this looks like it's going to be something important.'"[2] It was; *Toy Story* opened to universal raves—for its technical prowess, its script, and for the vocal efforts of Hanks et al. After a year in release, it had grossed nearly $200 million in the US, and it doubled that number in its worldwide release, where it was dubbed into dozens of foreign languages. Lasseter won an Academy Award for Special Achievement, and *Toy Story* became the first animated feature to snare an Oscar nomination for Best Original Screenplay, which was won that year by *The Usual Suspects* writer Christopher McQuarrie.

Don was hot again at the age of seventy, and he rode the double-barrel blast of *Casino* and *Toy Story* into 1996. In January, he played three nights at Caesars in Atlantic City, where he was billed as "Don Rickles: Star of Hollywood's 'Casino' and 'Toy Story,'" and he was now morphing into an elder statesman of comedy, distancing himself from some of the younger, cruder comics making names for themselves, including Andrew Dice Clay. "They cross the line," Don told a reporter. "They took a flavor of Don Rickles and then they cross the line. Whatever they do more power to them, but it's not what I do. My claim to fame is that I'm different. I've always prided myself on being a different kind of guy as a performer. That's the only thing that keeps my success going."[3] Jack E. Leonard, long dead, was unable to respond.

"It wasn't that Don wasn't working, that he wasn't visible, but it just didn't all reach the same level that he reached earlier," recalled Paul Shefrin, who took over handling Don's publicity from his father, Gene, when he retired in 1987. "And then all of a sudden, with *Toy Story* and *Casino* . . . I mean, a lot of things just started falling into place. And that wasn't over a period of two months, obviously, it was over an extended period of time, but there were things happening that made it all go on a 'skyrocket' phase again."

They included late-night television, Don's home away from home since the mid-1960s. Now, thirty plus years later, he found himself adapting to the rhythms and sensibilities of the younger generation of late-night hosts, notably Johnny Carson's *Tonight Show* successor, Jay Leno, and David Letterman over on CBS, whose acerbic, biting style gibed with Don's comic sensibilities. "When Johnny retired, Don was a little reticent to do other shows," Shefrin said. "Johnny epitomized to him the way talk shows should be done, and he only wanted to do it with the best. It was that kind of thinking. And it took some convincing to get him to do some of those other shows."

Don had been a guest on *Late Night with David Letterman* but had yet to appear on Letterman's *Late Show*. Peter Lassally, one of Carson's top *Tonight Show* producers, had migrated with Letterman to CBS. He knew Don, of course, and they were friendly with one another. One night, Lassally, *Late Show* producer Bob Morton, and

Letterman flew to Vegas to see Don's act in a bid to convince him to appear on *The Late Show*, and after Don departed to the usual thunderous applause, they took him out to dinner. "From that point forward, the door was now open for Don to do Letterman, not because Letterman had not been working for Don, but because Don just needed to feel comfortable with David," Shefrin said. "And he did. And they became pretty good friends and he did the show probably twenty odd times after that.

"Don called me one day—we were going to New York to do Letterman—and he said, 'Do you think Dave would want to have dinner with us?' And I said, 'I don't know, Dave tends to be a little reclusive, but let me call his assistant and ask.' So I did, and she got back to me and said, 'Yes, Dave would love to.' Well, that was interesting in and of itself, but the night we're doing the show, Dave comes on the air and he's talking and he said, 'I've been doing this show for years and during that entire time, no other guest has ever asked me out to dinner. But tonight, I am going out to dinner with Don Rickles.' And I immediately called Dave's assistant and said, 'I'm so sorry. You better be prepared for the onslaught of phone calls tomorrow. Everyone is going to want to have dinner with Dave.'"[4]

Jay Leno recalled how quickly Don was able to adjust his appearances on *The Tonight Show* depending on the mood of the audience. "He would always come out with some insult, and if it didn't work, he had another insult. It was funny, and he used to make me laugh because Don knew nothing about cars, and he would go, 'Jay, you're putting the clutch in the front seat.' He would play some automotive term that didn't work. That used to make me laugh.

"And he was a real comic, a nightclub comic, which is what we all were," he said. "You know, a lot of guys are TV comics, they write a joke and they say it on TV and if it doesn't get a laugh, they sweep it in. But when you're a nightclub comic, you can't sweep a joke. It's gotta be funny. You gotta be loud, direct, you gotta make your point, you gotta look right at the audience. You can't look away. It was funny to watch Don when it wasn't working to see him being like, 'Where am I going with this?' And Don knew how to do it. When a joke bombed he would just keep coming back. That's what made it funny. And a lot of it was Don's physicality, too. It wasn't even the joke, it was the way he barked at the person or yelled at them, or feigned that anger. 'What do you want, a cookie?!' He knew the words."

Despite the box-office success and critical acclaim generated by *Casino*, Don was not bombarded with movie offers. He was content enough, at this stage of his career, to continue his big-screen career by lending his voice to Mr. Potato Head in *Toy Story 2* (1999) and in *Toy Story 3* (2010), which grossed more than the first two movies combined and pushed the franchise past the $1 billion mark globally, according to the studio. The movies also added to Don's cachet with his two young grandsons, Ethan and Harrison. (Mindy married writer Ed Mann in 1997.) "I busted my bird for sixty years in the business," Don said, "but my grandkids only know me as Mr. Potato Head."[5]

In 2014, Don signed on for *Toy Story 4*, but he died while the movie was still being written. No matter—the film's director, Josh Cooley, said that Don's family reached out and asked if he could construct a role for Mr. Potato Head around preexisting recordings of Don. "Unfortunately we did not get a chance to record him for the film. But we went through, jeez, 25 years of everything we didn't use for *Toy Story* 1, 2, 3, the theme parks, the ice capades, the video games—everything that he's recorded for Mr. Potato Head," Cooley said at the time. "And we were able to do that. And so I'm very honored that they asked us to do that, and I'm very honored that he's in the film. Nobody can replace him."[6]

The small screen still welcomed Don Rickles with open arms— not for the big, splashy, star-studded prime-time specials of years past, but for guest-starring roles on popular sitcoms. In the three years following the release of *Casino* and *Toy Story*, he played himself on HBO's *The Larry Sanders Show*—Garry Shandling's hip, satiric take on late-night talk shows (and their hosts)—was Dr. Dick Sloan in an episode of the NBC sitcom *The Single Guy* (costarring Don's old friend

Ernest Borgnine), and made a cameo appearance as one of Murphy's (Candice Bergen) secretaries in the final season of *Murphy Brown* in 1998. Murphy's short-lived secretaries were a running gag on the series, and Don joined a long list of celebrity cameos (ninety-three in total) including John F. Kennedy Jr., Sally Field, Bette Midler, Marcia Wallace (from *The Bob Newhart Show*—Newhart himself showed up in an episode to win back her job), and Hillary Clinton. There were even published reports that he was being considered for a supporting role in Jackie Chan's next movie.

"Amazingly, though, my dance card is as full as it's ever been," he said. "At this stage of my life, I figured my workload would taper off considerably. But a new generation is seeing my films or watching me on the Leno, Letterman, or Larry King shows, which keep asking me back."[7]

CHAPTER 20

The winds of change were blowing through the world of comedy as Don neared his fortieth year as a headliner in Vegas. The city's hotels and casinos were no longer run by the Mob, and it was now a more family-friendly destination dotted with amusement-park rides, light shows, and kitschy hotels built to replicate the Pyramids, the canals of Venice, and the New York skyline. Don's days of signing long-term deals in Sin City were behind him now; he was still a top draw, but he opted for short-term contracts that took him up and down the strip to the Golden Nugget (with Sinatra), the Tropicana, the MGM Grand, and the Stardust. Later, he moved off the strip for a longer-term residency at the Orleans Hotel and Casino. "There's an atmosphere, and my style of humor is well-suited for this kind of town," he said. "If you look at the crowd, it's that kind of—I'm not saying mob guys, but the high roller. The guy with the ring. The wife with the jewelry and the fur coat. You don't see that anymore. But I bring in those kind of people."[1]

He refused to change his act, which was still rife with ethnic insults, and as the twenty-first century approached, he was out of step with the younger generation of comedians. He didn't care. The act was Don Rickles and Don Rickles was the act. The *New York Times*, August 25, 1996: "Don Rickles peers into the front row of the Hollywood Theater at the MGM Grand Hotel in Las Vegas . . . He spies a young man. 'Look at this kid staring. That comes from locking yourself in the bathroom too much.' The audience howls. He sees a Black waiter and starts to shuffle. 'Yeah, I make fun of Blacks, and why not?' he asks. 'I'm not a Black.'"

If he wasn't your cup of tea, so be it. He was an institution, a remnant of the old guard, the Last Man Standing on the front lines of old showbiz, where you wore a bathrobe over your bow tie and tuxedo shirt but no pants—sitting would ruin the sharp creases—and had a drink or two before striding onto the stage to wild applause. "That was the thing about Don. If there was any kind of change, or people would say to him, 'The times are changing,' he stuck to his guns. 'This is who I am and this is what I do and I'm not changing,'" recalled Lorna Luft, one of Don's regular opening acts in those years. "He watched the whole world change in front of him, he watched people change, everybody updating this or that, and he wouldn't do it. And I took my hat off to him."[2]

"Sometimes he was talking about the 'colored guy' in the audience when no one had used that word in ten years," said comedian Tom Dreesen. "Today, the politically correct police would try to destroy him. He sometimes said things that people thought and he pushed the envelope. And I think that's what people like in certain comics. Lenny Bruce, Jack E. Leonard, they went places other comics wouldn't go. Like it or not, Don was different from all the other acts. That might be the best way to express it: 'Like it or not.'"[3]

"He was sort of grandfathered in. He had done what he had done, it was who he was and it was accepted, even though we went into a different era of correctness," recalled Don's longtime publicist Paul Shefrin. "It was still accepted for Don Rickles and I think there were a couple of reasons. One is that people knew, they really did know, where he was coming from. He wasn't being nasty; he wasn't going after you in such a way that it would be really hurtful. He was embellishing and having fun and people considered it a badge of honor to be 'insulted' by Don Rickles. And if you saw his show, you knew where he was coming from. I'm not talking about six minutes on a talk show . . . but if you went and sat for an hour and watched Don, you would understand where his heart was. People knew that."[4]

Stand-up comics were now looking for their big breaks in . . . prime-time television, where Jerry Seinfeld, Drew Carey, Tim Allen,

Brett Butler, and Ray Romano were all thriving in network sitcoms across the board on NBC, ABC, and CBS. They also had something in common: career-advancing appearances at the Just for Laughs comedy festival in Montreal, thriving since its inception, in French, in 1983 (the English-language festival followed two years later).

At the age of seventy Don Rickles was an institution, not only in the United States but in all of North America. He was always a hit in Canada, even back in the days when he was a jobbing, unknown comedian working the clubs in Montreal and Quebec: "The Man with the Glass Head." And what wasn't to admire about Don Rickles, who popularized "hockey puck" as a term of derision—while simultaneously calling attention to the country's national pastime?

In 1998, Don was invited to perform at the Just for Laughs comedy festival at the St. Denis Theatre in Montreal, where he was given a Lifetime Achievement Award and inducted into its Comedy Hall of Fame, which already counted George Burns and Milton Berle among its members. He tore through a set that still had them talking over twenty years later—more so than the sets of those who had preceded him at the festival in prior years: Jerry Lewis, Alan King, Jonathan Winters, Bob Newhart, and George Burns. Don had been at the top of festival cofounder Andy Nulman's short list of "must have" comedians, and it took several years to finally work it out.

"There was a certain point where Don really became this elder statesman and [was] hip again, for lack of a better term, and we got him at that very moment," Nulman recalled. "There was a resurgence and love for this guy." When Don and Tony O. arrived in Montreal in mid-July for the festival, Nulman had yet to meet The Merchant of Venom. "Tony O. is a real character, but I have to tell you, the sweetest, nicest guy you could meet," he said. "He said, 'This is what Don's going to do, this is how it's going to work.' It was all done through Tony O."

Don was nearly late to his first appearance at the festival when his limo driver got stuck in traffic after picking him up at his hotel. He arrived about ten minutes before he was scheduled to go on stage and introduce the performers. "He comes in like a bull, walks down the stairs, and goes backstage, and I say, 'Welcome, Mr. Rickles, I would like to apologize,' and he says, 'I don't care!' And slaps me, and he goes, 'Come here, *bubbale*, I'm kidding,' and he gives me a big hug," Nulman said. Then it was on to another crisis—Don was having trouble reading the teleprompter. "Tony O. was very cool and calm and he goes, 'Don, come here, listen, let's go, we're going to fix it.' There were certain moments in the show where Don couldn't read the teleprompter, but he didn't care; the writers wrote these intros for him, but he would say, 'Who gives a damn?' and he improvised. What an amazing night that was. We didn't realize how much the audience would really love the guy, and he walks on to that stage, to that music, and does the show and it's an incredible night.

"He did a whole bunch of stuff that night. A lot of audience participation. I will never forget the Iwo Jima number. I was saying, 'Who remembers Iwo Jima?' Nobody gave a shit. They were just so happy to see this guy, to hear the insults, to have him pick on them. It was a badge of honor. He sang. It was amazing. I don't know if people realize what a great singing voice he had. Harry Goins took care of Don on the road, and he was this amazing, old-school valet. Harry was there as soon as Don walked off the stage. He gave him his vodka and put on Don's robe. It was almost like James Brown."[5]

Nulman's father had Parkinson's disease and his mother, who had just been diagnosed with cancer, would die three months later. But Don made them feel special after his performance. "I told Don that my parents were both ill, and you cannot believe how he made these people feel when he walked backstage," Nulman recalled. "He was saying, 'This kid is amazing, you should be proud of your boy.' That's what a parent wants to hear. And there is a great picture of him and my parents, and my mother was wearing a wig and her skin was very white and she is just beaming."

Don received his Just for Laughs Lifetime Achievement Award from comedian Bobby Slayton, aka "The Pit Bull of Comedy," who was assisted by Montreal Canadiens legend Jean Beliveau. "My grandfather used to be a furrier, and he did the fur coats for all the Canadiens players," Nulman said. "He did stuff for Beliveau's wife, so I had this contact to Jean Beliveau. So he came on stage and did the whole induction ceremony. He has this gorgeous, baritone voice with the French accent."

Bruce Hills, who worked with Nulman organizing the festival, was on hand to witness the ceremony. "They presented him with the award, and Jean Beliveau thanked Don for making the hockey puck a household word," he recalled. "Obviously that was written for him, but Jean was in on it. He knew Don Rickles because he comes from that era. He probably saw Rickles in Montreal with Sinatra, because in the fifties Montreal was rocking and Rickles was here all the time."[6]

Don spent the rest of that summer finishing his tour of the US with Joan Rivers as his opening act. There were a few more movie appearances, including his role alongside Monty Python member Eric Idle as a two-headed dragon in *Quest for Camelot*, an animated Warner Bros. movie—Idle was the polite dragon, Don (of course) the wiseass—and a cameo appearance as a theater owner in *Dirty Work*, a comedy directed by Bob Saget with stars Norm Macdonald and Artie Lange. *Toy Story 2* opened in November 1999 and, once again, pleased the critics and the public alike, no mean feat for a sequel to its game-changing predecessor. "The screenplay," Roger Ebert wrote in the *Chicago Sun-Times*, "isn't just a series of adventures (although there are plenty of those), but a kind of inside job in which we discover that all toys think the way every kid knows his toys think."[7]

CHAPTER 21

F rank Sinatra died on May 14, 1998, at the age of eighty-two. His health had been declining for several years; in November 1995, he made his last onstage appearance, at the Shrine Auditorium in L.A. to sing the final line of "New York, New York" during the taping of Sinatra: 80 Years My Way, an ABC special produced by George Schlatter. Don was there, of course, just one of the stars who turned out to pay tribute to Frank, who, by this point, was struggling with his memory.

The special aired on December 14, 1995. "It starts well enough with Springsteen, Natalie Cole and Ray Charles, hits a lull from Angela Lansbury to Luis Miguel, and ends with a bag so mixed that Don Rickles comes off as affectionate and funny," noted *Variety*.[1] Eleven days later, Dean Martin died on Christmas Day at the age of seventy-eight, hours after a final phone call from Frank—leaving Joey Bishop as the last living member of Sinatra's swinging sixties-era Rat Pack. (Bishop died in 2007 at the age of eighty-nine.)

Don was a pallbearer at Frank's funeral at Good Shepherd Church in Beverly Hills on May 20, carrying the gardenia-covered casket along with Tom Dreesen, Steve Lawrence, Tony O., Frank Sinatra Jr., Eliot Weisman, and several others; Paul Anka, Mia Farrow, Sophia Loren, Nancy Reagan, Bob Newhart, Robert Wagner, Liza Minnelli, Kirk Douglas, and Bruce Springsteen were among the many mourners. "The casket was extremely heavy," Weisman recalled in *The Way It Was: My Life with Frank Sinatra*. "We were halfway down the stairs when I felt a tremendous strain on my shoulder. Rickles, who was behind me, had suddenly let go. After the casket was inside the hearse, I turned around and said, 'You're kidding me. Why did you

289

let go?' 'Jews don't do this kind of work,' he said. I didn't find it at all funny."[2] Tony O. recalled seeing Don, "looking pale and strained," leaning on the casket in the church after the funeral service while talking to Peggy Lee, who was staring at his arm on the casket. She pointed that out to him. "Why should things change now?" he said. "I've been leaning on Frank all my life."[3]

Frank was buried alongside his parents and Jilly Rizzo in a vault at Desert Memorial Park in Cathedral City. Don was in mourning, but decided to forge ahead that weekend and perform, as scheduled, at Harrah's in Reno.

His circle of friends from the old days was closing tighter now as the new century began. Old pal and *Kelly's Heroes* costar Carroll O'Connor, who grew up near Don in Queens, died in 2001. The cause of death was listed as complications from diabetes, but he never recovered from the death of his troubled son, Hugh, who committed suicide in 1995. Don's idol, Milton Berle, died in 2002 at the age of ninety-three. "From the first days of my career, he was one of my comedic heroes," Don said in a statement. "He was always a great mentor. His style of comedy will never be replaced."[4] In June 2003, Buddy Hackett shuffled off this mortal coil at his home in Malibu, felled by heart disease at the age of seventy-eight. Alan King and Rodney Dangerfield were next in 2004, King killed by lung cancer at the age of seventy-six and Dangerfield, five years Don's senior, succumbing to heart problems.

In January 2005, Johnny Carson, who more than anyone was instrumental in launching Don's television career, passed away at the age of seventy-nine from emphysema—a sad reminder of the night, nearly thirty years before, when Don broke Johnny's cigarette box on *The Tonight Show*. In the wake of his death, Don and Bob Newhart appeared together on Jay Leno's *Tonight Show* to eulogize Johnny. Eight months later, death took eighty-two-year-old *Get Smart* star Don Adams, one of Don's dearest friends and his frequent collaborator on television in the sixties, seventies, and eighties.

In May 2001, Don turned seventy-five, but age did not seem to slow him down. His jam-packed schedule of nightclub dates would have exhausted a performer half his age. His health was good, so why not? Eliot Weisman diversified Don's entertainment portfolio to include corporate dates and television commercials and, over time, increased Don's fees to $75,000 per show.[5]

He was playing the Stardust in Las Vegas with Lorna Luft when the world changed forever on September 11, 2001. "The hotel made us do a show. And Don didn't want to do it, out of respect, out of everything that happened," Luft recalled. "The hotel said, 'You know, you have a contract and we have people that are basically stuck in a hotel and you have to do the show.' He was beside himself. He said, 'How do I go out there? How do I say anything?' We had two or three days off and I was in Los Angeles and we were driving back to Vegas—me, Tony O., and my husband—and there were phone calls with Don saying, 'I just can't do this.'

"My manager at the time, Eliot Weisman, who was also Don's manager, was saying, 'You have to do this.' And so we met in the dressing room when I got to the hotel and I said, 'Okay, I will go out and say something.' And he said, 'Great, you do it. Go out and say something poignant.' It was an awful, terrifying, hideous situation for the entire country, and he had to go out there and try to make people laugh. Don was so upset. That entire time was so strange because people in the audience all looked stunned. A lot of people were wearing American flag bandanas on their heads. Usually, when Don came out, people would scream and yell. They just all sat there." "It is not easy to do at this time," Don told *Variety* columnist Army Archerd on September 18, "but I'll do it if it makes someone feel better."

Don spent the rest of the decade doing what he did best. The Toy Story franchise rolled on with Don along for the ride as Mr. Potato Head. The television appearances were fewer and farther between now. He guest-starred on an episode of *The Bernie Mac Show* on Fox and played a supporting role in *The Wool Cap*, William H. Macy's updated take on the Jackie Gleason movie *Gigot* that aired in 2004 on cable network TNT.

"When Atlantic City got back on track there for a little while, that really helped Don get going again," recalled business manager Bill Braunstein. "The whole world was changing. That whole business of Vegas and the owners and understanding him and his humor . . . are you going to bring in a Celine Dion–type of person? Sinatra was gone. Sammy Davis Jr. was gone. Dean Martin was gone. That whole world was dying off. Rickles really was the last man standing. Everything was changing and it took some time to readjust and let people know that he is still here and still funny."[6]

Late night remained his television bread and butter, with frequent stops at CBS with David Letterman and NBC with Jay Leno. In January 2003, Jimmy Kimmel entered the arena with *Jimmy Kimmel Live!* on ABC—and that, in time (it took a few years), became another destination for The Merchant of Venom, as did *The Late Late Show with Craig Ferguson*, which followed Letterman's *Late Show* at 12:30 p.m. and was produced by Peter Lassally, who went way back with Don from his days as Johnny Carson's producer on *The Tonight Show*. "Peter was the one who said, hey, you should do Craig's show," recalled Don's publicist, Paul Shefrin. "And he ended up doing quite a few appearances with Craig. It wasn't that he wasn't looked for by the talk shows. He was. But it was Don deciding when he wanted to do them."[7]

And then he became an author.

In the fall of 2006, Don signed a deal with Simon & Schuster to write his memoirs and announced the news in typical Rickles fashion: "I can say anything I want now that Frank's gone." The tome, *Rickles' Book*, was cowritten by David Ritz, a noted celebrity collaborator (including books with Ray Charles, Smokey Robinson, Jerry Wexler, and Aretha Franklin).

"We went through a bunch of drafts and he was very conscientious," Ritz recalled. "He was very easy to deal with. One of the hard things is to catch up with these people—they don't want to talk to you, they get the deal, they don't care about the book, they don't prioritize, you have a meeting and they don't show up. It was the opposite with Don. He was home, and I would go over there. I guess we spent about thirty hours together."

Rickles' Book was billed as a memoir, but there was little biographical information or deep introspection throughout its 239 pages. The narrative shoe, in this case, fit snugly, since that was never Don's style. "I wanted to write about the outstanding incidents that I could recall from my career and my life."[8]

The book was written in his voice, by Ritz, and unfolded in short vignettes—each chapter was two or three pages long—and covered the touchstones of Don's life in mostly whimsical fashion: Max and Etta, his naval service during World War II, the American Academy of Dramatic Arts, his nightclub and television work, Joe Scandore, Sinatra, meeting and marrying Barbara, etc.

"Milton Berle was his idol, and in many ways, he mirrored Milton," Ritz said. "I mean, he was very strong. Milton's mother actually pushed him onto the stage. Don's mother wasn't to that degree. Part of the challenge was to get his sort of nastiness in the book and not alienate the reader, because his humor is based on sort of a nasty persona and basically he is not a nasty guy. But in our interviews he was not calling me names and he was not doing his shtick, so that was part of his talent—to create that voice that the reader knew about and to get that anger."[9]

Rickles' Book: A Memoir was released by Simon & Schuster on May 6, 2007, Don's eighty-first birthday. Eighty thousand copies were printed, and the *New York Times* excerpted the first chapter, which helped draw attention to the project. The critics were not bowled over but were, for the most part, gentle in their assessments. *The Palm Beach Post*, for example, said: "It's a breezy, superficial and serviceable memoir."

Don visited all the late-night talk shows to promote the book, which spent five weeks on the bestseller list and spawned a sequel, *Rickles' Letters*, published in November 2008, in which Don, again with the help of David Ritz, wrote (fake) letters to celebrities and historical figures. "It was Don and I getting together and kind of jamming," Ritz said. "It was an improvisation of crazy letters he might have written." (To Mary Todd Lincoln: "Sorry you had problems at Ford's Theatre last night, but could you get me a couple of aisle tickets for the Saturday matinee?") *Rickles' Letters* did not make the bestseller lists.

The publicity surrounding the publication of *Rickles' Book* drew attention to another Rickles-centric project in the works: a documentary about Don's life directed by John Landis, who first met Don when he was a gofer on the set of *Kelly's Heroes*. It was tentatively titled *The Rickles Project* and was set to premiere later in the year on HBO. In early March 2007, Landis screened some of the work-in-progress footage at the US Comedy Arts Festival in Aspen, where Don was honored with its first-ever Pinnacle Award. (Don to a reporter: "It's a real great honor—but you won't know about that. You've never got one.") "I'm really proud of what Landis has done," Don said at the time. "It goes all the way back to Heights, where I was born, and to Queens, where I grew up. He's interviewed just about everybody in the business, my family and friends, and it includes all of those trips my wife and I took with the Bob Newharts—when we were still speaking to them."[10] (Don was surprised by Newhart at a festival dinner in Aspen that week.)

Larry Rickles was a producer on the project. Don's son, now thirty-seven, had worked on a number of network sitcoms and participated in a writing workshop at Warner Bros. He joined the writing staff of *Murphy Brown* in 1997, the same season that Don played one of Murphy's interchangeable secretaries.

The documentary was Larry's idea; when he pitched it to his father, Don was initially reluctant, since it would include parts of his onstage act, which he did not want to be filmed. He eventually relented, and was glad he did so. "In a magical moment it all came together," he wrote in *Rickles' Letters*. "The fact that it's a father-and-son project makes it one of the highlights of my life." Its title was changed to *Mr. Warmth: The Don Rickles Project*, when it premiered in December 2007 on HBO.

"Don was nervous about us shooting the documentary because he didn't want to give his show away," recalled Mike Richardson, one of the four producers of *Mr. Warmth* along with Larry, John Landis, and Bob Engleman. "It didn't matter. The audience was there to see him. They just loved to watch him in person."

Richardson, who founded Dark Horse Comics in 1986, had met Larry several years earlier, when they were introduced by an agent and started talking about collaborating on a documentary about Don. "We have Dark Horse Entertainment so I produced a number of projects," Richardson said. "My agent at the time was John Levin and he introduced me to Larry, but that was some time earlier and I didn't really think about it after that. But John Landis is a good friend of mine, and we were supposed to go out for dinner one night, and he called me and had to cancel because he was going out to dinner with Don Rickles. I told him that if he didn't get me into that dinner, I would never speak to him again."

Landis obliged and took Richardson to Don's house in Beverly Hills before dinner. "Don finally turned to me and said, 'So you're the goy.' He said, 'Michael, come with me,' and he took me in the back room and fixed me a drink and we sat down and just started talking. That was the beginning of it." At their dinner in the restaurant, Don turned to Richardson. "And he said to me, 'You know, Mike, one of the disappointments of my life, I wish somebody would do a biography on my life because I've had an amazing life.'" I said, 'You know, I've got this independent division of a company and we've got funding for it, so we could do this.' And Don just looked at me and said, 'You wouldn't stab me in the heart? Build up my hopes?' And I said, 'No, of course not,' and John Landis was there and he said, 'I'm directing' so the project started there."[11]

Mr. Warmth was almost scrapped when the company financing Dark Horse Entertainment was the subject of a hostile takeover. "We couldn't get the money and John had assembled everyone in Las Vegas and was ready to go and I was flying that afternoon—and just before I left, the plug was pulled, financially," Richardson said.

"So I flew to Vegas and gave John my American Express card to pay the bills and that's what we filmed [the documentary] on—my American Express card."

Landis constructed the documentary largely around Don's performance at the Stardust Resort and Casino in Las Vegas in November 2006; the hotel closed its doors at the end of the year and was demolished the following March—yet another remnant of Don's past (literally) biting the dust. (Don was also filmed at the Golden Nugget.) The eighty-nine-minute film included home movies, archival footage, rare photographs, clips from Don's movies and television appearances—notably from those raucous visits to Johnny Carson's *Tonight Show*—and interviews with thirty-nine friends, colleagues, and admirers, including Ernest Borgnine, Carl Reiner, Robert De Niro, Robin Williams, Debbie Reynolds, Sidney Poitier, and Keely Smith—whose history with Don stretched back nearly fifty years to his 1959 premiere in Vegas, when he opened for Keely and Louis Prima in the Sahara's Casbar Lounge. Red Buttons was to have appeared in *Mr. Warmth*, too; he died in July 2006, the day before his scheduled interview with Landis.

Mr. Warmth: The Don Rickles Project was screened on October 13, 2007, at the New York Film Festival, after Don's performance there. He cracked a rib later that week when he fell off an exercise bike in his hotel room, and was shelved from performing for about a month. He no longer played golf or tennis—a cranky back, he said—and, at the age of eighty-one, he was a bit stooped now and was being treated for Type 2 diabetes. It was clear to anyone watching Don's performing in *Mr. Warmth* that whatever physical maladies were creeping up on him vanished as soon as he strode onto that stage, as if, when the lights went on, he flicked an internal switch and transformed into The Merchant of Venom. The act was all that mattered. "In the old days, he strode on stage with a confident swagger, leading with that bulldog jaw. These days, his legs are bowed from age, he looks at the floor beneath him and he walks a bit unsteadily to the center of the stage, dressed, of course, in a tuxedo," the *San Francisco Chronicle* noted in its review of *Mr. Warmth.* "Age may have stiffened the joints, but, judging by the bits from recent performances included in Landis' film, his wit is as sharp as ever."[12]

Mr. Warmth premiered December 2 on HBO and, from the outset, generated nearly unanimous praise across the board. "Nothing particularly innovative distinguishes John Landis' documentary on Don Rickles—no digital bells and whistles, revelations of untold tragedies or self-destructive demons," *Variety* opined. "Rather, interviews edited with fine comic timing, judiciously selected clips and extended stretches of a routine with its own inimitable internal rhythms make for an unheard-of curio: a hilarious movie about a surprisingly funny man."[13]

Mr. Warmth was nominated for two Emmy Awards—the documentary itself for Outstanding Variety, Music or Comedy Special, and Don for Outstanding Individual Performance in a Variety or Music Program, alongside Stephen Colbert (*The Colbert Report*), Tina Fey (*Saturday Night Live*), David Letterman (*The Late Show with David Letterman*), and Jon Stewart (for hosting the 80th Academy Awards). It won in both categories, and 12.2 million television viewers watched on September 21, 2008, as Don, not as spry as he once was, walked up to the Nokia Theatre stage in L.A. to accept his Emmy Award from Neil Patrick Harris and Kristin Chenoweth. The band, of course, played him up to the podium with "The Bullfighter's Song"—his signature theme.

"It's a mistake," he said with a big smile on his face. "I'm just stunned by this. I've been in the business fifty-five years and the biggest award I got was an ashtray from the Friars in New York. He thanked "my son, Larry Rickles . . . who made it happen"; Mike Richardson, "who came up with a money truck and said, 'Here's four dollars, Jew, try to make it work'"; John Landis, "who I met on a picture called *Kelly's Heroes* forty-five years ago, a picture in which I carried Clint Eastwood"; and, of course, Barbara, gazing lovingly up at Don as he hauled out his standard line about her "sitting on the beach in Malibu with the jewelry signaling ships." Everyone had heard it a million times before, but they all laughed. It was Rickles. He thanked the National Academy of Television Arts and Sciences and, as was his custom, signed off with blowing a kiss to his late mother: "Etta, darling, I love you and I'm listening for you." Don was the last recipient to receive an Emmy in that particular category, which was dropped thereafter.

"Jerry Lewis called us after he saw the Don Rickles documentary and he really wanted us . . . to do a documentary on him like we did for Don," Mike Richardson recalled. "But in the end he wanted to have the final cut, and John [Landis] doesn't do that. Don didn't try to sway the project at all. He did not try to influence the final picture. Jerry wanted to have the final cut—and John was not interested."[14]

Mr. Warmth would be Don's last hurrah on the big screen, at least in human form. He continued to voice Mr. Potato Head in different iterations—*Toy Story 3* in 2010 and a handful of short films and TV specials. In 2011, at the age of eighty-five, he made his final sitcom appearances on the hit TV Land series *Hot in Cleveland*, playing Bobby, the dead husband of Elka (Betty White), in the Season 2 finale. He returned in Season 3; it turned out that Bobby had faked his own death, and Elka now had to choose between Bobby, Max, and Fred (the latter two characters played by Carl Reiner and Buck Henry).

CHAPTER 22

There was sadness, too, in Don's life that year. His beloved son, Larry, an Emmy winner for *Mr. Warmth: The Don Rickles Project*, passed away suddenly on December 3 from respiratory failure after contracting pneumonia. He was only forty-one. "Larry developed a very severe acid reflux and was occasionally spitting up blood," Tony O. recalled. "He went into the hospital and his immune system evidently was weaker than they thought and he picked up some kind of bacterial infection and they were trying to get rid of it. They did a combination of things . . . and after about two-and-a-half weeks he ended up succumbing to respiratory failure."

The Rickles family was shattered beyond words. "When Larry passed away I was shocked," recalled *Mr. Warmth* producer Mike Richardson. "I know Don was so happy when we got the Emmy and he was so proud of his son, that he was part of it. He told me that. He thanked me for getting the project going because Larry benefited from it. I couldn't bring myself to ever bring it up with Don, either. I knew he was devastated."

Don was booked to play a New Year's Eve gig at Harrah's Marina Casino in Atlantic City just weeks after Larry's death; overcome with grief, he wanted to cancel the performance. "I said, 'Don, Larry would be the first one who would be very upset that you're canceling the gig. It will be therapeutic, trust me," Tony O. said. "And he reluctantly went, and I had Tony DeSare on the show, a really fantastic piano player and singer. We did the show, and a few minutes before midnight, Don did something that he rarely did—and I'm shocked that she went along with it—he brought Barbara out onto the stage and they brought in the

New Year together. They needed each other that badly. From then on, he would say 'good night' to Larry at the end of every show."

Four years later, Don sat for a one-on-one interview with Dan Rather for his AXS television show, *The Big Interview with Dan Rather*, in which Don spoke openly, and emotionally, about his late son. At one point, he broke down in tears when Rather asked him about the worst thing that ever happened to him. "It never goes away. I lost my son," Don said. "I don't want to get too emotional, but he was only forty years old. He was everything to us. He has a sister, thank God, she has two children and she's great . . . to lose a son at forty, God forbid, it was a horror. It absolutely broke my heart . . . with my son, it was the only time I fell apart a little bit."

Don's grief over Larry's death never went away, but somehow he soldiered on, with Barbara at his side. The work, at least, helped him forget his sorrow, if only for a few hours. Don eventually returned to the circuit after mourning Larry's passing and, at times, he was still firing on all cylinders.

In 2012, he was invited by the American Film Institute to cele- brate Shirley MacLaine, who was receiving the AFI's 40th Lifetime Achievement Award at a black-tie event held at Sony Pictures Studios in L.A. Don and Shirley knew each other from way back, from their days as honorary members of Sinatra's Rat Pack in those swingin' days in Vegas in the early sixties. When Don stood up to make a few remarks, he shocked everyone by taking aim at a person who was not in attendance—proving that he had not changed the act a bit, political correctness be damned. "I shouldn't make fun of the Blacks," he said. "President Obama is a personal friend of mine. He was over to the house yesterday, but the mop broke." The audience, including Sidney Poitier, gasped and a hush fell over the room—this was Hollywood, where liberals outnumbered conservatives by quite a wide margin, and Don's joke about the country's first Black president went over like a lead balloon . . . at first. As he continued his verbal barrage, the laugh- ter returned. He spotted actor Dennis Haysbert in the audience; five years earlier, Don had guest-starred on Haysbert's CBS drama series,

The Unit—as a priest. "Oh, there's the Black guy from *The Unit*," he said. "Now he works for Allstate." He also took shots at MacLaine's brother, Warren Beatty—"I know your brother very well, and I never liked him"—and at L.A. Lakers superfan Jack Nicholson, who was sitting in the audience laughing along with everyone else. "He's not here tonight," Don said, "he's with the Lakers, oiling their jocks."[1]

Don's controversial rip about Obama was cut from the ninety-minute telecast when it aired on TV Land in late June; Don's camp insisted he was not censored. "Before all of this started, we knew Don's spot would be cut a bit for time, as would others, including possibly Shirley herself, since the show ran over and we knew it was likely that he might be edited," his rep told *The Hollywood Reporter*.

Don struck out once again when he went over the line with Black comedian and actor Kevin Hart, who related the incident to Terry Gross on her National Public Radio show, *Fresh Air*. "I'm at a *Vanity Fair* party. It's a very true story. And [someone] says, 'Don Rickles wants to meet you. He's a huge fan.' I said, 'Aw man, Don Rickles?' Comedian legend. This man is unbelievable. He's just a legend just for who he is and what he's done for comedy. I go meet Don Rickles. Don Rickles, he sees me, gives me a hug, taps my cheek, and says, 'Look at you, you're like a cute little monkey.' Don Rickles was always known for edgy, crazy material. He always said crazy things out of his mouth. At this moment, I say, 'Wow. He just called me a monkey. Let me just get out of here. Let me just leave.' Good meeting you, man. I don't want to sit here and tell people that Don Rickles just pissed me off. I'm just going to go and leave. It's very easy for me to leave. It's very easy for me to say at that moment, 'Hey, this ain't for me. I'm out.'"[2] Hart repeated the story to Howard Stern on his SiriusXM radio show. "I know disrespect when I see it," he said. "I just got called a little monkey by an old white man and he grabbed my face when he did it. What do I do? I can't push Don Rickles. I can't go, 'What the fuck did he just say?' . . . I immediately knew it was unintentional racism. It was unintentional. It wasn't done with the intent to hurt and diminish, it was his bit."[3]

•   •   •

In 2013, Don was diagnosed with a flesh-eating disease in his left leg called necrotizing fasciitis, a bacterial infection that spreads quickly and destroys tissue under the skin. He underwent three surgical debridement procedures to remove the infected tissue and endured a skin graft. The operations forced him to cancel several engagements and stay off his feet while he recovered. "He almost lost his leg from the knee down," Tony O. recalled. "He was terrified, like, 'That's it, my career is over,' and I said, 'No, don't be so quick to think that.'"

"He went off the road for a long time to recover between surgeries," Paul Shefrin recalled. "He had been laying down with his leg propped up for a long period of time and he had to do rehab to get himself where he could be out there physically at all. It came to a point where it wasn't going to get any better. He wasn't a young kid. So his show had to be adjusted a little bit to compensate for that."

Don felt well enough the following year to pay a return visit to the Just for Laughs Festival in Montreal, his first appearance there in sixteen years—and what now seemed like a lifetime ago. Comedians Alonzo Bodden, Tom Papa, Caroline Rhea, and Australian comic Adam Hills were his warm-up acts. "By this time, he was a lot older and also couldn't really walk, so he did most of his show in a chair," recalled festival cofounder Andy Nulman. "Again, nobody cared or gave a shit, least of all Don. Because he did what he had to do—got on stage, sat down, and did his show."

The festival producers, including Bruce Hills, were sensitive to Don's inability to walk onto the stage due to his leg problems. "We knew we were definitely getting an older version of this legend, but we also knew that, when the light hit him, he would be fine," he said. "And that is exactly what happened." In an effort to make The Merchant of Venom feel less self-conscious, he was camouflaged by dancers so the audience could not see his approach to the stage. "And then he was on a seat because we wanted him to be Don," Hills said. "We wanted to set the table for him and he killed it. Two shows. He killed it."

Earlier, on May 4—two days before his eighty-eighth birthday—
Don had been honored at the Apollo Theater in Harlem at an all-star
event hosted by Jerry Seinfeld and recorded for a television special, *Don
Rickles: One Night Only*, that aired in May on cable's Spike TV (which
later morphed into the Paramount Network). "They took out every seat
and turned the theater into a nightclub," recalled Bob Booker, who was
invited to the taping. "It wasn't really a roast; it was more of a tribute.
The opening act was Jerry Seinfeld, okay? I mean, it was everybody in
the world, closing with David Letterman, who never appeared on anything for anybody, ever. It was like an explosion when he came out."[4]

The two-hour event featured clips from Don's television and
movie career and tributes from comedians and friends, including
Bob Newhart, Eddie Murphy, Robert De Niro, Martin Scorsese,
Tracy Morgan, Regis Philbin . . . and actor Johnny Depp, who had
met Don for the first time at the taping of Frank Sinatra's eightieth
birthday special.

"They hit it off," recalled Paul Shefrin, who was backstage with
Don when Depp approached him. "They got into a conversation,
and I remember a few days later Depp was on with Jay Leno, and
Jay said to John, 'Is there anyone in particular that you met,' and
he said, 'Yeah, Don Rickles,' and Jay was kind of like, 'Don Rickles
and you? Is he a fan of yours?' and John said, 'Apparently.' From
that point on Johnny Depp started communicating with Don. He
would call Don from Japan."

Behind the scenes, the *Don Rickles: One Night Only* special marked
the end of Don's business relationship with his manager, Eliot Weisman, who had succeeded Joe Scandore twenty-two years earlier. Weisman recalled how he sent a bill to Don's office for the Apollo Theater
booking and received back only half of what he billed. By that point,
Weisman and Don's agent at William Morris, Rob Heller, had agreed
to cut their percentages from Don's commissions several times for various reasons, including one instance, according to Weisman, where
Don needed some extra cash to help out his son-in-law. Now Don
wanted to pay Weisman 5 percent "to do nothing, but only if I agreed

to never speak publicly about our relationship and all the things that had occurred over the years," Weisman wrote in *The Way It Was: My Life with Frank Sinatra.* "He wanted editorial control over what I could say about him. It seemed crazy and downright insulting. Even Sinatra never asked me for that." In the summer of 2014, they terminated their business relationship. "The Don Rickles I knew was a loyal, stand-up guy who paid his dues and his debts," Weisman wrote. "He was a great talent and I was sorry he was no longer a good friend. He did the one thing Sinatra never did: He forgot where he came from."[5]

There would be no more Don Rickles bounding around the stage like a caged animal, drenched in sweat, picking off audience members with laser-like barbs aimed at Blacks, Hispanics, Jews, Asians, Italians, or whatever ethnic variety was on the menu that night. "Now I sit in a chair with a cane and they still laugh so I'm happy about that," he told the author in an interview with the *New York Post.* "And if I don't do standup, I'll be sitting in a chair and taking questions and talking about my life. As long as they show up and see me."[6]

Following Don's bout with the necrotizing fasciitis, Tony O. rebuilt his stage show. "I stopped having opening acts and . . . I put all kinds of video in the show," he said. "I would announce the show and have the orchestra play Don's overture, which ended in a big hoopla and then I would say, 'And now some classic moments with Mr. Warmth,' and I would run video clips that I edited together, and while the curtain was closing the audience was watching that. I would walk Don onto the stage, so they didn't see him walking with a cane and limping, and at the end of the video we'd play the music, the announcer would say, 'And now, here he is, the Emmy Award–winning Mr. Warmth himself, Don Rickles!' and the drape would fly open and there he was. He would do a tribute to Frank and I would show clips of him with Frank."

In better days, Don had included a bit of dancing in the act. He was unable to do that now, but he could still sing "Yankee Doodle Dandy" accompanied by patriotic clips of him and his pals on the USS *Cyrene* during World War II and in the Philippines, and photos of Don in his Navy uniform with his parents. "At the end of the show, after he would do his normal bits," Tony O. recalled, "while the audience was applauding and I'm playing his playoff signature music, I started to show video clips, and as he's waving to the audience and they're standing and applauding, the curtain closed and that closing music continued to play until the video ended. So that's how we continued to work for another four years."

Don also teamed with his friend Regis Philbin for a series of shows in which they shared the stage, sitting side by side, with Philbin holding index cards given to him beforehand by Tony O. so he could talk about subjects that would lead to specific video clips, ending with a question-and-answer session.

"It became basically a conversation with Don, and Regis emceeing it," said Don's publicist, Paul Shefrin. "That took some of the pressure off of Don. They would ask people in the audience if they had questions, and somebody would be out there with a microphone and they would line them up to ask their questions, and Don would kid with the audience members in that way, rather than calling out the guy in the third row and giving him grief about something. He loved being out there with the audiences. It was important to his life, but again, he gave that back to the fans."

Don and Regis Philbin shared a long history, dating back to the early sixties, when Regis was a local radio and television host in San Diego and L.A. and Don was a frequent guest whenever he was in town. Their friendship continued through Philbin's sidekick years on *The Joey Bishop Show* and into his move to New York to host the nationally syndicated talk show *Live with Regis and Kathie Lee*, later *Live with Kelly and Ryan* when Kathie Lee Gifford retired and was replaced by Kelly Ripa (Don was a guest on both iterations).

In the 1980s, Philbin was putting together an act of his own—singing, some patter—and opened for Don at Resorts International in Atlantic City and at the Westbury Music Fair on Long Island. In early 2000, when Philbin was riding high as the host of ABC's *Who Wants to*

Be a Millionaire, he and Don embarked on a tour of Florida. "They sold out every show. They were so great," recalled Ken DiCamillo, Philbin's agent at William Morris, who arranged the tour. "Rickles would close the show, because there is no way you could follow Rickles. Regis would be done with his show, and he couldn't wait to get out in the audience to see Rickles. He was just amazed by Don's ability to think so fast on his feet."[7]

Don was not on his feet anymore in front of an audience, but he shared an easygoing rapport with Philbin, and their shows together sold out in every venue—Don sitting at a table being interviewed by Regis, who would show clips of his movies and television work. "Don would sit in a chair and the curtain would rise and the two of them would talk about their careers," DiCamillo recalled. "It was so great to see these two giants together. Don was like Regis, and I understood why they got along so well. Neither one would put on airs. Neither one had attitude. They treated the mail room boy with the same respect as the CEO. And Don would never give you the high hat.

"I'll never forget, my mother, God rest her soul, went to the same high school as Don in Queens. Newtown High School. They were a year apart. My mother was a year older than Don. She was diagnosed with cancer in 2001, and I said to Don, 'You and my mom went to the same high school. She has been dealing with cancer. Would you mind saying hello to her?' I put her on the phone, and he made my mother laugh when she was going through chemotherapy. He was such a gentleman when it came to people."[8]

Don refused to stop working despite his physical condition. He was stooped over now and appeared shrunken, but he continued to appear with Philbin and occasionally showed up on the late-night talk shows, including *The Tonight Show*, now hosted by Jimmy Fallon, and *The Late Show*, where, in May 2015, he was one of departing host David Letterman's final guests, nearly sinking into his chair, his cane beside him. "The problem with some of the talk show appearances that he did at the end was, he's doing references . . . to a singer from the forties where the audience has no connection, instead of doing Justin Timberlake or somebody like that," author/ archivist Paul Brownstein said. "The audience had no connection, but the hosts were so thrilled to have him."[9]

He guested several times on *Jimmy Kimmel Live*—including a sweet, thirteen-minute appearance there with John Stamos in 2016, where they reminisced about their friendship. Don's voice wasn't as strong as it once was, but he was in fine form with Stamos, ripping everyone from Stamos's former *Full House* costar (and their mutual friend) Bob Saget to Regis Philbin ("He's not here tonight—he's in Ireland, hoping they recognize him"), and recalling how Dodgers announcer Vin Scully reached out to him after Larry passed away. Later that year, he and Barbara put their two-story, four-bedroom, five-bath Malibu home on the market for $8 million as Don prepared for what would be his final project.

It was a Web series called *Dinner with Don*, which began shooting in the late fall of 2016 as the maiden project for AARP Studios, the new in-house production arm of AARP, the national organization focusing on the interests and issues of people over fifty. AARP, with its national membership of over 38 million, was looking to expand its reach across the digital landscape in movies and on television. *Dinner with Don* was a coproduction with Stamper Lumber Media Group, whose cofounder Bobby Bauer had jumped at the chance to meet with Don's manager, Tony O., and his partners, Michael Guarnera and Vincent Desalvo. They wanted to talk with Bauer about a new project with the ninety-year-old Merchant of Venom.

"We met at the Smokehouse in Burbank, so it was kind of fitting because it's an old Hollywood place," Bauer recalled. "They had this idea of doing a talk show with Don . . . but their intention was to do a half hour and to take it to the marketplace and I just didn't see that as being the appetite of the marketplace at the time. We had a good meeting of the minds, and I came up with a more specific version, *Dinner with Don*, as a short-form series, with each episode between six and fifteen minutes." After their meeting, Tony O. put Bauer on the phone with Don, who did not understand how the short-form series would work. "He said, 'I'll put myself in your hands,'" Bauer recalled. "'If you can make it work, great.' That was the genesis of it."

The series was not an easy sell, especially to younger industry executives who thought the market for a show featuring a ninety-year-old comic was nonexistent, even if he was Don Rickles. Bauer disagreed. "There was something about sitting with somebody that has a lot less road ahead of them but such an amazing road behind them that we could sit with and talk with and go 'What have you seen?' and 'What does the future look like?'" he said. "And I just didn't give up." *Dinner with Don* eventually landed at AARP Studios, where the concept was enthusiastically embraced by the studio head, Jeffrey Eagle, who gave Bauer the green light to proceed. "They were sitting on this," Bauer said, "and I was like, 'You know he's ninety years old? You know that time is not our friend.' I was being pushy about getting it done, and to Jeffrey's credit, he really understood that and he had to pull a lot of levers that had not been pulled. This was new ground for AARP."

The series was shot in a restaurant setting, a natural milieu for Don and more comfortable for him than an antiseptic studio. Each episode of *Dinner with Don* featured him breaking bread with a celebrity guest and talking about his life and career. Bauer directed every episode and brought in his friend, writer/comedian Wayne Federman, to help him "write in the moment" as the guests arrived. "We basically chapterized Don's life and created dossiers for the guests and then let them kind of go where they wanted and let the conversation take the direction it wanted to take," Bauer said. "And then we would muscle it or nudge it along one way or another and pick up on cues that we heard."

Bauer, Don, and Tony O. agreed to shoot the series in six of Don's favorite L.A. restaurants: Dan Tana's, Mr Chow, Craig's, Madeo, Vincenti, and The Palm. Bauer shot two episodes each day, using a three-camera setup. "We got there before they opened for night service," he said. "I think we started around 11 a.m. or noon. I invited guests, friends of the crew, Tony O., myself, and Don. So it was a 'live' restaurant."

"I would confer with Bobby Bauer and whatever talent was going to be doing that specific episode and give them a list of subjects that they were going to ask Don to talk about," Tony O. said. "I would bring Don to whatever venue we were going to to tape that particular episode . . . and casually I would say, 'Don, tell me that story again about that thing at the Copa' and blah, blah, blah, and I was planting the seed knowing what the people were going to discuss with him that day, so it would be fresh in his mind. If he ever caught on that that's what I was doing, I don't know. He never said a word."

The first two episodes were shot at Madeo, with Rich Eisen and actor Jonathan Silverman as Don's first two guests. "Jonathan had gone to school with Mindy and his father was Don's rabbi. As a kid, he'd been at Don's house for many years, so I knew there was a relationship there," Bauer recalled. "I said, 'Look, you guys are going to be the first through the wall—it could be a little bloody but . . . I sort of protected myself with my friends." Bauer had yet to meet Don in person, and when The Merchant of Venom arrived, he was shocked by what he saw. "Don came in in a wheelchair with a baseball hat and aviators on, and I swear to God, it didn't look good," he said. "He looked like a billion years old. I turned to Wayne and I was like, 'Jesus Christ, I don't think we are going to make it through the day.' And we got the theme music ['The Bullfighter's Song'] going and Don came in. He wasn't saying very much at all. He was very low energy. I get Don touched up, I'm about to call 'action,' and Rich Eisen is going to walk in. I didn't let any of the guests talk to Don off-camera beforehand. I wanted it all to unfold on camera. I swear to God, as soon as I called 'action!' and the lights were on, Don dropped forty years in that moment. You just saw this consummate professional showman. He sat up and the first words out of his mouth, after everybody applauded and Rich came and they sat down, were 'Okay, can I get my check and go home?' When everybody cracked up, Don fed off of that."

Bauer shot thirteen episodes of *Dinner with Don*, with a guest list including Jimmy Kimmel, Vince Vaughn, Sarah Silverman, Snoop Dogg, Marisa Tomei, Paul Rudd, Judd Apatow, and Billy Crystal. "Don was very clear that his body wasn't working at the same functionality that his mind was," Bauer said. "He was pissed about that. The second day that we shot with Jimmy Kimmel and Sarah Silverman, it was more pronounced." Following their meals, each guest sat for a short on-camera interview and shared their feelings about Don and about the experience.

"It was really bittersweet," Bauer said. "I realized that some of these people that really knew him just recognized . . . that a guy like Don comes around once in a lifetime. He won't be replicated. You'll get something else, but not what we witnessed, what we came to know about Don Rickles. It will never be again." Billy Crystal noted how long it had been since he last saw Don in person. "Afterwards, it became clear that he probably would not see Don again," Bauer said.

On January 27, 2017, Don taped the season's final episode of *Dinner with Don* at Craig's, where he was joined by guests Martin Scorsese and Robert De Niro as they reminisced about *Casino* and shared some lighthearted banter. Don was fashionably dressed, as always, wearing a white shirt under a red sweater, but he looked extremely weak and frail and seemed, at times, to struggle to get his words out. He spoke in a low whisper, but never failed to make both men laugh. "In retrospect, I could see, watching the videos, that he was beginning to have difficulty," recalled Tony O. "I had a list of people from Kevin Hart to Whoopi Goldberg to Queen Latifah, J.J. Abrams . . . the line was out the door of people wanting to do the show. And then Don took ill, so we had to put it on hold—and we never got to revisit it."

Don's health took a turn for the worse. His *Dinner with Don* episode with Scorsese and De Niro turned out to be his final on-camera appearance. "Don got a bacterial infection and ended up in the hospital," said Tony O. "And when he recovered from that, then all of the sudden his kidneys began to fail. His doctor, God bless him, was able to get that all calmed down and Don was sent home and we were teaching his staff . . . how to use a portable dialysis machine that we could take on a private jet with us so that he could continue to work—because he wanted to continue to work."

Don's condition improved a bit. On April 4, Tony O. drove over to the Rickles residence to meet with Don and go over a few bits of business, including future episodes of *Dinner with Don* and a few upcoming dates in Vegas where he was scheduled to reopen the Mirage. "We were working the Orleans because they tore the Stardust down, but Don was passionate about wanting to be back on the Strip," he said. "I told him, 'I'm going to go through your act with you because I didn't cancel any of the gigs that we haven't done since we were shooting *Dinner with Don*. I postponed everything and people know that you haven't been exactly 100 percent, health-wise, and the last thing we need is you going out on the road and doing a mediocre performance.' And he said, 'You're so right, I'm sure my performance is falling by the wayside.' And so I leaned over and gave him a kiss on the cheek and I said, 'Okay, listen, I'll see you Thursday.' And as I'm walking out of his room, he calls to me and I turn around and look back at him, and he says, 'Keep my name alive.'"

Don slipped away on April 6, 2017, one month shy of his ninety-first birthday. He was survived by Barbara; Mindy; her husband, Ed Mann; and their two sons, Ethan and Harrison. Just one month before, Don and Barbara had celebrated a milestone, which Don acknowledged on his Twitter account, @DonRickles, one of his few concessions to the digital age: "We are celebrating our 52nd Wedding Anniversary March 14th. Happy Anniversary, my dear wife, Barbara. You are my life."

Funeral services were private, and the family suggested that, in lieu of flowers, donations be made to the Larry Rickles Endowment Fund at Children's Hospital Los Angeles. Don was buried near Larry at Mount Sinai Memorial Park in the Hollywood Hills.

His death made national headlines, with lengthy obituaries recounting the arc of his life and career. This from the *New York Times*: "For more than half a century, on nightclub stages, in concert halls and on television, Mr. Rickles made outrageously derisive comments about people . . . He didn't discriminate: His incendiary unpleasantries were aimed at the biggest stars in show business."[10]

The tributes poured in. "He was called 'The Merchant of Venom,' but in truth, he was one of the kindest, caring and most sensitive human beings we have ever known," Bob and Ginny Newhart said in a joint statement released to the media. "We are devastated and our world will never be the same. We were totally unprepared for this." Don's death was "a giant loss," Billy Crystal tweeted, while Samuel L. Jackson posted a message on Instagram: "Farewell to a comic legend & dear friend, Don Rickles. I know you're cracking them up in the Great Beyond!"

"Don Rickles was a giant, a legend," Martin Scorsese said. "And I can hear his voice now, skewering me for being so lofty . . . We became friends over the years and I had the honor of being roasted by him more than once—sometimes when I didn't expect it. He just started showing up at places and insulting me . . . He made comedy into an art form." "I'm a little disappointed with Don," said Robert De Niro. "He had promised me he would live to be at least 95. In all seriousness, he was not only a great friend, he was a great man with a great heart."

Associated Press reporter Lynn Elber wrote a thoughtful piece on Don a few days later, summing up his appeal. "Offstage, the self-described 'shy and frightened kid' was invariably kind and caring, fellow celebrities said after his death Thursday at age 90. So are many other worthy people. But Rickles, only Rickles, could leave that sweet man offstage and turn into a smirking, hairless attack dog who chewed out fans and famous pals alike with brutal insult after insult. Everyone ate it up, because he practiced an equal-opportunity brand of humor that targeted people by race, religion, appearance and anything else he could find to mock. And because his career was born in the 1950s, when racist and sexist broadsides delivered by white male comedians were OK, and he got grandfathered in for the remainder."[11]

Tony O. spoke at Don's memorial service, which was held at Temple Sinai in L.A. "Half of Hollywood was there," he said. "I was explaining to the people in attendance that, in Don's mind, comedy is the single best disinfectant to the most sensitive subjects in the world, so that's how he would deal with everything, through comedy."

CHAPTER 23

I n August 2017, Don and Barbara's house in Malibu, on the market since December 2016, was sold for $6.5 million. *Dinner with Don* premiered on September 25, 2017, on AARP's YouTube channel. It was both a sad reminder of Don's ebbing mortality and an eloquent send-off celebrating a one-of-a-kind performer. The series was nominated for a 2018 Webby Award, the top honor for an Internet series, and that same year it was honored by the Telly Awards as a Bronze Winner for a non-scripted Web series.

Barbara passed away of complications from non-Hodgkin's lymphoma on March 14, 2021—what would have been Don and Barbara's fifty-sixth wedding anniversary. She was eighty-four and was buried alongside Don and Larry in Mount Sinai Memorial Park.

"Barbara was his backbone," said Don's longtime business manager, Bill Braunstein. "I think that's important to know about the whole Rickles story. She helped keep him together through the times he was ill, not feeling well, getting older. She went on the road with him everywhere. Barbara was Jack Gilardi's secretary, and Don came in and did a little of his shtick and she said, basically, 'Go away,' because she was from Philly so she had that Philly attitude. Of course they ended up getting married and being tremendously in love all those years."[1]

In August 2021, Don and Barbara's four-bedroom Mediterranean-style villa in Century City, their home since 1990, was sold for $6.4 million by trustees of their estate. That was followed in January 2022 by a live online auction of their personal belongings from the house, including Don's collection of autographed photos with ink inscriptions (Elizabeth Taylor, Sinatra, Lauren Bacall, Ernest Borgnine, Sammy Davis Jr., among them), his many mementos and a baseball signed and inscribed by Willie Mays.

"He had no real competition," Jay Leno observed, four years after Don's passing. "People have tried to copy him. They either come across as too mean, or 'Whoa, that is racist.' With Don, there was a gentleness to his harshness, if that makes sense. Because you realize that he is not going for the throat, he is going for the funny bone. And that was the key."

In the end, Don's greatest epitaph were the eloquent words inscribed on his tombstone:

Beloved Husband, Dad, Pop,

Brother-In-Law And Friend

The World Was A Brighter And Better Place

Because You Were Here

You Will Be Remembered Forever And Ever

With Great Love In Our Hearts

So Very Missed!!

Rest In Peace

Notes

CHAPTER 1

1. "History of Fair Housing," Program Offices, U.S. Department of Housing and Urban Development, https://www.hud.gov/program_offices/fair_housing_ equal_opp/aboutfheo/history.
2. Don Rickles with David Ritz, *Rickles' Book: A Memoir* (New York: Simon & Schuster, 2007), 11.
3. Etta Rickles, "Don Rickles (as told by his mother, Etta)," interview by Douglas Cooper, WNYC, Jan. 1, 1971, the Douglas P. Cooper Distinguished Contemporaries Collection (1967–74), https://www.wnyc.org/story/etta-rickles/.
4. Etta Rickles, "Don Rickles (as told by his mother) . . ."
5. Rickles with Ritz, *Rickles' Book*, 9.
6. Edith Efron, "Don Rickles??," *TV Guide*, March 16, 1968, 14–17.
7. Alex Witchel, "I'm No Howard Stern, You Dummy," *New York Times*, Aug. 25, 1996, 26, https://www.nytimes.com/1996/08/25/magazine/i-m-no-howard-stern-you-dummy.html.
8. Rickles with Ritz, *Rickles' Book*, 9.
9. Rickles with Ritz, *Rickles' Book*, 13.
10. "Don Rickles: The Insult King from Queens," *Wall Street Journal*, July 20, 2015, https://www.wsj.com/articles/don-rickles-the-insult-king-from-queens-1437406094.
11. Rickles with Ritz, *Rickles' Book*, 14.
12. Rickles with Ritz, *Rickles' Book*, 17.
13. Interview with Jack Cafferty, "Live at Five," WNBC, New York, May 16, 1985.
14. Rickles with Ritz, *Rickles' Book*, 19.
15. Rickles, "Don Rickles (as told by his mother, Etta)."
16. Rickles with Ritz, *Rickles' Book*, 22.

CHAPTER 2

1. Terry Gross, "In 'Rickles Letters,' 'Mr. Warmth' Goes Postal," *Fresh Air*, NPR, Dec. 1, 2008, https://www.npr.org/2008/12/01/97637201/in-rickles-letters-mr-warmth-goes-postal.
2. Lance M. Bacon, "5 Questions for Don Rickles on Release of 'CPO Sharkey,'" *Navy Times*, June 10, 2015, https://www.navytimes.com/off-duty/movies-video-games/2015/06/10/5-questions-for-don-rickles-on-release-of-cpo-sharkey/.
3. Sol Weinstein, "Playboy Interview: Don Rickles," *Playboy*, Nov. 1968, 75–90.
4. Lynn Elber, "Rickles: The Man Was Sweet, but Oh That On-stage Bite," Associated Press, April 7, 2017, https://apnews.com/article/0486b783af1347fca349e797e2479f3c.

5. Alex Witchel, "I'm No Howard Stern, You Dummy," *New York Times*, Aug. 25, 1996, 26, https://www.nytimes.com/1996/08/25/magazine/i-m-no-howard-stern-you-dummy.html.

6. Don Rickles with David Ritz, *Rickles' Book: A Memoir* (New York: Simon & Schuster, 2007), 26.

7. Sander Vanocur, "Don Rickles Is Tickled That *Sharkey*'s Renewed," *Fort Lauderdale News*, May 15, 1977, 54.

CHAPTER 3

1. Don Rickles with David Ritz, *Rickles' Book: A Memoir* (New York: Simon & Schuster, 2007), 33.

2. Sander Vanocur, "Don Rickles Is Tickled That *Sharkey*'s Renewed," *Fort Lauderdale News*, May 15, 1977, 54.

CHAPTER 4

1. Anthony Ramirez, "The Last Clown in His Class," *New York Times*, Oct. 7, 2004, B3, https://www.nytimes.com/2004/10/07/nyregion/the-last-clown-in-his-class.html.

2. Sol Weinstein, "Playboy Interview: Don Rickles," *Playboy*, Nov. 1968, 75–90.

3. Allan Sherman, *A Gift of Laughter: The Autobiography of Allan Sherman* (New York: Atheneum, 1965), 96.

4. Etta Rickles, "Don Rickles (as told by his mother, Etta)," interview by Douglas Cooper, WNYC, Jan. 1, 1971, the Douglas P. Cooper Distinguished Contemporaries Collection (1967–74), https://www.wnyc.org/story/etta-rickles/.

5. Don Page, "Don Rickles: The Ever-Busy Insult Comic Who Never Writes Anything Down," *Los Angeles Times*, Oct. 13, 1967, https://www.latimes.com/entertainment/tv/la-et-from-the-archives-don-rickles-interview-20170406-story.html, 71.

6. Weinstein, "Playboy Interview: Don Rickles," 75–90.

CHAPTER 5

1. Kliph Nesteroff, *The Comedians: Drunks, Thieves, Scoundrels and the History of American Comedy* (New York: Grove Press, 2015), 151.

2. Author interview.

3. Author interview.

4. Percy Shain, "Put Down Champ Comes into His Own," *Boston Globe*, Sept. 1, 1968, 2.

5. Stan Wyman, "Young Comedian Has Two Objectives in Life," *Brooklyn Daily*, May 14, 1957, 4.

6. Art Ryon, "Ham on Ryon," *Los Angeles Times*, July 29, 1957, 5.

7. Harold Whitehead, "Don Rickles Stars Chez Paree Show," *Montreal Gazette*, Oct. 4, 1956, 12.

CHAPTER 6

1. Author interview.

2. "Boosters to Convene," The Rounder, *Los Angeles Mirror News*, July 16, 1957, 15.

3. "Slate Boys Open Nitery," The Rounder, *Los Angeles Mirror News*, July 20, 1957, 18.

4. Author interview.

5. Debra Birnbaum, "Carl Reiner Pays Tribute to Don Rickles: 'We All Knew of Don's Heart,'" *Variety*, April 11, 2017, https://variety.com/2017/tv/news/carl-reiner-don-rickles-tribute-1202027778/#!.

6. Brad Lewis, *Hollywood's Celebrity Gangster: The Incredible Life and Times of Mickey Cohen* (2007; repr., North Charleston, SC: BookSurge, 2009), 199.

7. Janis Paige, "One of Don Rickles' First Insult 'Victims' Explains How She Dealt with It," *Hollywood Reporter*, April 7, 2017, https://www.hollywoodreporter.com/movies/movie-news/don-rickles-janis-paige-was-one-his-first-insult-victims-991978/#!.

8. Author interview.

9. Dean Gysel, "Don Rickles Works Over Show Biz Celebrities," *Passaic Herald-News*, Feb. 17, 1968, 9.

10. Eve Starr, "Don Rickles Looms as Good Bet," *Allentown (PA) Morning Call*, May 19, 1958, 22.

11. Harvey Pack, "Jonathan Winters on for Hour Tonight," *Rockland Journal-News*, Feb. 20, 1964, 42.

12. Author interview.

13. Edith Efron, "Don Rickles??," *TV Guide*, March 16, 1968, 14–17.

14. Author interview.

15. Efron, "Don Rickles??"

16. Author interview.

17. Author interview.

18. Author interview.

19. Percy Shain, "Put Down Champ Comes into His Own," *Boston Globe*, Sept. 1, 1968, 2.

20. Starr, "Don Rickles Looms as Good Bet."

21. Don Rickles with David Ritz, *Rickles' Book: A Memoir* (New York: Simon & Schuster, 2007), 81.

22. Alex Witchel, "I'm No Howard Stern, You Dummy," *New York Times*, Aug. 25, 1996, 26, https://www.nytimes.com/1996/08/25/magazine/i-m-no-howard-stern-you-dummy.html.

23. Marc Weingarten, "Good News for All the Hockey Pucks," *New York Times*, Dec. 2, 2007, https://www.nytimes.com/2007/12/02/arts/television/02wein.html?searchResultPosition=1.

24. Dorothy Manners, "All at Sea, but Screen Team Found Star," *San Francisco Examiner*, Aug. 23, 1958, 33.

25. Mike Connolly, "Salmon and Eggs," *Pasadena Independent*, Oct. 29, 1957, 6.

CHAPTER 7

1. Earl Wilson, "It Happened Last Night," *Petersburg Virginia Progress-Index*, Aug. 21, 1959, 4.

2. James Gavin, *Is That All There Is?: The Strange Life of Peggy Lee* (New York: Atria, 2014), 345.

3. "History of the Sahara Hotel," Las Vegas Strip Historical Site, https://web.archive.org/web/20200223220516/http://www.lvstriphistory.com/ie/sahara56.htm

4. John L. Scott, "Aqua Show Set at Marineland," *Los Angeles Times*, May 2, 1959, 3.

5. Mike Weatherford, *Cult Vegas: The Weirdest! The Wildest! The Swingin'est Town on Earth!* (Las Vegas: Huntington, 2001), 63.

6. John L. Scott, "MacRaes Score; Davis Returns," *Los Angeles Times*, May 9, 1959, 15.

7. Weatherford, *Cult Vegas*, 63.

8. Author interview.

9. Author interview.

10. Harrison Carroll, "In Hollywood," *Lancaster Eagle-Gazette (OH)*, May 19, 1959, 6.

11. Author interview.

12. Evan Hammonds, "Don Rickles: Quick Wit, Fast Horse," Bloodhorse, April 7, 2017, https://www.bloodhorse.com/horse-racing/articles/220857/don-rickles-quick-wit-fast-horse.

13. Jim McCulley, "95G Wood to Francis S., 50,055 Bet $4.7 Million," *New York Daily News*, April 24, 1960, 129.

14. Associated Press, "Tompion Victor in Travers by 6," *Miami News*, Aug. 21, 1960, 6C.

15. Author interview.

16. Don Rickles with David Ritz, *Rickles' Book: A Memoir* (New York: Simon & Schuster, 2007), 91.

17. Associated Press, "Sands Closing Sunday," *The Racine (Wisc.) Journal Times*, June 27, 1996, 2A.

18. Jerry Fink, "At 81, Still Partial to Putdowns," *Las Vegas Sun*, March 19, 2008. https://lasvegassun.com/news/2008/mar/19/q-don-rickles/.

19. Dick Williams, "McHugh Learned the Telephone Always Rings Twice," *Oakland Tribune*, Aug. 14, 1960, 18B.

20. Author interview.

21. Author interview.

22. Ernest Borgnine, *Ernie: The Autobiography* (New York: Citadel Press, 2008), https://erenow.net/biographies/ernie-the-autobiography/35.php.

23. Author interview.

24. Dorothy Kilgallen, "The Voice of Broadway," *Asbury Park (NJ) Press*, July 12, 1960, 14.

25. Earl Wilson, "It Happened Last Night," *Camden (NJ) Courier-Post*, Aug. 6, 1960, 5.

26. Wilson, "It Happened Last Night," 5.

27. Herb Lyon, "Tower Ticker," *Chicago Tribune*, Sept. 23, 1960, 5.

28. Earl Wilson, "Insults for Profit," *San Francisco Examiner*, Oct. 24, 1960, 10.

29. Lee Mortimer, "Walter Winchell," *Wilkes-Barre Times-Leader*, Feb. 7, 1961, 2.

30. Lee Mortimer, "New York Confidential," *Glen-Falls Post-Star*, Jan. 30, 1961, 11.

CHAPTER 8

1. Herb Kelly, "Show Scene," *Miami News*, Feb. 28, 1961, 6B.

2. Mark Beltaire, "The Town Crier," *Detroit Free Press*, May 19, 1961, 56.

3. Beltaire, "The Town Crier," 56.

4. Dick Nolan, "The City," *San Francisco Examiner*, July 26, 1961, 31.

5. Charles McHarry, "On the Town," *New York Daily News*, Oct. 7, 1961, C12.

6. Harrison Carroll, "Behind the Scenes in Hollywood," *Wilkes-Barre (PA) Record*, Feb. 12, 1962, 13.

7. "TV Scouts," *Philadelphia Daily News*, Nov. 20, 1961, 24.

8. Author interview.

CHAPTER 9

1. Walter Winchell, "Millions of Ransom Lined Fidel's Pocket," *Cincinnati Enquirer*, April 17, 1963, 16.

2. Author interview.

3. Erskine Johnson, "Too Honest to Be Sexy," *New Brunswick Daily Home News*, Nov. 7, 1963, 18.

4. Author interview.
5. Author interview.
6. Author interview.
7. *The Beatles Anthology* (San Francisco: Chronicle Books, 2000), 123.
8. *Beatles Anthology*, 123.
9. Harvey Pack, "Don Rickles Makes Darn Good Living from Insulting Ringsider," *Rockland (NY) Journal-News*, April 12, 1965, 20.
10. Herb Kelly, "Oscar Nominee Almost Faints at the Big News," *Miami News*, Feb. 22, 1966, 6B.
11. Don Rickles with David Ritz, *Rickles' Book: A Memoir* (New York: Simon & Schuster, 2007), 139.

CHAPTER 10

1. Don Rickles with David Ritz, *Rickles' Book: A Memoir* (New York: Simon & Schuster, 2007), 98.
2. Rona Barrett, "Inside Hollywood," *Paterson (NJ) Morning Call*, Dec. 8, 1964, 16.
3. Edith Efron, "Don Rickles??," *TV Guide*, March 16, 1968, 16.
4. Author interview.
5. Erskine Johnson, "Insults Are His Bread and Butter," *Philadelphia Daily News*, April 12, 1965, 20.
6. Dick Kleiner, "Brassy Comic Has Heart of Gold," *Raleigh (VA) Register*, March 5, 1965, 4.
7. *The Journal-News*, Oct. 19, 1967.
8. *The Fort Worth Star-Telegram*, Nov. 18, 1965.
9. *The Los Angeles Times*, Dec. 19, 1965.

CHAPTER 11

1. Don Rickles with David Ritz, *Rickles' Book: A Memoir* (New York: Simon & Schuster, 2007), 133.
2. Michael Starr, "Don Rickles: I Was Too Mean for TV," *New York Post*, Oct. 15, 2015, https://nypost.com/2015/10/15/don-rickles-i-was-too-mean-for-tv/.
3. Zoë Heller, "Don't Call Me Sir: Don Rickles and the Art of the Insult," *New Yorker*, Aug. 2, 2004, 38.
4. Roger Ebert, "Enter Laughing," https://www.rogerebert.com/reviews/enter-laughing-1967.
5. Charles McHarry, "On the Town," *New York Daily News*, Sept. 10, 1966, C16.
6. Gay Talese, "Frank Sinatra Has a Cold," *Esquire*, April 1966, 19.
7. Frank Langley, "Hope Likes Other Comics; Particularly Don Rickles," *Elmira (NY) Star-Gazette*, March 11, 1967, 10.
8. Don Page, "Don Rickles: Insulting His Way to Fortune," *Los Angeles Times*, Oct. 13, 1967, 17.
9. Burt Prelutsky, "Bard of the Barb," *Los Angeles Times*, Nov. 12, 1967, 6.
10. Dorothy Manners, "Mia's Career Return Could Be Short Lived," *Tampa Bay Times*, March 14, 1967, 6D.
11. Jeanne Miller, "Off Stage, the Terror Really Is Quite Gentle," *San Francisco Examiner*, April 8, 1967, 9.
12. Ernest Borgnine, *Ernie: The Autobiography* (New York: Citadel Press, 2008), https://erenow.net/biographies/ernie-the-autobiography/35.php.
13. Florabel Muir, "Looking at Hollywood," *Colorado Springs Gazette-Telegraph*, April 23, 1967, 7E.

14. Borgnine, *Ernie*, https://erenow.net/biographies/ernie-the-autobiography/35. php.
15. Author interview.
16. Borgnine, *Ernie*, https://erenow.net/biographies/ernie-the-autobiography/35. php.
17. Clifford Terry, "Belly Robber Borgnine Makes It as Bronx Butcher," *Chicago Tribune*, May 21, 1967, 42.
18. Perry Phillips, "Night Sounds," *Oakland Tribune*, Sept. 1, 1967, 55.
19. Miller, "Off Stage, the Terror Really Is Quite Gentle."
20. Donald Freeman, "The Bigger the Star, the Harder He Hits," *Fort Worth Star-Telegram*, April 9, 1967, 26.
21. Prelutsky, "Bard of the Barb," 7.
22. Earl Wilson, "My Readers Tell Me Off," *Paterson (NJ) Morning Call*, Aug. 24, 1967, 20.
23. Samuel Livingston, MD, "Jests About Epilepsy Are Deplored," *Baltimore Evening Sun*, May 24, 1967, A26.
24. "The Merchant of Venom," *Newsweek*, Sept. 25, 1967, 118.
25. Edith Efron, "Don Rickles??," *TV Guide*, March 16, 196 14–17.
26. Bob Ellison, "Would You Believe It," *Chicago Tribune*, June 30, 1968, 181.
27. Key TV Syndicate, "Modern Game Shows Compete with Movies," Feb. 4, 1968.
28. Burt Prelutsky, "Bard of the Barb," *Los Angeles Times*, Nov. 12, 1967, 7.
29. Bob Mackenzie, "The Funniest Violinist," *Oakland Tribune*, Nov. 2, 1967, 18.
30. Efron, "Don Rickles??," 14–17.
31. Dean Gysel, "Making Up for Lost Time: Over-Exposure Is No Worry to Don Rickles," *Corpus-Christi (Texas) Caller-Times*, Feb. 25, 1968, 60.
32. Bob Mackenzie, "Abandoning Hope," *Oakland Tribune*, Nov. 9, 1967, 36.
33. Richard K. Shull, "An Unbearable Idea, Making Bear Lovable," *Indianapolis News*, Oct. 24, 1967, 9.
34. "Bernie Kopell," interview by Jim Colucci, The Interviews: 25 Years, April 19, 2017, Television Academy Foundation, https://interviews.televisionacademy. com/interviews/bernie-kopell."

CHAPTER 12

1. Robert Sylvester, "Around & About," *New York Daily News*, Jan. 16, 1968, 56.
2. Bob Ellison, "Would You Believe It," *Chicago Tribune*, June 30, 1968, 181.
3. Barry Westgate, "Billboard Sucks in the Suckers," *Edmonton Journal*, Jan. 23, 1968, 13.
4. Frank Penn, "Physically Un-phit," *Ottawa Citizen*, Jan. 23, 1968, 15.
5. Earl Wilson, "It Happened Last Night," *Camden (NJ) Courier-Post*, Jan. 25, 1968, 31.
6. Television Film Fare, "He Predominates as a Stand-In," *Decatur (IL) Daily Review*, April 4, 1968, 17.
7. Bob Ellison, "Would You Believe It," 181.
8. Author interview.
9. "W7 Interview: Don Rickles," *Los Angeles Times*, May 19, 1968, 31.
10. Rick Du Brow, "TV Critic Tags Emmy Awards All-Out Disaster," *Lawton (OK) Constitution*, May 20, 1968, 11.
11. Percy Shain, "Emmy Grim About Awards," *Boston Globe*, May 20, 1968, 25.
12. Charles Petzold, "Comics' Defense Is Ad Lib Script," *Philadelphia Daily News*, June 2, 1969, 27.
13. Author interview.

14. Bob Foster, "Screenings," *San Mateo (CA) Times*, Aug. 1, 1968, 16.
15. "Don Rickles – 'Hello, Dummy,' (Full Album)," YouTube video, https://www. youtube.com/watch?v=n9pSG1FM-I4.
16. Murray Ball, "Record Corner," *Calgary Herald*, July 19, 1968, 59.
17. James Wilber, "New Rickles Album Is 'Live,'" *Cincinnati Enquirer*, June 11, 1968, 9.
18. "Jack Riley with Emerson College," interview by Bill Dana and Jenni Matz, Feb. 14, 2007, American Comedy Archives at Emerson College, The Interviews: 25 Years, Television Academy Foundation, https://interviews.televisionacademy. com/interviews/jack-riley-with-emerson-college.
19. Harris Katleman and Nick Katleman, *You Can't Fall Off the Floor and Other Lessons from a Life in Hollywood* (New York: RosettaBooks, 2019, https://www.google. com/books/edition/You_Can_t_Fall_Off_the_Floor/HJ-RDwAAQBAJ?hl=en &gbpv=1&dq=harris+katleman+don+rickles&pg=PT76&printsec=frontcover.
20. Bernard Dube, "Once More, with Feeling," *Montreal Gazette*, Sept. 11, 1968, 51.
21. Will Jones, "Rickles Show Insults Viewer," *Minneapolis Star Tribune*, Sept. 28, 1968, 13.
22. John Heisner, "Conned Rickles?," *Rochester (NY) Democrat and Chronicle*, Sept. 28, 1968, 40.
23. Richard K. Shull, "Rickles Without Booze Was Foam-Rubber Bomb," *Indianapolis News*, Sept. 28, 1968, 9.
24. Dwight Newton, "Tom, Dick, and Ed Fly; Don Flops," *San Francisco Examiner*, Sept. 30, 1968, 23.
25. Hal Humphrey, "Don Rickles Puts Verve in Comedy," *Los Angeles Times*, Sept. 28, 1968, 35.
26. Kay Gardella, "Rickles: Man in Middle Riots Television Audience," *New York Daily News*, Sept. 28, 1968, 14.
27. Ernie Kreiling, "A Closer Look," *Van Nuys (CA) Valley News*, Dec. 15, 1968, 54.
28. Ben Gross, "'Insults' Don't Pay Off as a Regular TV Feature," *New York Daily News*, Nov. 15, 1968, 92.
29. Author interview.

CHAPTER 13

1. Don Rickles with David Ritz, *Rickles' Book: A Memoir* (New York: Simon & Schuster, 2007), 126.
2. Cecil Smith, "Funnyman Don an Actor First," *Akron (OH) Beacon Journal*, March 5, 1969, 39.
3. Don Rickles, "Don Rickles Roasts Ed Sullivan [Live on The Ed Sullivan Show, June 29, 1969]," https://www.allmusic.com/song/don-rickles-roasts-ed-sullivan-mt0058132853.
4. Author interview.
5. Author interview.
6. Sheilah Graham, "Academy Awards Remain Dull Show," *Orlando Evening Star*, April 18, 1969, 24.
7. "ABC13 film from press junket in 1968 on the set of Kelly's Heroes," YouTube video, March 30, 2020, https://www.youtube.com/ watch?v=VrZjWhM0TGQ&t=190s.
8. The Projection Booth, "Episode 514: Kelly's Heroes (1970)," April 7, 2021, https://www.projectionboothpodcast.com/2021/04/episode-514-kellys-heroes-1970.html.

9. Thomas Blakley, "Don Rickles Trades Barbs for Rifle," *Pittsburgh Press*, Dec. 10, 1969, 87.

10. Author interview.

11. Julia Imman, "Adams Hour Gave You New Improved Rickles," *Indianapolis Star*, Feb. 27, 1970, 19.

12. Author interview.

13. "Laugh Track," *San Antonio Express and News*, July 5, 1970, 26.

14. Ann Guarino, "Forced War Comedy Has Action Aplenty," *New York Daily News*, June 24, 1970, 36.

15. Joe Baltake, "'Kelly's Heroes' on Scene at Fox," *Philadelphia Daily News*, June 25, 1970, 41.

16. Larry Townsend, "Don Rickles: A Long Way with the Old Insult Routine," *Chicago Tribune*, Nov. 27, 1970, 49.

17. Author interview.

18. Harvey Pack, "Now Folks—The Paper Clown!," *Allentown (PA) Morning Call*, Feb. 2, 1971, 22.

19. Author interview.

20. Jack O'Brian, "June Allyson May Get Touring Plum," *San Francisco Examiner*, Nov. 8, 1971, 35.

21. Ed Sullivan, "Coast to Coast," *New York Daily News*, Nov. 5, 1971, 326.

CHAPTER 14

1. Sam Denoff, Archive of American Television.

2. Author interview.

3. Author interview.

4. L. Ian MacDonald, "Canadian Cigarette Firms Spent Less in Media," *Montreal Gazette*, June 11, 1971, 21.

5. Earl Wilson, "It Happened Last Night," *Camden (NJ) Courier-Post*, April 17, 1971, 10.

6. Author interview.

7. Norman Mark, "'Mr. Nice Guy' Polishes Image for Mid-Season Comedy Show," *Miami Herald*, Nov. 23, 1971, 43.

8. Bill Davidson, "Mr. Warmth Spreads a Little Joy Around," *TV Guide*, April 22–28, 1972, 28–32.

9. Don Rickles with David Ritz, *Rickles' Book: A Memoir* (New York: Simon & Schuster, 2007), 194.

10. "TV Scout Previews," *Philadelphia Daily News*, Dec. 14, 1971, 19.

11. Author interview.

12. Sam Denoff, Archive of American Television.

13. Davidson, "Mr. Warmth Spreads a Little Joy Around."

14. Marilyn Beck, "There'll Be No Barbs on Don's New Series," *Dayton (OH) Journal Herald*, Dec. 14, 1971, 49.

15. Vernon Scott, "Rickles Is a Pussycat on TV, but Watch Out," (Phoenix) *Arizona Republic*, Feb. 3, 1972, 34.

16. Clarence Petersen, "Checking the Comedy Situation: They're Fast Becoming Funnier," *Chicago Tribune*, Jan. 5, 1972, 55.

17. Val Adams, "'Sanford and Son' Abounds in Warmth and Laughter," *New York Daily News*, Jan. 15, 1972, 9.

18. Cynthia Lowry, "TV Review," *Valparaiso (IN) Vidette-Messenger*, Jan. 17, 1972, 12.

19. Lou Cedrone, "Jack Lemmon and 'Chimp,'" *Baltimore Sun*, Jan. 14, 1972, 23.

20. Cleveland Amory, "The Don Rickles Show," *TV Guide*, Feb. 19, 1972, 36.
21. Author interview.
22. Author interview.
23. Bill Libby, "A Day in the Mouth of Don Rickles," *Los Angeles Times*, June 18, 1972, 9.
24. Bill Martin, "'Favorite Bigot' Archie in Reno," *Reno Gazette-Journal*, April 1, 1972, 11.
25. Earl Wilson, "Boss Is Sold on Don Rickles," *Lansing State Journal (MI)*, May 14, 1972, 45.
26. Libby Slate, "Mr. Warmth Is Hotter Than Ever," May 5, 2010, https://www.emmys.com/news/news/mr-warmth-hotter-ever.
27. Author interview.

CHAPTER 15

1. Author interview.
2. "Greg Garrison," interview by Henry Colman, Oct. 8, 1998, The Interviews: 25 Years, Television Academy Foundation, https://interviews.televisionacademy.com/interviews/greg-garrison.
3. Author interview.
4. Author interview.
5. Author interview.
6. Marilyn Beck, "'73 Rickles Series Next?," *Edmonton Journal*, Dec. 4, 1972, 22.
7. Marilyn Beck, "Rickles Dons Role of Purring Pussy," *Orlando Sentinel*, Jan. 11, 1973, 22.
8. United Press International, "Carson Plotter Got Tip on TV," *San Francisco Examiner*, April 26, 1973,. 7.
9. Laurence Leamer, *King of the Night: The Life of Johnny Carson* (St. Martin's Paperbacks, New York: 1990), 169.
10. Author interview.
11. Al Cohn, "Rickles: A Really Nice Guy with a Bad-Mouth Reputation," *Calgary Herald*, Sept. 20, 1974, 84.
12. Author interview.
13. Paul Jones, "Family TV Zone Wins Viewer Praise," *Atlanta Journal-Constitution*, Jan. 24, 1975, 41.

CHAPTER 16

1. "Aaron Ruben," interview by Morrie Gelman, Feb. 25, 1999, The Interviews: 25 Years, Television Academy Foundation, https://interviews.televisionacademy.com/interviews/aaron-ruben#interview-clips, Chapter 6: "On creating and producing CPO Sharkey starring Don Rickles."
2. United Press International, "'C.P.O. Sharkey' May be Rickles' Last Chance on TV," *Shreveport Times*, Nov. 30, 1976, 6.
3. Author interview.
4. Author interview.
5. Bill Cosford, "Rickles Muzzled Again, Alas," *Miami Herald*, Dec. 5, 1976, 33.
6. Sander Vanocur, "Rickles' Humor Finally Succeeds," *Indianapolis Star*, Dec. 2, 1976, 19.
7. Author interview.
8. Author interview.
9. Author interview.

10. Author interview.
11. Noel Holston, "Rickles Bites to Save 'Sharkey,'" *Orlando Sentinel*, Jan. 25, 1978, 8B.
12. "Aaron Ruben," interview by Morrie Gelman, Feb. 25, 1999.
13. Rudy Maxa, "'Mr. Warmth' Strikes Again," *Victoria (TX) Advocate*, Aug. 20, 1978, 18.

CHAPTER 17

1. "TV Previews," *Albuquerque Journal*, Jan. 10, 1984, 11.
2. Sylvia Lawler, "Mr. Nice Guy and Mr. Insult Meet the Press," *Allentown (PA) Morning Call*, Aug. 5, 1984, 1.
3. Tom Shales, "The Super Duper Supernaugural! TV's Rush to Gush All Day," *Washington Post*, Jan. 21, 1985, https://www.washingtonpost.com/archive/lifestyle/1985/01/21/the-super-duper-supernaugural-tvs-rush-to-gush-all-day/9e166bec-5424-49fd-804e-0ace6897cb6f/.
4. Don Rickles with David Ritz, *Rickles' Book: A Memoir* (New York: Simon & Schuster, 2007), 202.

CHAPTER 18

1. Evan Hammonds, "Don Rickles: Quick Wit, Fast Horse," Bloodhorse, April 7, 2017, https://www.bloodhorse.com/horse-racing/articles/220857/don-rickles-quick-wit-fast-horse.
2. Don Rickles with David Ritz, *Rickles' Book: A Memoir* (New York: Simon & Schuster, 2007), 212.
3. Mary K. Jacob, "$6.5M Offer Made on Don Rickles' Longtime Home After Only a Week on the Market," *New York Post*, July 22, 2021, https://nypost.com/2021/07/22/offer-made-on-don-rickles-longtime-home-after-only-a-week/.
4. Author interview.
5. Associated Press, "Don Rickles Ad Libs Way Through Special," *Sioux City (IA) Journal*, Aug. 24, 1986, 36.
6. Kay Gardella, "This Is Funny?," *New York Daily News*, Aug. 22, 1986, .97.
7. Rickles with Ritz, *Rickles' Book*, 207.
8. Author interview.
9. Eliot Weisman and Jennifer Valoppi, *The Way It Was: My Life with Frank Sinatra* (New York: Hachette, 2017), 217.
10. Associated Press, "Mr. Warmth Still on a Roll," *Fond du Lac (WI) Reporter*, March 24, 1993, 15.
11. Author interview.
12. Author interview.
13. Rickles with Ritz, *Rickles' Book*, 215.
14. Alex Witchel, "I'm No Howard Stern, You Dummy," *New York Times*, Aug. 25, 1996, 26, https://www.nytimes.com/1996/08/25/magazine/i-m-no-howard-stern-you-dummy.html.
15. Rickles with Ritz, *Rickles' Book*, 216.
16. Steve Daly, "*Toy Story* and *Casino*: Don Rickles' Big-Screen Comeback," *Entertainment Weekly*, Nov. 24, 1995, https://ew.com/article/1995/11/24/don-rickles-big-screen-comeback/.

CHAPTER 19

1. Susan Wloszczyna, "Don Rickles Is Hot, Playing in 'Casino' and 'Toy Story,'" *Louisville Courier-Journal*, Nov. 23, 1995, 55.
2. Todd Camp, "It's a Toy's Life," *Fort Worth Star-Telegram*, Nov. 24, 1995, 20.
3. Randy Cordoza, "Successful Don Rickles Says It's All in Fun," *Minneapolis Star-Tribune*, April 4, 1996, 41.
4. Author interview.
5. Patrick Carone, "Notorious Insult Comic Don Rickles Reveals His Darkest Secret of All: He's Actually Nice," *Maxim*, April 6, 2017, https://www.maxim.com/entertainment/interview-icon-don-rickles/.
6. Marc Sneitker, "Here's How *Toy Story 4* Will Honor the Late Don Rickles as Mr. Potato Head," *Entertainment Weekly*, March 28, 2019, https://ew.com/movies/2019/03/28/toy-story-4-potato-head/.
7. Bill Brownstein, "Emperor of Insult Still Fills the Big Rooms," *Calgary Herald*, July 5, 1998, E3.

CHAPTER 20

1. Mike Weatherford, "Las Vegas Was a Special Place for Don Rickles," *Las Vegas Review-Journal*, April 7, 2017, https://www.reviewjournal.com/entertainment/shows/las-vegas-was-a-special-place-for-don-rickles/.
2. Author interview.
3. Author interview.
4. Author interview.
5. Author interview.
6. Author interview.
7. Roger Ebert, "'Toy Story 2,'" *Chicago Sun-Times,* Nov. 22, 1995; reprinted at https://www.rogerebert.com/reviews/toy-story-2-1999.

CHAPTER 21

1. Phil Gallo, "Sinatra: 80 Years My Way," *Variety*, Dec. 13, 1995, https://variety.com/1995/tv/reviews/sinatra-80-years-my-way-1200444080/.
2. Eliot Weisman and Jennifer Valoppi, *The Way It Was: My Life with Frank Sinatra* (New York: Hachette, 2017), 282.
3. Tony Oppedisano with Mary Jane Ross, *Sinatra and Me: In the Wee Small Hours* (New York: Scribner, 2021), 270.
4. Hal Boedeker, "Legendary 'Mr. Television' Dies at 93," *Orlando Sentinel*, March 28, 2002, https://www.orlandosentinel.com/news/os-xpm-2002-03-28-0203280268-story.html.
5. Weisman and Valoppi, *The Way It Was*, 218.
6. Author interview.
7. Author interview.
8. Daniel Durchholz, "Hockey Pucks and Potato Heads, but No Jokes Please," *St. Louis Post-Dispatch*, Sept. 27, 2007; reprinted at https://www.danieldurchholz.com/don-rickles.html.
9. Author interview.
10. Phil Roura, "Still Shtickin' It to 'Em," *New York Daily News*, March 11, 2007, 41.
11. Author interview.
12. David Wiegand, "Review: How Don Rickles Heaps Abuse and Keeps You Laughing," *San Francisco Chronicle*, Dec. 1, 2007, https://www.sfgate.com/news/article/Review-How-Don-Rickles-heaps-abuse-and-leaves-3300260.php.

13. Ronnie Scheib, "Mr. Warmth: The Don Rickles Project," *Variety*, Oct. 13, 2007, https://variety.com/2007/film/reviews/mr-warmth-the-don-rickles-project-1200555365/.
14. Author interview.

CHAPTER 22

1. Gregg Kilday, "Don Rickles Shocks Hollywood Crowd with Racial Obama Joke," *Hollywood Reporter*, June 8, 2012, https://www.hollywoodreporter.com/news/general-news/don-rickles-president-obama-shirley-maclaine-335308/.
2. Terry Gross, "Kevin Hart Says Comedy's Full of 'Flawed but Funny' People, Himself Included," *Fresh Air*, Jan. 10, 2019, https://www.npr.org/2019/01/10/683598263/kevin-hart-says-comedy-is-full-of-flawed-but-funny-people-himself-included.
3. "Kevin Hart on Dining with Eddie Murphy, Getting Disrespected by Don Rickles, and Finding Happiness Amid a Sea of Criticism," *Howard Stern Show*, Jan. 27, 2021, https://www.howardstern.com/news/2021/01/27/kevin-hart-on-dining-with-eddie-murphy-getting-disrespected-by-don-rickles-and-finding-happiness-amid-a-sea-of-criticism/.
4. Author interview.
5. Eliot Weisman and Jennifer Valoppi, *The Way It Was: My Life with Frank Sinatra* (New York: Hachette, 2017), 219.
6. Michael Starr, "Don Rickles: I Was Too Mean for TV," *New York Post*, Oct. 15, 2015, https://nypost.com/2015/10/15/don-rickles-i-was-too-mean-for-tv/.
7. Author interview.
8. Author interview.
9. Author interview.
10. Peter Keepnews and Richard Severo, "Don Rickles, Comedy's Equal Opportunity Offender, Dies at 90," *New York Times*, April 6, 2017, https://www.nytimes.com/2017/04/06/arts/television/don-rickles-dead-comedian.html?searchResultPosition=1.
11. Lynn Elber, Associated Press, "Rickles Was Sweet, but Oh That On-stage Bite," April 7, 2017, https://apnews.com/article/0486b783af1347fca349e797e2479f3c.

CHAPTER 23

1. Author interview.

Index

327